STUDIES IN IMPERIALISM

general editor John M. MacKenzie

Established in the belief that imperialism as a cultural
phenomenon had as significant an effect on the dominant
as on the subordinate societies, Studies in Imperialism
seeks to develop the new socio-cultural approach which
has emerged through cross-disciplinary work on popular
culture, media studies, art history, the study of education
and religion, sports history and children's literature.
The cultural emphasis embraces studies of migration and
race, while the older political and constitutional,
economic and military concerns will never be far away.
It incorporates comparative work on European and
American empire-building, with the chronological focus
primarily, though not exclusively, on the nineteenth and
twentieth centuries, when these cultural exchanges were
most powerfully at work.

Law, history, colonialism

D1528608

MANCHESTER
UNIVERSITY PRESS

AVAILABLE IN THE SERIES

Law, history, colonialism

THE REACH OF EMPIRE

edited by Diane Kirkby
and Catharine Coleborne

MANCHESTER
UNIVERSITY PRESS
Manchester and New York

distributed exclusively in the USA by
PALGRAVE

Published by Manchester University Press
Oxford Road, Manchester M13 9NR, UK
and Room 400, 175 Fifth Avenue, New York, NY 10010, USA
www.manchesteruniversitypress.co.uk

Distributed exclusively in the USA by
Palgrave, 175 Fifth Avenue, New York NY 10010, USA

Distributed exclusively in Canada by
UBC Press, University of British Columbia, 2029 West Mall,
Vancouver, BC, Canada V6T 1Z2

British Library Cataloguing-in-Publication Data
A catalogue record for this book is available from the British Library

Library of Congress Cataloging-in-Publication Data
A catalog record for this book is available from the Library of Congress

ISBN 10: 0 7190 8195 5

ISBN 13: 978 0 7190 8195 8

First published 2001 by Manchester University Press

First digital, on-demand edition produced by Lightning Source 2010

CONTENTS

[v]

CONTENTS

Part III Justice, custom and the common law

Part IV Land, sovereignty and imperial frontiers

Part V Colonialism's legacy

GENERAL EDITOR'S INTRODUCTION

Western concepts of law were deeply embedded in both the practice and the propaganda of imperialism. Empire's beneficent cargo included 'the rule of law', and an early generation of imperial historians were interested in the high-flown principles of the globalization of western legal ideas and their application in international and constitutional notions, in legislation, and in the courts. Although the eighteenth century saw some efforts at creating legal syncretism in India, the sub-continent became a significant location for the expression of English legal traditions, not least in the external expressions of the architecture of court houses and the garb of judges and lawyers. As the British Empire extended its reach, these distinctive characteristics of an organic English (as opposed to Scottish or Continental European) inventing of legal conventions were extended throughout the so-called white dominions and the 'dependent' territories. Such manifestations remain one of the continuities of the post-colonial era, even if appeals to the judicial committee of the British privy council are becoming increasingly rare.

But for many years, as the celebratory and justificatory narration of imperial practice has fallen out of fashion, the legal history of empire has been a relatively untouched field. Yet many modern controversies were notably bound up with these inescapable legal pasts, most notably those relating to indigenous land rights and the status of first peoples within their own territories and landscapes. Within the past decade, a new and radical legal historiography has arisen. This book constitutes a highly significant illustration of the important work now being done in this field.

To inject a personal note, my own interest in colonial law developed in the 1980s when I set out to analyse (in my book *The Empire of Nature*) the exploitation of animal resources in selected areas of the British Empire, the development of game law, and the emergence of conservation movements. Without fully realizing it at the time, I had stumbled upon an exceptionally important area of imperial law. Such game law was inevitably connected with the long tradition of game regulations and law-making that stretched back to the European Middle Ages, but it also neatly represented the international character of imperialism. The British promulgated game legislation in their Asian territories, but they also drew heavily on German examples derived from Africa. In defining who could hunt and by what methods, such laws were racially and technologically specific. They excluded indigenous hunters from long-standing practices of sport and protein enhancement. But they also introduced concepts of game frontiers, of land specialization and use, as well as detailed regulations concerning 'seasons', 'permits', zoological definition (for example, in the contrast between 'royal game' and 'vermin'), and appropriate killing techniques. But in many ways the law became so detailed and complex as to be self-defeating. There was a very apparent gulf between intention and effect, well illustrated by the relatively small number of cases brought under the game legislation. In short, through a study of the human interaction with animals and the environment in empire, I was inevitably brought face to face with key aspects of imperial law (through ordinances issued by essentially autocratic systems) and practice. Moreover, since such laws dealt with animals and land, they well represented the processes of state-making (and their limitations) that are central to the imperial process.

As it happens, this book touches on game law only tangentially. But there is much else here. The contributions deal with legal concepts and their role in the extension of authority, with race and definitions of citizenship, with indigenous and imperial systems grappling with each other, with questions of land rights and property, with the body, gender, and aspects of the law of the environment. We have here much evidence of the bold new directions in which the legal history of imperialism is moving.

John M. MacKenzie

NOTES ON CONTRIBUTORS

Constance Backhouse is Professor of Law at the University of Ottawa, Canada. Her Book *Petticoats and Prejudice: Women and Law in Nineteenth Century Canada* won the 1992 Willard Hurst Prize in American Legal History awarded by the Law & Society Association.

John Borrows B.A., M.A., LL.B., LL.M. (Toronto), D.Jur. (Osgoode Hall) is Associate Professor in the Faculty of Law at the University of Toronto. He formerly worked as an Associate Professor and Director of First Nations Legal Studies in the Faculty of Law at the University of British Columbia, and as an Associate Professor and Director of the Intensive Programme in Lands, Resources and First Nations Governments at Osgoode Hall Law School. Professor Borrows is a visiting professor and Executive Director of the Indian Legal Program at Arizona State University's College of Law in Phoenix, in 2000–2001. He teaches in the broad area that encompasses constitutional law, Aboriginal law, natural resources, law and the environment, and land-use planning. He is Anishinabe/Ojibway and a member of the Chippewa of the Nawash First Nation in Ontario.

Christine Choo M.Soc.Wk., Ph.D. formerly worked for the Western Australian Aboriginal Legal Service in Perth. She is an honorary research fellow at the Department of Social Work and Social Policy at the University of Western Australia and works as a consultant historian on native title cases.

Catharine Coleborne completed her Ph.D. in history at La Trobe University, Melbourne, and is now a lecturer at Waikato University, New Zealand. She teaches world history, Australian history and social histories of sickness and health and has published work on lunacy legislation, patient case-books, official inquiries and psychiatry in the museum.

Ann Curthoys is Professor of History at the Australian National University in Canberra. She has published extensively on race and gender in Australian history and is currently writing a book on the 1960s. She is the author of *For and Against Feminism: A Personal Journey into Feminist Theory and History* (1988).

Radha D'Souza is a Ph.D. candidate at the University of Auckland, New Zealand, working on international environment law. Radha studied arts and law at the University of Bombay and is a Member of the Bar, High Court of Bombay. Radha has published a number of papers and chapters in books and is a human rights and labour rights activist.

Ian Duncanson works in the areas of legal–social theory, law and history and legal education. On the theme of law, imperialism and postcolonialism he has published most recently in the *Canadian Journal of Law and Society* (2000), *Postcolonial Studies* (2000), *The Inter-national Journal for the Semiotics of*

NOTES ON CONTRIBUTORS

Law (2000) and in Gideon Calder, Edward Garret and Jess Shannon (eds), *Liberalism and Social Justice: International Perspectives* (2000). When Ian is unable to be in Apollo Bay, Victoria, he lives in Melbourne.

Julie Evans is Australian Research Council Postdoctoral Fellow in the Department of History, University of Melbourne. She is particularly interested in nineteenth-century comparative colonial history and law and is co-author of *Grounds For Dispute* (forthcoming).

Peter Fitzpatrick is Anniversary Professor of Law at Birkbeck College, University of London, and has taught at universities in Europe, North America and Papua New Guinea. He has published numerous works on law and social theory, law and racism, and imperialism, including *The Mythology of Modern Law* (1992) and *Modernism and the Grounds of Law* (2001).

Helen Gardner completed her doctoral dissertation in Pacific history at La Trobe University, Melbourne, where she now works as a research associate. She was awarded a scholarship to the Research School of Pacific and Asian Studies at the Australian National University and more recently has published an article in *Messy Entanglements*, the proceedings of the 10th Pacific History Conference in 1996.

Hilary Golder completed her undergraduate degree at Oxford University and her Ph.D. at the University of New South Wales, Sydney. She has published several books on the history of law in Australia, including *Divorce in Nineteenth Century New South Wales* (1985) and *High and Responsible Office: A History of the Magistracy in New South Wales* (1991), and is now a Research Associate at La Trobe University, Melbourne.

Patricia Grimshaw is Max Crawford Professor of History at the University of Melbourne. She has published extensively on women's history of New Zealand, Australia and the Pacific, and is currently working on a collaborative project, which will be published under the title *Grounds for Dispute:Indigenous Peoples and Citizenship in Nineteenth-Century Settler Societies* (forthcoming from Manchester University Press)

Diane Kirkby is Reader in History, La Trobe University, Melbourne, and President of the Australian and New Zealand Law and History Society. Her book *Alice Henry: The Power of Pen and Voice* (1991) won the W.K. Hancock Prize awarded by the Australian Historical Association. She is the editor of *Sex, Power and Justice: Historical Perspectives on Law in Australia* (1995) and author of *Barmaids: A History of Women's Work in Pubs* (1997).

John McLaren is Lansdowne Professor of Law, University of Victoria, British Columbia. He has co-edited books on the legal history of British Columbia and the Yukon and of the North American West, and has several more under way. A co-edited book of essays, *Land and Freedom: Law, Property and the British Diaspora*, is in press

[x]

NOTES ON CONTRIBUTORS

Ann Parsonson is Senior Lecturer in History at the University of Canterbury, New Zealand. Since the late 1980s she has worked with Maori in respect of their claims against the Crown, presenting historical reports on behalf of both Ngai Tahu and the Taranaki tribes in Waitangi Tribunal hearings, and providing historical research for the Tainui Settlement of 1995.

David Philips is Associate Professor in History at the University of Melbourne. He was born in South Africa and educated there and at Oxford University. He has published extensively on law and policing in British and Australian history and is also engaged in the collaborative research project on comparative colonial states, to be published with the title *Grounds For Dispute*.

Robert Reynolds is a Postdoctoral Fellow in History at the University of Sydney, working jointly on the large research project *Grounds for Dispute*, tracing the comparative franchise status of indigenous people in British settler societies.

Shurlee Swain teaches history at the Australian Catholic University in Melbourne. She has been the recipient of a number of large research grants and has published extensively on welfare and social justice history, including *Single Mothers and Their Children*. She, too, is currently involved in the collaborative research project *Grounds For Dispute*.

Christopher Tomlins has a Ph.D. in American history from Johns Hopkins University. He has taught at La Trobe University and has been a research fellow at the American Bar Foundation since 1992. He was recently awarded the American Historical Association's Littleton-Griswold Fund Fellowship for Research in American Legal History, and has published *Law, Labor and Ideology in the Early American Republic* (1993) which was awarded the J. Willard Hurst Prize of the Law and Society Association. He is the editor of the *Law and History Review*.

Mark Walters wrote his doctoral dissertation at University College, Oxford, on Aboriginal customs under British law in Colonial Canada. He has published work on indigenous peoples and law in the *Queen's Law Journal*, the *University of Toronto Law Journal* and the *Osgoode Hall Law Journal*. He now teaches in the Faculty of Law, Queen's University, Canada.

John Weaver is Professor of History and former Dean of Graduate Studies at McMaster University, Hamilton, Canada. He has published extensively on law and history in leading international journals.

Nancy Wright has published interdisciplinary studies of law and literature in journals such as *English Literary History* and the *Australian Journal of Legal History*. She is Director of the Research Centre for the Interdisciplinary Study of Property Rights at the University of Newcastle, where she and Andrew Buck convened 'Land and Freedom', the 18th Annual Conference of the Australia and New Zealand Law and History Society.

ACKNOWLEDGEMENTS

Editing this book has been a joint enterprise, heavily dependant on the assistance and cooperation of many different people. We are indebted to Robert Kenny for his hard work and advice in preparing the manuscript; Margaret Thornton who guided our editorial process in the early stages; Ian Duncanson, Rosemary Hunter and John McLaren whose ideas and suggestions for conference themes and speakers proved to be inspired; Christopher Tomlins, who is always ready with assistance when required; and Gayle Maddigan whose art work captured the themes and goals of our conference so well.

We are particularly grateful for the financial support we received from the Vice-Chancellor of La Trobe University for the initial organization of the conference in 1998 and for the subsequent editing of these papers, and to Alan Frost, Head of the Department of History, for his on-going support of the project. Thanks also to new colleagues in the Department of History at the University of Waikato, New Zealand, for their ongoing assistance and friendship, and special thanks to Craig Hight, Alexander Hyslop, Michael and Zoë Kirkby for their cheerful support. Lastly, we have appreciated the professionalism and cooperative spirit of each and every one of our contributors. Ultimately it was this which made the task of editing both possible and enjoyable.

Introduction

Diane Kirkby and Catharine Coleborne

> Everything about human history is rooted in the earth, which has meant
> that we must think about habitation, but it has also meant that people
> have planned to have more territory and therefore must do something
> about its indigenous residents.[1]

Empires, colonies and their legal cultures formed the subject of the
17th Annual Law and History Conference organized by members of the
Australian and New Zealand Law and History Society (ANZLHS), with
the assistance of the Canadian Law and Society Association, in July
1998. Matters of indigenous land rights, racial definitions and exclu-
sions, colonial authority, sovereignty, custom and citizenship were key
areas of discussion to conference delegates, reflecting the immediate
contemporary importance of these issues in 'settler societies' and
revealing a burgeoning interdisciplinary scholarship on law, history
and colonialism. This collection is drawn from the papers presented at
that conference.

While the papers published here represent only a small sample of the
diverse range presented at the conference, they are nevertheless representative of the international mix of conference delegates and topics.
Papers have been selected for inclusion in this collection for the illu-
mination they provide on key areas of colonialism and legality. What
unites them is a common concern for the reach of empire and a critical awareness that what we know is very much a result of how we
know it,[2] that it is the task of historians and legal scholars, engaging in
interdisciplinary projects, to unravel the intricacies by which such
imperial relations are maintained.

This exploration of law and history began in Australia in 1982 when
a small group of lawyers and historians teaching at La Trobe University
in Melbourne and the University of Adelaide in South Australia organized the first Law and History Conference.[3] By the early 1990s that
small group had expanded: the conference had become an annual event

catering to well over 100 academics and practitioners from a range of disciplines, and a formal organization had been constituted. Today the disciplines of law and history are being brought together in new and exciting ways. As concepts like 'land', 'native title', 'citizenship' and 'human rights' are contested in courtrooms, parliaments and the media, old historical certainties are challenged and new demands for a professionally active historical profession come to the fore. Law has never been a marginal player in imperialism: in some specific instances it has been legal codes alone that have created boundaries and empowered the enforcement of differentiation.[4] But history, too, has been both partial and powerful in creating knowledge of past (in)justice(s) and territorial expansions. Scholars are increasingly turning their attention to questions of colonialism and postcoloniality, to the meaning and consequences of imperialism, and to the dynamics of imperialist institutions and the colonial enterprise. As they do they encounter the conjunction of the disciplines of 'law' and 'history' as one such matrix of imperial power.

Imperialism and *colonialism* are words deeply imbued with political meaning. Indeed it is hard to imagine how these terms might be discussed without reference to the power relationships they constitute. Processes of learning are not unaffected by the imperial cultures in which we live. Most of the world's peoples live in situations where colonialism and 'race' are defining features of everyday life.[5] 'Law' and 'history' are culturally specific ways of knowing and ordering experience, inherently implicated in relations of power. In a postcolonial world, for indigenous people and for colonizers, these power relationships are being amplified in new and sometimes confrontational ways.

There is thus a growing field of empire studies to which this book is intended as a contribution. Drawing together many scholars who work at the interface of legal and historical studies, it concentrates on locating contemporary legal issues of empires and colonies, of imperial pasts and presents, into their spatial, temporal and historical contexts.

'Law' and 'history' in settler societies

If we may misquote and paraphrase Homi Bhaba: colonialism takes its power in the name of history, yet it repeatedly exercises its authority through the drama of the law.[6] As the 1998 conference organizers, we envisaged a very broad sweep when deciding on the theme of empires and colonies yet far and away the bulk of the papers presented at the conference concentrated on the Empire of England and its outreaches. This is perhaps not surprising. As early as 1820 the British Empire had already absorbed almost one-quarter of the world's population,[7] and schoolchildren in the mid-twentieth century were well familiar with world maps exhibiting the vast expanses of red that depicted countries belonging to this Empire. Thus, while seemingly narrowing the conference focus, this bias towards the major imperial power of the nineteenth century actually gave a coherence to the conference, which we can see reflected in this collection.

English colonization nearly always took the form of conquest by settlement, giving rise to a group of colonial states now known as 'settler societies'.[8] These societies are characterized by their having an indigenous population displaced from the land and replaced with instititions of authority and government imposed by the imperial power. As a contribution to a recent collection of essays argues: 'Settler societies have both embraced and refused history, rejected it and been obsessed with it.'[9] This book's contributors engage with the many histories 'embraced' and yet 'refused' by settler societies in examining for themselves the meanings of 'law' and 'imperialism'.

The settler societies discussed in this study – those of Australia, New Zealand/Aotearoa, South Africa, Canada and the United States' east-coast, together with India and parts of the Pacific – are presented here as case-studies for the implications of imperialism in the contemporary world, particularly for indigenous peoples in those regions. Some of the essays in this book also explore the effects of the presence of indigenous peoples on the modification, interpretation and inheritance of British laws and the legal ideology by white law-makers. For colonialism was not simply a one-way imposition, 'a crushing progress' of triumph for the colonizers.[10] As Ann Stoler and Frederick Cooper have pointed out, colonialism was shaped in struggle as it 'was made both possible and vulnerable at the same time'.[11]

Law, the rule of law, was at the heart of the English colonial enterprise. The five sections of this book explore the varied articulations of the effects and experiences of legal imperialism in these societies. Beginning with historical explications of the very 'legalities' of colonialism, where authors 'map' the territory of colonialism, legal authority, imperial law and colonial encounters, the book goes on to deal with the creation of 'citizens', 'nations' and notions of 'race' within and outside of the law. It then discusses the production of the serious and contested concept of 'sovereignty' and the modifications to legal practices made necessary by a reconsideration of both common law and customary law, by looking at specific instances of judicial decision-making, and more abstractly, at the relevance and appropriateness of issues of 'custom' and 'culture' in the courtroom. The book deals more directly with land and property at and around the actual and imagined frontiers of settler societies; and finally, it comments on the legacies of colonialism for both legal praxis and academic studies. The broader reaches of imperial power are also examined in explorations of the work of colonial missionaries and exponents of psychiatric medicine.

The reach of empire – the central theme of this book's writers – is a key to understanding the twentieth century. While it is fundamental to histories of indigenous peoples and their struggles, 'race' and national identity are not issues only for minorities. The imperial project also made Europeans and Englishness 'back home'.[12] Imperialism therefore should also be central to an understanding of the creation of official and unofficial narratives of the past. What kinds of 'national' histories have been produced, and how do they perpetuate that empire's reach? How have history and its writing shaped national histories and contemporary legal issues?

As Peter Fitzpatrick, one of our contributors, has suggested elsewhere: 'the correspondence between law and nation is remarkable in many ways ... That theme of exclusion and otherness and its constitutive power is one which accumulates force ...'.[13] And Ann Stoler has remarked that 'empire figured in the bourgeois politics of liberalism and nationalism in ways we have only begun to explore'.[14] This volume continues that enquiry as it explores what Philippa Levine once called 'the complex reach of empire'[15] in specific moments in the dynamics of law, history and colonialism.

Notes

1 Edward W. Said, *Culture and Imperialism* (London, Vintage [1993] 1994, p. 5).
2 A point also made by Haleh Afshar and Mary Maynard, *The Dynamics of 'Race' and Gender: Some Feminist Interventions* (London, Taylor & Francis, 1994), p. 4.
3 Ian Duncanson and Christopher Tomlins, 'Law, History, Australia: Three Actors in Search of a Play', *Law and History in Australia*, 1 (1983), pp. 1–15.
4 Ann Laura Stoler, *Race and the Education of Desire* (Ann Arbor, University of Michigan Press, 1994), p. 47; for an example see Peggy Brock, 'Aboriginal Families and the Law in the Era of Assimilation and Segregation, 1890s–1950s', in Diane Kirkby (ed.), *Sex Power and Justice: Historical Perspectives on Law in Australia* (Melbourne, Oxford University Press, 1995), pp. 133–49.
5 Afshar and Maynard, *The Dynamics of 'Race'*, p. 1.
6 Homi Bhabha's actual words are 'If colonialism takes power in the name of history it repeatedly exercises its authority through the figures of farce', see 'Of Mimicry and Man: The Ambivalence of Colonial Discourse', in Frederick Cooper and Ann Laura Stoler (eds,), *Tensions of Empire: Colonial Cultures in a Bourgeois World* (Berkeley and Los Angeles, University of California Press, 1997), p. 153.
7 Susan Thorne, ' The Conversion of Englishmen and the Conversion of the World Inseparable: Missionary Imperialism and the Language of Class in Early Industrial Britain', in Cooper and Stoler, *Tensions of Empire*, p. 154.
8 See e.g. Donald Denoon, *Settler Capitalism: The Dynamics of Dependent Development in the Southern Hemisphere* (Oxford, Clarendon Press, 1983).
9 Klaus Neumann, Nicholas Thomas and Hilary Eriksen (eds,), *Quicksands: Foundational Histories in Australia and Aotearoa New Zealand* (Sydney, UNSW Press, 1999), p. 238.

INTRODUCTION

10 John L. Comaroff, 'Images of Empire, Contests of Conscience: Models of Colonial Domination in South Africa', in Cooper and Stoler, *Tensions of Empire*, p. 165.
11 Cooper and Stoler, *Tensions of Empire*, pp. viii, ix.
12 Catherine Hall, *White, Male and Middle Class: Explorations in Feminism and History*, (New York, Routledge, 1992), p. 20; see also Ruth Roach Pierson and Nupur Chaudhuri, *Nation, Empire, Colony: Historicizing Gender and Race* (Bloomington, Indiana University Press, 1998).
13 Peter Fitzpatrick, *Nationalism, Racism and the Rule of Law* (Brookfield, VI, Dartmouth Publishing Co., 1995), pp. xiii, xix.
14 Stoler, *Race and Desire*, p. 130
15 Philippa Levine on the dustjacket of Clare Midgley (ed.), *Gender and Imperialism*, (Manchester, Manchester University Press, 1998).

PART I

Colonialism's legality

Legalism accompanied and facilitated European colonial expansion into the New World in the fifteenth and sixteenth centuries, and it was at the core of the colonialist enterprise from the seventeenth to the nineteenth century. Here we see the processes of colonialism's legality, the internal dynamics of law's theories, the external politics of law's rule.

CHAPTER ONE

Terminal legality: imperialism and the (de)composition of law

Peter Fitzpatrick

Introduction

To start with what may seem paradoxical, even quirky, in the following argument: that imperial law fails because it does not fail enough. It is not sufficiently insufficient. For this argument Francisco de Vitoria is a telling figure: the Vitoria received as the benign humanist who erected a basic defence of Indian *dominium* in the Americas – *dominium* as a combination of sovereign and proprietary title – and fathered international law – and provided a consummate legitimation for one of the more spectacularly rapacious imperial powers. Beginning with Vitoria and that ambivalence, this chapter offers a brief history of imperial law, focusing ultimately on its terminal failure in colonialism. What this failure reveals is the necessity of the responsive quality in law, a quality denied in standard and stultifying affirmations of the distinct determinative force of modern legality. And it is this outcome, this end of a history, which may be of some relevance to the chronic inadequacy of national legal systems in North America and Australia in accommodating claims of indigenous peoples.

The ambivalence of Vitoria

There could hardly be two more divergent views of the primal text of international law than those which have come to accompany Francisco de Vitoria's *De Indis*.[1] In one view, Vitoria is seen as getting international law off to an aptly exalted start in the early sixteenth century with his universalist, humanitarian espousal of the interests of the Indian during the Spanish colonization of the Americas.[2] With the other view, Vitoria certainly did bequeath the enduring lineaments of international law, but he did so by way of providing a refined framework and justification for colonial oppression.[3] These views, I will now try to show, are compatible.

A preliminary outline of what Vitoria said can intimate both claims readily enough. Vitoria set his lectures in opposition to the more predatory and the more resolutely genocidal among the Spanish colonists. In distinguishing Spanish settlement from other forms of acquisition – including acquisition by conquest and the full ownership bestowed by the law of nations on the first occupant of deserted regions – Vitoria found that 'the Indies' had not been 'without an owner': the Indians had rights of *dominium* over the land and, furthermore, they were basically human beings even if ones with considerable, but remediable, shortcomings. These rights had, however, to adjust to the expansive rights of all people, including the Spanish, to travel, trade, 'sojourn' and, in the cause of Christianity, to proselytize. There was also something of a right to enforce natural law. Such rights could not be aggressively asserted unless they were resisted by the Indians. But when so resisted, these rights could be asserted to the full extent of conquest and dispossession.[4]

Convenient as Vitoria's humanism has been in providing virtuous origins of international law, or in offering support for the recognition of rights of indigenous peoples or of Indian title to land in the United States,[5] it is not a humanism manifest in Vitoria's work. This work, along with that of his contemporaries and disciples clustering around it, was a large exercise in scholastic theology, its presiding genius being Thomas Aquinas. Not only does the whole scheme derive from Aquinas: Aquinas provides the impelling point of departure, the affirmation that infidels could exercise *dominium*.[6] There is some semblance of the secular here, for Vitoria used this point in opposition to papal pronouncements which others had used to support the contrary view. Vitoria relied on the precept of Thomist natural law which attached *dominium* to all 'men', to all rational beings. Natural law of this kind could be ascertained by observing the practice of all, or the majority, of peoples. Such a natural law would rule even if the godhead did not exist.[7] So, Vitoria perceived that the Indians did have the accoutrements of natural law. They lived in communities, had families, hierarchical government, legal institutions, and something like religion.

If the case for Vitoria as a fount of secular humanism begins now to look arguable, it collapses completely when confronted with the overall picture of Thomist natural law. Since all of natural law issues ultimately from the deity, God cannot be dead, even speculatively. The 'secondary precepts' of this natural law, such as the attachment of *dominium* to all rational beings, must accord with 'primary precepts' more intimate to the divinity. True, Vitoria does not emphasize this dimension of natural law so much, but he does not really have to. It is at one with the whole theologic ethos in which he worked. So, in his going on to adopt a superordinate, universalist and Eurocentric position denying Indians what had just been magnanimously allowed them, Vitoria is not, contrary to the charge often laid against him, being hugely inconsistent. He has nothing to be inconsistent about because he is simply demonstrating what is inexorably so, and why.

In this demonstration or exposition, Vitoria attaches to his list of the accoutrements of natural law, which are engagingly similar to those of the Spanish, another list of what is contrary to natural law and repulsively different.[8] The Indian people, initially included in the universal embrace of the first list, are now rejected in terms of the second as distinct and at best remotely redeemable. Either they were so deviant as to be placed beyond the reach of natural law or, where there was some recognizable similarity keeping them within the pale, the Indian qualities were downgraded as inadequate or inferior. The Indian may well have been blessed with family, religion, government and law, but these were of a decidedly defective kind. As for the utterly deviant, the list of horrors was even then quite standard, ranging from the instantly egregious, such as cannibalism and sexual perversion, to more picayune affronts to European taboos of diet and dress – nudity, consuming food raw, eating reptiles, and so, considerably, on.

These two types of exclusion were markedly divergent in their presuppositions. The observation of similarity in religion, family, law and government, when combined with the deficiencies of the Indian in such things, imported a call for the Indian to change and become the same as the European, even if that would take a conveniently long time.[9] Unmitigated exclusion assumed a more chasmic separation, one also grounded in natural law. Natural law did not only prescribe right conduct as obligatory: conduct was right in the sense of being accurate, of being in itself what that conduct truly and properly was. Unfortunate appetites, then, would place the Indian altogether beyond the reach of a natural law which found the true and the proper in what it was to be Christian or civilized. That which is beyond what is universally true and proper can only 'be' entirely, absolutely, beyond. What the various indications of utter exclusion also revealed was an inability on the part of the Indian to distinguish the truly human from the non-human and to act accordingly.[10] Humans were not food, they did not have sexual intercourse with other species; only wild beasts ate raw food, and so on. This comes close to denying the Indians the capacity to overcome their morbid tastes, even if that capacity must also be allowed to them as humans. It is indicative, then, that the Spanish saw the condition of the Indian as embedded in custom and, as such, well-nigh impervious to a reforming natural reason.[11]

And so, as Antony Anghie puts it, the Indian in Vitoria's lectures had to be 'schizophrenic', encompassed in the sameness of a universal humanity yet set apart from it.[12] It was the recalcitrance thrust upon the Indian people which ultimately justified their conquest and dispossession by the Spanish. As we saw earlier, others had a right to travel, sojourn, trade and proselytize in Indian lands. This was a natural right and, hence, the Indian people had to allow and respond positively to the presence and ministrations of the Spanish. And it was crucial that in this way active relations be established between peoples because this was seen as essential to building up that human consensus which revealed an operative content for natural law.[13] But the Indian people were designated in such a way as to put them, for a very long time at least, beyond the range of the effectively and reflectively human. They were incapable, for example, of agreeing a just peace. The Spanish would always be either at war or at risk unless the Indians were thoroughly subjugated.

The law of all peoples

In Anghie's elegant analysis, Vitoria's lauded origin of international law is not so much to do with its conventional concern, the relation between sovereign states, as with the colonial domination of people burdened with radical difference.[14] Perhaps it could now also be said that Vitoria's scheme massively implies that it is the colonial domination which effects the relation between sovereign states. The *ius gentium*, the law of all peoples, relies on the already existent gentes. It says nothing of the quality positively endowing the people or nation. This comes about negatively in the imperial division between the *barbari*, who are not sovereign or Christian or civilized, and the specular European nations, which are. With that primal divide, distinct national identity is taken on in the assertion of a sovereignty in opposition to the non-sovereign. The negativity of sovereign assertion imports a denial of the primary and positive force of relatedness 'in' the nation. Nation thence becomes complete in its sovereignty and need only relate as a secondary or incidental matter. The relatedness, the 'non-sovereignty', which persists with-in the nation, becomes a negative attribute projected onto the *barbari* and other inadequates. The now international community of sovereign nations can generate that consensus-forming international law as natural law in its tellurian domain, and do so even if God did not exist, through the coherence endowed in the common rejection of the *barbari*. For Vitoria, however, this natural law still ultimately cohered in the Christian God or, more exactly, in a Thomist eternal law which conveniently has never assumed any definite content. Some ironic allowance could then be made for Vitoria as a secular humanist since, in his inhuman scheme, international law can subsist without religious authority. The degraded *barbari* substitute for the elevated god as the formative point of coherence. In all, this new scheme initiated an imperial legality which could extend universally, naturally, to all 'men', yet effect and rely on an exclusion of some in constituting this very universality. And it was the *barbari*, furthermore, which carried the resulting contradiction 'in' imperial legality by being both utterly excluded yet always includable.

The deflating of grandiloquent claims made for Vitoria is at least implicitly countered by another branch of revisionist scholarship, one which would tell us that it was only in the early nineteenth century that international law 'started contracting into a regional (purely European) legal system, abandoning its centuries-old tradition of universality based on the natural law doctrine. ... International law shrank to regional dimensions though it still carried the label of universality.'[15] Vitoria must then be absolved. The 'natural universality of the law of nations' contrasts fundamentally with a straitened universality arrogated to itself by Europe and confirmed in its claims by the 'writers of the positivist school in the nineteenth century'.[16] Some such thesis of radical discontinuity is now often advanced but it is somewhat overdrawn. Without subscribing to the potted genealogies of the trade, which would trace an unbroken line of development in international law from beyond ancient Greece until now, there are significant continuities into the modern period. Ancestor figures such as Vitoria and Grotius are readily relied on to support the universal range of the law of nations, but closer observation would qualify this reliance and reveal that they too resorted to a more focused illimitability. The prior proto-modern conception of the *ius gentium* was unresolved over whether it extended to all people or to most of them. Following on from Vitoria, the immense influence of Grotius maintained an ambivalence between a universal natural law pertaining to all 'men' and the law-generating practice of some of them who happened to be Christian or civilized. Even civilization did not provide an assured entry since heathens and barbarians, even when civilized, were considered to be inadequate and much in need of conversion to standards typified by Europe.[17]

Granted some similarity in terms of exclusion, significant differences did nonetheless supervene in the modern period, differences which amounted to more than a matter of degree. Here Grotius can be seen as a transitional figure. Despite his manifest continuities with a medieval Europe, Grotius is received as the embodiment of that modern international law emerging from the Peace of Westphalia of

1648, even though this came after his writings. That settlement of the engulfing Thirty Years War in Europe was set against an encompassing or 'universal' religious authority, and in this it accentuated the separate and sovereign quality of the 'European' nation-state. All of which served to 'found' international law in the supposed society of supposedly independent nation-states. Sovereignty became the pivotal notion. It marked the contained independence of the nation-state, its free-standing completeness, and it was the qualification for entry into the society of nations. The range of peoples admissible to such a society came to be more and more confined in terms of European systems of sovereign rule. From the eighteenth century, formerly acceptable civilizations mysteriously degenerated and became uncivilized. Legal systems of the once civilized lost their international character in a colonial reduction of their laws to what was local and folkish.[18]

New criteria of separation and distinction replaced the naturalism of the *ius gentium*. It was Vattel who, from the mid-eighteenth century, assumed a pivotal significance here. For Vattel, the society of nations was not to have any overarching commonality or authority or even to involve any of its members 'yield[ing] … rights to the general body': each independent state claims to be, and actually is, 'independent of all the others'.[19] There was, however, a 'natural society' of nations akin to the primitive state of nature 'among men in general' – an identification which was, of course, to become commonplace.[20] The problem which now confronted, or should have confronted, Vattel was how an international society of sovereign states, which he saw as civilized, could be distinguished from its savage or barbaric counterpart.

The solution impacted in Vattel's text is territory. Like Grotius, he foresaw a scheme of things. What he anticipated was the advent of nationalism whence nation became 'actually' identified with its distinct territory and a people gainfully attached to it. This 'positivist' affixing of the national idea to a reassuring materiality was effected in the reinforcing of an existent divide: the opposition between a civilized territoriality and those not explicitly enough attached to the earth – those 'wandering tribes whose small numbers can not populate the whole county', and whose 'uncertain occupancy' cannot be 'a real and lawful taking of possession'. It is, then, 'entirely lawful' to occupy such a country.[21] But savagery of the nomadic kind was only the extreme of inadequacy, the ultimate instance of a definitive deficiency – the inability to hold the land or to combine with a sufficiently delineated portion of it. This, it should be stressed, is an adequacy which remains ever elusive. The nomads and hunter–gathers are obviously Vattel's extreme but even a settled agricultural or pastoral existence remained conveniently 'uncertain' if it were of a savage variety. So despite according all 'men' universal natural rights of dominion, like Vitoria, Vattel ultimately denied any positive content to such rights when held by certain peoples. What apparently counted 'from the point of view of international law as it existed in the middle of the eighteenth century' was that, to take a specific example, 'the Indians of North America had never inhabited any territory to an extent sufficient to preclude newcomers'; and so, *ex hypothesi*, this international law regarded 'their land as unoccupied and amenable to the acquisition of sovereignty'.[22] To this day, and in the same way, territory remains the ground of sovereign completeness.[23]

The savage hold on the land could only ever be elusive, not just because of its constitutive inadequacy but for related practical reasons. Clear criteria of adequate occupation would mean that savages could attain adequacy and may even have done so already. And what would be equally disruptive of the whole imperial scheme, many scant colonial occupations would fail to meet substantial criteria. The unavoidable consequence was that colonists could not erect general and clear criteria to justify occupation and found territoriality. This inability underscored the negative constitution of the putative right to hold the land. Sovereignty and proprietary title became existent and adequate only in their negative relation to the intrinsically inadequate other. This key configuration of the 'ground' of imperial law is encapsulated in the 'international law' of discovery.

Discovery, or the doctrine of discovery as it is called with an indulgent exactitude, has a very long history, but its modern manifestation can be extracted from one of its more notorious instances, the account given by Columbus of his claims to 'the Indies'.[24] Understandably enough, Columbus did draw on pre-modern modes of legitimating discovery – the invocation of a deity and of the 'marvellous', the emphasis on naming so as to take land out of the category of *terra incognita*, and the perfunctory contact sufficient to 'take possession' – but he was more modern in the obsessive resort to certain other legitimations.[25] There was an obviously felt need for legal justification. Columbus's appropriations were seen as valid only when authorized by a sovereign power.[26] And he usually insisted on some legalistic recording by a notary. There was also an indefinite imperative to mark the land in some way and to record presence. The modes of doing these things were legion and there was no general test of their adequacy. Marks and records were aimed at establishing the fact of occupation but they were usually saturated with legality as well. But, in all, there were no internationally agreed rituals nor fixed general prescriptions determining the efficacy of claims made on discovery and after.

The inability to devise clear criteria was compounded by inter-imperial rivalry. Soon after the somewhat cavalier annexations by

Columbus, other imperial powers, most notably France and England, objected to the sufficiency of some of the Spanish claims, objected to the Spanish having simply 'touched here and there', as Elizabeth of England put it.[27] Such disputes, unlike those with indigenous peoples, could not be resolved by negating the inadequate other, and they came to be settled in terms of the intensity of a fixed and fixing connection to the land – in terms of the comparative effectiveness of occupation.[28] The older tradition which recognized a minimal marking or presence as enough to establish title against indigenous peoples carried over to the situation because of the necessity for the imperial discoverer to be allowed a toe-hold on the land as preliminary to effecting fuller occupation. This now took the form of the doctrine of inchoate title. The initial presence or mark or claim conferred a conditional title which had eventually to be 'consummated' through 'adequate possession'.[29] However neither the quality of the initial contact nor the open-ended prospect of consummation were or could be clearly specified.

In short, the adequacy of imperial title could not be endowed with positive content. In a move which refigured Vitoria's template, it was made adequate negatively by setting it against the inadequacy of the savage. As Vattel's telling contribution indicated, the modern sign of inadequacy was the cultivation of territory, either its lack or insufficiency. The inadequacy of the savage in this was intrinsic and irredeemable. Any imperial occupation surpassed whatever the savage did upon the land.

What was made crucially operative here was the long occidental romance between law and agriculture. The relationship has been brilliantly observed by Vismann in the analogy between law's fixity of determination and agriculture's sharp delineation of the land.[30] In the late eighteenth and early nineteenth centuries, the occidental belief that law comes into existence with agriculture is expressed in notions of the stages of progress or improvement in humanity.[31] And that belief now extended to the concurrent emergence of state sovereignty. Hegel definitively concentrated the fateful triad of agriculture, law and sovereignty in a way which denied a 'barbarian' people effective right: lacking in this combination and thence being deficient in 'essential moments of the state', such a people has neither sovereignty nor a correlative 'universally valid embodiment in laws ... and as a result it fails to secure recognition from others'.[32]

There did remain, however, an intriguing trace of the tradition in international law which accorded some 'rights' to the savage and the *barbari*, including rights of *dominium*. These were, however, no more assured under this dispensation than they were with Vitoria. Here they had two possible sources. One was the fitful incorporation in international law of natural rights, a source which was to disappear in the nineteenth century. The other was bolstered by imperial utility. Conceding some title to the savages was not a response to their being more or less adequately attached to the land but, rather, a response to the varying exigencies of colonial occupation. When people impertinently resisted conquest or where colonial occupation was tenuous, the savages were often found to have proprietary rights after all, rights which could then be transferred to settlers. Yet imperial right was still founded on the negating of these same people, with the result that their 'rights' were thoroughly subordinate and could never amount to or reflect that 'holding ... the land' which grounds the occidental 'right of sovereignty'.[33]

Yet, if under the aimless feet of the savage the earth is marked at most desultorily, this same encompassed being is also *too* attached to the earth, a creature of blood and soil, debarred from relating to anything beyond the entirety of its all-too-bounded plot. In this inescapable particularity, the savage, the barbarian and such become simply incapable of relating to or reciprocating with others beyond their territory.[34] Relation became negatively the preserve of those nations cast in the European mould, just as sovereign entirety became so in its opposition to the feckless, deracinated savage. It was, in a considerable feat of legerdemain, a transcendent custom now released from place and particularity which constituted the source of a manifestly self-serving international law – an international law in which its elect subjects could simply and marvellously be as they (customarily) are, each entire yet all related to one another. There is, in short, a projection of this irresolution between entirety and relation onto a supposedly exterior savagery which provides the subject's point of coherence.

So, in its contradictory consolidation in the nineteenth century, international law constituently opposed a savagery which must be quite other to it.[35] In laying out 'the principles of international law', Westlake found in 1894 that 'of uncivilized nations international law takes no account'.[36] Or, as J S Mill declaimed, doubtless as an inveterate advocate of liberal principle: 'To characterize any conduct whatever towards a barbarous people as a violation of the law of nations, only shows that he who so speaks has never considered the subject.'[37] The exasperating problem for the barbarians was that they 'have no rights as a *nation*, except a right to such treatment as may, at the earliest possible period, fit them for becoming one'.[38] Indeed, to continue in a heavily ironic vein, in the work most closely associated with him, *On Liberty*, Mill decreed that 'despotism is a legitimate mode of government in dealing with barbarians providing the end be their improvement'.[39]

The sainted Mill does, however, introduce the redeeming element, the right of the barbarians to be subjected to the occident's benevolent civilizing mission so as to rectify their deficiency. And the convenient duty of the occident to civilize meant that its identity could be sustained in a response to the challenging proximity of the other. The insuperable difficulty with the 'particular' alterity of the savage and the barbarian was that they were not only called to become civilized and the same as the occidental, but they must, as the negative coherence of occidental identity, remain ever distinct and excluded from civilization, remain eternally unmixed. Again and again, international law extended itself in a quasi-universal way to include and be with the savage other, only to then draw back and reassert an exclusive completeness, a kind of superordinate sufficiency. So, Westlake seems to soften his brutal exclusion of the 'uncivilized native' by going on to allow them 'rights' which then turn into the occasion of their abasement. Specifically, the exclusion from the reach of international law 'does not mean that all rights are denied to such natives, but that the appreciation of their rights is left to the conscience of the state within whose recognized territorial sovereignty they are comprised ...'.[40]

Laws of colonialism

This dubious duty brings into play a further law of imperialism, colonial law, and heightens a certain artificiality in the distinction between this and international law. Whether it comes from the universalist arrogation of international law, or from the exemplarity of each of the imperial nations, or from the exaltation of that comity which came to combine them, it remains the same quality of law and civilization which is formed in its opposition to the savage and obdurate other. All the 'sources' of law come to be fused in the ambient discourse which gave imperial legal action its justification. The 'discovery' of territory, for example, was obviously an extraversion of a specific imperial nation, but the discovery could not simply be something that a colonizing nation smugly held to itself; it had to be recognized as an effective discovery, be projected forward and secure continuing recognition among the community of nations for it to come into and remain in being.

What was crucial for the consistent and civilized character of this testing international domain, and what was crucial for the commonality of civilized identity among nations, was that the variety of encountered others all be rendered similar. Thus, these others had a remarkably common set of characteristics which remarkably contrasted to the common characteristics of elect nations. This was a world made for ready comparison, and one suited to the emergent disciplines of comparative law and comparative anthropology. For the identity of the elect to be held inviolate, the characteristics of the others had to be determinantly, eternally, set. Yet modern imperialism itself, in its expansionary encounters, had to be responsively accommodating. And given its universalizing redemptive prospectus, the encountered were somehow to be brought within the fold of civilization.

It would be difficult to imagine a scene more adapted to 'resolution' through law, at least in so far as law could match its determinant and responsive dimensions. And to the imperial eye law was pre-eminent among the 'gifts' of an expansive civilization, one which could extend in its abounding generosity to the entire globe.[41] This was the same law which had assumed in modernity a civilizing mission within the national territory, and for this purpose had become 'a flexible, indefinitely extensible, and modifiable instrument'.[42] The gift was not perceived, however, simply as one coming from its immediate national donor. It was the gift of a universal (European) civilization, and it was itself composed of universal principles.[43]

But if imperial law was a gift of civilization, it was also, like its national equivalent, a 'grim present', as the more perceptive of the colonists recognized.[44] Law had responsively to extend towards new found worlds but, having done so, it sought their subjugation also in a determined order. The supreme justification of imperial rule was that it brought order to chaos, reined in 'archaic instincts', and all this aptly enough through subjection to 'laws'.[45] Looked at another way, the violence of imperialism was legitimated in its being exercised through law. Imperial violence was explicitly elevated as the motor-force of an implacable progress.[46] That same violence, as Fitzjames Stephen would have it, was 'forced, disciplined and regulated in the form of law, [which] played the leading part in the creation of civilization'.[47] The pale texts of the law itself were not without their flaring passion. Thus, a leading authority on international law revealed, with the 'discoveries' in the interior of 'the Dark Continent ... the earth-hunger of the Old world had been aroused'; but passion of this kind somehow took form in a law which could 'tame ... [the] wild passion' of the savage on whom it was brought to bear.[48] 'Every civilized and independent political community', the same authority revealed, 'possesses in greater or less abundance such things as palaces, museums, ships, forts, arsenals, arms, ammunition, pictures and jewels'.[49] As the prominence of instruments of war in this little list would indicate, this was 'a belligerent civilization', something Fitzjames Stephen proudly proclaimed.[50] A stable order was to be miraculously wrought in a disordering violence. Here, yet again, we find an ambivalence in occidental self-constitution imposed upon the necessarily obliging savage who had to be violently disordered, and thus ever needful of a settled subordination, and at the same time inertly over-ordered, ever awaiting the transforming dynamism of colonization. Positively, it was law which combined exuberant violence with contained order.

The parallel with law in its national setting now becomes strained. Law in that setting was integral to 'the state's social mission' of 'homogenizing and hegemonizing ... a society conceived as inherently fragmented, atomized and centerless'.[51] Law played a key part in this by seeking to effect a direct and primary relation between the state and the individual citizen and, in so doing, to eliminate or dominate all 'intermediate' orders. In the colonies, however, the savage was the carrier of the irresolution in occidental identity and the constituent negation of its civilization and, so, had to be maintained as intractably apart from that identity and that civilization. Such an utterly antithetical being could not be brought within the replete realm of civilization, much less integrated into its emphatic instrument, the metropolitan state. The savage, in short, was denied a participative legal personality.[52] It was solely the colonist who was to provide civil and civilized order. There were no rights for the savages in this scheme, apart from 'rights' to have things done to them so as to bring them within the ambit of civilization.[53]

The savage, then, had to become the same as the civilized colonists yet remain unalterably different from them. That unsettled ambivalence permeated the whole of colonial settlement. The colonist took on the 'burden' of pervasive powers in the cause of an inclusive civilization, only to use them to exclude, dissipate and generally 'hold down' the savage as incorrigibly deviant. Comprehensive and draconic legal regimes sought to separate out and stultify not only the colonized but the traditional or customary institutions and processes imputed to them. All of which was enshrouded in ethical imperatives of 'conservation', of 'protecting' the native, especially from too disruptive an exposure to the benison of civilization. And any native who assumed a precipitate civility would be checked by a tentacular 'native regulation' or by something more brutally informal. Nothing so readily reveals the native as a projection of an irresolution in occidental identity itself than the hysterical and aggressive response of the colonist to the impertinent *évolué* who successfully takes on civilized abilities, denies deep or intractable difference, and thus exposes the fragility of imperial rule at its seemingly confident core.

What the response to the *évolué* reveals is that the imperial project was decidedly less about a bringing into the fold of civilization and definitively more about a creation and containment as different. The torpid incapacity of the savage was one which not only prevented the assumption of civilized behaviour but also denied the ability to act transformatively at all. The savage, that is, could not become anything other than what it had to be in its specular relation to the dynamism of European identity. Some effective action had to be allowed to the native, however, because of the poverty of colonial rule. Various systems of 'indirect rule', of 'recognition' of native modes necessarily proliferated. Yet the reach of such effective action was always severely circumscribed. Not only was it characterized as static, repetitive and mimetic but, for good measure, it was held, or attempted to be held, within a supervisory system of administration. Custom, for example, was 'recognized' solely in subordination to the law of the colonist and denied such recognition where it was 'repugnant to natural justice, equity, and good conscience', or contrary to 'the general principles of humanity', to take two standard and revealing formulations.

This pervasion of rule accords with the prime place set for law in the imperial project. Given the separation and containment of the natives and the denial to them of effective modes of engagement – 'strictly contractual relations are not possible'[54] – there is no space, as it were, for the development of social relations of a more 'organic' kind, relations which would ease and mediate the demands made on an overweening law. The necessity of distance was made a dubious virtue. Like a lawgiver of antiquity, the colonist claimed to bring law from the outside, a civilized law of universal valency free from polluting involvement with the particularity of the local scene.[55] This stance was imbued with the colonist's more general claim to be able to stand objectively and transcendently apart from the squabbling diversity of the natives and from that vantage not just to resolve their differences but to encompass and determine their very destiny. The progressive and evolutionary assumptions of imperial rule placed the colonist in a position which enveloped all lesser conditions of existence. From this exalted position, therefore, the colonist could know and speak for the natives better than they could themselves – and thence decide to act with an appropriate force. So, even when a customary legal system was allowed some operative effect, its aberrations and inadequacies could be put right by superior prescription. And even if, to take another example, some legal or quasi-legal capacity is allowed to the native to effect the conclusion of a treaty with the colonist, the treaty can still be disregarded when some higher imperative of civilization supervenes.

Termination

This deathly disregard of the other marks an extremity of legal determination. It could, in one way, be seen as the apotheosis of legality, its perfected achievement. Here is law supposedly in its ultimate, its full determinative force. It has no responsive regard for its subjects, or objects, who are, to borrow Maine's and Bagehot's definitive descriptions, 'caught ... in distinct spots', 'stationary societies' for ever 'stopped' in their development.[56] But the stasis and comprehensive containment visited on the savage comprise the very conditions of this law. Caught itself in an ultimacy of exclusion and denial, colonial law is fixedly restrained in law's responsive dimension. The resulting hiatus is 'filled' with an imperial responsibility *for*, one on the side of determination, rather than a responsibility *to*. A premonitory indication of this disjunction can be discerned from the colonial governor of Bombay in the middle of the nineteenth century when he remarked on 'the perilous experiment of continuing to legislate for millions of people, with few means of knowing, except by a rebellion, whether the laws suited them or not'.[57] Rebellion would eventually show they did not.

Studies of resistance to colonial rule tend nowadays to be just as unregarded as the resistance itself. They invited this fate because, all too often, these were studies of the evanescent and marginal, worlds lost and passing pathologies of desperate revolt, or they were studies of precarious persistence in stark opposition to the colonial and the modern. But effective resistances can only ever be engaged with what they resist. Such resistances should not be viewed as essentially apart from that which they resist but, rather, as integral to it. The colonial situation is now revealed in numerous histories no longer as the assumed dissemination of an *imperium* marginally resisted but as a scene of endemic contest, one in which colonial rule and its incipient successors were continually shaped and constituted in the engagement with resistances to it.[58] That situation could not be responded to or even be perceived in terms of a civilizing law which had always to be determinedly apart – 'insulated, complete and universal'.[59] Such a law could not but fail in this persistent denial of law's intrinsic need to be responsive, to respond adequately to that which it would determine. Modern imperialism, in all, marks a terminal extremity of law.

Notes

Many thanks to Diane Kirkby for the generous invitation to give and publish this talk, to Cornelia Vismann for sending the papers of hers which play such a significant part in it, to Sarah Kyambi for an engaged translation of one of those papers, and to Greg Marks for telling me of his important work on Vitoria.

1 F. de Vitoria, *De Indis*, in J.B. Scott, *The Spanish Origin of International Law: Francisco de Vitoria and His Law of Nations* (Oxford, Clarendon Press, 1934). For a wider range of reference to *De Indis* and to other works of Vitoria connected with it, and for important critical engagements, see A. Anghie, 'Francisco de Vitoria and the Colonial Origins of International Law', in E. Darian-Smith and P. Fitzpatrick (eds), *Laws of the Postcolonial* (Ann Arbor, University of Michigan Press, 1999); G.C. Marks, 'Indigenous Peoples in International Law: The Significance of Francisco de

Vitoria and Bartolome de las Casas', *The Australian Year Book of International Law*, 13 (1992), 1–51; A. Pagden, *The Fall of Natural Man* (Cambridge, Cambridge University Press, 1982), chapter 4; and R. Williams, *The American Indian in Western Legal Thought: The Discourses of Conquest* (New York, Oxford University Press, 1990), pp. 96–108, 114–18. Each of these makes a compendious yet highly significant contribution, but it is Pagden's which is central to my concerns here.

2 E.g. J.B. Scott, *The Spanish Origin of International Law: Francisco de Vitoria and His Law of Nations* (Oxford, Clarendon Press, 1934).

3 E.g. Williams, *The American Indian*, pp. 96–108.

4 For specific coverage of these points see Vitoria, *De Indis*, xiii–xiv (section I, para. 24), xxvii–viii, xxxix, xli–ii (section III, paras 3, 4, 6, 9, 10, 12)).

5 As to both of which see e.g. F. Cohen, *The Legal Conscience: Selected Papers of Felix S. Cohen* (New Haven, CT, Yale University Press, 1960), pp. 230–52; Marks, 'Indigenous Peoples'.

6 Cf. Williams, *The American Indian*, p. 57 n.100.

7 Pagden, *The Fall of Natural Man*, pp. 62–5.

8 See Pagden, *The Fall of Natural Man*, pp. 86–91, where the list is extended to take some account of Vitoria's antecedents and near contemporaries.

9 Pagden, *The Fall of Natural Man*, pp. 100–3.

10 See Pagden, *The Fall of Natural Man*, pp. 85–9.

11 Pagden, *The Fall of Natural Man*, p. 101.

12 Anghie, 'Francisco de Vitoria', p. 96; cf. H. White, *Tropics of Discourse: Essays in Cultural Criticism* (Baltimore and London, Johns Hopkins University Press, 1978), pp. 103–4.

13 Pagden, *The Fall of Natural Man*, p. 77.

14 Anghie, 'Francisco de Vitoria'.

15 C.H. Alexandrowicz, *An Introduction to the History of the Law of Nations in the East Indies* (Oxford, Clarendon Press, 1967), p. 2.

16 Alexandrowicz, *An Introduction*, p. 57.

17 See Vitoria, *De Indis*, xxxix, xli (section III, paras. 9 and 10); H. Grotius, *De Jure Belli ac Pacis*, vol. 1 (n.p. , Sijthoff, 1919), p. 28.

18 See J. Strawson, 'Islamic Law and English Texts', in E. Darian–Smith and P. Fitzpatrick (eds), *Laws of the Postcolonial* (Ann Arbor, University of Michigan Press, 1999).

19 E. de Vattel, *The Law of Nations, or the Principles of National Law Applied to the Conduct and to the Affairs of Nations and Sovereigns* trans. C.G. Fenwick (Washington, Carnegie Institute, 1916), vol. 3, p. 9.

20 *Ibid.*

21 E. de Vattel, 'Emer de Vattel on the Occupation of Territory', in P.D. Curtin (ed.), *Imperialism* (London, Macmillan, 1971), pp. 44–5.

22 L.C. Green, 'Claims to Territory in Colonial America', in L.C. Green and O.P. Dickason (eds), *The Law of Nations and the New World* (Alberta, University of Alberta Press, 1989), p. 75.

23 Cf. G. Torres and K. Milun, 'Stories and Standing: The Legal Meaning of Identity', in D. Danielsen and K. Engle (eds), *After Identity: A Reader in Law and Culture* (New York, Routledge, 1995).

24 The texts relied on here come from S. Greenblatt, *Marvelous Possessions: The Wonder of the New World* (Oxford, Clarendon Press, 1991), throughout chapter 2 but especially at p. 52 with the modification of that translation at p. 58. For a diversity of modalities of appropriation see P. Seed, *Ceremonies of Possession in European Conquest of the New World, 1492–1640* (Cambridge, Cambridge University Press, 1995).

25 The division here should not, of course, be seen as a sharp one. 'The marvel of the divine gift', which is how Columbus saw the Indies, 'is at once a legitimation and a transcendence of the legal act' (Greenblatt, *Marvelous Possessions*, p. 80).

26 See C. Vismann, 'Terra Nullius: Zum Feindbegriff im Völkerrecht', in Armin Adam and Martin Stingelin (eds), *Übertragung und Gesetz: Gründungsmythen, Kriegstheater und Unterwerfungstechniken von Institutionen* (Berlin, Akademie Verlag, 1995), p. 168.

27 See Vismann, 'Terra Nullius', p. 169; C. Vismann, 'Starting from Scratch, Concepts of Order in No Man's Land', in B. Höppauf (ed.), *War, Violence and the Modern Condition* (Berlin and New York, Walter de Gruyter, 1997), p. 50.

28 Vismann, 'Starting from Scratch', pp. 50–1.

29 E.g. Green, 'Claims to Territory' p. 81; I.A. Shearer, *Starke's International Law*, 11th edn (London, Butterworths, 1994), pp. 147–8.

30 Vismann, 'Starting from Scratch', p. 46.

31 P. Fitzpatrick, *The Mythology of Modern Law*, (London, Routledge, 1992), pp. 72–91.

32 G.W.H. Hegel, *Philosophy of Right*, trans. T.M. Knox (Oxford, Clarendon Press, 1952), pp. 218–19.

33 Cf. J.-J. Rousseau, *The Social Contract* (London, Penguin, 1968), p. 67; and see Vismann, 'Terra Nullius', p. 167.

34 See P. Passavant, 'A Moral Geography of Liberty: John Stuart Mill and American Free-Speech Discourse', in E. Darian-Smith and P. Fitzpatrick (eds), *Laws of the Postcolonial* (Ann Arbor, University of Michigan Press, 1999), pp. 67–75.

35 See A. Riles, 'Aspiration and Control: International Legal Rhetoric and the Essentialization of Culture', *Harvard Law Review*, 106:3 (1993), pp. 723–40.

36 J. Westlake, 'John Westlake on the Title to Sovereignty', in P.D. Curtin (ed.), *Imperialism* (London and Basingstoke, Macmillan, 1971), p. 47.

37 J.S. Mill, *Essays on Politics and Culture* (New York, Doubleday, 1962), p. 406. On this score, Passavant, 'A Moral Geography', provides a remarkably searching demystification of Mill.

38 Mill, *Essays*, p. 406.

39 J.S. Mill, *On Liberty*, in *Utilitarianism, On Liberty, Essays on Bentham* (n.p., Fontana, 1962), p. 136.

40 Westlake, 'Title to Sovereignty', pp. 47, 50–1.

41 P. Darby, *Three Faces of Imperialism, British and American Approaches to Asia and Africa 1870–1970* (New Haven, CT, Yale University Press, 1987), p. 37; Lord Lugard, *The Dual Mandate in British Tropical Africa*, 5th edn (London, Frank Cass, 1965), pp. 546–7.

42 G. Poggi, *The Development of the Modern State: A Sociological Introduction* (London, Hutchinson, 1978), pp. 73–4.

43 See E. Stokes, *The English Utilitarians and India* (Oxford, Clarendon Press, 1959), p. 118, for a significant example. No matter what the national or imperial rivalries among the 'great powers', they did see each other as the carriers of a civilization common to them all. For his 'General or Universal Jurisprudence', Austin had only to extract its principles from a few great legal systems; see J. Austin, *The Province of Jurisprudence Determined*, 2nd edn and Lectures on Jurisprudence, 3 vols, (London, John Murray, 1861–63), vol. I, pp. 350, 356–7.

44 See Stokes, *The English Utilitarians*, p. 299.

45 See Stokes, *The English Utilitarians*, p. 299; E.W. Said, *Orientalism* (Harmondsworth, Penguin, 1985), p. 219.

46 See e.g. A. Nandy, *The Intimate Enemy: Loss and Recovery of Self Under Colonialism* (Delhi, Oxford University Press, 1983), p. 69.

47 See Stokes, *The English Utilitarians*, p. 294.

48 See Riles, 'Aspiration and Control' (pp. 730–1) for this instance, and her whole note for an abundance of others accompanied with much analytical verve.

49 See Riles, 'Aspiration and Control' p. 735.

50 See Stokes, *The English Utilitarians*, p. 288.

51 Poggi, *Development*, p. 121.

52 Some colonial powers allowed some rights of metropolitan citizenship but the overall position of the colonized remained very far from even formal equality.

53 A.P. Thornton, *Doctrines of Imperialism* (New York, John Wiley & Sons, 1965), p. 158.

54 J. Maquet, 'Inborn Differences and the Premise of Inequality', in P. Baxter and B. Sansom (eds), *Race and Social Difference* (Harmondsworth, Penguin) 1972, p. 232.

55 Stokes, *The English Utilitarians*, p. 178.

56 W. Bagehot, *Physics and Politics, or Thoughts on the Application of the Principles of Natural Selection and Inheritance to Political Society* (London, Kegan Paul, Trench & Trubner, n.d.), pp. 29–30; H. Maine, *Ancient Law* (London, Oxford University Press, 1931), pp. 18–19, 64, 141.
57 Thornton, *Doctrines*, p. 181.
58 E.g. J. Axtell, *The Invasion Within: The Conquest of Cultures in Colonial North America* (New York, Oxford University Press, 1985).
59 S. Swain, 'Postmodern Narratives and the Absurdity of Law', in S. Earnshaw (ed.), *Just Postmodernism* (Amsterdam, Editions Rodopi B.V., 1997), p. 22.

CHAPTER TWO

Law's empire: chartering English colonies on the American mainland in the seventeenth century

Christopher Tomlins

Curiously, much of the 'colonial' era of American history (understood as the period from the first English encroachments on the North Atlantic seaboard in the late sixteenth century until the end of the War of Independence in 1783) has been written of as a history not of colonizing at all, but of settlement. 'Colonial America', in traditional parlance, is not *colonized* America. Rather, it is what precedes the United States in the larger story of revolutionary climacteric and subsequent national development. One experiences a history of colonial encounter and colonizing process that disregards colonization as an interpretive perspective of relevance to this or any later period of American history, treating the arrival and presence of the English in America more or less as a given from which point history is written, not a problem to be incorporated in historical explanation. It is of course quite justifiable to treat English colonies in mainland America as islands in a spreading English archipelago. But their presence needs to be rendered explicitly part of that archipelago, not assumed. That is, one needs to do for the English in America what Donna Merwick has done for the Dutch – namely, draw attention to them. Instead, American historians have tended to write the history of the colonial era largely as an inside narrative of the formation of the settler societies that eventually became building blocks of a new nation.[1]

This essay approaches mainland settlement from the outside, as first and foremost an expression of, largely English, colonizing impulses. To *colonize* means, fundamentally, to appropriate, to take possession. What is appropriated varies. In the Americas, the Spanish appropriated both metallic wealth and an indigenous population to extract it. The Dutch appropriated routes, connections, to sustain commerce. The English appropriated territory, which required that they find ways either of sharing it with a pre-existing population or of depopulating it – mostly the latter. Appropriation is conventionally material but not necessarily so; how appropriation is implemented is therefore complex, because it has many dimensions. Force, obviously, is one major instrumentality. But at least as important are the techniques that permit one to plan, explain and justify one's appropriations, to and for oneself. Colonization, this suggests, has an epistemology of its own – a theory of knowing that enables the processes of 'discovery' and ordering (or more accurately re-ordering) inherent in appropriation to take place. Colonization is a matter of intellectual as well as material possessing that, in the act of taking, re-invents what it appropriates for its own purposes.

So understood, the process of colonization in the American case was in good part a legal construct, expressed in the numerous charters and letters patent secured over the course of the seventeenth century by English proponents of Western planting to define, describe and justify their activities. It is hardly novel to investigate things American as constructs of English law. Much of American historiography assumes English legal culture as a foundation, notably as a font of liberties more perfectly realized in a revolutionary America. Not for some considerable time has it been thought worth exploring whether the substance of the English template should be sought in an examination of the forms that authorized colonizing adventures, rather than through the more usual exercise of seeking out colonial reactions to doctrines or theories current in metropolitan common-law texts, courtrooms, or constitutional discourse.

Why, then, engage in that exploration? First, the elaborated legality of chartering clearly provided the necessary legitimacy for colonizing projects. Second, and more interesting, chartering as a legal process offered projectors means to plan and implement enterprises whose practical dimensions, for obvious reasons, could not be known with any certainty. Charters allowed projectors to define and pursue territorial claims formulated, necessarily, in abstract; they provided a medium in which to declare, with precision, the order of things and people that would desirably eventuate; and they provided means by which that order and the specific socio-legal structures in which it was embodied could be projected onto unmapped transatlantic landscapes.

The essay has a further and complementary objective. In implementing their designs, English projectors encountered competing conceptions and, consequently, conflicts. Historians have tended to treat departures from projectors' plans as inevitable corrections brought about by the intrusion of local environmental realities upon projectors' fantasies, or as the necessary consequence of an implicit evolutionary logic of legal–political maturation. But competition and conflict can also be seen to stem from the collision of different English legal cultures brought by migration into unavoidable proximity, legal cultures expressed on the one hand in the structures of authoritative socio-legal order planned by colonizing projectors, and on the other implicit in the massed migrations of actual settlers. Persistent variety, not a singular developmental logic, is the distinguishing characteristic of the English settlement of America. Just as David Hackett Fischer has disassembled a wide array of metropolitan practices and institutions into regional variations and shown their persisting influence as reconstituted American regionalisms,[2] it makes sense to investigate to what extent the process of designing and implementing settlement gave expression to distinct legal cultures originating in differing British locales, bred up there by distinct institutional trajectories, histories and local practices.

The most informative early discussion of English colonization can be found in the work of two cousins, both named Richard Hakluyt, who wrote extensively on the subject between 1570 and 1610.[3] Long identified as prolific ideologists of colonization, the Hakluyts are particularly remarkable for the extraordinarily 'applied' quality of their work. They outlined not simply an ideology of expansion but also offered a methodology for appropriation (in both the material and the intellectual sense) based on four powerful interrelated components – Christianity, commerce, geography and law. But while all four played crucial parts in the Hakluyts' discourse, their relative significance differed. Were one to isolate the key to the colonizing project described in their writings – bluntly stated by the elder Hakluyt as determining, once a country or province had been conquered, how 'to man it, to plant it, and to keepe it'[4] – one would find Christianity and commerce assuming a reduced role. When expansionists turned to the measures necessary for the realization of colonization's essential processes, what they mobilized were geography and law.

Christian evangelism provided a general underpinning for the ambitions of both Hakluyts, as it had for two centuries for all European expansion overseas. The English claims the Hakluyts propagandized were founded on the papal-asserted rights of Christian rulers to authorize occupation of the lands of non-Christian rulers and convert their inhabitants. Thus, the younger Hakluyt's contemporaneous *Discourse of Western Planting* (1584) took as its point of departure 'That this westerne discoverie will be greately for the enlargement of the gospell of Christe'. But although Christian ambition furnished both general impetus and grandiose justification it did not furnish instruments. Before the younger Hakluyt's opening exposition was a quarter complete, he had moved on to by 'what meanes ... this most godly and Christian work may be perfourmed'. His answer was 'by plantinge colonies of our nation'. And, from that point on, *planting* took centre

[28]

stage in Hakluyt's discourse, its secular characteristics his abiding concern – revival of trades, production of commodities, employment of the idle, and withal a general accretion in 'the strengthe of our Realme'.[5] Similarly, commerce, in principle a civilizing and mutually beneficial 'trafficke' between peoples, appeared in the Hakluyts' discourse as an activity with rather limited prospects – likely to be successful only to the extent that it was divorced from any dependence on the involvement of the indigenous population, an expression of wholly intra-European relationships between *colon* occupants of new territories and their metropolitan sponsors.[6] Nor, in either case, was the activity independently self-realizing. Both Christianity and commerce required planting as a pre-condition of their success. Neither furnished instrumentalities or technologies that were conditions of planting's success.

Success in planting was far more dependent upon the other discourses mobilized by the Hakluyts – geography and law. Each furnished means to formulate the precise statements of relationships, existing or desired, between places and people, that were crucial to successful planting. Each offered means to design and implement those relationships. Finally, each provided a potent medium for the imposition of meaning on the activities engendered.

In the late sixteenth century, geography was one in a spectrum of interrelated techniques for study and measurement of the world. At one end of that spectrum lay *chorography*, which denoted the narrative description of specific regions – their topography, inhabitants, institutions, cultures. At the other end lay *cosmography*, which combined techniques of terrestrial and celestial observation in predominantly representational and abstract attempts to map the world as a whole. Geography filled the range between: its horizons wider than the chorographer's region, its goals more substantively descriptive than the cosmographer's representations of the world.

Cosmography, within the intellectual sphere primarily of the younger Hakluyt, was an essential instrumentality of successful navigation. The younger Hakluyt, however, also cast geographic knowledge as a means for the projection of national political and economic ambitions onto newly discovered worlds. Such a connection of geography to colonizing should not be unduly surprising. Matthew Edney's recent study of the geographical construction of British India has stressed how 'geography and empire are ... intimately and thoroughly interwoven ... both fundamentally concerned with territory and knowledge', how British scientific–intellectual activity in India created a representation of what 'India' comprised that conformed it to British purpose. Two centuries earlier, Hakluyt's *Discourse* helped begin the creation of a similar *English* representation of America.[7]

Yet although geographic knowledge was thus as instrumental to this late sixteenth-century invention of empire overseas as it would be to its Asian subcontinental extension 200 years later, the younger Hakluyt was at a disadvantage relative to his descendants. Their techniques were born in the Enlightenment's general commitments to rigorous rational inquiry and empirical certainty. In India, British access to particular technologies of systematic measurement – geodetic triangulation, statistical survey and so forth – allowed them to discipline the subcontinent with their science, transforming India, as Edney puts it, 'from an exotic and largely unknown region into a well-defined and knowable geographic entity'. Hakluyt in contrast, was reliant on scraps of impressionistic second-hand narrative. His resources were far more limited, and the results less organized.[8]

Certainly, the achievement of intellectual control over appropriated territory through survey and mapping would become an essential aspect of European expansion and overseas colonizing. Maps enabled their creators and their sponsors to take 'effective visual and conceptual possession' of whatever they represented. They were important instrumentalities for the creation of new identities, the consolidation of new intrusions of authority, throughout the first English overseas empire. Yet it is also the case that maps did not do so in detail. Colonial survey was neither consistently scientific in its methods nor definitive in its results, nor was visual mapping a routine practice for recording outcomes. Rather than being visually recorded, territory was summarized and possessed by written description – enumerations of assets, narratives of features 'parcel by parcel, by means of lists of bounds and abuttals.'[9]

This description reminds us of the centrality of narrative to chorography; but it also takes us further afield, to a distinct though closely related technology, conceptually no less powerful in matters of possession than mapping's cartographic descriptions and representations, and certainly as authoritative: that is, law. For the documents that enabled land to be possessed and surveyed, sold and bought, used, valued, taxed, inherited were, of course, legal documents. Everywhere the English went in North America, as Richard Bushman argues, 'legal texts' constructed the particular objects of their industry – the fields and fences, the farmhouses and ordinaries, the characters who inhabited them, their transactions, their relationships, the 'habits of living, actions, dangers, and rewards' that motivated them. Collectively and over time, law created 'a set of deep routines … of social interaction and human purpose' – in effect an inventory of exemplary activities that helped to constitute the cultural field in which action occurred, and to establish authoritative identities for the subjects within the field's parameters, whether people, places, institutions, activities or relationships.[10]

[30]

In the case of colonizing, this was almost invariably a prospective inventory – a means of anticipating, and planning, what would come to be. Take as one of the first available examples the so-called *Notes on Colonization* drawn up by the elder Hakluyt in 1578 to instruct Sir Humfrey Gylberte in his pursuit of a project of discovery and colonization authorized by Elizabeth I. Drafted at the request of Gylberte's backers, the *Notes* are analogous in form to the shipping instructions by which merchants commissioned captains and directed them in the performance of voyages: they prescribe how Gylberte should implement Elizabeth's patent. They combine several elements: first, a list of technical tasks to be performed – materials and sustenance to be secured, territory to be scouted, a harbour located, commodities planted and processed; second, a speculation on what resources might be found and commodified – 'golde, silver, copper, quicksilver ... Rootes, Berries, Fruites, wood or earth fitte for dying ... hides of beastes fitte for sole Lether ... Figges, Almondes, Sugar Canes'. In both these respects the *Notes* comprise a catalogue of practical activity and a canvassing of contingencies.

Overriding the whole was a portentous invocation of the kind of society required to facilitate such development, and the kind of statecraft required to give it ascendancy over the 'savages'. It was to be a permanent settlement. It was to aspire to dominion over its region. Above all it was to be a 'Citie' – a permanent settlement of brick and stone, of houses and roofs and walls, of all the 'thinges without which no ... people [may] in civill sorte be kept together'. In this way the *Notes* announce the effective theme of the coming century of English expansion, which consisted of repeated efforts to define precisely those 'thinges' – both material and ideational. Gylberte's original letters patent, together with Hakluyt's *Notes*, constitute the initial example of an authoritative plan of colonizing activities that employed law for planning and eventually, in the projected ascendancy of the colonial *civitas* governing its region, for implementing the appropriation of territory and its domination.[11]

Gylberte's letters did not become the basis of permanent settlements, nor did the more elaborate exercise surrounding the planning of Ralegh's expedition to Roanoke several years later. The first comprehensive illustration of the English model at work is on display in the first charter of Virginia, granted in 1606. The charter licensed two colonies 'of sundry of our People' to be established in 'that part of America commonly called VIRGINIA', territory 'not now actually possessed by any Christian Prince or People'. Neither was to be established within 100 miles of the other. Each colony's patentees were granted 'all the lands, Tenements, and Hereditaments' within its precincts, to be held of the Crown, 'as of our Manor at East-Greenwich, in the County of Kent, in free and common Soccage only, and not in Capite', whereon they might 'inhabit ... build and fortify' at their discretion. Each colony was to have its own council, to 'govern ... according to such Laws, Ordinances, and Instructions, as shall be, in that behalf, given and signed with Our Hand'. Both were granted particular privileges (for example, unencumbered flows of people and armaments), tending to confirm them in physical and economic command of their own borders.[12]

Using the charter to plan and distribute powers and institutions of government, grant subsidies and define and dispose of land and minerals was an exercise in the creation of jurisdictions. The charter was also used to confirm other crucial jurisdictional arrangements governing the disposition of vital resources, notably population. First, it expressed the crown's supervening jurisdictional authority over its subjects by explicitly permitting their departure for purposes of colonizing. Second, it extended a common civic status to the inhabitants of the Virginia settlements, and simultaneously situated the settlements within a web of like polities among which population was (in civic personality) fungible. All persons being the crown's subjects, dwelling and inhabiting within both colonies had 'all [the] Liberties, Franchises, and Immunities within any of our other Dominions', as if abiding and born within England 'or any other of our said Dominions'. In both respects the charter offers an interesting contrast between its representation of the prospective population – transportable, interchangeable, but jurisdictionally organized and culturally 'settled' in appropriate civic order – and the actual indigenous inhabitants, who were invoked as a preliminary only to establish that their want of civic personality rendered them unsettled, and therefore unfit to occupy what they, in fact, occupied. They lived 'in Darkness and miserable Ignorance of the true Knowledge and Worship of God'. Theirs was not a *civitas*. Only the creation of colonies, the charter claimed, might 'bring the Infidels and Savages ... to a settled and quiet Government'.[13]

Future charters – of which there were many – differed in the extent of their claims and the terms in which they were made, but performed in essence the same role, mobilizing legal discourses both instrumentally and imaginatively to imprint *England* on America. In each case the document that was used to permit colonization simultaneously supplied a medium in which to plan its expression. Coloniszation's essential features – physical (location), economic (the distribution of rights over land and other resources, the control of flows of population), political (the structure of government) and civic (the legal character of colonial personhood, hence the basis upon which all other listed privileges might be claimed) – were all given points of English reference that enabled, instrumentally, the process to take place. This gave the process a language – law – in which it could take place and in which, more important, it could become transactionally aligned with myriad enabling processes. Collectively these functioned as signs of colonization's legitimacy to English audiences, and as specifications of the process's limits and boundaries. The whole comprised serial authoritative re-presentations of a vast and remote tract of territory – from 'Florida to the Circle Articke' as Hakluyt described it – in familiar English designs that underscored English possession and simultaneously rendered competing occupants and their practices, to English intents and purposes, practically invisible.

The charters were often inconsistent with each other, their conflicts and overlaps a sign of intense competition for territory. Charles M. Andrews commented many years ago: 'One wonders if any of the crown lawyers or chancery officials ever consulted the old patents in making out a new one, or ever studied the geography of the regions they so easily gave away.'[14] Perhaps one should take this as a sign of disorganization or indeed of the relative unimportance of chartering as compared with 'facts on the ground' – the physical creation of settlements. But colonizing impulses will find different expressions in different places for different purposes. Which was the more impressive or the more informative from a metropolitan standpoint – the thin scattering of actual English settlements up and down the mainland coast in the seventeenth century or the dense and elaborate tapestry of possessory and jurisdictional claims that blanketed it?

In the charters, in any case, physical occupancy and legalized claim overlap as expressions of colonizing. For example, all the charters are catalogues of intense creative activity. All foreshadow systematic transformative action on the land. The New England Charter of 1620, for example, endows 'Adventurers intending to erect and establish fishery, trade and plantations'.[15] Charters in general underscored possession of fisheries, harbours and soils. Later charters give greater emphasis to cultural signs of occupation rather than specificities of use – the division of lands, the erection of churches, manors and fortifications, towns and markets. All, however, imply substantial constructive activity.

It is well established, of course, that the claim of legitimacy of appropriation by use or constructive occupation meant that previous or current occupants did not use (or constructively occupy) the space in question. The 'natives' were savage both by dint of their paganism but also by dint of their failure (in the English imagination) to cultivate or 'improve'. Thus the evangelical and appropriative justifications tended to merge into one characterization of a prior 'emptiness' that permitted occupancy. This could be a claim of actual physical empti-ness – as in the New England case, where 'God's Visitation', the char-ter stated, had 'raigned a wonderfull Plague' wherefore 'those large and goodly Territoryes, deserted as it were by their naturall Inhabitants, should be possessed and enjoyed by ... our Subjects'. Before the end of the century, however, it had become a claim to a general spiritual–ideological emptiness to which the actual presence or absence of an indigenous population was irrelevant. The Pennsylvania Charter, for example, defined the colony's general objects in language that could simultaneously acknowledge the physical presence of an existing indigenous population while denying that presence any political or legal significance:

> Our well-beloved Subject, William Penn, Esquire ... out of a commend-able Desire to enlarge our English Empire, and promote such usefull comodities as may bee of Benefit to us and Our Dominions, as also to reduce the savage Natives by gentle and just manners to the Love of Civil Societie and Christian Religion, hath humbly besought Leave of Us to transport an ample Colonie unto a certaine Countrey ... in the Partes of America *not yet cultivated and planted.*

The natives did not occupy anything because they did not cultivate. They were simply ... there.[16]

As interesting as the actual territorial grants and the claims to occu-pancy that their aspiring possessors invoked – where there is consider-able continuity in English discourse – are the structures of authority through which claimants proposed to pursue control of and organize activity in their territories (that is, build states). Here continuities are less apparent.

Between 1606, the date of the first Virginia Charter, and 1681 the Pennsylvania Charter, some twenty-eight major territorial charters and grants were promulgated, dealing with the establishment, re-estab-lishment or confirmation of English, and one Scottish, settlements on the North American mainland. Each described a particular territory and the particular institutional and cultural forms in which authority would be applied to that territory. Those forms changed over time. As is well known, the initial expression of English colonizing was pre-dominantly one of commercialized settlement through incorporated trading companies. During the 1620s the incorporated company as institutional model for the colonial 'state' was succeeded by territorial lordship, a distinctly different expression of jurisdiction. Forms of authority considered appropriate to control over commodities were increasingly replaced by forms of proprietorial authority appropriate to control over people and expanse, a transition that occurred precisely as metropolitan concerns about migration and the control of territorial extent through transplantation of population became more and more prominent.

In fact the proprietorial idea layered additional discourses of authority and jurisdiction onto familiar conceptions of territorial lordship. From 1623 on, English charters made *palatine*, that is to say *vice-regal*, authority and institutions key features of North American colonization. Palatine powers invoked and conveyed distinctly seigneurial capacities. The idea expressed the ambition shared by crown and proprietors alike to control England's American territorial claims through institutions and powers designed for remote and contested regions that allowed local authorities to exercise effective regional sovereignty.

Proprietorial colonization climaxed after the Restoration. The post-Restoration grants were notable for the size of the territories involved and, in two cases at least – Carolina and Pennsylvania – for the density and sophistication of the civic establishment they envisaged. The Carolina Charter of 1663 and the *Fundamental Constitutions of Carolina*, written six years later by the young John Locke, are quite fascinating – by far the most elaborated statement of English proprietorial colonization's mapping of authority onto an expanse of mainland territory.[17] Here, however, let us give more attention to William Penn's 1681 charter for Pennsylvania, because it was the last of the great seventeenth-century proprietorial grants and hence closes this part of the story.

Although the smallest of the major Restoration proprietaries, Penn's grant was substantial. But it was a departure in both its territorial and its institutional aspects from those that had preceded it. First, the way it described territory hinted at the intrusion of new scientific conceptions of territorial marking onto the chorographic perambulations of metes and bounds that had until that point formed the descriptive basis of the American charters.[18] This foreshadows the abstract measurement and command of territory that would become such a marked feature of post-Enlightenment imperialism. Second, the way the charter described jurisdiction invoked the imperial as well as the proprietorial state much more explicitly than had previous charters.

Previous charters had never extended their concern for local detail beyond topographical marking and the appropriation of resources. They were all metropolitan products. Local political institutions, the local economy and local culture were all re-presented in a welter of English impositions. In this regard, Penn's charter was no exception at all. All its points of social, economic, political and cultural reference projected *Englishness* onto the mainland. Penn himself was made a

[35]

'true and absolute' proprietor, holding the land in free and common socage. He was granted 'free and absolute' power to divide the country into 'Townes, Hundreds and Counties', to 'erect and incorporate Townes into Borroughs, and Borroughs into Citties, and to make and constitute ffaires and Marketts'. He was to be free to 'assigne, alien, Grant, demise, or enfeoffe' without restriction. He was to be free to 'erect any parcells of Land ... into Mannor's and in every one such to have and hold Court-Baron, and View of ffrank-pledge'.[19]

Within that English context, however, Penn's charter signified a diminution of capacity, the closing of an era of extensive delegation of colonizing responsibilities and governing authority. Though proprietorial, Pennsylvania was not palatine. Penn's charter powers were not as extensive as those of the Carolina proprietors, nor of the Calverts in Maryland before them. Like them he could make laws, with the approbation of the province's freemen, and appoint 'Judges and Justices, Magistrates and Officers ... for what Causes soever'. But the Privy Council had oversight of provincial laws; and the king retained the right to hear appeals. Proprietorial discretion in the disposition of land was constrained by restrictions on subinfeudation. Proprietorial discretion in the control of trade was constrained by the requirement of strict adherence to the acts of navigation. Proprietorial control of the economy was limited by royal claims of a right (with parliamentary consent) to impose taxes. By the 1680s, in fact, what Penn's charter revealed in its English context was that the proprietorial design for English colonization was fast being eclipsed by the expanding English State. Colonization, as before it had not been, was re-presented as an enterprise of an imperial state and an expression of nation.[20]

To see colonial charters in this light helps us refine our perception of the dynamics of the relationship between law and European colonial expansion. John and Jean Comaroff have argued forcefully against what they see as a scholarly tendency to insist upon the absolute centrality of law in the colonization of the non-European world. As scholars investigate how 'Eurocentric hegemonies and colonial subjects' are made, say the Comaroffs, they turn over and over to law, as the source of the necessary 'tools of domination and disempowerment', the 'blunt instruments' needed by 'states, ruling classes, reigning regimes'. The Comaroffs dispute the sufficiency of this line of scholarship. Coloniszation's legalities, they argue, were less an instrumental facilitation of a 'linear, coherent, coercive process' than an imaginative resource not entirely under the colonizer's control. Clearly law could have instrumental effects in discrete circumstances, but considered as a general phenomenon law was and is 'inherently ambivalent, contradictory'.[21]

Examination of the charters that authorized English intrusions onto the American mainland both relativizes and reinforces the Comaroffs' critique. The claim is relativized because, considered from the outside simply as a genus of legal activity, chartering was quite linear and not at all self-contradictory. Its purpose was not at all ambiguous – it was the creation of English colonies. And considered as such it was clearly a success. It is true that in the second empire, centred on India and southern Africa, indigenous colonial subjects were able to discover how to mobilize the colonizer's legalities in their own struggles against him; but it is also true that the first, Atlantic, Empire offers much less evidence of this. The design of seventeenth-century English colonizing was insular and monocultural. It expressed a dramatic social, cultural and economic separation between the colonizers, who were 'settled', and civically endowed, and the indigenous world that they had entered, which was unsettled and 'savage'. In that Empire much less was shared.

Considered on its own terms, however – that is from *within* an initial characterisation as a legal activity expressing and projecting Englishness and English rule – chartering's linearity becomes far less evident. Here then is an important degree of reinforcement for the Comaroffs' observation. First, as we have seen, one encounters in the genre itself a variety of expressions of Englishness, and successive differing modalities of rule – commercial, proprietorial, national. Seventeenth-century England was not singular but plural, not Albion but 'poly-Olbion'.[22] What chartering accomplished, that is, was the appropriation of territory to English variety. Second, in institutional terms all those expressions were highly prescriptive representations of the English *civitas*. There is much to be gained by investigating them as such, for it is important to remember that English settlement did not occur in vacant legal–conceptual space, anymore than it did in vacant physical space. Study of the charters allows us to inquire into the varied composition of colonization's legalities, precisely because it recalls to our attention the institutional and political contexts for settler legal culture that existed beyond those in evidence on the spot. The legal history of early America written over the last fifteen years has been primarily social–historical in nature, written from the ground up, as if the only significant referent were the quotidien social behaviour of the colonies' settler populations. The charters offer a different context, a different set of references for what colonization, rather than simply settlement, entailed.

Finally, and now admitting the importance of ground-up behaviour and influences in the formation of early American settler legal cultures, what light do the charters throw on the process of *their* composition?

Was there an ineffaceable common fund of 'English' legality on which all impositions of England on America drew, chartering elites and migrating masses alike, or did there exist fundamental distinctions in English legal culture that transferred with English colonists? If the latter, what were their origins, and what were their effects once transported?

Here we can be informed by *Albion's Seed,* in which David Hackett Fischer proposes that the several waves of British migration into North America occurring during the seventeenth century created distinct societies, each based on a core movement of people and folkways from a particular region of the British Isles.[23] Fischer calls such settler core groups 'elites'; but before *we* can call them that we must distinguish them from the metropolitan magnates and courtiers who negotiated the colonial charters and who really were elites, few of whom were participants in the actual process of settlement. Among the actual settlers, 'elites' were generally quite unremarkable in their social origins – at best minor gentry and substantial householders. They were elites only relative to the even more modest social composition of the mass of migrants.

What is important about the settler elites is that they were overwhelmingly regional in their original solidarities. In other words, the cultural resources – knowledge, relationships, ascendancies – upon which core migrants relied to establish rules of engagement with each other were regional not national in their points of reference.

Historians like George Haskins and David Konig, and more recently Cornelia Dayton and William Offutt, have shown that among all the means to the establishment of local rules of engagement, law enjoyed considerable prominence.[24] We have already seen that processes of colonization were framed by the discourse of legalities, both as general legitimation and as a more specific matter of designing procedures for the occupation of territory and the organisation and government of settler populations. But the legal cultures actually created in the regions of mainland settlement departed from many of the prescriptions to be found in the colonial charters. They also differed from each other. Colonization no more exhibited a common national legal culture in action than any other facet of Albion's social seeding.

Early-modern England was dense in law and its institutions, but there was nothing particularly unitary about English law as a cultural field. Critics labelled it 'dispersed and uncertain', unsystematic and unimproved, uncivilized, 'barbaric'. Richard Helgerson points to Sir Edward Coke's Tudor–Stuart era project of 'writing English law' as the product of Coke's 'persistent awareness' of external rivals, like continental roman law, 'against which English law had to defend and define itself'. But the rivals were also internal, and Coke's passion for national–legal consolidation had 'a double-face ... turned inward to find out and eliminate those practices and those institutions that failed to reflect back its own unitary image' as well as outward 'to declare its defining difference'.[25]

The sources of English law's interior diversity were both regional and social. Regional plurality in English legal culture was revealed by the very same chorographic texts that recorded the diversity of the country's institutions and topographical features. Take the work of the Kent Justice of the Peace William Lambarde. His *Perambulation of Kent* (1576), the first history of an English county, made law an important part of the narrative of Kent's distinctiveness, discussing at some length the peculiarities of Kentish inheritance practices.[26] As to *social* differentiation, we may observe that although law was assuredly an essential element of the so-called 'great tradition' of supra-local patrician culture, it was no great tradition monopoly – except, perhaps, in its most ritual presentations. For commoners in general, law was 'part of popular culture ... something which people used and participated in'. Though the singularity 'law' implies unity in meaning, the existence of such differentiated social opinions about law can also be taken to stand for distinct conceptions of what 'law' actually was.[27]

Evidence of both social and regional difference in English conceptions of legal order, and more generally of authority, is abundant. Keith Wrightson, for example, contrasts the intensifying 'infrastructural reach' of the Tudor–Stuart state with the endemic 'variability in contexts and options' exhibited across the country's 9,000 parishes. Studies underlining the continued importance of locally oriented manor courts in local dispute settlement have also stressed how the 'wide variation of practice and jurisdiction' among those courts belies 'the uniformity implicit in the legal handbooks of the day'.[28]

More systematic analysis of legal–cultural variation may be possible. Margaret Somers, for example, has attempted to establish an historical sociology of law grounded on the hypothesis that the legal culture of localities in Britain varied according to whether they were to be found in 'arable' or 'pastoral' regions. The country, she claims, manifested two distinct 'types' of legal culture, pastoral regions tending to manifest a substantially greater consciousness of legal right and of entitlement to participate in law-making processes than arable. In arable regions, strong manorial institutions created private spheres of power and 'a hierarchical chain of relationships'. In pastoral highland and woodland regions manorialism was weak or non-existent and the population primarily one of 'small free-holding peasant villagers who farmed and lived in scattered villages and hamlets'. Pastoral communities were more self-contained than arable, family cohesion was higher, powerful elite figures from outside the immediate locale were less in evidence, officeholders closer to the people.[29]

Historians will always want to treat such generalizations with some caution, if for no other reason than that ideal-type analysis necessarily abstracts from actual empirical example. Nevertheless, both conceptually, and in some important particulars empirically, Somers's hypotheses are relevant to our understanding of the legal cultures that migrants established on the early North American mainland. The migrant streams that fed New England and the Delaware Valley, for example, had important 'pastoral' resonances through their roots in, respectively, southern East Anglia and the Pennine northwest. Migration to the Chesapeake meanwhile had sufficient elite connection to downland southern England to mark the Chesapeake's legal culture as, potentially, quite distinct.

In the American case colonization was (as we have seen) designed by elites, but it was precisely people from the 'plebeian' strata – both above and including the labouring poor – who constituted the mass of each of the three major seventeenth-century transatlantic migrant streams. Hence one may propose that the movement of socially identifiable strata of the population implied the movement of socially identifiable legal cultures. Given, further, that migration to each of the three mainland regions of primary reception had identifiable regional characteristics, one may propose, similarly, that transatlantic movement implied the movement of regionally distinct legal cultures.

Recognizing early American history as a true 'colonial' history does not excuse one from writing the history of migration and settlement. But it does recommend situating the dynamics of migration and settlement anew, within the history of colonization. Here I have used the colonial charters as a means of invoking and characterizing the phenomenon of colonization in the American case. As an endeavour ultimately dependent upon the importation of population to confirm the boundaries established, to process resources and to cement occupancy on the ground, colonization was not simply a unitary enterprise of legal claiming and naming; it was necessarily one dependent upon the movement of people, which in turn meant the transference of social and cultural plurality. At the same time, the movement of people has no meaning if separated from the context of colonizing. Interaction between the process of colonization and the plurality it imported, this suggests, may be seen as the prime mover of early American history. In acknowledging both the process of colonization and the importation of people in all their variety, historians will find themselves in a position to interpret early American history anew.

Conclusion

'More vividly perhaps than any other developments during the first century', Jack Greene has argued, 'the number and range of [colonizing] experiments illustrates the extent to which America had been identified among Europeans as a site for the realization of dreams and hopes that could not be achieved in the Old World'. Greene is referring here to the charter designs with which the bulk of this paper has been concerned. 'Of course', he continues, 'all of these efforts were failures' and their failure was 'almost immediate.' Intricate designs yielded to cruder material realities of resource allocation, demography and economy. New World settlers substituted as 'their principal collective social goal the creation of some sort of recognisable version of the metropolitan society'.[30]

One can be thus confident of the 'failure' of English colonization designs only if one has first assumed a position on the interior of the history of English expansion. Viewed from the outside, where were the failures? The first objective of colonial chartering was to sanction the planting of colonies; the second, to employ the discourses and methodologies to hand to impress Englishness in detail on the American mainland, and to displace competitors. Both were attained. A third objective was to design particular political economies and state forms for the colonies themselves. Here some degree of failure is more evident, although neither as quickly nor as finally as Greene implies. Ideologically, Massachusetts's loss of its charter half a century after the founding of the colony was deeply traumatic – hardly a sign of the charter's irrelevance. Both the politics and the expression of proprietorial design were of continuing influence in the development of both Maryland and Pennsylvania well into the second half of the eighteenth century. The work of John Reid and others on conceptions of rights and liberties in the revolutionary epoch also suggests that the provisions of the colonial charters remained a crucial point of civic reference.[31] More generally, the discourse of appropriation, occupation, construction, improvement – ubiquitous in the charters – was embraced everywhere. Seen for what they were – means to express colonization and expansion and displacement – the founding designs for English mainland colonies do not seem at all irrelevant to the mainland's subsequent history.

If declarations of the irrelevance of foundational designs for English colonization thus seem worth at least a degree of reconsideration, so does the companion assertion that what settlers substituted was an approximation or amalgam of '*the* metropolitan society'. It is not clear how the capacity to approximate or amalgamate a metropolitan culture would be developed or set in play. In language, it is true, many settlers enjoyed one common cultural trait upon which they could draw in forming colonial societies. It is unclear how many other commonalities they shared. As Fischer has proposed, it is more realistic to hypothesize that the settler cultures of the North American mainland tended to establish and reproduce serial locally or regionally specific English cultures rather than a homogenous national culture. It is debatable whether the regional migrations Fischer describes were quite as solidary in all cases as he claims, but it is indisputable that each of the recipient regions became home to influential pluralities who were, in their origins, distinctive and who brought many elements of that distinctiveness to bear in the 'settling' of their new environment.

The legal field is not the least of those in which cultural variation may be observed. Although crude, the distinction between *arable* and *pastoral* legal cultures offers us a means of conceptual purchase in understanding systematically differences in the nature, ideology and institutional organization of legal and social authority in different areas of settlement. It is also worth considering to what extent tensions between settler legal cultures and chartered authority arose from a cultural dissociation between the two that stemmed from processes of migration which confronted people from one English region with authority structures designed on the basis of practice in another. Endemic proprietor–settler conflicts in Maryland and, especially, in Pennsylvania might well be analyzed in such terms.

What, finally, should one say now of law as a constituent element in the process of colonization? First, it seems clear that law as a discourse of authority-in-general had a crucial role to play in the processes by which English colonizers claimed, planted, manned and kept the American mainland. Second, as a discourse of authority-in-detail (as a modality of home rule, so to speak), law continued to play that considerable role, though subject to the rather more considerable refractions of widespread cultural and institutional variation.

Here we might insert as a coda a last reflection on the Comaroffs' view of law not as colonization's blunt instrument but instead as its rather more ambivalent legacy. As the seventeenth century became the eighteenth, English colonization of the American mainland became more and more completely a self-colonization; no longer, that is, primarily a visitation of power upon a colonized 'other' but a labour of transformation wrought by the English upon themselves. This labour of self-transformation, which in the North American context has been labelled Anglicization, was expressed in processes of institution- and state-formation that challenged prevailing cultural affinities, rearranged hierarchies of rule and sought uniformities of practice where previously there had existed plurality and custom. In the mainland

[42]

colonies, as in Britain itself – for Britain was undergoing 'Anglicization' at more or less the same time – law proved an important medium for the realization of social transformation. But also, through both its charter-founded civic claims and its persistent regionalisms, colonial law proved an important means of resistance to the process, particularly as the century wore on and the process of transformation took on increasingly imperial overtones that exposed creole colonials not, after all, as 'English' at all, despite their protestations, but as provincial 'others'.

Thus we find ourselves back at that magnetic late eighteenth-century climacteric, where law, the modality of imperial state formation, becomes also the modality of resistance to the English imperial state. Anglo-Americans distilled from English law the rights of the colonies to claim their independence. They did so to free themselves from imperial constraints that restrained their own colonizing (in more anodyne phraseology, their 'westward movement') so as to realize and release their energies as self-conscious subjects of their own, newly American, history, and thereby – at the expense of others – make manifest their destiny as 'new men'.[32] What one discovers in the legal history of colonization and settlement are some of the greatest continuities of early-modern and modern American history.

Notes

1 Donna Merwick, *Possessing Albany, 1630–1710: The Dutch and English Experiences* (Cambridge and New York, Cambridge University Press, 1990).
2 David Hackett Fischer, *Albion's Seed: Four British Folkways in America* (New York, Oxford University Press, 1989).
3 See generally E.G.R. Taylor, 'Introduction: The Two Richard Hakluyts', in *The Original Writings and Correspondence of the Two Richard Hakluyts* (London, Hakluyt Society, 1935), vol. I, pp. 1–66.
4 'Pamphlet for the Virginia Enterprise By Richard Hakluyt, Lawyer, 1585', in *Original Writings and Correspondence*, vol. II, p. 334.
5 *Discourse of Western Planting*, in *Original Writings and Correspondence*, vol. II, pp. 211, 214, 215, 270, 313–19.
6 'Pamphlet for the Virginia Enterprise', pp. 332–4.
7 Matthew H. Edney, *Mapping an Empire: The Geographical Construction of British India, 1765–1843* (Chicago, IL, University of Chicago Press, 1997), pp. 1–36; Richard Helgerson, *Forms of Nationhood: The Elizabethan Writing of England* (Chicago, IL, University of Chicago Press, 1992), pp. 152–3.
8 Edney, *Mapping an Empire*, pp. 318, 333–4; Helgerson, *Forms of Nationhood*, p. 165.
9 Roger J.P. Kain and Elizabeth Baigent, *The Cadastral Map in the Service of the State: A History of Property Mapping* (Chiago, IL, University of Chicago Press, 1992), pp. 5–6. On early surveying and the absence of cadastral mapping, see Edward T. Price, *Dividing the Land: Early American Beginnings of Our Private Property Mosaic* (Chicago, IL, University of Chicago Press, 1995), pp. 121, 129, 331–2, 349–53.
10 Richard Lyman Bushman, 'Farmers in Court: Orange County, North Carolina, 1750–1776', in Christopher Tomlins and Bruce H. Mann (eds), *The Many Legalities of Early America* (Chapel Hill, NC, University of North Carolina Press, 2001).
11 Richard Hakluyt, *Notes on Colonization*, in *Original Writings and Correspondence*,

Vol. I, pp. 116–22. On the significance of 'city' and *civitas* in the discourse of European expansion, see Anthony Pagden, *Lords of all the World: Ideologies of Empire in Spain, Britain and France, c.1500–1800* (New Haven, CT, Yale University Press, 1995), pp. 18–28.

12 'First Charter of Virginia, 1606', in Francis Newton Thorpe (comp.), *The Federal and State Constitutions, Colonial Charters, and other Organic Laws of the States, Territories, and Colonies now or heretofore Forming the United States of America* (repr. edn, Buffalo, NY, William S. Hein, 1993), Vol. VII, pp. 3783–9.

13 *Ibid.*

14 Hakluyt, *Discourse of Western Planting*, p. 213; Charles M. Andrews, *The Colonial Period of American History*, 2nd edn (New Haven, CT, Yale University Press, 1964), vol. I, p. 323.

15 'Charter of New England', in Thorpe, *Federal and State Constitutions*, vol. III, pp. 1828f.

16 *Ibid.*, pp. 1828–9; 'Charter for the Province of Pennsylvania' (1681), in *ibid.*, vol. V, p. 3036.

17 'Charter of Carolina' (1663) and 'The Fundamental Constitutions of Carolina' (1669), both in *ibid.*, vol. V, pp. 2743–53, 2772–86.

18 'Charter for the Province of Pennsylvania' (1681), in *ibid.*, vol. V, p. 3036.

19 *Ibid.*, pp. 3040–3.

20 Andrews, *Colonial Period*, vol. III, p. 225.

21 John L. Comaroff and Jean Comaroff, *Of Revelation and Revolution (II): The Dialectics of Modernity on a South African Frontier* (Chicago, IL, University of Chicago Press, 1997), pp. 365–7; John L. Comaroff, 'Foreword', in Mindie Lazarus-Black and Susan F. Hirsch (eds), *Contested States: Law, Hegemony and Resistance* (New York and London, Routledge, 1994), pp. ix–xiii.

22 'Poly-Olbion' refers to the work of the same name by Michael Drayton (1612), which, Richard Helgerson argues, epitomizes a movement from nation singularly embodied in the Crown to nation plurally embodied in country. See Helgerson, *Forms of Nationhood*, pp. 117–47.

23 See above, note 2.

24 See George L. Haskins, *Law and Authority in Early Massachusetts: A Study in Tradition and Design* (New York, MacMillan, 1960); David Konig, *Law and Society in Puritan Massachusetts: Essex County, 1629–92* (Chapel Hill, NC, University of North Carolina Press, 1979), particularly pp. xii–xiii; Cornelia Hughes Dayton, *Women Before the Bar: Gender, Law and Society in Connecticut, 1639–1789* (Chapel Hill, NC, University of North Carolina Press, 1995); William N. Offutt, *Of 'Good Laws' and 'Good Men': Law and Society in the Delaware Valley, 1680–1710* (Urbana, IL, University of Illinois Press, 1995), particularly pp. 22–4.

25 Helgerson, *Forms of Nationhood*, p. 71.

26 *Ibid.*, pp. 136–8. In *William Lambarde and Local Government: His 'Ephemeris' and Twenty-Nine Charges to Juries and Commissions* (Ithaca, NY, Cornell University Press, 1962), Conyers Read notes that Lambarde's famous study of the office of the justice of peace, *Eirenarcha*, was wholly based on Lambarde's experience as a justice in Kent, and that his focus in that office was entirely local, see pp. 7–8, 60.

27 James Sharpe, 'The People and the Law', in Barry Reay (ed.), *Popular Culture in Seventeenth-Century England* (New York, St. Martin's Press, 1985), pp. 244–70, 261, 262. See also Andy Wood, 'Custom, Identity and Resistance: English Free Miners and their Law, c.1550–1800', in Paul Griffiths, Adam Fox and Steve Hindle (eds), *The Experience of Authority in Early Modern England* (New York, St. Martin's Press, 1996), pp. 249–85.

28 Keith Wrightson, 'The Politics of the Parish in Early Modern England', in Griffiths *et al.*, (eds), *Experience of Authority*, pp. 10–46, at p. 31; Christopher Harrison, 'Manor Courts and the Governance of Tudor England', in Christopher Brooks and Michael Lobban (eds), *Communities and Courts in Britain, 1150–1900* (London, Hambledon Press, 1997), p. 46.

29 Margaret R. Somers, 'Rights, Relationality and Membership: Rethinking the Making

[44]

and Meaning of Citizenship', *Law & Social Inquiry*, 19:1 (1994), 97; and 'Law, Community and Political Culture in the Transition to Democracy', *American Sociological Review*, 58:5 (1993), 593, 601.

30 Jack P. Greene, *The Intellectual Construction of America: Exceptionalism and Identity from 1492 to 1800* (Chapel Hill, NC, University of North Carolina Press, 1993), pp. 58, 66.

31 John P. Reid, 'Law and History', *Loyola of Los Angeles Law Review*, 27 (1993), 214–17.

32 James Willard Hurst, *Law and the Conditions of Freedom in the Nineteenth Century United States* (Madison, WI, University of Wisconsin Press, 1956).

CHAPTER THREE

Reflections on the rule of law: the Georgian colonies of New South Wales and Upper Canada, 1788–1837

John McLaren

'Liberty' was a shared constitutional and legal concept in the thought of the eighteenth century Anglo-American world.[1] It lay at the crux of a balance between arbitrary power on the one hand and licentiousness on the other, and was open to varying interpretations. Competing constructions of liberty were reflected in divergent views about the rule of law as its guarantee. Conservatives tended to hew to a narrow conception that tied legitimacy to the satisfaction of essentially formal requirements of a decision according to law. By contrast, radical and reformist Whigs were inclined to relate it to the achievement of greater political equality, the placing of constitutional limitations on government power and the redress of various political, social and economic grievances.

These competing ideas were translated from Britain to the American colonies. They set the ideological stage for conflict between the British Government and its colonial loyalist supporters, on the one hand, and patriot colonists, on the other.[2] The reverberations of those disagreements over the meaning of the rule of law were to be felt within the British Empire for decades after the conclusion of the hostilities in North America.

The late nineteenth-century Diceyan conception of the rule of law with its positivist focus on courts and judges is of limited value in assessing ideas and claims about law, governance and the subject in the late eighteenth and early nineteenth centuries. Then the line between its legal and political meanings was ill defined.[3] Colonial as well as legal historians have illuminated for us two important issues: first, what people in the eighteenth and early nineteenth centuries actually understood by the rule of law; second, the extent to which political and legal change or resistance to the rule of law in one part of the British Empire reverberated elsewhere within the imperial system. In this paper I speak to both matters as I explore the deployment of the rule of law at both an ideological and a practical level in two very different British colonies established within three years of each other, New South Wales (1788) and Upper Canada (1791), through to the late 1830s.

Interpretations of liberty and the rule of law within the Anglo-American world in the eighteenth and early nineteenth centuries also need to take account of a tension between law as a centralized system of decision-making, and law as a product of local and particular custom. Christopher Hill points out how in seventeenth-century England many middling and poor folk perceived both legislation and the common law as inimical to their interests.[4] For them the powerful invoked these systems to subvert and abolish ancient customary rights in the commons and the waste. Enforced change by centralized systems of law promoting enclosure engendered resistance to the removal of 'liberties' that had survived the 'Norman yoke' and constituted *their* rule of law. In folk lore and contemporary literature the themes of oppression and reaction were played out in tales of Robin Hood, pirates, smugglers, gypsies, vagabonds and even indigenous peoples as heroic representatives of a craved pristine freedom.[5]

Local law and its administration lived on in both practice and the realm of ideas in Britain. Jack Greene notes that after the demise of the Stuart kings there was a significant withdrawal of central authority from local affairs in England. Thus the eighteenth century, far from being a period of consolidation of centralized power, witnessed a reaffirmation of the dominance of localized privilege and special jurisdictions.[6] Most people still experienced law and administration as the product of decisions of local magnates and the gentry, whether in regulating their economic and social relations, or subjecting them to the processes and penalties of the criminal law.

What was true of the relationship between national and local governance in Britain, was amplified in the relations between Great Britain and the American colonies. Distance, periods of imperial disinterest, and the growth of a strong North American sense of political community had produced democratic organs of local government and justice administration that wielded considerable power and enjoyed support among settlers. As a consequence, unique domestic legal solutions to colonial problems were devised.[7]

The rule of law can embrace not only generic imperial, national or colony-wide law and justice, but also law and justice embodying local community aspirations and needs. Thus, when tension developed between an imperial Government committed to preserving deference, order and imperial hierarchy and a colonial majority pressing for political equality and the removal of constitutional and legal impediments to their development, the notion of the rule of law could be passionately and honestly invoked by both sides.[8]

After the American Revolution, as John Manning Ward pointed out, Britain's conservative leaders decided that greater rather than less imperial control over colonies was needed if the remaining Empire was to survive.[9] In Upper Canada the full range of political and legal institutions previously enjoyed by the American colonies was granted to the settlers. However, the British Government believed that, with strong executive control by a lieutenant-governor supported by officials and judges appointed from London (removable at pleasure), the replication of an elite, whether landed or of merit, along with an established Church, would keep the colonists in line. This structure would ensure that – as John Graves Simcoe, the first lieutenant-governor, put it – the colonial constitution would be 'a Perfect Image and Transcript' of the British constitution, but at the same time clearly subordinate to it.[10]

Ward also stressed that imperial policy on colonial constitutional development was an experimental and pragmatic process. It took account not only of historical expectations that the settlers took with them, but of the multifarious nature of the territories which Britain controlled and its objectives in settling them, added to the diversity of their populations and of the tensions existing within them. Multi-racial colonies in which slavery was an issue, and special-purpose colonies like New South Wales, could expect little or no local autonomy.[11]

Ward's third point was that the British Government's experience with law and politics in some colonies affected its development of constitutional arrangements and policies elsewhere. The two colonies of Upper and Lower Canada were endowed with the classic range of governing and legal institutions – legislative councils and assemblies, common law courts and trial by jury. However, the fractiousness and unrest experienced in both persuaded London that in subsequent settler colonies executive power should be further reinforced and local legislative autonomy constrained or delayed.[12] Thus in the first effective free settler colony in Australia, South Australia established in 1836, the governor was vested with exclusive executive and legislative powers over law and order. Only later was a legislative council added. A legislative assembly had to await the grant of responsible government, in the mid-1850s.[13]

Earlier I pointed to the development of conflicting interpretations of the rule of law, both within Britain itself, and their translation to the thirteen American colonies. Events in Ireland were also to be significant.

If Britain had been insufficiently solicitous of its American colonies and their governance, quite the reverse was true of Ireland.[14] There, British anxieties about the loyalty of the majority of the population of its oldest and nearest colony had resulted in close and oppressive rule by a lord lieutenant appointed and instructed from London. The Irish Parliament was exclusively Protestant, and was largely in the pockets of English or ascendancy landlords. Moreover, most Irish judges were notoriously servile to British interests. Although there were episodic local protests and uprisings by members of the Roman Catholic majority, the political opposition in Ireland lay primarily among Anglo-Irish and Presbyterian reformers.[15] Given these realities, British treatment of Ireland proved an emotional spur to the patriot cause in the American colonies. Conversely their struggle struck a responsive chord in Ireland.

When American Whigs needed ammunition to show how Parliament had perverted British constitutionalism they had only to point to Ireland and its sad legacy. The American Revolution in its turn had a significant effect on events in Ireland.[16] A conjunction of Irish Whig reformism inspired by the success of the independence war in America and a transitory willingness in Westminster to make concessions led to ostensible reform of the constitutional relationship between Ireland and Great Britain in 1782. However, what the Irish reformers hailed as autonomy and as a compact between the Irish people and the Crown was quickly subverted by the continuation of executive control from London and through parliamentary resistance by the conservative wing of the Anglo-Irish ascendancy. Frustration born of the failure of the reform agenda in 'Henry Grattan's' Parliament combined with admiration for the French Revolution had induced Protestant radicals by 1795 to seek independence for Ireland by force of arms and to establish a republican government, leading to the rebellion of 1798.[17] Fierce suppression by British forces and militia, widespread hangings and transportation to Australia and the absorption of Ireland into Great Britain through the 1800 Act of Union, followed in its wake.[18] Thus ended the short-lived Irish Whig constitutional experiment, although not necessarily its ideological legacy.

There are clear connections between events in America and Ireland, and the founding and early histories of the two new colonies of New South Wales and Upper Canada. New South Wales owed its establishment to the closing of America to convict transportation.[19] Although envisaged as a colony in which convicts would be treated as free men, the humanitarian instincts of the first governor, Arthur Phillip, and his immediate successors meant in practice a form of government which blended close control and regulation of convicts and their lives with the use of executive discretion in granting complete or partial emancipation to those who had served their time or seemed likely to live responsibly.[20] Among those who went to New South Wales as military or government personnel and then settled, or who went as original free settlers, were men who projected a rather different vision of what an ordered colony should be.

The first and most powerful example of an Australian conservative colonial family elite, the Macarthurs, assumed that commitment to order, deference and hierarchy characteristic of eighteenth-century British and North American conservatives.[21] They believed that it would be through their efforts and leadership that New South Wales would develop and prosper. Convicts or former convicts did not feature as rulers in this equation. While their earliest brushes were with colonial governors who shared their conservative mindset, but disliked their opportunism and exclusiveness in seeking to shape the colony in their image, the Macarthurs were, in time, to find reformist foes committed to more liberal or radical notions of constitutionalism and the rule of law.

Events in Ireland were also to affect the political and legal development of New South Wales. The presence of growing numbers of political prisoners from Ireland through the late 1790s and beyond was in the short term to create special security problems for the authorities.[22] Some of these convicts fomented insurrection.[23]

By contrast Upper Canada was established in response to loyalist exiles from the former American colonies pressing for space to live under both British rule and the common law. Upper Canada's constitutional arrangements were carefully constructed to serve British interests.[24] They were designed to ensure the colony's fealty and subordination to Britain, not to mention the benefits of adherence to the British Whig constitution and the providentially ordered society that it supported. All of this seemed more pressing not only in buttressing Canada against military defeat or gradual absorption by the United States, but because the French Revolution was causing anxiety in British Government ranks.

Preserving these conservative credentials was the responsibility of the British administrators and judges and, later, of an indigenous North American colonial elite comprising original loyalists and their offspring who secured preferment in government, judicial or ecclesiastical ranks. Colonial judges, unlike their counterparts in England, served at pleasure. Contrary to British assumptions, among the loyalists there were those who, while loyal to the Crown and the British connection, recognized themselves as North Americans first and were drawn to more liberal and democratic beliefs about government and its purpose.[25] In time, as a greater number of migrants with republican, radical or reformist pedigrees moved from the south to Upper Canada, and from Britain itself, links with conservative loyalism were weakened even further and challenged more firmly.

[50]

The immediate influence of Irish events and the ideas in Upper Canada was more benign than in New South Wales, although not entirely unproblematic. Protestant Irishmen settled in Upper Canada in the late 1790s and the early 1800s. Most came to Upper Canada purely to seek opportunity or to escape the unrest in their native land. Several of Irish Whig persuasion became active in political life as reformers. They reacted unfavourably against what they saw as oppressive laws and arbitrary conduct on the part of the executive. Although several disappeared quickly from the provincial scene,[26] one, William Warren Baldwin, was active as a lawyer and more generally in public life until the early 1840s.

This man, a physician and lawyer, often described as the father of responsible government in the colony, brought to Upper Canadian constitutional debate the beliefs of Irish Whigs to which his father had subscribed in Ireland.[27] In particular, Baldwin viewed the Upper Canadian constitution as representing a compact between monarch and people in which both undertook rights and obligations. Part of the Government's duty was to listen to and resolve grievances. The primary role of the constitution and the law was to afford rights to people and to protect them from arbitrary executive action. Following the Irish constitutional model of the 1780s, Baldwin believed that colonies should be recognized as co-equals with the colonial power in almost all matters. He also argued vigorously that as the 1791 Constitution Act was a compact with the people of Upper Canada it enjoyed special status and could not be repealed by the British Parliament without the colonists' consent.[28]

The constitutional and legal history of the first five decades of New South Wales and Upper Canada reflect the tensions between conservative and more liberal notions of the rule of law and its significance in those societies. It also illustrates the conflicting pulls of centralism and localism in government and the administration of justice. How debate and conflict were played out, and who stood where on the rule of law and its meaning, reflected the peculiarities of Britain's colonial policies in the particular jurisdiction and the way power was distributed at both formal and practical levels.

In its first decade, tensions developed in Upper Canada between colonial government, intent on introducing a centralized court system, and local commercial interests content with the system of local lay courts with simplified procedures inherited from Quebec.[29] The Government's granting of monopolies to its friends exacerbated the feelings of frustration. At the same time there was evidence of disharmony within loyalist ranks. This tension reflected differences of opinion about what it meant to be a British North American, as well as resentment among some of the immigrants about favouritism in land settlement and preferment of both a loyalist elite and military officers.[30]

Conflict over the meaning of the rule of law intensified between 1800 and the War of 1812. The colonial government, concerned about security in an era of high anxiety over American designs and those of Irish exiles and fearful of war with the French, reacted offensively. It took measures to stifle dissent, to strengthen the hold of both the political and the ecclesiastical elite on decision-making and to prefer its supporters in filling governmental and judicial appointments at a local level. The passage of the Sedition Act of 1804[31] on the initiative of the lieutenant-governor and the Legislative Council was particularly divisive. It provided for the expulsion of anyone who had been in the colony for less than six months, or had not taken an oath of allegiance, who had caused or was suspected of causing disaffection against the Crown or of disturbing the tranquility of the colony with seditious intent. The process was summary and the accused subject to a reverse onus.[32] The Act's passage helped inspire the first legislative opposition by Irish reformers, notably lawyer William Weekes and Judge Robert Thorpe.[33]

In New South Wales during the same period, the lack of conventional legislative bodies and the single-minded commitment of governors to establishing and maintaining a convict colony meant a comparative lack of open debate over the meaning of the rule of law. Among the convicts, of course, especially those transported for political crimes, various forms of radicalism and even republicanism were evident.[34] As long as they were convicts and subject to penal law, however, they had no public and legal forum for their views. Normally, their only effective means of action to change things were insurrection, refusal to work or attempts to escape. The only example of insurrection in 1804, by Irish prisoners, was quickly suppressed.[35] Lesser forms of resistance could result in re-transportation, or flogging. Escape attempts typically resulted in recapture or death.

The rule of law was not, however, an entirely irrelevant consideration to the life of the colony. Convicts, some of whom continued to nurse the radical and reformist views for which they had been transported, were pardoned and emancipated. Even those still under penal sanction were, if literate and well educated, capable of 'troublesome' appeals to liberty and the rule of law through manifestos, letters and complaints to governors or to the Colonial Office.[36] At a more systemic level, as John Hirst and Bruce Kercher have shown, government in the colony was not entirely autocratic and oppressive.[37] Although New South Wales was subject to a unique form of quasi-military rule and convicts were harshly treated, the colony possessed a legal system that had some sensitivity to the rule of law. Convicts, for instance, could not be punished without orders issued by magistrates or the judge-advocate.[38]

More importantly, however, a legal system developed from the practices of the governors and from decisions of legal officials that had some claim to suiting the local needs of the colony. This system treated the convicts – who by English law would have had no legal rights and status under felony attaint – as persons to whom the law would provide some protection, especially in civil matters, and restored full civil rights to them when they were released or pardoned. Conditional pardons and tickets of leave, both gubernatorial inventions, helped to propel convicts towards restoration of their rights earlier than usual.[39] To the extent that the rule of law, could take account of locally produced law, both convicts and the emancipated had law by which they were ruled and by which their relations were governed, and to which they could appeal when their rights were in jeopardy.

There were disagreements about legitimacy and authority between governors and free settlers. Tensions existed between the colonial Government, on the one hand, and active and retired members of the New South Wales Corps – one of whom, John Macarthur, had assumed the leadership of the free settlers – on the other. Here there is some resemblance to conditions in Upper Canada. The officers of the 'Rum Corps' had established a monopoly on trade in the colony, and several of its former members, including John Macarthur, had secured vast stretches of land and moved into commercial grazing.[40] Other free settlers, lacking the elite's economic power, and emancipists (former convicts), who ranged from substantial entrepreneurs and landholders to smallholders and trades people, resented both the exercise of monopoly and the securing of the best land by this exclusionary group. When governors and judge-advocates sought to do justice by protecting smallholders from powerful creditors the conservative elite criticized them for their pains. The charge levelled by this 'compact' group was that the colonial government was acting arbitrarily and infringing their rights as landholders and entrepreneurs.

The earliest judicial appointments in Upper Canada assumed that the judges would share conservative leadership and act as sources of constitutional and legal advice to the colonial Government. William Osgoode, the first chief justice, assumed the combined functions of judge, executive officer and legislator, a pattern which, while it offended notions of the separation of powers, was common in British imperial practice.[41]

Close association in Upper Canada between the judiciary and the colonial executive, and the further blurring of the political and judicial roles of the judges, was to intensify after the War of 1812, and especially during the 1820s and 1830s. This period marks the emergence of the so-called Family Compact, a group of conservative politicians, lawyers and judges, the offspring of early loyalists. The members of this group, especially its leader John Beverley Robinson, were unalterably wedded to the imperial connection, believed ardently in replicating the values of the late eighteenth-century British constitution, and were archly conservative in political and social ideology. They were strong exponents of a limited formal definition of the rule of law.[42]

These people incorporated into their opinions, addresses and judgements changes wrought in the common law and British legislation. However, they saw no reason to countenance constitutional change in the colony, especially where it would rob them of power and influence and afford unnecessary legal protection to radicals and other political 'trouble-makers'. They were virulently opposed to the system of government in the United States and thus to republican and even democratic sentiments. Operating variously as law officers of the Crown, as judges and as members of executive and legislative bodies, they were ready to manipulate the administration of justice to secure the interests of the conservative cause. This they did in the selection of administrators and magistrates, and in the conduct of political trials. As advisers and confidantes of the well-intentioned, but blinkered, senior army officers sent out to rule the colony, they were able to influence significantly the exercise of executive power.[43] The offences of criminal and seditious libel, which reflected older, elitist notions of the need to protect the State and great men from criticism, provided the weapons that the Compact could use to silence opposition and harass their opponents through the court process. These offences were particularly appealing, as, unlike tortious defamation, truth was no defence.[44]

The Compact's manipulation of the administration of justice is evident in several prosecutions of radicals and reformers for sedition. John Beverley Robinson and Henry Boulton, as law officers of the Crown, invoked the special procedures under the Sedition Act against the Scottish radical Robert Gourlay, in 1818. This led to his banishment from the colony by the judiciary, on the advice of the law officers given in secret, even though he had already been acquitted of sedition by two juries.[45] In the late 1820s Attorney General Robinson hounded Francis Collins, a radical newspaper publisher, in several libel prosecutions.[46] Among other things Collins had pointed to the malfeasance of the law officers in not prosecuting Tory bully-boys, including students-at-law from Robinson's office, who had destroyed the printing press of radical newspaper editor William Lyon MacKenzie in 1825. The latter had committed the sin of inveighing intemperately against the Compact.

During the 1820s, members of the Compact committed themselves to a legislative agenda classifying as aliens and denaturalizing all those who had migrated from the United States after the first wave of loyalist exiles.[47] This obsessive campaign, designed to rid the colony of disloyalty, or, more especially, potential sites of opposition to Tory rule, was finally scotched by disallowance in Westminster.

If these stratagems were not sufficient to cast doubts on the motives of Compact 'justice', there were further calculated instances of violence by supporters of the Tory elite against radical and reform interests. One of the most infamous was the tarring and feathering in Ancaster of George Rolph, the Gore district's clerk of the peace and brother of reformer John Rolph, by ten men with blackened faces and dressed in sheets. The assailants included two local magistrates, the deputy clerk of the Crown and two attorneys.[48] Here was the concept of ordered liberty turned upside down.[49] The activities of Compact members in subverting the rule of law, even in the narrow sense which they gave to it, were contested by moderates and radicals, especially those within the ranks of the legal profession.[50] In their actions and discourse the emphasis of these men was on the importance of rights and protection within the British constitutional tradition. They pointed to the freedom of Englishmen, and thus of colonists, to dissent and to voice their displeasure with government, and to the need for judges and the law officers to respect that tradition and for the courts to act impartially at all times.

When William Warren Baldwin wrote as treasurer of the Law Society to Attorney General John Beverley Robinson in 1828,[51] reproving him for not taking disciplinary action against the young lawyers and students-at-law who had trashed Mackenzie's printing press, he reminded the attorney general of the oath of barristers to uphold the constitution and defend the rights of their fellow-citizens. Here was the invocation of a broader, more political, notion of the rule of law that embodied liberal Whig constitutional notions and recognized their importance in protecting people from arbitrary government and state-approved vigilantism.[52]

In Upper Canada the threat to the rule of law during this period was from the political and legal conservative elite who had the ear of the lieutenant-governor. Opposition that was based on more liberal and democratic notions of constitutionalism and the rule of law was located both within the legal profession and the Legislative Assembly.

For a short period in the mid and late 1830s the Upper Canadian political stage was seized by the republican agenda of William Lyon MacKenzie on the one hand and by the conservative reaction of the colonial Government of Sir Francis Bond Head and his Compact supporters on the other.[53] During this period debate on constitutionalism and the rule of law within the British tradition was briefly pre-empted. When it re-emerged, as it did after the rebellions of 1837 and 1838, it was in the far less frenzied context of movement towards responsible self-government, and a realignment in politics in which extreme radicalism was disavowed and moderation became a pervasive value at both ends of the political spectrum.[54] The consensus on constitutional values that emerged reflected both conservative and reformist understandings, and Upper Canadian as well as British expectations. The emphasis, as in all British colonial constitutions of the era, was on peace, order and good governance. The rule of law in an era of legislative ascendancy was to lose its potency as a principle embracing both liberty and the more formal interpretations of law's limiting role on state action, and to take on more clearly the trappings of Dicey's definition.[55]

If the rule of law was in jeopardy in Upper Canada primarily from colonial conservatives in elite political and legal positions who unduly influenced the lieutenant-governor, in New South Wales it was in the main the governors themselves who tended to ignore or subvert it. There was, it is true, an embryonic colonial elite ready to impress its image of governance and society on the colony. The role of the exclusionists (i.e. those opposed to convict emancipation) in seeking to secure their social and economic ends has already been noted. While they were to receive a rebuff in the wake of the Rum Rebellion of 1808, their disgrace was only short lived. The exclusionists cultivated strong connections with conservative politicians in Britain and sought to exercise influence both with the British government and at home in Australia.[56] They comprised the group from which the local magistracy was selected, which meant they were able to secure considerable power at a local level. With varying degrees of success they sought to put pressure on governors to further their aims of ultimate involvement in the government of the colony.

The 'Family Compact' was not as consistently influential in New South Wales as it was in Upper Canada. Until 1823 New South Wales lacked the executive and legislative bodies in which exclusivists were able to locate and work their will consistently on the political process. Their pressure operated somewhat vicariously in that they had to secure their ends through allies in the expatriate colonial administration. During the period under review they had no access to professional judicial office. The first legally qualified judge who was actually effective in the role, Ellis Bent, was not appointed until 1810.[57] For the next three decades all of the judicial appointments in the colony were of English barristers or those who had trained in England. These judges differed in their attitudes to 'Compact politics'. The short-lived Jeffrey Bent had cordial relations with the colonial conservatives in the mid-1810s because of mutually conservative views and a shared distaste for Governor Macquarie and his promotion of emancipists.[58] By contrast, the first chief justice of the colony, Francis Forbes, a liberal, appointed in 1824, took positions contrary to their values and attempts to monopolize government.[59]

That it was governors who were less than solicitous of the rule of law should not surprise us. Up to and including Macquarie they were enlisted to run a penal colony as a semi-military and highly disciplined penal operation. While they enjoyed the widest administrative powers, as would befit prison wardens, they lacked explicit legislative powers with which to govern. The latter lay in Westminster. As Macquarie in particular found, this was a serious limitation on a governor's freedom of action, particularly as free settlement increased, and more and more convicts were released, many settling down to normal productive lives. He was faced increasingly with economic and social problems of growing complexity associated with a conventional settler colony with an expanding population, while continuing to run an open prison.[60] This was at a time when the imperial Tory Government was effectively distracted from providing firm and effective guidance by the last few years of the Napoleonic Wars, including the so-called North American War of 1812.[61]

It was perhaps inevitable that governors used to ruling by administrative *diktat* and military orders would run into criticism from professional lawyers and judges appointed from London. Tensions between the Governors and the judiciary were to reach a peak in the 1820s. This was attributable partly to the more formal introduction of English law and the establishment of a conventional Superior Court system on the civil side. It also reflected the differing personalities and political ideologies of the governor, Ralph Darling, and the chief justice, Francis Forbes. Darling was a former general with some skill in that role. He was, however, endowed with a conservative's suspicion and mistrust of change, he was quick to judge others unfavourably, especially if they disagreed with him, and was unreceptive to criticism. At the same time, as a military man he was impatient with lack of action and the niceties of process.[62] Francis Forbes by contrast was a liberal in political and social terms. He was born not in England but in Bermuda.[63] Forbes had trained as barrister in London, and before going to Sydney, in 1823, had been chief justice of Newfoundland. In that role he had developed a reputation as a liberal because of his belief that law should reflect and respond to local commercial conditions and needs.[64] As a learned and precise judge, Forbes recognized the need to bring English law and the rule of law much more fully into New South Wales.[65] At the same time, as a sophisticated observer of British imperialism, he was aware of the need to balance concern for centralization and system with appreciation of the realities of the history and population of the colony.

In Upper Canada there was a mutuality of interest and a shared ideology between the lieutenant-governor and his colonist judges and legal advisers. By contrast, a gulf existed between the chief justice and the governor of New South Wales in the middle and late 1820s in their 'visions of legality.' If, in Murray Greenwood's words, the Compact judges in the Canadian colony were Baconian in their understanding of their role – that is, one of service to government above all else[66] – Francis Forbes had some claim to being Cokeian in his approach to law and politics. His view was that judges needed to stand up to the irresponsible and arbitrary use of executive power.

A major *casus belli* between Governor Darling and Chief Justice Forbes and his colleagues on the bench was press freedom. By the mid-1820s there were three newspaper editors in the colony – William Charles Wentworth, Edward Hall and Robert Wardell – who represented reformist opinion and favoured full emancipist involvement in the political and legal life of the colony.[67] When these men attacked Darling in their newspapers for resisting reform and described him as a tyrant he moved to muzzle them.

He introduced legislation requiring those publishing newspapers only to do so with a license granted at his discretion, and to impose a stamp duty, ostensibly designed to fund the Government's printing programme but intended to ruin his adversaries. The chief justice, exercising power of review under the New South Wales Act, found the Licensing Act repugnant to the laws of England, and he denied certification. Forbes characterized the statute as subversive of freedom of the press, and went on to describe this freedom as a constitutional privilege. As Bruce Kercher has observed, 'that was as much a statement of political aspiration as law, given the repressive nature of English press laws'.[68] The judge was also persuaded, after initially approving it, that the stamp duty was invalid, once he became aware of the actual motive behind it.

Forbes as chief justice was clearly not prepared to allow the colony to continue with repressive governance in which the governor was subject to no local authority other than his own. He set out to curb the exercise of gubernatorial discretion by invoking a liberal view of constitutional rights and of the rule of law. It is true that renewed efforts by Governor Darling to silence his press critics by libel prosecutions were successful and landed several editors in jail.[69] Forbes had, however, made it clear that freedom of the press was in New South Wales an important element in the political process, and that it was for judges and juries, not the governor, to determine whether the limits of tolerance had been exceeded.

[58]

A further point of tension within the administration of governance and justice in the colony, and one that it shared with Upper Canada, was the identification of the magistracy with the conservative elite. In New South Wales conservative exclusionists were able to exercise significant power by their control of local administration and justice.[70]

As constitutional argument and the protection of rights shifted into the political and legislative sphere, and the rule of law became essentially a court-based and legal doctrine in Canada, so it did to a degree in Australia as the grant of responsible government became a reality. The initiative for legal change shifted to the legislatures, although in several colonies the courts were faced with the challenge of resolving the legislative stalemate caused by conflicts between assemblies and councils elected using different franchises.[71]

These short descriptions of the operation of the rule of law in two Georgian colonies show clearly that the differences in interpreting and understanding its meaning – vigorously debated in the latter half of the eighteenth century in Britain, the American colonies and Ireland – lived on into the later British Empire. On the one side, conservatives liked to stress the need for order, deference and political and social hierarchy, a limited notion of rights and a narrow legal conception of the rule of law. Radicals and reformers, by contrast, stressed rights and freedom, the desirability of enshrining them in constitutional form and the need to protect citizens from arbitrary government. In both Upper Canada and New South Wales this was the ideological and rhetorical matrix in which debates about governance and law took place, whether in legislative bodies, on the hustings or in the courts.

The advocates of these conflicting visions were not a uniform or unified class in each colony. This diversity reflected the differing reasons for the foundation of the colonies and their different cultural development. What both colonies did share was the experience of contested conservative and liberal interpretations of the rule of law that had their roots in the Anglo-American world of the seventeenth and eighteenth centuries. These interpretations were refracted through the particular colonial experience, and in that sense were authentic. They were subject to further development as the impact of new, predominantly reformist, ideas from outside the colonies were felt, and rearguard action was mounted by the forces of conservatism both within the Government and among the settler elite in the colonies. Where the balance settled during particular periods depended on a variety of factors. These included imperial policy on and experience in colonies established for very different purposes, political and strategic considerations relating to both the Empire as a whole and to particular territories, and the relative political, economic and social strength of the interests and personalities involved in those colonies. We have noted that constitutional argument and the protection of rights shifted into the legislative sphere, and that the rule of law became more clearly a court-based and legal doctrine, as the grant of responsible government became a reality and judicial positivism emerged. Despite the fading of the rule of law as a progressive political inspiration in judge-made law as the nineteenth century wore on, its spirit was to live on in constitutional debate, discourse and wrangling for the remainder of the century and beyond. Insofar as it embodied classical notions of liberty, its ghost has been converted once again to matter, as both Australia and Canada sought during the twentieth century to round out or articulate the constitutional values to which each subscribes.

Notes

This paper was completed while on a Visiting Research Fellowship at the Humanities Research Centre, Canberra.

1 John Phillip Reid, *The Concept of Liberty in the Age of the American Revolution* (Chicago, University of Chicago Press, 1988); Janice Potter, *The Liberty We Seek: Loyalist Ideology in Colonial New York and Massachusetts* (Cambridge, MA, Harvard University Press, 1983).
2 Potter, *The Liberty We Seek.*
3 Paul Romney, 'Very Late Loyalist Fantasies: Nostalgic Tory History and the Rule of Law in Upper Canada', in W. Wesley Pue and Barry Wright (eds), *Canadian Perspectives on Law and Society: Issues in Canadian Legal History* (Ottawa, Carleton University Press, 1988), p. 119; David Neal, *The Rule of Law in a Penal Colony: Law and Power in Early New South Wales* (Cambridge, Cambridge University Press, 1991).
4 Christopher Hill, *Liberty Against the Law: Some Seventeenth-Century Controversies* (Harmondsworth, Penguin, 1996).
5 *Ibid.*
6 Jack P. Greene, *Negotiated Authorities: Essays in Colonial Political and Constitutional History* (Charlettesville, University Press of Virginia, 1994), pp. 36–7.
7 *Ibid.*, pp. 78–130.
8 John Phillip Reid, *In a Defiant Stance: The Conditions of Law in Massachusetts Bay, the Irish Comparison and the Coming of the American Revolution* (University Park, Pennsylvania State University Press, 1977).
9 John Manning Ward, *Colonial Self-Government: The British Experience 1759–1856,* (Toronto, University of Toronto Press, 1976), pp. 1–3.
10 J.M. Bliss, *Canadian History in Documents, 1763–1966* (Toronto, Ryerson Press 1966) pp. 34–6.
11 Ward, *Colonial Self-Government*, pp. 82–123, 124–71.
12 *Ibid.*, pp. 38–81.
13 Douglas Pike, *Paradise of Dissent: South Australia, 1829–1857*, 2nd edn (Melbourne, Melbourne University Press, 1967).
14 Reid, *In a Defiant Stance*, pp. 135–49.
15 On the general history of Ireland in the late eighteenth century, see Robert Kee, *The Green Flag*, vol. 1: *The Most Distressful Country* (Harmondsworth, Penguin Books, 1983), pp. 21–159.
16 Reid, *In a Defiant Stance.*

17 Kee, *Distressful Country*, pp. 21–159.
18 Act of Union between Great Britain and Ireland (1800), 40 Geo. III, c. 67.
19 John Manning Ward, *James Macarthur: Colonial Conservative, 1798–1867* (Sydney, Sydney University Press, 1981), pp. 1–2.
20 Alan Atkinson, *The Europeans in Australia: A History*, vol. 1 (Melbourne, Oxford University Press, 1998), pp. 66–78.
21 Ward, *James Macarthur.*
22 Anne-Maree Whitaker, *Unfinished Revolution: United Irishmen in New South Wales, 1800–1810* (Sydney, Crossing Press, 1994).
23 *Ibid.*, pp. 89–115.
24 Robert L. Fraser, *Provincial Justice: Upper Canadian Legal Portraits* (Toronto, Osgoode Society, 1992), pp. xxv–xxx.
25 Jane Errington, *The Lion, the Eagle and Upper Canada: A Developing Colonial Ideology* (Kingston and Montreal, McGill-Queen's University Press), pp. 13–54.
26 Fraser, *Provincial Justice*, pp. lviii–lix; and see entries for Weekes, pp. 285–6, and Thorpe, pp. 188–91.
27 *Ibid.*, pp. 201–21, entry for William Baldwin.
28 (1791) 30–1 Geo. III, c. 31. For other influences, see Errington, *The Lion, the Eagle and Upper Canada*, pp. 97–118.
29 Fraser, *Provincial Justice*, p. xlii. See also William Wylie, 'Instruments of Commerce and Authority: The Civil Courts in Upper Canada 1789–1812', in David Flaherty (ed.), *Essays in the History of Canadian Law*, (Toronto, Osgoode Society, 1983), vol. 2, p. 3.
30 *Ibid.*, p. xlvii–l.
31 The Sedition Act (1804), 44 Geo. III, c. 1.
32 *Ibid.*, s. 1.
33 Fraser, *Provincial Justice* li; and F. Murray Greenwood and Barry Wright (eds), *Law, Politics and Security Measures 1608–1837* vol I: *Canadian State Trials* (Toronto, Osgoode Society, 1996), p. 380.
34 See Lynette Ramsey Silver, *The Battle of Vinegar Hill: Australia's Irish Rebellion, 1804* (Sydney, Doubleday, 1989), pp. 128–30, for pen portraits of Maurice Margarot and Thomas Fyshe Palmer ('Scottish Martyrs'), Joseph Holt (United Irishmen) and George Mealmaker (republican).
35 Whitaker, *Unfinished Revolution*, pp. 99, 119.
36 Yvonne Cramer (ed.), *This Beauteous, Wicked Place: Letters and Journals of John Grant, Gentleman Convict* (Canberra, National Library of Australia, 2000), pp. 89–153, especially his letters to Governor King.
37 J.B. Hirst, *Convict Society and its Enemies: A History of Early New South Wales* (Sydney, Allen & Unwin, 1983), pp. 106–33; Bruce Kercher, *An Unruly Child: A History of Law in Australia* (Sydney, Allen & Unwin, 1995), pp. 22–42.
38 Kercher, *An Unruly Child*, pp. 25–6.
39 *Ibid.*, pp. 29–30.
40 See Hirst, *Convict Society and its Enemies*, pp. 37–8. On John Macarthur, see *Australian Dictionary of Biography*, (*ADB*), (Melbourne, Melbourne University Press, 1967), vol. 2, pp. 153–9.
41 Fraser, *Provincial Justice*, pp. xxvi, x, and entry for William Osgoode, pp. 129–34.
42 *Ibid.*, pp. xxiv–xxxix, and entry for Robinson, pp. 153–75; Patrick Brode, *Sir John Beverley Robinson: Bone and Sinew of the Compact* (Toronto, Osgoode Society, 1984).
43 Paul Romney, *Mr. Attorney: The Attorney General for Ontario in Court, Cabinet and Legislature 1791–1899* (Toronto, Osgoode Society, 1986), pp. 62–157.
44 James Fitzjames Stephen, *A General View of the Criminal Law of England* (London, MacMillan, 1863), p. 146.
45 Barry Wright, 'The Gourlay Affair: Seditious Libel and the Sedition Act in Upper Canada, 1818–19', in Greenwood and Wright (eds), *Law, Politics and Security Measures*, pp. 487–504.
46 Paul Romney, 'Upper Canada in the 1820s: Criminal Prosecution and the Case of

Francis Collins', ibid., pp. 505–21.

47 Fraser, *Provincial Justice*, p. lxviii; Errington, *The Lion, the Eagle and Upper Canada*, pp. 166–84.
48 Romney, *Mr. Attorney*, pp. 109–14.
49 Carol Wilton, '"Lawless Law": Political Violence in Upper Canada, 1818–41', *Law and History*, 13 (1995), 111.
50 Fraser, *Provincial Justice*, pp. lxv–lxxiv.
51 Romney, 'Very Late Loyalist Fantasies', pp. 131–2.
52 *Ibid.*, p. 132
53 Gerald Craig, *Upper Canada: The Formative Years, 1784–1841* (Toronto, McClelland & Stewart, 1963), pp. 226–51.
54 *Ibid.*, pp. 252–75; J.M.S. Careless, *The Union of the Canadas: The Growth of Canadian Institutions, 1841–1857* (Toronto, McClelland & Stewart, 1967).
55 See Paul Romney, 'From the Rule of Law to Responsible Government: Ontario Political Culture and the Origins of Canadian Statism', *Canadian Historical Association Papers* (1988), 86.
56 See e.g. J.J. Eddy, *Britain and the Australian Colonies 1818–1831: The Technique of Government* (Oxford, Clarendon Press, 1969), pp. 68–70.
57 Richard Dore, a lawyer, was appointed judge-advocate in 1798, but died two years later; see Kercher, *An Unruly Child*, pp. 47–48.
58 Neal, *The Rule of Law in a Penal Colony*, p. 175.
59 See e.g. Kercher, *An Unruly Child*, pp. 82–6.
60 Anthony Hewison, *The Macquarie Decade* (Sydney, Cassells Australia, 1972). On Macquarie, see *ABD*, vol. 2, pp. 187–95.
61 Eddy, *Britain and the Australian Colonies*, pp. x–xi.
62 On Darling, see Neal, *The Rule of Law in a Penal Colony*, p. 108, and *ADB*, vol. 1, pp. 317–20.
63 Alex C. Castles, *An Australian Legal History* (Sydney Law Book Company, 1982), pp. 182–4.
64 C.H. Currey, *Sir Francis Forbes: The First Chief Justice of the Supreme Court of New South Wales* (Sydney, Angus & Robertson, 1968).
65 Letter from Forbes to J.R. Wilmot Horton, MP, 6 March 1827, in J.M. Bennett and Alex C. Castles, *A Source Book of Australian Legal History: Source Materials from the Eighteenth to the Twentieth Centuries* (Sydney, Law Book Company, 1979), pp. 70–1. On Forbes' judicial career and views see J.M. Bennett (ed) *Some Papers of Sir Francis Forbes, First Chief Justice of Australia* (Sydney, Parliament of New South Wales, 1998).
66 Murray Greenwood, *Legacies of Fear: Law and Politics in Quebec in the Era of the French Revolution* (Toronto, Osgoode Society, 1993), pp. 27–8.
67 W.C. Wentworth, *Description of the Colony of New South Wales* (London, Whittaker, 1819).
68 Kercher, *An Unruly Child*, pp. 85–6. See also Brendan Edgeworth, 'Defamation Law and the Emergence of a Critical Press in Colonial New South Wales (1824–1831)' *Australian Journal of Law and Society*, 6 (1990–91), pp. 67–70.
69 Edgeworth, 'Defamation Law', pp. 50, 67–70.
70 Neal, *The Rule of Law in a Penal Colony*, pp. 115–40.
71 Paul Finn, *Law and Government in Colonial Australia* (Melbourne, Oxford University Press, 1987); Alastair Davidson, *The Invisible State: The Formation of the Australian State, 1788–1901* (Cambridge, Cambridge University Press, 1991).

PART II

Imperialism and citizenship

These chapters foreground racial differentiation at the heart of colonialism, and the work of law(s), courts and legislatures, in defining a colonial population and in categorizing and excluding colonized populations from citizenship in specific localities.

CHAPTER FOUR

'Race' definition run amuck: 'slaying the dragon of Eskimo status' before the Supreme Court of Canada, 1939

Constance Backhouse

As a colony Canada inherited both English and French law, was pummelled by American influences, and asserted imperialistic powers of its own across racial boundaries *vis-à-vis* First Nations' and Aboriginal communities. This paper focuses on the legal definition of 'race', an area riddled with Canadian imperialist thought and practice, at the moment when the issue of 'Eskimo status' was catapulted before the Supreme Court of Canada. The crucial question posed in the case was whether 'Eskimos' were 'Indians' under the Canadian constitutional framework.

At the time, the affirmative decision was derisively labelled 'an absurd little mouse' by Diamond Jenness, a leading white Canadian anthropologist, who borrowed it from the Latin of Horace. The original – *Parturiunt montes; nascetur ridiculous mus* – 'The mountains are in labour. From their womb will issue an absurd little mouse.' Such was Jenness's disdain for the ruling issued by the Supreme Court of Canada on 5 April 1939 and for the reasoning of its eminent judges.[1] The judges had definitively held that 'Eskimos' were 'Indians' within the Canadian constitutional framework. A landmark judicial opinion on racial definition, the case's most noteworthy feature was the breath-taking sense of certainty that accompanied the court's pronouncement.[2] The legal definition of 'Indian' had long occupied Canadian legislators and judges, who tinkered and fretted over the language in the successive enactments of the Indian Act. The federal Government never enacted an Eskimo Act to be the counterpoint of the Indian Act and seemed of two minds whether to include 'Eskimo' under the latter. In 1924, Parliament debated the matter, and resolved not to do so. Now the perplexing question of whether the word 'Eskimo' was subsumed within the word 'Indian' was at last resolved by the court. And Jenness was properly irked. As well he might have been, since he had testified as an expert witness that 'Eskimos' and 'Indians' were 'racially' distinct.

Diamond Jenness was, by all accounts, a fascinating and irrepressible scholar, possessed of a bitingly funny wit and apt to dispense disarmingly frank, droll comments on any range of intellectual issues. Born in Wellington, New Zealand, he obtained his academic degrees at the University of New Zealand and Oxford, where he trained in classics. Jenness held an M.A. degree in honours classics from the University of New Zealand, and an honours M.A. in classics from Oxford. In 1910, he was awarded a diploma in the 'relatively new field' of anthropology under Dr R.R. Marett. At the time of testifying, he held an honourary doctorate of literature from New Zealand University, and served as a Fellow of the Royal Society of Canada, an honourary corresponding member of the Danish Geographical Society and as President of the Society for American Archaeology. Towards the end of his studies he embraced the subject of anthropology and picked up a 'diploma' in the newly emergent discipline. In 1911, he began his field work in the steamy jungles of Papua New Guinea, and then in 1913, looking for a change of pace, he joined Vilhaljmur Stefansson's Arctic Expedition. Jenness spent an extraordinary three years travelling and living among the Arctic peoples, examining their culture and recording his observations for posterity. In 1926, he was appointed chief anthropologist for the National Museum of Canada, where his steady stream of papers, articles and books inspired others to christen him 'Canada's most distinguished anthropologist' and 'one of the world's most respected Eskimologists'.[3]

Testifying before the Supreme Court, Diamond Jenness had offered his opinion that both Eskimos and Indians had 'a very strong infusion or percentage of Mongoloid blood', and that there was a 'strong racial resemblance, a strong community of race between all the inhabitants' of North and South America. There were, however, sharp distinctions. In addition to different language, customs and religion, the Eskimo 'diverge[d] considerably from the other aborigines' in physical appearance. 'The Eskimo may well have inherited some of the same racial features as the Indians', noted Jenness, 'but may have deviated so greatly, owing to his peculiar environment, that he now forms a distinct sub-type'.

Trying to clarify matters, one of the lawyers had asked Jenness whether the difference between the Eskimo and the Pacific coast Indians, for example, could be compared 'with the difference between the Englishman and the Hindu'. Although he was careful to qualify his answer, noting that it was 'hard to define the uniform Englishman or the uniform Hindu', Jenness had no difficulty formulating a reply. A man with a genius for calculating his words, Jenness may have gazed steadily out at the bench of six white Supreme Court judges when he offered up this astute assessment: 'I should think the difference between the Eskimo and your Siwash [Indians] on the Pacific coast would be about as great as between, say, an Englishman and an Italian or Greek; possibly between an Englishman and certain Hindus.'[4]

This evidence must have given some pause. The judges were a bit out of their league in trying to assess the racial affinity between the 'Eskimo' and the 'Indian', lacking any personal reference base from their own sense of the world. Now the litigants were attempting to lob the problem back into more familiar territory. All of the judges knew instinctively what an 'Englishman' was. Some of them were such. Had they glanced down the bench, they would have found no one of Italian or Greek heritage. Nor was there anyone who professed the Hindu religion. With the exception of one justice, whose mother was a Francophone, all of them came from a homogeneous English, Scottish or Irish background.[5]

The evidence must have left the judges in quite a quandary. Did they surreptitiously scan the faces of their colleagues, searching for skin pigmentation, skull shapes, nasal apertures and eye characteristics? Just how distinct did they feel themselves, linguistically, socially, economically, culturally and physically from Hindus, Italians and Greeks?

Background to the case

The case, styled 'Re Eskimos' was provoked by a dispute between the federal Government and the province of Quebec over who should have to pick up the tab for the meagre relief rations that were being distributed to Aboriginal communities on the Ungava Peninsula of Hudson's Bay. The people who inhabited the region called themselves 'Inuit', meaning 'the people' in their language of Inuktitut. Europeans erroneously called them 'Eskimos', a term that may have originated from an Algonquin word meaning 'eaters of raw meat' or from a Montagnais word meaning 'those who speak a strange language'.[6]

Although the majority of the Inuit in Canada lived along the Arctic and sub-Arctic coasts and islands of the Northwest Territories and the Yukon, a smaller population settled on lands that eventually became part of Quebec. A geographic expanse initially referred to as the Ungava Peninsula, this area later came to be known as Nouveau Quebec and then Nunavik. Inuit spokespersons still register surprise as they describe how their traditional lands seemed to change hands at the stroke of a pen, without any consultation with the native inhabitants. Zebedee Nungak writes:

> If I go back to 1670, when King Charles issued a proclamation naming not only this vast geographic area, indeed all the area where the rivers

flow into Hudson and James Bay, as Rupert's Land, I can describe that as the first political earthquake that happened. This act gave a political status to a geographic area that did not involve the consent or involvement of the people who lived there. It was known as Rupert's Land for the next two hundred years. In 1870, three years after the Dominion of Canada was proclaimed as a country, this geographic area was transferred ... to the Dominion of Canada ... gaining the label of the Northwest Territories ... This was the second political earthquake that took place without the involvement or even the information of our forefathers. Then in 1912, another event took place, where the Parliament of Canada extended the boundaries of what was then Quebec to the geographic area that it is now. The third political earthquake that happened in the time of my great-grandfather was when he woke up one morning in 1912, a newly minted citizen of La Belle province – not ever having been informed of such.[7]

The Inuit had inhabited the northern reaches of Canada for centuries by the time European explorers first recorded contact. Aboriginal peoples migrated across the Arctic in waves, the 'Paleo-Eskimo' group around 2000 BC, the 'Pre-Dorset' until 800 BC, the 'Dorset' until AD 1000 and the 'Thule' until AD 1600, spreading west from Alaska to Greenland. Despite the harsh climate, the Inuit subsisted on a rich bounty of sea-mammals, caribou, musk-oxen, polar bears, birds and fish.[8] Diamond Jenness, who claimed an intimacy with Inuit culture atypical of most whites, picturesquely recorded the expertise of the indigenous hunters. Although his idyllic portrayals of some aspects of Inuit culture can be contrasted with others more patronizing and dismissive in tone, Jenness described how Inuit tracked the 'breathing holes of the seals in the ice that mantles the winter sea', how they approached their quarry 'within harpoon range' as the seals 'drowsed in the sun on the surface of the ice', how they drove 'whole herds of caribou into snares or ambushes, or into lakes and rivers where the hunters could pursue the swimming animals in their kayaks and slaughter them with their lances'. He marvelled at how the Inuit seemed to thrive in the face of 'howling blizzards', recounting the example of an Inuit woman, 'crouched down in the lee of her sled, during a winter migration', who withdrew 'her naked baby from under her fur coat' and calmly changed 'its tiny caribou-fur diaper, although the temperature was 30 degrees fahrenheit below zero and a thirty-mile-an-hour gale was whipping the snow against our faces'.[9]

Survival was always precarious in the Arctic. But beginning in the nineteenth century, with the penetration of European whalers, the Inuit experienced significant cultural, economic and political dislocation. The social upheaval increased when the whaling industry was supplanted by the fur-trade, which dramatically transformed traditional hunting patterns. With the worldwide recession in the 1930s, the bottom dropped out of the fur market. Jenness wrote agonizingly of 'lonely Eskimo trappers' who died of starvation while their tents 'overflowed with furs'.[10] Stepping in to forestall starvation, parsimonious government bureaucrats selected dried buffalo meat for distribution, aware that 'the Eskimos are not particularly fond of it and consequently are not likely to ask for it unless they are in real need'. Another problem was the fat content. Buffalo meat did not contain enough fat to be much use in the Arctic climate, but federal officials suggested that the Inuit might supplement it with 'seal or walrus meat [to] provide a very nourishing diet'.[11]

The only remaining question was: which government should be on the hook for the financial bailout of the Inuit in northern Quebec, paltry though the sum may have been? Quebec lawyers argued that the federal government was responsible, since under the Canadian constitution, the federal government had sole jurisdiction over 'Indians and Lands Reserved for Indians'. The federal government insisted that Eskimos were distinct from Indians, and that the cost should be shouldered by the province of Quebec. As for Diamond Jenness, he called it 'bureaucracy in inaction', 'steering without a compass' and 'shamelessly passing the buck'.[12]

The issue was framed as a 'reference', a lawsuit that allowed the government to obtain advisory opinions on important matters of law from the Supreme Court of Canada. There was no legal barrier to having representation from Aboriginal communities during the lawsuit. Indeed, the court was authorized to direct that all 'interested parties' be heard, and was permitted to appoint counsel to represent such parties. Yet just as there had been no consultation with the Inuit regarding the political claims on their land, no-one seems to have thought to ask their opinion concerning their national and racial identity. There were no 'Indian' or 'Eskimo' parties to the proceeding. Had the court taken proper care to solicit the perspectives of Aboriginal peoples, it might have sought input from any number of First Nations with whom it had negotiated treaties in the past. The collective view of the Inuit might have been somewhat more difficult to discern, since there had as yet been no treaty-making, and there were no hierarchically situated 'chiefs' or associations to approach among the scattered camps and outposts in the north. However, there were many elders, shamans and other leaders whose ideas would have been invaluable to the proceeding. Instead, six white Supreme Court of Canada judges and two sets of white government lawyers all set about contemplating the weighty question: 'Are Eskimos Indians?'[13]

Anthropological 'expertise'

There were a host of anthropological theories available to provide expertise on this thorny question. In 1939, the concepts of 'race' and 'racial classification' were in some flux. According to government census documents, there were only four races. Officials surveyed the Canadian nation every decade, relegating each member of the population into one of four 'racial' boxes: 'white', 'red', 'yellow' and 'black'. At issue would have been whether to consign 'Eskimos' to the 'red' or 'yellow' category.[14] Scientific understandings of race on the other hand were considerably more intricate, with Blumenbach delineating five races, Nott and Gliddon seven, and Deniker no fewer than seventeen main races with twenty-nine sub-races.[15] The late nineteenth and early twentieth centuries witnessed a peak of scholarly research on racial identification. Dismissive of the early racial theorists, who catalogued and classified largely on the basis of anecdotal commentary from world travellers, the new scholars showed themselves anxious to demonstrate the superiority of the 'scientific method'. Physicians, biologists, psychologists and ethnologists conducted scores of studies. They measured head length, head width, face height, nose height, nose width, facial angle, stature, eye colour, hair colour and form, thickness of lips and beard characteristics.[16]

Debates erupted over gradations of skin colour. The original idea that the 'American race' was properly designated as 'red' gave way to scholarly critique, with some conjecturing the real shade was 'bronze', 'coppery', 'burnt coffee' or 'cinnamon'.[17] One anthropologist postulated that there were no fewer than thirty-four shades of skin colour differentiating the races.[18] Then there was always the question of whether the skin being measured had been properly cleaned, with some fretting that smoke and dirt could sully the accuracy of findings.[19] Others struggled over precisely where on a subject's body skin colour should be tested. Data had traditionally been based on facial colouration, but more reflective minds suggested that researchers should examine a spot better protected from the elements, 'from the inside of the forearm and not from the face'.[20]

Skull measurement was touted as a quintessential characteristic, since scientists believed that intelligence was equated with brain size.[21] Problems arose when the theories ran foul of the data. Shaken researchers discovered that Eskimos, Lapps, Malays and Tartars had larger cranial capacity than 'most civilized people of Europe'.[22] Instead of reordering the racial hierarchy, anthropologists circumvented the problem, claiming that brain size and intelligence 'might not correlate' at the upper end of the scale.[23] Some speculated that the remarkable size of the Eskimo skull might harken back to 'the masticatory apparatus', which had seen extraordinary development as a result of their flesh and fish diet and 'the energetic uses to which they put their teeth'. A steady diet of chewy raw seal and whale had purportedly distorted the facial size and shape with enormous chewing muscle.[24]

Similar problems arose over arms. Scientists had advanced the theory that a long forearm was 'more characteristic of the ape' and thus indicative of lower racial stock. The data seemed intact when measurements showed blacks to have longer forearms than whites, but everything ran amuck when Eskimos and Australian Aborigines turned out to have shorter forearms than either. Some suggested, at least in the case of Eskimos, that frigid Arctic weather might have stunted arm growth.[25] Some researchers maintained that racial characteristics could differ by gender. Birket-Smith, known as 'the doyen of Danish Eskimologists', confided that Eskimo women had a 'more Mongoloid appearance than the men', attributing this strange finding to the fact that they were 'fuller in the face'. Nor did he stop with faces. 'The breasts of quite young women are often conical', noted Birket-Smith, 'but soon begin to hang and before long resemble a pair of long, loose bags'. One wonders what comparison base he was using when he drew this particular assessment.[26]

Of course, when considering whether Eskimos were Indians, one had to have some base-line definition of 'Indians' against which to make comparisons. The definition of 'Indian' had posed a conundrum for years. Since 1850, when the earliest statute defining 'Indian' appeared in Lower Canada, a host of federal and provincial legislative definitions had tampered and tinkered with a complex amalgamation of concepts and designs.[27] A rash of theories competed for pre-eminence. Some made reference to having 'Indian blood', or 'residing among Indians'. Others included those 'reputed' to belong to a tribe, or those living the 'Indian mode of life'. Once again, there had never been any consultation with First Nations' communities. The full arrogance of government authorities was transparently obvious in the 1876 Indian Act, which contained the rather startling statement that the word 'person' did not include 'Indian'.[28]

In the hands of the courts, the definition of 'Indian' was embellished still further. Judges scrutinized variables such as language, lifestyle, skin pigmentation, attire, diet, occupational history, demeanour, wealth, religion, place of residence, whether one paid taxes or voted, even the company one kept. In what seems to a new millenial perspective most bizarre of all, Canadian courts routinely made racial assessments based on whether the individual concerned 'wore moccasins'.[29]

Throughout all the weighing, measuring and testing, the issue of racial purity seemed to flutter at the margins. Most anthropologists conceded that racial intermixture flourished almost everywhere, that it was many thousands of years too late to speak of 'pure races'. Given that within fifteen generations, one individual can trace back 32,000 direct ancestors, this is not surprising.[30] The Arctic was perhaps something of an exception. As Diamond Jenness pointed out, 'two grim sentinels, Cold and Silence, guarded the retreats of the Eskimos', repelling European adventurers who tried to 'storm their gates'. But by the late nineteenth century, even here intrepid whalers from Britain, Holland, Spain, France, Russia and the United States had 'breached the walls', routinely striking up sexual liaisons with Inuit women. After the whalers came fur-traders, police, missionaries and anthropologists, many of whom contributed to the cross-fertilization. Inuit also intermarried with Algonkian peoples in the eastern Arctic, and with Africans, Asians and Polynesians on the west coast.[31]

The 'discovery' of 'blonde Eskimos' in a remote area near the Bering Strait set anthropological tongues to wagging in earnest, until researchers unveiled the puzzle. Lacking access to water in frigid months of winter, some Inuit women washed their hair in 'stale urine', with a pronounced bleaching effect. The red beards of the men were attributable to daily drinking of 'scalding blood soup'. Blue eyes, which were initially diagnosed as pathological, were apparently brought on by frequent attacks of snow-blindness.[32] When astonished anthropologists discovered an alleged 'Eskimo skull' in France and another at Obercassel, near Bonn, in Germany, consternation knew no bounds. Jenness proffered one explanation: 'Theoretically, it would seem not impossible that the generalized Eskimo type established itself somewhere in the Old World towards the close of the Glacial period, and that some of its representatives penetrated to western Europe.'[33] But if Eskimos had migrated to France and Germany, what were the implications for the theory of racial purity?

Racial blending made mincemeat of the already imponderable task of quantifying and delineating racial characteristics. The most incredible thing was how few seemed to recognize that before one could articulate racial characteristics one had to be certain of exactly who one was measuring. Yet no one ventured to whisper 'The Emperor has no clothes'.

The Supreme Court hearing and decision

In the face of this appalling lack of certainty, government lawyers waded in with arguments and summations before the Supreme Court of Canada. The task was monumental. It took two full years merely to prepare arguments, compile voluminous exhibits and publish detailed, intricate facta. Counsel picked away at 'bones, flesh and blood' as they fashioned their arguments, but they also filed copious entries from old dictionaries, as well as correspondence from missionaries, clergy, cartographers, geographers, government officials and nineteenth-century Hudson's Bay Company records. The oral submissions stretched across nine months.

The complex case took the judges considerable effort to resolve. The decision required fourteen months of deliberation, prompting Diamond Jenness to suggest mockingly that the court must have needed 'the fullness of time'. The long-awaited judgment, released in April of 1939, seemed surprisingly bold and succinct. The Supreme Court ruled unanimously that 'Eskimos' were 'Indians'. In the final resort, the court seems to have preferred the 'hard' evidence of American dictionaries, European missionaries, British Hudson's Bay Company officials and the like, over the intricate and confusing data of scientific anthropologists. Records showed that many whites in the nineteenth and early twentieth centuries had equated Eskimos and Indians, some even coining the phrase 'Eskimaux Indians' as a unifying construct, and it was these the Court relied on for authority. When the Supreme Court discovered correspondence between two federal government officials dating back to the late nineteenth century, promising to provide funds for the relief of destitute Eskimos on the north shore of the St Lawrence, the judges seized on this with glee. They used the correspondence to conclude that the Fathers of Confederation must always have understood 'Indians' to include 'all aborigines living within the territories in North America under British authority'.[34]

Diamond Jenness must have been miffed to see that the final decision contained not a whit of reference to his testimony classifying Eskimos as racially distinct. Perhaps the judges found it easier to disagree with Canada's most respected Eskimologist without attracting attention to the fact. Perhaps 'Eskimos' and 'Indians' were so obviously on a different physical, social and cultural plane from other Canadian groups that there was no need to call up 'scientific' data before equating them. Perhaps the judges discerned a chasm between white communities (on the one hand) and Aboriginal and Inuit communities (on the other) that was so large that even Jenness's reference to equating Englishmen with Italians, Greeks and 'certain Hindus' did not dissuade. In rendering the constitutional opinion equating Eskimos and Indians, the Supreme Court relied entirely on opinions of persons of European heritage. Colonial representatives of imperial British power led the pack, supplemented by compilers of United States' dictionaries. No one of Aboriginal heritage was consulted or permitted to speak. No one seems to have thought this omission worthy of comment.

In the end the judges shrank from entangling themselves in the mire of race classification. Legislation, judicial cases and scientific data threw up an amazing morass of variables to use in the legal construction of 'race' in Canadian history. Perhaps the single most fascinating aspect of the Supreme Court's decision was the judges' failure to articulate any unifying, concrete, legal criteria for race categorization. The court made no attempt to sort through the profuse, rambling list of factors, nor to offer guidance on matters of racial designation for the future. It simply declared as a matter of Canadian law, because the framers of the British North America Act had done so, that Inuit would be equated part of the 'Indian race' forever.

Racial categorization is not a minor matter: despite the appalling emptiness of racial categories, and the artificiality and impermanence of such terminology, racial concepts have had important economic, social and political consequences for those affected by them. The legal system has played a major part in this process. Of the judgment *Re Eskimos* in 1939 Diamond Jenness, ultimately claiming the final word, quipped that the powers that be had 'unweariedly fought the dragon of Eskimo status' and law, not science, had won. In the end, he concluded with some finality, the 'august body' of the Supreme Court of Canada had settled the question 'once and for all'.[35]

Notes

I am indebted to Betty Brewster, Susan Enuaraq, Sandra Inutiq, Leetia Janes, Eric Jamie, Bernadette Makpah, Julia Olayuk, Sarah Papatsie, Pauline Pemik, Louisa Pootoolik, Paul Quassa and Helen Tologanak, all students of the Jump-Start Inuit Legal Studies Programme in Iqaluit in 1997, and Signa Daum Shanks and Debbie Rollier, students at the University of Western Ontario, for assisting me in this research. I am also indebted to Brenda Mowbray and Gayle Jessop of the Nunavut Arctic College Library, Nunatta Campus, as well as Richard Diubaldo, who generously shared with me his sources on this case. Funds from the Law Foundation of Ontario and the Social Sciences and Humanities Research Council of Canada are gratefully acknowledged. A fuller discussion of this case is published in Constance Backhouse (ed.), *Colour-Coded: A Legal History of Racism in Canada, 1900-1950* (Toronto, University of Toronto Press, 1999), Chapter 2 (pp. 18–55).

1 Richard J. Diubaldo, 'The Absurd Little Mouse: When Eskimos Became Indians', *Journal of Canadian Studies*, 16:2 (1981), 34.
2 *Re Eskimos* (1939) 80 SCR 104; [1939] 2 DLR 417.
3 William E. Taylor, Jr, 'Foreword' in Diamond Jenness, *Indians of Canada* (Ottawa, National Museum of Canada, 1932; republished by Ministry of Supply and Services Canada, 1977), p. v; Case on Behalf of the Attorney General of Canada, in the Supreme Court of Canada, In the Matter of a Reference as to Whether the Term 'Indians' in Head 24 of Section 91 of the British North America Act, 1867, Includes Eskimo Inhabitants of the Province of Quebec (Ottawa, King's Printer, 1938), p. 16; B.L. Clark, 'Diamond Jenness 1886–1969', in the NMC's *Development of Caribou*

Eskimo Culture – A Diamond Jenness Memorial Volume (Ottawa, National Museum of Canada, 1977); 'Jenness, Diamond', entry in W. Stewart Wallace (ed.), *The Macmillan Dictionary of Canadian Biography*, 4th edn (Toronto, Macmillan of Canada, 1978), p. 390.

4 Factum on Behalf of the Attorney General of Canada, in the Supreme Court of Canada, In the Matter of a Reference as to whether the term 'Indians' in Head 24 of Section 91 of the British North America Act, 1867, includes Eskimo inhabitants of the Province of Quebec, pp. 19–20.

5 The ethnic and religious diversification of the Supreme Court of Canada would begin decades later. Bora Laskin became the first Jewish Supreme Court justice, when he was appointed in 1970. John Sopinka, whose parents emigrated from the Ukraine, appears to have been the first appointee to the Supreme Court of Canada to identify himself as a member of an 'ethnic minority'. Frank Iacobucci, whose parents were Italian-Canadian, was appointed in 1991. As yet, there have been no Supreme Court justices with Greek, South Asian, Chinese, Japanese, African-Canadian or Aboriginal heritage.

6 Pauktuutit, *The Inuit Way: A Guie to Inuit Culture* (Ottawa, Pauktuutit, Inuit Women's Association, 1989), p. 4; David Damas (ed.), 'Arctic', entry in William C. Sturtevant (ed.), *Handbook of North American Indians*, (Washington, Smithsonian Institution, 1984), vol. 5, pp. 6–7.

7 Zebedee Nungak, 'Quebecker?? Canadian? ... Inuk!', in Bruce W. Hodgins and Kerry A. Cannon (eds), *On the Land: Confronting the Challenges to Aboriginal Self-Determination in Northern Quebec and Labrador* (Toronto, Betelgeuse, 1995), p. 19. Mary Ellen Turpel-Lafond notes, in 'Oui the People? Conflicting Visions of Self-Determination in Quebec' (*ibid.*, p. 66), that these land transfers fly in the face of Inuit national heritage: 'The Inuit in Quebec have stated that they are part of one Inuit nation in Canada and part of a larger Inuit nation in the Circumpolar Region.' See also the comments of Grand Chief Matthew Coon Come, in 'Clearing the Smokescreen' (*ibid.*, pp. 8–9).

8 Alan D. McMillan, *Native Peoples and Cultures of Canada* (Vancouver, Douglas & McIntyre, 1988), pp. 240–6; James S. Frideres, *Aboriginal Peoples in Canada: Contemporary Conflicts*, 5th edn (Scarborough, Prentice-Hall, 1998), p. 391.

9 Diamond Jenness, *Eskimo Administration: II. Canada* (Calgary, Alberta, Arctic Institute of North America, 1964), pp. 25, 146. For a critical assessment of Jenness's contributions on Inuit culture, see Sidney L. Harring, 'The Rich Men of the Country: Canadian Law in the Land of the Copper Inuit, 1914–1930', *Ottawa Law Review*, 21:1 (1989), 1.

10 Penny Petrone (ed.), *Northern Voices: Inuit Writing in English* (Toronto, University of Toronto Press, 1988), pp. 103–286; W.C.E. Rasing, *'Too Many People': Order and Nonconformity in Iglulingmiut Social Process* (Nijmegen, Katholieke Universiteit, Faculteit Der Rechtsgeleerdheid, 1994), p. 63; McMillan, *Native Peoples*, pp. 264–6; Jenness, *Eskimo Administration*, pp. 10–25, 50–2; Keith J. Crowe, *A History of the Original Peoples of Northern Canada* (Montreal, McGill-Queen's University Press, 1974), pp. 111f.; Richard Diubaldo, *The Government of Canada and the Inuit: 1900–1967* (Canada, Research Branch, Corporate Policy, Indian and Northern Affairs Canada, 1985), p. 12.

11 Jenness, *Eskimo Administration*, p. 52, citing *Canada Department of the Interior Annual Report, 1933–34*, p. 35, and W.C. Bethune, *Canada's Eastern Arctic, its History, Resources, Population and Administration* (Ottawa, Department of Interior, 1934), filed as Exhibit Q-3 in 'Case on Behalf of the Attorney General of Quebec', p. 161. Jenness also notes that the 500 green buffalo hides that were distributed in addition to the meat 'were too thick for clothing, but made tolerable bed-robes, rather heavy, however, to carry on the back during the summer months'.

12 British North America Act, 1867, 30–1 Vic., c. 3 (UK); Jenness, *Eskimo Administration*, pp. 17, 30, 43, 49, 55, 90.

13 Barry L. Strayer, *The Canadian Constitution and the Courts: The Function and Scope of Judicial Review*, 3rd edn (Toronto, Butterworths, 1988), p. 313.

14 'Instructions to Officers taking the Dominion Census, Introduction to the Census Report of Canada for 1901', *Fourth Census of Canada 1901* (Ottawa, S.E. Dawson, 1902), vol.1, sections 47–54, pp. xviii–xix, as quoted in In re Coal Mines Regulation Act and Amendment Act, 1903 (1904) 10 BCR 408, (BCSC) p. 427. The instructions also contain a fifth category: 'Persons of mixed white and red blood – commonly known as "breeds" – will be described by the addition of the initial letters "f.b." for French breed, "e.b." for English breed, "s.b." for Scotch breed, "i.b." for Irish breed … Other mixtures of Indians besides the four above specified are rare, and may be described by the letters "o.b." for other breed.' These criteria were not altered until the census of 1951.

15 Otto Klineberg, *Race Differences* (New York, Harper, 1935), p. 20, citing J.F. Blumenbach, *Anthropological Treatises*, (London, 1865), J.C. Nott and G.R. Gliddon, *Types of Mankind* (Philadelphia, 1854), and J. Deniker, *The Races of Man* (New York, 1900).

16 See, for example, H.L. Shapiro, *The Alaskan Eskimo: A Study of the Relationship Between the Eskimo and the Chipewyan Indians of Central Canada* (New York, American Museum of Natural History, 1931).

17 Griffith Taylor, *Environment Race and Migration* (Toronto, University of Toronto Press, 1945), p. 252. See also 'Extract from M'Culloch Geographical Dictionary' (London, 1866), Exhibit Q-138 p. 444; 'Extract from Encyclopedia Americana' (1919), Exhibit Q-169 p. 549, from 'Case on Behalf of the Attorney General of Quebec'.

18 Thomas F. Gossett, *Race: The History of an Idea in America* (Dallas, Southern Methodist University Press, 1963), p. 69, citing Paul Broca, who founded the Anthropological Society in Paris in 1859.

19 See, for example, Exhibit C-125, Extract from 'The Polar Regions' by Sir John Richardson (1861) pp. 298–303, in Case on Behalf of the Attorney General of Canada p. 138; and Exhibit C-100, Extract from Samuel George Morton, *Crania Americana: or A Comparative View of the Skulls of Various Aboriginal Nations of North and South America: to which is prefixed An Essay on the Varieties of the Human Species* (1839), also from Case on Behalf of the Attorney General of Canada p. 385, where he notes that 'the color' of 'the Polar family' is 'brown, lighter or darker, but often disguised by accumulated filth'.

20 Shapiro, *The Alaskan Eskimo*. See also Taylor, *Environment, Race and Migration*, p. 51.

21 Taylor, *Environment, Race and Migration*, pp. 59–60.

22 Gisela Kaplan and Lesley J. Rogers, 'Race and Gender Fallacies: The Paucity of Biological Determinist Explanations of Difference', in Ethel Tobach and Betty Rosoff (eds), *Challenging Racism and Sexism: Alternatives to Genetic Explanations* (New York, Feminist Press, 1994), p. 71.

23 Otto Klineberg, *Race Differences*, pp. 36, 77.

24 Kaj Birket-Smith, *The Eskimos* (London, Methuen, [1936] 1959; 1st Danish edn 1927), p. 42; Extract from H.L. Shapiro, *Some Observations on the Origin of the Eskimo* (Toronto, 1934), Exhibit Q-190 p. 665; Shapiro, *Monograph on the Indian Origin of the Eskimo* (New York, 1937), Exhibit Q-193 p. 698, both in Case on Behalf of the Attorney General of Quebec.

25 Paul Broca 'Sur les proportions relatives du bras, de l'avant bras et de la clavicule chez les négres et les europèens', *Bulletin Sociètè d'Anthropologie Paris*, 3:2 (1862), 11. See Extracts from A. Fullerton & Co., *Gazetteer of the World* (London, 1857) Exhibit Q-133, in Case on Behalf of the Attorney General of Quebec, p. 401, for reference to the 'diminutive stature' of 'Eastern Esquimaux', attributed to 'their mode of living, which continually exposes them to every hardship and privation'.

26 Birket-Smith, *Eskimos*, pp. 30–1.

27 An Act for the better protection of the Lands and Property of the Indians in Lower Canada, S.Prov.C., 1850, c. 42, s. 5, was the first such statute. For a detailed account of other legislative definitions prior to 1950, see Backhouse, *Colour-Coded*.

28 The Indian Act, 1876, S.C., 1876, c. 18, s. 3(12), states: 'The term "person" means an individual other than an Indian, unless the context clearly requires another

construction.' The Indian Act, R.S.C., 1886, c. 43, s. 2(c), states: 'The expression "person" means any individual other than an Indian.' See also Indian Act, R.S.C., 1906, c. 81, s. 2(c); An Act respecting Indians, R.S.C., 1927, c. 98, s. 2(i). This offensive provision was not removed until 1951: see An Act respecting Indians, S.C., 1951, c. 29.

29 See, for example, *Rex* v. *Tronson* (1931), 57 C.C.C. 383 (B.C. County Ct); *Regina* v. *Howson* (1894), 1 Terr. LR 492 (N.W.T.S.C.); *The Queen* v. *Mellon* (1900), 7 C.C.C. 179 (N.W.T.S.C.); *The King* v. *Pickard* (1908), 14 C.C.C. 33 (Edm. Dist. Ct); *Rex* v. *Verdi* (1914), 23 C.C.C. 47 (Halifax Co. Ct).

30 Jack Forbes, 'The Manipulation of Race, Caste and Identity: Classifying Afro-Americans, Native Americans and Red-Black People', *The Journal of Ethnic Studies*, 17:4 (1990), 37–8.

31 Jenness, *Eskimo Administration*, pp. 10–13, 22, 26; Bobbie Kalman and Ken Faris, *Arctic Whales and Whaling* (New York, Crabtree, 1988); William R. Morrison, *Under the Flag: Canadian Sovereignty and the Native People in Northern Canada* (Ottawa, Indian and Northern Affairs Canada, 1984), pp. 71–141; Factum on Behalf of the Attorney General of the Province of Quebec, p. 24, citing Jenness; Emoke J.E. Szathmary 'Human Biology of the Arctic', in Sturtevant (ed.), *Handbook of North American Indians*, p. 64.

32 Birket-Smith, *Eskimos*, pp. 36–7. For an early reference to the 'flaxen'-haired Eskimo, see Extracts from Thomas Jeffreys, *The Natural and Civil History of the French Dominions in North and South America* ... (London, 1760), Exhibit Q-88 in Case on Behalf of the Attorney General of Quebec, p. 216.

33 Factum on Behalf of the Attorney General of the Province of Quebec, p. 7. The original reference comes from Jenness, *Indians of Canada*, p. 247.

34 The decisive exhibit contained correspondence between Prime Minister Sir John A. Macdonald and Sir Hector Langevin, in 1879, in which the federal Government promised to provide money for the relief of the 'Eskimo on the north shore of the St. Lawrence'. This resulted in the expenditure of $2,000 to aid the 'Montagnais and Eskimaux Indians' in the Lower St. Lawrence in 1880.

35 Jenness, *Eskimo Administration*, pp. 40–1.

CHAPTER FIVE

The paradox of 'ultra-democratic' government: indigenous civil rights in nineteenth-century New Zealand, Canada and Australia

Patricia Grimshaw, Robert Reynolds and Shurlee Swain

The colonial and dominion franchise status of the first peoples of Australia, Canada and New Zealand was formed through a potent mixture of racism, anxiety and calculation. In 1870, Earl Grey, secretary of state for colonies from 1846 to 1852, expressed his fear that the New Zealand settlers' rush to manhood suffrage would disadvantage Maori people. The new 'ultra-democratic government', he wrote, 'in which the Maoris cannot be allowed their fair share of power, will not long abstain from giving them cause for discontent'.[1]

It was a shrewd prediction. With the withdrawal of the Crown from the management of Maori affairs, the rapid influx of new settlers and with all white men enfranchised, who would adjudicate between the expansionist desires of the settlers and the beleaguered and increasingly dispossessed original inhabitants of New Zealand?

Earl Grey's pessimism could equally have been directed at the British settler societies of Australia and Canada where settlers sought political independence from a conservative Mother Country, but used this independence to contain indigenous peoples' rights and powers, negating the very democracy and egalitarianism so vaunted as a hallmark of their own progressive states. In each of these societies settlers moved quickly to counter any threat, real or imagined, that indigenous peoples might pose to white hegemony in the body politic. In 1870, Maori still constituted a very sizeable minority of New Zealand's population. That indigenous people constituted, or could have been thought to constitute, any threat to settler political dominance in Canada or Australia might seem far less obvious. Yet, here too, the place of indigenes in their national franchises was shaped by similar concerns: settlers acted out the paradox of independence and democracy for themselves, and marginalization or exclusion for indigenes.

This outcome stemmed not simply from an unmediated racism, but from a pragmatic and anxious appraisal of the potential power indigenous voting blocs could pose to white dominance. This is not to deny the particular and potent power of racist thought which cast the indigenous subject as inherently incapable of exercising the rights and responsibilities of citizenship. Rather, we would suggest, such racist ideology informed a calculated settler appraisal of the potential political agency of indigenous peoples.

Australia's racialized federation

At federation, in 1901, Aboriginal Australians constituted a tiny minority in the new nation, but any such calculation disguised the concentration of Aborigines in the west and the north. Politicians from these areas made it clear that their potential could not be discounted.

In 1902, NSW Senator Richard O'Connor introduced a bill to enfranchise women, Aborigines and naturalized immigrants of colour. The reaction from Queensland and Western Australian senators was swift. 'It is all very well for honourable senators to be benevolently inclined towards aboriginals and coloured aliens', complained Senator Glassey, 'but that policy means letting loose a large number of persons who will be able to affect our elections in Queensland in a manner that will be detrimental to the interests of that State and of the whole Commonwealth'.[2] Another Queenslander, Senator Stewart, urged 'honourable senators from other States to be guided by us in this matter'.[3] At the behest of Senator Matheson (WA), an amendment which effectively excluded most Australian indigenes from the franchise was ultimately passed by both Houses. It was the frontier states of Queensland and Western Australia which led the charge. But even in Queensland and Western Australia the numbers of Aborigines could not seriously threaten the numerical and electoral dominance of white settlers. Why then did white legislators feel so threatened?

In introducing manhood suffrage the south-eastern colonies had not explicitly excluded Aboriginal people. However, various residential qualifications and charitable receipt clauses effectively disenfranchised most. Only in South Australia is there clear evidence of groups of Aborigines voting in colonial elections, although one NSW MHR claimed he had seen Aborigines voting in his home state.[4] For Queensland and Western Australia, with their more recent frontier history, the strategy of disenfranchisement through stealth was not enough. Instead, Queensland in 1885 moved to explicitly disenfranchise indigenous peoples, by maintaining a race-specific freehold qualification set at a prohibitive £100.[5] In 1893 and 1899, Western Australia followed suit.[6] In these colonies, where the frontier remained unclosed, electoral arrangements reflected the racial anxieties of white legislators. Within the Queensland

Parliament, support for the disenfranchisement of the indigenous population was widespread. 'Is there a single member who would give votes to aborigines, Japanese, Chinese, Hindus, negroes, and South Sea Islanders?' Charles Powers declared: 'I do not think there is one.'[7]

In attempting, in 1902, to create a uniform national franchise, federal parliamentarians had to negotiate these different state franchise qualifications, the competing readings of section 41 of the constitution (which guaranteed the Commonwealth vote to any elector already registered on a state roll), and the racial anxieties of the frontier states. Senator Stainforth Smith (WA) argued that the bill 'would be all right for Tasmania, where there are no blacks, and probably all right for such States as New South Wales or Victoria; but to give the vote to most of the aboriginals in Western Australia would be a very serious matter indeed'.[8] Matheson was insistent: 'we must take some steps to prevent any aboriginal taken at large, chosen anywhere, from acquiring the right to vote'.[9] O'Connor suggested that the number of Aborigines in Western Australia was 'comparatively trifling'.[10] Aborigines, he argued, were a 'failing race' – and where they weren't failing they were becoming civilized and thus 'quite as well qualified to vote as are a great number of persons who already possess the franchise'.[11] But the senators from Western Australia and Queensland would not be reassured. Passing the bill, Senator Glassey (Queensland) declared, would be 'antagonistic to the sentiments of public opinion in the State I represent'.[12]

At first glance, the federal franchise debate was all about demography, but the actual number of potential Aboriginal voters was less important than the symbolic threat of Aboriginal citizenship. The mere potential of an Aboriginal vote posed a threat to the identity of a white Australia, particularly in Queensland and Western Australia where the colonial frontier still operated powerfully in the settler imagination as a place of danger, risk and threat. The debate marked a shift in anxiety from earlier colonial imagining of the Aborigine as a murderous and vengeful subject who had to be conquered to that of the passive object who could be manipulated by others. Nevertheless, a sense of threat and anxiety remained.

Nor were these fears confined to frontier states. John Watson, a MHR from NSW agreed that in 'the more settled districts of the eastern coasts, the matter is of little importance, because the number of aborigines is few and they are scattered'. But Watson was anxiously concerned about areas where 'vast numbers of practically uncivilised blacks' could be manipulated to 'turn the tide at an election'. While Watson argued that he had no objection 'in principle' to an educated Aboriginal voting, he wanted to 'prevent these savages and slaves ... in the northern and western portions of Australia, from running the electorates in the districts in which they reside'.[13] This sentiment was shared by many other south-eastern representatives, including some of the nation's leading liberals.

The legacy of frontier conflict – and perhaps a barely unconscious guilt and anxiety – was written upon the soul of White Australia. And yet an acknowledgment of this brutal past and present was too difficult for most to bear. In this first Commonwealth Parliament, it was as if the mere prospect of Aboriginal citizenship was an affront to the white colonization of Australia. The threat here was less the realistic prospect of Aboriginal influence in the Parliament than the return of a repressed history of invasion and conquest which might undermine the legitimacy of this proudly democratic and youthful country. '[It is] absurd', Senator Playford (SA) argued, 'that we should say we are so frightened of the original inhabitants that we dare not allow them to vote'.[14] And yet this was exactly what transpired. A fear of the original inhabitants of Australia, and the threat of having to grapple with a shameful history of race relations, saw the Aboriginal people denied that most potent symbol of modern citizenship – the vote.

Canada and the 'status Indian'

Although Canada had a longer and more complex history of white–indigenous interaction than did Australia, there were parallels when its national legislature debated the introduction of a uniform franchise in 1885. The proportion of indigenous peoples in the Canadian population was small, but in the western provinces, which had more recently entered the confederation, First Nations' peoples were far more numerous. As with Australia, the fear that enfranchised indigenous peoples could outweigh white voters in individual electorates helped shape the outcome of the national debate. While there is little evidence of indigenous peoples arguing for inclusion – indeed there were powerful reasons why they believed they would be compromised by participating in settler government[15] – they figured prominently in the fears and the imaginings of politicians intent on preserving settler hegemony.

Canada had entered into confederation in 1867 without a uniform franchise, its constitution ensuring simply that 'every man who has now a vote in his own Province should continue to have a vote in choosing a representative to the first Federal Parliament'.[16] Provincial franchises encoded considerable diversity, not only in relation to property qualification but also in the definition of the word 'man', which, at least in the eastern provinces, had allowed some indigenous people to register and vote.[17] When Prime Minister J.A. Macdonald set out to

[81]

standardize the federal franchise, it was these differences which had to be resolved.

When responsible government was first under consideration there were some Canadians who shared Earl Grey's concerns about the fate of indigenous peoples. Commending the way in which the 'mother country' had protected the rights of 'Indians',[18] Mr Neilson (MLA, United Canada, 1841) noted: 'If they get into the hands of the Colonial Government it would lead to dissatisfaction and difficulty.'[19] In 1860 Britain, ignoring indigenous protests,[20] transferred its protective powers to the newly responsible governments, who in turn vested these responsibilities in the Federal Government after confederation. This set in train a process through which policies developed in the eastern provinces would be applied across the nation.

The most important of these was the Gradual Civilization Act passed by the Canadian provincial legislature in 1857. This had created the category of the 'status Indian' standing outside of, and in opposition to, the 'Canadian citizen'. 'Status Indians' could continue to exercise their treaty rights, but they would do so under government supervision.[21] This status was considered both temporary and inferior, offering indigenous peoples the prospect of 'enfranchisement' or access to Canadian citizenship conditional upon abandonment of their Indian status.[22] Its aim was to remove, over time, the distinctions between indigenous and other British subjects established by the Royal Proclamation of 1763, which had constructed indigenous peoples as dependent and in need of protection while simultaneously recognizing their sovereignty in their own land.[23]

Yet only in Ontario was the exclusion of indigenous peoples from the franchise framed within the understandings of the Gradual Civilization Act. The new provinces in the west of Canada followed the Nova Scotian precedent excluding all indigenous peoples from manhood suffrage introduced in 1854.[24] Parliamentarians in British Columbia – where, in 1870, the 10,000 settlers were outnumbered by an estimated 40,000 indigenous peoples[25] – claimed to represent the indigenous population while denying its right to have a say in that representation. 'They contribute as much to the revenue as a Canadian ... [and] are entitled to be represented as well as white men'.[26] Yet in revising the local franchise, the same legislators voted to exclude all indigenous peoples (and Chinese) irrespective of their economic standing.[27]

Macdonald's 1885 Federal Franchise Bill initially cast aside such distinctions, applying a uniform property franchise across the nation irrespective of race. The belief that the bill appeared to be extending the vote to indigenous people who actively resisted Canadian citizenship, while removing it from adult males, enfranchised under the more liberal property qualifications in their individual provinces, was the source of much of the anger generated during the debate. In defence of their argument that a stake in the country was an essential prerequisite for citizenship, conservatives were prepared to extend the franchise to suitably qualified indigenous people (although, significantly, not to Chinese). The liberals, arguing that the vote was a privilege only for those who were 'free', opposed this extension, arguing that Macdonald wanted to enfranchise indigenous people for his own political advantage, assuming that, as wards of the Indian Department, they would direct their votes towards his party. The fact that the debate was taking place during the final stages of an Indian uprising in the west introduced a third element into the argument, with members from frontier provinces arguing that the success of Macdonald's proposals could threaten settler control of the political process.[28]

Richard Bartlett has suggested that Macdonald was advancing a race-blind notion of the privileges of the British subject, forcing his liberal opponents to put forward a range of often inconsistent objections arguing that indigenous people were incompetent in law, wards rather than adults, subject to government control, dependents not tax-payers, and inherently rebellious.[29] Yet the difference between the two sides was never so absolute. The language of race permeated the debate, with all members arguing for an expansion of the franchise only so long as it would not endanger their particular conception of a settler-controlled polity. The threat was understood in very local terms. Even in the east, where the European majority was clearly secure, members identified individual electorates in which indigenous people could determine the outcome of the poll. 'The Indians to be enfranchised', George Casey (Elgin, West Riding, Ontario) argued, 'are distributed in counties which either return prominent members of the Opposition or have returned supporters of the Government by a very narrow margin'.[30]

Numbers provide a constant subtext to the parliamentary debate, with individual members advancing their own estimates of the dimensions of the threat. To Philippe Casgrain (L'Islet, Quebec), the 131,952 indigenous people would produce 60,000 voters, constituting one-fifth of the total electorate.[31] On the local level the implications could be far more threatening. New Brunswick representative George King, faced with the loss of 500 of his existing 2,000 constituents because of the higher property qualification, declared that 'the proposition to enfranchise the 1,500 Indians there is an insult to the white settlers'. More frightening, however, was the prospect that the bill might have 'the effect of enfranchising 50,000 or 60,000 Indians in British Columbia, whose votes may swamp those of the white people in the Maritime Provinces'.[32] The message from the frontier areas was even more direct:

'If a band of 40 or 50 Indians came up to the polling booth in Manitoba and attempted to kill the votes of an equal number of white men who pay the taxes, who build the roads and bridges and support all the expenses of Government, it would raise a rebellion', Robert Watson (Manitoba) warned.[33]

As definitions of citizenship became more democratic, race was increasingly central. Just as the perceived threat of manhood suffrage underlay Macdonald's support for a uniform and race-blind property franchise, the possibility of indigenous enfranchisement threatened widescale acceptance of the principle of manhood suffrage, advocated by his opponents. The compromise position adopted in the Franchise Act of 1885 restricted the franchise to the so-called 'civilized Indians' in the east, defusing the possibility of the white vote being 'swamped' from the 'wild Indians' of the west. Even this limited franchise was abandoned in 1898 by the Liberal Federal Government, which returned to elections based on the provincial rolls. Although this legislation prohibited provinces excluding from voting classes of otherwise qualified people, these clauses were not interpreted as applying to indigenous peoples.[34]

As provincial franchises became more democratic, restrictions on indigenous participation intensified. Ontario retained a property qualification for indigenous people enfranchised under the Gradual Civilization Act for twenty years after manhood suffrage was adopted for the non-indigenous population in 1888.[35] When Prince Edward Island (1902) and Quebec (1915) introduced manhood suffrage, indigenous people domiciled or resident on a reserve were explicitly excluded. In New Brunswick, which introduced manhood suffrage in 1916, indigenous people were excluded, leaving only Nova Scotia (1920) – where they had voted since 1863[36] – with no racial bar.[37] By 1920, when the federal Government again took control of its own franchise, disqualifications on the basis of gender and property had been removed,[38] yet indigenous peoples were more effectively excluded from political participation than ever before.[39]

New Zealand's empty compromises

New Zealand was the one nation state of the three under consideration that emerged from a single colonial experience, having refused overtures from the Australian colonies to become part of the Australian Commonwealth. The situation about politics and franchise was therefore less ambiguous. The Maori were politically organized and had shown themselves capable of standing up to the British army. Debates about their political place were grounded in genuine fears of renewed and effective, if ultimately futile, armed resistance. These factors, perhaps, account for the apparently fairer outcomes for Maori people as the settler colony moved to universal male and, later, female suffrage. Nevertheless, Maori political marginalization was very real and aligned this country's experience with the other two British dominions more closely than at first might be apparent.

Addressing the first national legislature in 1854, Governor Gore Browne advised the settler representatives to demonstrate through 'prudence and moderation, the fitness of our countrymen for representative self-government and free institutions'. For the Governor, a key indicator of this prudence was for the settlers, 'the pioneers for its colonisation by the Anglo Saxon race ... to preserve and to advance the scale of civilisation of the Native inhabitants of these Islands'.[40] Writing privately to the Colonial Office, the governor confided his fear that the settlers would take a 'one-sided view of the native affairs'.[41]

Initially the Crown retained primary responsibility for Maori affairs, although settler representatives bristled at the suggestion that their relationships with the Maori were anything less than harmonious. In the Assembly debate on responsible government, only Thomas Forsaith dared to suggest that the interests of the settlers and the Maori were not identical.

> When they [Maori] consented to the establishment of British authority in these Islands they voluntarily agreed to rely upon Her Majesty, as their guardian and defender. Would they be satisfied with such an arrangement as that which proposes to transfer this power from the hands of the Queen to those of a party?[42]

For his trouble, Forsaith was roundly berated, retreating, by the close of the debate, to the claim that 'his sentiments had been misrepresented'.[43]

As in other British settler societies, there was no explicit racial bar in the 1852 New Zealand constitution. A relatively low property franchise meant that in theory 'property holders, leaseholders and householders could vote regardless of their colour (but not their sex)'.[44] The reality was somewhat different. Maori communal land tenure prevented them from qualifying for a franchise based upon individual property ownership. Moreover, they were effectively disenfranchised 'through the divorce of Maoris from the European politics or administration', which included, at its most explicit, the excision of the most heavily populated Maori areas in the North Island from electoral districts.[45] Although some Maori did vote during the 1850s, an 1859 ruling that they could not vote as landowners unless they had a Crown grant limited this practice.[46]

Settler representatives were more concerned to contain than to protect Maori interests. In 1858, when Maori constituted 56.5 per cent of

New Zealand's 115,000 people these fears were grounded in demography. By 1874 Maori constituted only 13.7 per cent of a population of 334,000,[47] but racial anxieties remained acute. More cynically, some North Island politicians during the 1850s were reported to have enrolled Maori voters in order to manipulate their votes.[48] Variously describing the registration of Maori voters as a 'plot' and 'a dangerous weapon', superintendent Featherstone warned that settlers, as a 'recourse in self defence to the dangerous weapon deployed against them', could just as easily register 'any number of Natives on the Roll, and to bring them up like a flock of sheep'.[49] The response from Auckland was just as revealing. Edward Stafford, himself a former superintendent of Nelson, expressed both a commitment to existing constitutional arrangements and a faith that these same liberal arrangements could adequately contain any political power the Maori might legally exercise. This liberality, however, rested upon Stafford's observation that, 'having regard to the limited number of Natives who possess an Electoral qualification, it does not appear that if they were all registered any fear need be entertained'.

Stafford's main objective was to maintain the semblance of racial harmony in order to protect the newly won system of responsible government. Any appearance of racial harmony, however, collapsed in the 1860s with the outbreak of war. So, too, did the restrictive electoral arrangements which had worked to assuage settler fears. In the wake of the prolonged New Zealand Wars, and the withdrawal of the Crown from the principle of trusteeship, new constitutional arrangements had to be created to contain both Maori political power and settler anxieties. Maori disenfranchisement through a property franchise was no longer tenable in a climate which demanded some sort of political settlement between Maori and Europeans. Indeed, Keith Jackson has argued that the 1860s' wars partly represented 'a desire by the Maoris to establish their own form of representation'.[50] In 1864 friendly Maori chiefs requested representation in the Assembly. 'Let us be ushered in, so that you may hear some of the growling of the native dogs without mouths [ie. not allowed to have a voice in public affairs], so that eye may come into contact with eye and tooth with tooth of both Maori and European.'[51] The challenge for the Government was to devise a system of Maori representation that did not endanger settler interests. Another word for this was 'containment'.

In introducing the Maori Representation Bill in 1867, Donald McLean[52] neatly encapsulated the political realities faced by the settler Government. The Maori paid taxes, owned three-fourths of the territory of the North Island, and, perhaps more importantly, were 'a people with whom the Government had been recently at war, and with whom it was desirous that peace should be established'. The introduction of special representation for Maori, he concluded, 'would tend to the best interests of the whole colony'.[53]

The creation of the four Maori seats in 1867 was not without some settler goodwill, but it was political pragmatism that demanded most representatives' attention. A genuine commitment to the democratic representation of Maori would have required the creation of at least sixteen Maori seats.[54] Attempts to increase the number of Maori seats during the 1870s and 1880s repeatedly failed. Given the 'temporary' and 'special' nature of the seats, most white representatives appeared to have imagined that the Maori representatives would hold observer status (with voting rights), and there was some surprise and consternation when Maori MPs demanded fuller participation.[55] The secret ballot, introduced in general electorates in 1870, was not adopted in Maori seats until 1937. Similarly, while electoral reform facilitated the redrawing of European electoral boundaries according to population changes, the Maori boundaries remained static. Although Maori men with individualized property freehold were allowed to vote in both Maori and European electorates until 1893,[56] the property qualification remained in place for Maori men after the 1879 electoral reforms had introduced manhood suffrage for settler males.

Settler fears remained acute despite continuing Maori population decline. The irony of such anxieties was that, in reality, it was the Pakeha, or white New Zealander, who had embarked on a process – demographic, economic, cultural and political – of swamping New Zealand's indigenous people.[57] In addition to the continuing diminution of Maori landholdings, a raft of legislation introduced around the same time as the Maori Representation Act – including the Native Lands Act (1865) which flagged the extinguishment of customary title, and the Education Act (1867) setting English as the language of education – accelerated this swamping process. By the late 1860s, the Government's policy of amalgamation had firmly brushed aside earlier Crown attempts to protect Maori interests.[58] Within this rhetoric of amalgamation lay the settler objective of containing the potential political power of the Maori.

The success of such policies by the 1890s eased settler anxieties. The Maori seats were increasingly seen as an irrelevance, a reminder of earlier, more anxious, years when the process of colonization was incomplete. From the European perspective, the existence of the Maori seats was now less about amalgamation and containment, and more the segregation of a dwindling indigenous population. For Maori MPs frustration grew. They began to organize to maximize their legislative strength. Others, however, looked to external forums, such as the Maori

Parliaments of the 1890s, where, they hoped, Maori would find a political voice and an autonomy denied them in the European Assembly. Maori women, along with Pakeha women, received the vote in 1893. Like their menfolk Maori women's voting was constrained to the four Maori-only electorates.[59]

In all three settler societies, racism was rife throughout the nineteenth century. This racism was reflected in the political accommodation which settler governments imposed upon the original inhabitants. That indigenous peoples, a minority in their own lands, were, by the early years of the twentieth century, marginalized, contained or excluded from the franchise may not appear surprising, given the terrible acts which had been perpetrated on them in the course of colonization. Indeed, given the history of violence in New Zealand, Canada and Australia, a history of the indigenous franchise may appear a less than pressing project. We believe, nevertheless, that such analysis of the marginalization of indigenous peoples from the white system of governance and representation is crucial to an understanding of the partial nature of settler democracy. Historians have not infrequently imbued the white settler sprint towards responsible and then democratic government with a decidedly triumphal hue. And yet, within this triumph of settler democracy, as barriers of birth, wealth, property and gender fell away, indigenous peoples' rights were increasingly circumscribed.

Notes

For a fuller discussion of the issues considered in this paper see P. Grimshaw, D. Philips, S. Swain and J. Evans, *Grounds for Dispute: Indigenous Peoples and Citizenship in Nineteenth-Century Settler Societies* (Manchester, Manchester University Press, in process).

1 Mitchell Library, Sydney, Earl Grey to Henry Sewell, 19 October 1870.
2 Australia, *Commonwealth Parliamentary Debates* (hereafter *CPD*), vol.9 (10 April 1902), p. 11596.
3 *CPD*, vol. 9 (10 April 1902), p. 11597.
4 Pat Stretton and Christine Finnimore, 'Black Fellow Citizens: Aborigines and the Commonwealth Franchise', *Australian Historical Studies*, 25 (1993), 522.
5 John Chesterman and Brian Galligan, *Citizens Without Rights: Aborigines and Australian Citizenship* (Melbourne, Cambridge University Press, 1997), p. 36.
6 Constitutional Amendment Act 1893 (WA), s. 21; Constitutional Amendment Act 1899 (WA), s. 26. See Patricia Grimshaw and Katherine Ellinghaus, 'White Women, Aboriginal Women and the Vote in Western Australia', in P. Crawford and J. Skene (eds), *Women and Citizenship: Suffrage Centenary*, special edition *Studies in Western Australian History*, 19 (1999), 1–19
7 *Queensland Parliamentary Debates*, (*QPD*), vol. 74 (18 October 1895), p. 1333.
8 *CPD*, vol. 10 (29 May 1902), p. 13003.
9 *CPD*, vol. 9 (9 April 1902), p. 11467.

10 *CPD*, vol. 9 (10 April 1902), p. 11584.
11 *CPD*, vol. 9 (9 April 1902), p. 11453.
12 *CPD*, vol. 9 (10 April 1902), p. 11596.
13 *CPD*, vol. 9 (24 April 1902), pp. 11975–6.
14 *CPD*, vol. 9 (10 April 1902), p. 11592.
15 *Royal Commission on Aboriginal Peoples* (hereafter *RCAP*), vol. 1: *Looking Forward, Looking Back* (Ottawa, The Commission, 1996), p. 24.
16 *Parliamentary Debates on the Subject of Confederation of the British North American Provinces*, 3rd Session, 8th Provincial Parliament of Canada, Quebec, 1865, p. 39.
17 F. Ouellet, *Lower Canada 1791–1840: Social Change and Nationalism*, (Toronto, McLelland & Stewart, 1980), p. 25.
18 The term 'Indian' where used in this paper is reflective of the terminology of the time.
19 Elizabeth Nish (ed.), *Debates of the Legislative Assembly of United Canada*, vol. 1 (Quebec, 1841 Présses de l'École des hautes études commerciale, (1841) p. 936.
20 *RCAP*, p. 273.
21 For an examination of Indian rights and liabilities under this and subsequent Acts, see J.L.Tobias, 'Indian Reserves in Western Canada: Indian Homelands or Devices for Assimilation?', in B. Cox (ed.), *Native People, Native Lands: Canadian Indians, Inuit and Metis* (Ottawa, Carleton University Press, 1992), pp. 148–56.
22 J.R. Miller, *Skyscrapers Hide the Heavens: A History of Indian–White Relations in Canada* (Toronto, University of Toronto Press, 1991), pp. 110–11.
23 Richard Bartlett, 'Citizens Minus: Indians and the Right to Vote', *Saskatchewan Law Review*, 44 (1979/80), 165, 167.
24 This clause was repealed when property qualifications were reintroduced nine years later: Elections Canada, *A History of the Vote in Canada* (Ottawa, Minister of Public Works and Government Services Canada, 1997), pp. 46–7.
25 This figure, which is clearly an estimate, comes from *Parliamentary Debates, Dominion of Canada*, 4th Session 34 Vic. 1871 (Ottawa, Queen's Printer, 1871), p. 664.
26 *Debate on the Subject of Confederation With Canada*, reprinted from *Government Gazette* extraordinary of March 1970 (Victoria, Government Printer, 1879, pp. 497, 541.
27 British Columbia, Qualification and Registration of Voters Act, 38 Vic. no. 1 1875.
28 *Commons Debates*, p. 1582.
29 Bartlett, 'Citizens Minus', p. 169.
30 *Commons Debates*, p. 1496.
31 *Commons Debates*, p. 1518.
32 The figure of 2,000 constituents refers only to King's electorate, while the figure of 1,500 Indians refers to the Province as a whole: *Commons Debates*, p. 1525. The estimate for the number of Indians in BC is substantially higher than the 33,000 cited earlier in the debate: *Commons Debates*, p. 1493.
33 *Commons Debates*, p. 1542.
34 Elections Canada, *A History*, pp. 52–3.
35 *Ontario Statutes 1888*, p. 11. Election Canada, *A History*, p. 53.
36 D. Bedford and S. Pobihushchy, 'On-Reserve Status Indian Voter Participation in the Maritimes', *Canadian Journal of Native Studies*, 15:2 (1995), 257.
37 Elections Canada, *A History*, p. 56
38 Except in Quebec, where women remained unenfranchised at the provincial level until 1940.
39 Bartlett, 'Citizens Minus', pp. 189–93.
40 *New Zealand Parliamentary Debates* (hereafter *NZPD*), *1854 and 1855* (Wellington, 1885), p. 13.
41 Keith Sinclair, *A History of New Zealand* (Harmondsworth, Middlesex, Penguin Books, 1980), p. 120.
42 *Ibid.*, p. 37.
43 *Ibid.*, p. 76.

44 G.A. Wood, 'The Electoral Bill and the Franchise Reform in Nineteenth Century New Zealand', *Political Science*, 28:1 (1976), 42.
45 W.K. Jackson and G.A. Wood, 'The New Zealand Parliament and Maori Representation', *Historical Studies: Australia and New Zealand*, 11:43 (1964), 384.
46 Keith Sinclair, *Kinds of Peace: Maori People After the Maori Wars, 1870–1885* (Auckland, Auckland University Press), p. 86.
47 Keith Jackson and Alan McRobie, *Historical Dictionary of New Zealand* (Boston, MA, Scarecrow Press, 1996), pp. 309–10.
48 Alan Ward, *A Show of Justice: Racial 'Amalgamation' in Nineteenth Century New Zealand* (Auckland, Auckland University Press, [1973] 1995), p. 153.
49 *Appendices to the Journals of the House of Representatives New Zealand), 1856.*
50 Keith Jackson, *New Zealand: Politics of Change* (Wellington, Reed Education, 1973), p. 69.
51 *Appendices to the Journals of the House of Representatives, 1864.*
52 James Belich, *Making Peoples: A History of New Zealanders* (Auckland, Penguin Press, 1996), p. 265.
53 *NZPD*, 2nd Session 4th Parliament, 1867, p. 336.
54 Paul Spoonley, 'Racism and Ethnicity', in Spoonley *et. al.* (eds), *New Zealand Society: A Sociological Introduction*, 2nd edn (Palmerston North, Dunmore Press, 1994), p. 85.
55 Alan McRobie, 'Ethnic Representation: The New Zealand Experience', in Evelyn Stokes (ed.), *Maori Representation in Parliament*, Centre for Maori Studies and Research, Occasional Paper No. 14 (University of Waikato, 1981), p. 5.
56 *Ibid.*, p. 6.
57 Belich, *Making Peoples*, p. 248.
58 Claudia Orange, *The Treaty of Waitangi* (Wellington, Allen & Unwin), p. 181.
59 Patricia Grimshaw, 'Settler Anxieties, Indigenous Peoples, and Women's Suffrage in the Colonies of Australia, New Zealand and Hawai'i, 1888 to 1902', *Pacific Historical Review*, 69:4 (2000).

CHAPTER SIX

'When there's no safety in numbers': fear and the franchise in South Africa – the case of Natal

Julie Evans and David Philips

It would be hard to overstate the importance, for twentieth-century South African history, of the franchise arrangement entrenched in the Constitution of the Union of South Africa in 1910. The Act of Union extended suffrage to almost all white adult males,[1] but excluded all non-whites from the franchise with the exception of the Cape Province, where a qualified colour-blind vote continued. The optimistic liberal scenario was that this initial compromise would be the start of a slow enfranchisement of the whole population, with a steadily increasing proportion of the African and the coloured population being admitted to the vote, with a gradual liberalization of the racial laws. This scenario proved to be completely wrong. South African history, for most of the century, instead followed a path of responding to the white electorate and removing even the political rights of non-white people in the Cape.

The new Government of the Union of South Africa showed, from the start, that it intended to govern in the interests of its white electorate. Almost immediately after Union, the Parliament passed the Natives Land Act of 1913 that reserved 87 per cent of the country for white ownership and became a key foundation-stone of subsequent apartheid. More such foundation-stones followed, with legislation entrenching an industrial colour bar in the 1920s, and further land legislation restricting the rights of Africans to own land in the urban areas in the 1930s.[2] Full-bodied apartheid was introduced in 1948, its path made easier by the direction taken by South African constitutional developments and racial legislation since 1910.

There was no further extension of the common franchise to any non-white people. In 1936, a coalition Government of the two main white parties provided the necessary two-thirds majority to remove Africans from the common voting roll; as token compensation, they were allowed to elect three white MPs and four white senators to represent specifically African interests, and were given an elected

'Natives' Representative Council' with no powers. In 1956, after a number of years of unscrupulous constitutional manoeuvring including packing the Senate and Appellate Division of the Supreme Court, the apartheid Government finally removed the Coloured voters from the common roll.[3] From 1956 on, the electorate which re-elected apartheid governments was entirely white; white and black South Africans were not again to vote on a common voters' roll until the first post-apartheid election in April 1994.

In this paper, we explore the historical development of the fear that informed the franchise arrangements of the 1910 Constitution. The question of an indigenous franchise had long been an issue central to politics in South Africa. The demographic structure of the former colonies, and then of the Union, clearly distinguished South Africa from other settler societies – at no point did the white population (English and Afrikaans) constitute more than about 21 per cent of the total population.[4] Commentators on South Africa have sometimes simplistically blamed everything about apartheid, and legislation to deny political rights to Blacks, on the Afrikaners. But through this case study of Natal, the most British of the four South African colonies, we can trace a growing awareness of the vulnerability of white hegemony in a colony in which Whites were overwhelmingly outnumbered. We demonstrate the correlation between that fear and the restrictive franchise legislation for indigenous and other non-white inhabitants. The peculiarly settler-colonial context of the crucial relationship between the possession of property, particularly the acquisition of individual (and therefore alienable) tenure, and franchise rights remains central to the analysis.

Franchise provisions
in the pre-Union South Africa colonies

By 1899, when the South African War began, the relatively independent African polities or chiefdoms of the Zulu, Swazi, Tswana, Pedi, Venda, Mpondo and Thembu peoples that had managed to survive two centuries of colonial incursion had finally been brought within the bounds of British or settler rule.[5] Apart from the three British Protectorates directly under the British Crown (Basutoland, Bechuanaland and Swaziland), the white-controlled states comprised two British colonies, the Cape Colony and Natal, and two independent Boer Republics, the Transvaal and the Orange Free State.

The two Boer Republics explicitly denied all political rights to black people; the vote was restricted to white adult male citizens. Indeed, the 1858 Transvaal Constitution proclaimed that 'the people desire to permit no equality between coloured people and the white inhabitants of the country, either in church or state'.[6]

The Colonial Office in London did not, however, allow the insertion of a legal colour bar into franchise provisions in the British settler states. From the initial grant of representative government in 1853 onwards, the Cape Colony had a colour-blind qualified manhood franchise. Any adult male, of whatever race, who occupied property worth £25 a year, or earned a salary of £50 (or £25 plus board and lodging), could qualify for the vote.

Despite these relatively liberal provisions, the political rights of blacks in the Cape steadily declined in the following decades. By the end of the nineteenth century, when the Cape franchise policy was often described as one of 'equal political rights for all civilized men', voting rights had become much more exclusive.[7] By 1909, when the South African colonies were discussing political union, the vote was restricted to any adult male British subject who could sign his name and write his address and occupation, and who either earned wages of at least £50 a year, or occupied a house or land together worth at least £75 a year. For land to qualify a man for the vote, it had to be in individual ownership; from 1889, communal tribal land could not count for this purpose.[8]

In Natal, on the other hand, given representative government in 1856 and responsible government in 1893, the system was manipulated to deny the vote to non-white men. Although the Royal Charter of 1856 had provided for a qualified non-racial franchise as in the Cape, restrictions on franchise rights were imposed soon after representative government was granted. All men with fixed property of £50, or paying £10 in annual rent, had initially been entitled to register,[9] but within the next decade legislation was passed to *disqualify* for the vote all people subject to Native Law. Any concerns about these restrictions contravening the Royal Charter were accommodated by further legislative provision enabling exemptions from Native Law for those deemed to have attained an increased social standing by 'abandoning Native practices and beliefs' and acquiring property.

Significantly, the other substantial non-white group in Natal, the Indians, also had their political rights made subject to the governor's discretionary power to grant exemptions from legislative provisions designed specifically to exclude them from the franchise. Originally brought to Natal in 1860 as indentured labourers to work in the sugar plantations, many Indians had settled in Natal; within a few decades, many white Natalians feared that the rapidly increasing numbers and the economic success of the Indians threatened white control of the country. By the end of the century, accordingly, most Indians had also been effectively disqualified from voting.

Such legislative restrictions on the franchise for non-Whites reflected the determination to preserve white minority rule in Natal. By 1907, Natal had a total electorate of nearly 24,000 men, almost all of them white; it contained only 150 Indians and six Africans – showing that the governor exercised his discretion to exempt Africans and Indians from the restrictions very rarely indeed. In effect, if not in legal theory, Natal had a franchise restricted to white males only.

Fear and the franchise: the case of Natal

Throughout the period with which we are concerned decisions about franchise rights for indigenous and other non-white peoples aroused considerable disquiet in the colonies as well as in Britain. Evidence of activism by those whose franchise rights had been denied or restricted is often limited, but certain petitions, newspaper articles and records of parliamentary debates provide important insights into the issues that activists regarded as central to their arguments against discriminatory franchise legislation.

It is clear from these documents, as well as from other official correspondence between local administrators and the Colonial Office, that decisions about the franchise held the capacity to reveal significant contradictions in British colonial policy and practice. A rhetorical commitment to equality among British subjects, so often reiterated by the Colonial Office in London, was often far less enthusiastically endorsed by settlers and administrators in the colonies. The question of the franchise held a more particular immediacy for Europeans in colonial communities, especially where they were outnumbered, than it ever could for politicians and colonial officials in Britain. But while the franchise became a potent indicator of white colonists' anxious determination to maintain exclusive minority rule, it also became a measure of the Home Government's unwillingness to redress such discrimination in practice.

This case study on Natal discusses the nineteenth-century context of that 1910 franchise decision which proved to be so important for twentieth-century South African history. We concentrate particularly on the correlation between white colonists' fears – that a more inclusive franchise threatened their economic, social and political power, and, indeed, at certain times, even their physical well-being – and the development of restrictive franchise legislation.

Securing life and property

During the frontier phase of settler colonization settlers were anxious to secure life and property in the face of indigenous resistance to colonial expansion. In 1851, for example, lieutenant-governor Pine noted that an outbreak of hostilities on the Natal frontier had occasioned panic among certain Europeans, notably those closest to the disturbances. His suggestion of recruiting a native force to quell the uprising met with strident opposition from some settlers but support from others. In a detailed response to those objecting to his proposals, Pine reflected in detail on the need to allay public panic and never to show any fear of 'the Natives'.[10] He upbraided his critics for not co-operating in his attempts to render assistance 'to our suffering fellow colonists on the Frontier', appealing 'to their self-interest and to their fears', claiming that:

> the battle on the Frontier concerns them as much as it does those who have to fight it, and that if rebellion be not speedily put down *there*, it will soon shew its terrible front *here*, if the flame be not extinguished *there*, it will soon spread into this district, and consume their property and themselves.[11]

In 1854, after visiting Natal, Assistant Commissioner Owen wrote to the secretary of state for the colonies, estimating a population of 5,000–6,000 Whites and 120,000 'Kaffirs or Zulus'. He judged that the Africans had made little progress towards civilization and that the two populations could not live together in mutual security. The best hope for the interests of the colony, he claimed, was to keep 'in strict and wholesome restraint the savage Kaffir population, whose overwhelming numbers at present render the carrying out of any stringent measures, however beneficial, unsafe without the presence of a large Military Force'.[12] Well aware that such a force would not be forthcoming, Owen endorsed the proposals of Natal's influential secretary for native affairs, Theophilus Shepstone, to withdraw 'a portion (say 50,000) of the superabundant black population from the District, and at the same time to induce, by all possible means, more white inhabitants to settle here'.[13] Such a plan, Owen emphasized, would provide 'a more equal balance of powers of the black and white population'. Moreover, Africans who remained in the district would be controlled more stringently, encouraged to abandon 'their barbarous customs' and their 'idle, vagabond, pastoral life' and to acquire 'habits of industry'. Specifically, as they moved from pastoralism to agriculture, those with indigenous or residential credentials would be encouraged to take up freehold and individual title – 'If they have property to lose they will not so wantonly engage in War!'

Owen's correspondence explicitly reveals the intimate connection evident throughout the settler colonies between the need to secure British hegemony and the sense of urgency surrounding the resolution of questions concerning entitlement to land and the nature of land ownership. Demographic imbalances further heightened the tensions that arose around these issues, especially in cases such as Natal where Europeans were so comprehensively outnumbered. As political rights depended upon the ownership of property, settler concerns about the Royal Charter's non-racial franchise became more apparent in Natal with the increase in both the number of Africans conforming to eligibility requirements and settler influence in local government.[14] Indeed, within the first few years of being granted responsible government, Natal's settlers were voicing their concerns about the local implications of the nexus between land ownership and voting rights established in the Royal Charter.

Grounding the right to vote – Africans, land and the franchise
There was general white agreement that settling Africans on land would facilitate efforts to 'civilize' them, as well as encourage them to abandon pastoralism in favour of agriculture, both of which, it was hoped, would contribute significantly to settlers' feelings of security. But the type of title Africans were to be accorded was a far more controversial question.

A local Select Committee Report of 1862, for example, strongly opposed the endorsement by the secretary of state and the Natal government of a Shepstone proposal to grant documentary *tribal* titles to land to Africans.[15] Under Shepstone's plan, such titles would initially be granted jointly to grouped tribes of Africans but would be vested in several trustees for an intermediate probationary period – considered 'absolutely necessary to precede the safe exercise of full political privileges'. As soon as the 'advancing civilization of the Natives' would allow, however, the land would be further subdivided into individual tribal and, eventually, individual family holdings.

The Select Committee objected strenuously to this form of title, claiming that the decision to include the chiefs among the trustees would increase, rather than diminish, both their power and the pull of tribalism generally. They argued that it had been clearly demonstrated that only the 'intermixture' of Europeans and Africans, and not segregation, would 'secure the peace of the colony'. Moreover, granting large numbers of Africans 'permanent exclusive possession' of 'rugged broken tracts of country' could result in 'danger and mischief' if they occupied these 'natural fastnesses' in cases of disturbance.

The Select Committee presented an alternative plan. Any land formally alienated to the 'Natives' should be granted on the basis of *individual* rather than *tribal* title, although a temporary period of trusteeship, again dependent upon the acquisition of civilized practices, would still apply. Under the Select Committee's proposal, trusteeship would be vested solely in the lieutenant-governor thereby precluding the possibility of any undue power accruing to chiefs and their headmen. Such lands would be 'for the use of the natives' but would 'be subsequently parcelled out to the natives under individual tenure according to civilized practices'.[16]

Significantly, though, the Select Committee condemned Shepstone's assertion that, in granting Africans *individual* title, there was also a legal obligation to extend to them the electoral franchise.[17] The Committee explicitly denied that Africans holding such tenure should become entitled to any ensuing political privileges, emphatically rejecting any constitutional link, for 'our Kafirs' at least, between individual title to land and the right to vote.[18]

The Committee considered that, in advocating a connection between individual title and franchise rights, Shepstone must have himself intended to withhold individual title for very many years to come, indeed, 'not until the white population has overtaken and far out numbered the black'.[19]

This extended discussion of the types of title that should be accorded to Africans emphasized that decisions about the nature of land ownership and the extent of franchise entitlement were intimately related to maintaining settler security and European control of the colony. By 1863, the Natal Legislative Council had passed resolutions conforming generally to the recommendations of the Select Committee Report.[20] The fifth resolution was specifically designed to disqualify from voting Africans accorded individual tenure, asserting that such title 'shall not confer the electoral franchise on its owner, except by a special act of release from such disability by the Legislature'.[21]

The lieutenant-governor, as an imperial official, was clearly disconcerted by the overt discrimination of such local decisions about land tenure and the franchise. Lieutenant-governor Scott advised the Legislative Council that the proposed resolutions 'so alter the scheme approved by Her Majesty's Secretary of State that they place the matter beyond the scope of any instructions the Lieutenant Governor has received'.[22] Specifically, the 'disfranchisement of the Natives' would require the enactment of a law, 'inasmuch as it involves an alteration in the Royal Charter, and is at variance with Her Majesty's Instructions'.[23]

In his despatch to the secretary of state, Scott revealed that his Executive Council had been split over the Legislative Council's resolve to break the nexus between property ownership and the right to vote. The colonial secretary, the treasurer and the secretary for native affairs 'considered that any Native having the property qualification required by the Charter was entitled to become a Voter', while the chief justice and attorney general argued that 'a Native could not claim the electoral franchise so long as he was subject to Native Law'.[24] Scott could see no reason why Africans, who were ostensibly under Native law but who had adopted civilized habits and had become 'proprietors of Land and occupiers of houses', could not claim the same rights or privileges as a white colonist.[25]

Fundamentally, however, Scott agreed with the settlers that 'it would be a positive evil to extend such a privilege to the Natives generally', and that it was not unjust 'to disqualify them from the exercise of such a political power' as long as they were in 'the exceptional position' of being subject to Native Laws. In this manner, Scott presented for the Home Government's approval proposed legislation to provide for 'the exemption of certain Natives from the operation of Native Law', which would appear to abide by the principles of the Charter while actually placing severe restrictions on the numbers of Africans to be enfranchised.

The first clause specifically disenfranchised Africans subject to Native law (with a further disqualification of those who had not been resident in the colony for a period of twelve years). The second clause provided for the enfranchisement of any African who had been exempted from Native law and who possessed the requisite property qualification. Letters of Exemption from Native law could be granted only by the lieutenant-governor acting on the advice and consent of a majority of the Executive Council.

The secretary of state for the colonies endorsed Scott's analysis of the issue, and indicated his approval of the proposed legislation:

> I consider it ... very undesirable, on the one hand, to extend the franchise largely among the Natives, and on the other hand, very advisable to admit them to it in moderate numbers as soon as they are fit to be admitted ...[26]

A law 'For relieving certain Persons from the operation of Native Law' was duly passed in 1864[27] while the law 'Disqualifying certain Natives from exercising the Electoral Franchise' was declared the following year.[28]

A petition from 'Micah Mkumananzi and seventeen other Natives exempted from Native Law', presented to the Legislative Council on 7 January 1880, indicated some local activism on the issue within the narrow constraints allowed by the petition form. The petitioners stated that they accepted their explicit disqualification from the franchise, citing Law no. 11, 1864, but they requested, as 'exempted Natives', the same rights under the ordinary laws of the colony as their European fellow-subjects. Claiming that they submitted 'contentedly' to having no voice in government as they did not 'well understand' the matters on which the Council deliberated, they were nevertheless concerned that their children should 'be in a position by education' to vote. The petitioners claimed, however, that 'the Government ... refuses them the assistance in educating their children which it extends to their wiser and richer white fellow-subjects'.[29]

The consequences of such legislative measures to disenfranchise Africans were immediate and comprehensive. As observed above, by 1907, only six Africans were registered as voters. But the Africans did not present the only threat to white supremacy in the colony; by the last decade of the century, the growing numbers of Indians residing in Natal presented a new and similarly frightening challenge to white minority rule.

The franchise as a race privilege

Britain's vast Indian Empire made the status of colonial Indians a more delicate subject. In contrast to the relative ease with which the disqualification of Africans had been achieved, the 1894 attempt to legislate the specific disenfranchisement of Indians in the colony attracted considerable protest in both England and Natal. Several deputations and petitions were presented to the secretary of state in London and to the local governor, while letters to newspapers and speeches in Parliament testified further to the considerable disquiet aroused by the Franchise Amendment Bill.

Debate surrounding the bill's intention to disqualify from voting 'persons belonging to Asiatic races not accustomed to the exercise of franchise rights under parliamentary institutions' clearly revealed the extent of white anxieties that their hold on power was under renewed threat. By the 1890s, the 40,000 Indians in the colony closely approximated the numbers of Europeans. Although only 300–400 Indians were enrolled as voters, such was the perceived danger of the sheer weight of their numbers in the community that the governor of Natal had 'grave reason to fear that [the number enrolled] will, from fresh arrivals, increase so as to give the Asiatic vote a strong influence in the elections'.[30] The proposed bill would preserve the rights of those Indians already enrolled, but allow no further registrations.

The prime minister, John Robinson, reiterated the conviction, 'universal amongst the European residents of the Colony,' that unless Indians were debarred from voting 'the Electorate will at no distant date be swamped by voters who are wholly unfitted by their inexperience and habits to exercise intelligently and independently franchise privileges.'[31]

In parliamentary debates, local members were prepared to use the fact that they had disqualified 450,000 Africans from the vote as a reason making it unjust to give the vote to Indians. The treasurer claimed general agreement, for example, that 'the Native, at any rate, would have more right to exercise the privilege than the [Indians]'.[32] But, he continued, it would be 'an utter anomaly' and 'contrary to all right principles' if Indians could ever comprise the majority of members in the Legislative Assembly. The Hon. Mr Arbuckle agreed, arguing: 'If we grant the franchise to the Asiatics, then we must do the same for the Natives; and if that were done the Government of the Colony would get into the hands of the coloured people, which I am sure no one desires to see.'[33]

In moving the second reading of the Bill in the House of Assembly, Prime Minister Robinson justified the disqualification of Indians on the grounds that 'the principle and practice of representative government were evolved in countries where race unity exists'.[34] In a wide-ranging speech, Robinson identified several cases where the consequences of according an 'indiscriminate' franchise supported his contention that 'in that fact of the plurality of the races rests one of the greatest political perplexities of the future'. According to Robinson, the experience of the United States and the Cape Colony clearly demonstrated that the difficulties of a liberal franchise were best avoided where 'race unity' patently did not exist. The Cape Colony, in particular, had been 'compelled at last' to cope with its franchise problems. Referring to increasing restrictions on the franchise in the Cape, Robinson declared that it could never be supposed that 'in an intelligent community like the Cape Colony such an evil – I might say such a curse – as what is called the "blanket vote" could be perpetuated'.[35]

Robinson congratulated his predecessors on acting to prevent such problems arising in Natal:

> Twenty-eight years ago a Law was passed which practically prevented the Natives of this Colony – at any rate, without great restrictions and safeguards – from exercising civil privileges, and I think we have every reason to be thankful that those who had charge of the legislation and the government of the country at that date, were prescient to that extent. I dare not contemplate what would have been the results in this Colony now had the Native inhabitants of this Colony had as free an access to the franchise as they had in the Cape Colony.[36]

The prime minister proceeded to outline his distinction between the 'essential, inalienable rights, irrespective of race or colour, of a every British subject', and the political privileges enjoyed only by certain designated sections of the population. While all British subjects were entitled to 'security to person and property, access to justice, freedom of speech, right of petition', the franchise right, by contrast, was 'a race privilege'. The right to vote was 'the most precious inheritance of an emancipated race ... the outcome of incessant struggle through six centuries ... the product of civilisation amongst Caucasian races, and especially among Anglo-Saxon races'.[37]

In undertaking to rule with generosity 'all the unenfranchised races under [European] control', Robinson specified the danger that the Indian community presented to the cause of representative government in Natal:

> Unless something be done to arrest this evil, this evil that threatens in a greater and greater degree day by day and year by year, we shall undoubt-edly ... run the risk of having the European electorate of this Colony swamped by the intrusion of voters who, by reason of their incapacity, will be liable to be swayed this way or that by venal, unscrupulous, or merely Party influences.[38]

It was his duty to South Africa, and, moreover, to the Empire at large, to face 'this evil at the outset.'[39]

Activists amongst the Indian community in Natal, including Hajee Mohamed Hajee Dada[40] and Mohandas Karamchand Gandhi,[41] mar-shalled local and metropolitan opposition to the proposals.

Despite the protests, the bill passed successfully through the local Assembly and Council. The Colonial Office, however, initially failed to endorse the Bill. Secretary of state Chamberlain objected that the Bill did not distinguish between aliens and British subjects, nor did it distinguish between 'the most ignorant and the most enlightened natives of India':

> I need not remind you that among the latter class there are to be found gentlemen whose position and attainments fully qualify them for all the duties and privileges of Citizenship, and you must be aware that in two cases within the last few years the Electors of important constituencies in *this* country have considered Indian gentlemen worthy not merely to exercise the franchise but to represent them in the House of Commons.[42]

Chamberlain claimed that while he appreciated 'local conditions', the Bill

> involves in a common disability all natives of India without exception, and provides no machinery by which an Indian can free himself from this disability, whatever his intelligence, his education, or his stake in the country; and to assent to this measure would be to put an affront upon the people of India such as no British Government could be party to.[43]

But Chamberlain gestured towards a canny solution to the problem, indicating that the ministers of government in Natal could devise a measure to achieve the aims of the bill in a way that 'will render it pos-sible for Her Majesty's Government to acquiesce in it'.

The bill was later approved by the secretary of state following amendments that replaced the explicit reference to 'persons belonging to Asiatic races' with 'certain persons' and 'natives of Countries which have not hitherto possessed elective representative institutions'.[44] In a minute forwarding the amendments and thanking Chamberlain for 'understanding the purpose of the Act', the ministers of Natal explained that there was not, and, indeed, could not be any difference of opinion among the European inhabitants of South Africa in regard to this question:

> The fact that the control and good government of half a million unenfranchised natives in Natal – to say nothing of millions of natives throughout South Africa – are closely bound up with this question, is a fact that cannot be too often reiterated.[45]

Conclusion

By the end of the nineteenth century, therefore, both Africans and Indians had effectively been excluded from the electorate in Natal. Although the Royal Charter had indicated that possessing equal property qualifications would guarantee both blacks and whites the right to vote in Natal, the local legislature had acted emphatically to soothe the fears of the minority white population that their privileged but tenuous hold on power could be overturned quite simply at the ballot box.

As the individual colonies in South Africa moved ever closer to Union in the period following the South African War, the quest to secure white rule continued to take precedence over the interests of Africans and Indians. For, despite the disenfranchisement of the vast majority of the population, legislative palliatives could only ever offer temporary relief from settler anxiety.

In the public debates about Union during the first decade of the new century, fear of Natal's isolation in dealing with 'the Native question' featured prominently in popular literature advocating Union. In his pamphlet 'Natal and Union', for example, the Reverend Frederick Mason declared that his greatest reason for supporting Union was 'Safety – Safety from native trouble':

> It won't come to-day or to-morrow on a big scale, but it is well known that the natives are combining now – chief and chief, tribe and tribe – as has never been known in the history of the country. As far as Natal is concerned, if a native rebellion were to break out, *where should we be if we were isolated and out of sympathy?*[46] (original emphasis)

No doubt given added force by the Bambatha Rebellion among the Zulu in 1906 when actual disturbances were evident or anticipated, the extent to which settlers were outnumbered induced acute fear in Europeans.

Such anxiety continued to be reflected in the increasingly severe restrictions that would be imposed on non-Whites in all spheres of their lives as the twentieth century unfolded, only to be expanded and more brutally enforced in the apartheid era. The prime minister of Natal summarized most succinctly, perhaps, the enduring nature of this anxiety when he stated in 1908 that 'the Native question' is 'not a problem to be solved in a word, or a phrase, or a Law, but ... is a problem, a living organism, which is always with us'.[47]

Notes

1 White women were enfranchised in 1930, while remaining property and income qualifications for white adult males were abolished in 1931.
2 See S. Plaatje, *Native Life in South Africa*, 2nd edn (Johannesburg, Ravan, 1916); G.M. Frederickson, *White Supremacy: A Comparative Study in American and South African History* (New York, Oxford University Press, 1981); N. Worden, *The Making of Modern South Africa: Conquest, Segregation and Apartheid*, 2nd edn (Oxford, Blackwell, 1995), ch. 4.
3 T.R.H. Davenport, *South Africa: A Modern History*, (London, Macmillan), pp. 276–87; 329–32; 342–3.
4 W. Beinart, *Twentieth Century South Africa* (Oxford, Oxford University Press, 1994), Appendix 1, Table 1.
5 Beinart, *Twentieth Century South Africa*, p. 1.
6 Quoted in Worden, *Making of Modern South Africa*, p. 70.
7 But despite greater restrictions on franchise rights for Blacks, by 1909, of a Cape electorate of 142,000, 10 per cent of the registered voters were 'Coloured', and nearly 5 per cent were African. In theory, at least, they could also stand for parliament, though no African or coloured man was ever elected to the Cape Parliament. But in several constituencies, their numbers were sufficient to compel the candidates of the two main parties to count their votes, and, as a result, the Cape Parliament paid more attention to the interests of non-Whites than did the legislatures of the other three settler-controlled colonies.
8 L. Thompson, *The Unification of South Africa 1902–1910* (Oxford, Clarendon Press, 1960), pp. 110–11. For a fuller discussion than is possible here of the complex developments in the Cape franchise over the period 1853–1910, see P. Grimshaw, D. Philips, S. Swain and J. Evans, *Grounds For Dispute: Indigenous Peoples and Citizenship in Nineteenth-Century Settler Societies* (Manchester, Manchester University Press, in preparation).
9 Worden, *Making of Modern South Africa*, p. 71.
10 At particular points in this paper, the words 'Native' and 'Kaffir' reflect contemporary terminology for Africans.
11 Lieutenant-Governor Benj. C.C. Pine, 'Reply to the Memorial ... ', 11 April 1851, enclosure no. 3 in Sir H. Smith to Earl Grey, no. 144, 15 August, 1851, CO 179/15, Public Record Office, London (henceforth PRO).
12 Assistant Commissioner Owen to Duke of Newcastle, 6 March, 1854, in Despatches, Reports on the Management of the Natives, Lt Gov. Pine and Mr Commr. Owen, Natal 1854, Vol. 4, CO 179/35, PRO.
13 Assistant Commissioner Owen to Duke of Newcastle, 6 March 1854, in Despatches, Reports on the Management of the Natives, Lt Gov. Pine and Mr Commr Owen, Natal 1854, Vol. 4, CO 179/35, PRO. The details of Shepstone's proposals are enclosed as Memorandum of Mr Shepstone, 23 January 1854.

14 Worden, *Making of Modern South Africa*, p. 71.
15 Select Committee Report, 5 August 1862, enclosed in Lt Gov. Scott to Duke of New-castle, no. 103, 24 September, 1863, CO 179/68, PRO.
16 The Select Committee Report also noted the need to stem the massive flow of African refugees. As a result of this population movement, the report claimed that the number of Natives residing within Natal's borders had increased from 11,000 in 1838, to 100,000 in 1848 to 180,000 in 1862.
17 Select Committee Report, 5 August 1862, enclosed in Lt Gov. Scott to Duke of Newcastle, no. 103, 24 September, 1863, CO 179/68, PRO.
18 *Ibid.*
19 *Ibid.*
20 Resolutions Passed by the Legislative Council of Natal, The 31st July, 1863, Respecting Granting to Natives Documentary Titles to Lands, enclosure no. 4, in Lt Gov. Scott to Duke of Newcastle, no. 104, 24 September, 1863, CO 179/68, PRO.
21 *Ibid.*, Resolution 5.
22 Lieutenant-Governor Scott to Natal Legislative Council, message no. 57, enclosure no. 5, in Lt Gov. Scott to Duke of Newcastle, no. 104, 24 September, 1863, CO 179/68, PRO.
23 *Ibid.*
24 Lieutenant-Governor Scott to Duke of Newcastle, no. 105, 25 September, 1863, CO 179/68, PRO. The attorney general and chief justice cited the twenty-eighth Article of Her Majesty's Instructions, given in 1848, and Ordinance no. 3 of 1849.
25 *Ibid.*
26 Duke of Newcastle to Lieutenant-Governor Scott, no. 355, 5 December, 1863, CO 179/68, PRO. A Colonial Office minute observed of the proposed legislation: 'Should all these measures be found practicable, a great stride will be made in the gradual civilization and advancement of the Native.' See Minutes, Lieutenant-Governor Scott to Duke of Newcastle, no. 105, 25 September, 1863, CO 179/68, PRO.
27 See Law no. 11, 1864: 'For Relieving certain Persons from the operation of Native Law', in Natal Acts, 1863–66, CO 180/3, PRO.
28 See Law no. 11, 1865: 'Disqualifying certain Natives from exercising the Electoral Franchise', in Natal Acts, 1863–66, CO 180/3, PRO.
29 Petition no. 14, 1880, from Micah Mkumananzi and 17 other Natives exempted from Native Law, praying for the granting to them of certain privileges under the general laws of the Colony', signed at Adamshurst, 10 December, 1879, presented to the Legislative Council on the 7 January, 1880, 2nd Session, 8th Council, 1879–80, Natal LegislativeCouncil, Sessional Papers, 1879–80, Rhodes House, Oxford.
30 Governor Hely-Hutchinson to Secretary of State, 16 July 1894, enclosed in Governor Hely-Hutchinson to High Commissioner, Cape Town, Confidential, 16 September, 1895, DO 119/92, PRO.
31 Ministers to Governor, 10 July 1894, enclosed in Governor Hely-Hutchinson to High Commissioner, Cape Town, Confidential, 16 September, 1895, DO 119/92, PRO.
32 Second Reading of the Franchise Law Amendment Bill, 4 July 1894, Natal Legislative Council, extracts of debates enclosed in Governor Hely-Hutchinson to High Commissioner, Cape Town, Confidential, 16 September, 1895, DO 119/92, PRO.
33 *Ibid.*
34 Prime Minister of Natal, John Robinson, Second Reading of Franchise Law Amendment Bill (no. 34, 1894), 20 June, 1894, Natal Legislative Assembly Debates, extracts of debates enclosed in Hely-Hutchinson to High Commissioner, Cape Town, Confidential, 16 September, 1895, DO 119/92, PRO.
35 *Ibid.* Note the significance of this contemporary use of the term 'blanket vote', which would have referred explicitly to the distinctive clothing of the 'tribal' Xhosa people in the eastern Cape.
36 *Ibid.*
37 *Ibid.*
38 *Ibid.*
39 *Ibid.*

40 Hajee Mohamed Hajee Dada and 500 other Indians from Durban and elsewhere to Legislative Assembly of the Colony of Natal, Petition no. 36, 1894, 28 June 1894, enclosed in Hely-Hutchinson to High Commissioner, Cape Town, Confidential, 16 September, 1895, DO 119/92, PRO.
41 M. K. Gandhi and others to Sir John Robinson, n.d., enclosed in Hely-Hutchinson to High Commissioner, Cape Town, Confidential, 16 September, 1895, DO 119/92, PRO.
42 Secretary of State Chamberlain to Governor Hely-Hutchinson, 12 September 1895, enclosure no. 1 in Hely-Hutchinson to High Commissioner, Confidential, 10 October, 1895, DO 119/92, PRO (italics added).
43 *Ibid.*
44 See Bill to Amend the Law Relating to the Franchise, enclosed in Governor to High Commissioner, Confidential, 21 October, 1895, DO 119/92, PRO.
45 Ministers' minute (no. 15/1895) to Governor of Natal, 18 October, 1895, enclosed in Governor to High Commissioner, Confidential, 21 October, 1895, DO 119/92, PRO.
46 Reverend Frederick Mason, 'Natal and Union', Miscellaneous Papers re. Natal and Union with South Africa, 1905–09, Coll. Misc. 0399, British Library of Political and Economic Science, London School of Economics.
47 Prime Minister of Natal, Second Reading of Native Administration Bill (no. 2/1908), 25 June, 1908, *Natal Legislative Assembly Debates*, 1908, vol. XLIV, p. 146, Rhodes House, Oxford.

CHAPTER SEVEN

Making 'mad' populations in settler colonies: the work of law and medicine in the creation of the colonial asylum

Catharine Coleborne

The colonial asylum in Australia and New Zealand was based largely on an English imperial model and became one site for the shaping of colonial identities in medicine. The 'casualties' of colonialism often found their way into this institution.[1] This paper examines the historical relationship between medicine and law that brought particular individuals into colonial institutional confinement in the settler colony of Victoria, and explores the impact and articulation of 'colonialism' on discourses around 'lunacy' and on asylum patient populations. It does this by drawing attention to representations of the small but perceptibly troubling population of Chinese inmates within the case-books of colonial Victoria's asylum. It argues that historians of the asylum, who have so often spoken from imperial centres, might fruitfully investigate the imperial reaches and effects of medical and legal practices and understandings of the nineteenth century by looking comparatively at settler colonies, and also at local asylum populations constructed on the colonial 'frontier'.

In the past decade or more, far from celebrating the history of European medicine, historians have increasingly turned to critique its effects and legacies both 'at home' and in colonial worlds. The assertion that European – read *imperial* – medicine can be understood as an 'agent of empire' has become almost commonplace. For example, Shula Marks comments that 'the history of medicine in the colonies is often an illuminating way to examine aspects of the power and limitations of colonialism and its ideas and discourses', while Lenore Manderson argues that colonial medicine is 'part of the front line of imperialism that strove to dominate by care and cure'.[2] Historians have shown that medicine embodied the aim of social reform; it became an aspect of the 'civic virtue' of colonial settler societies 'mimicking the grand configurations' of the metropoles.[3] In 1988 Milton Lewis and Roy Macleod provided the landmark volume *Disease, Medicine and*

Empire, which explored the problem of medicine as part of the imperial project. They argued that the period 1810–1910 was a period of colonial expansion, with medicine playing a role in the colonizing process.[4] Medicine did not only 'colonize'. Its character and presence in the colonies also signified the spread of intellectual and scientific imperial 'culture':

> Meeting similar patterns of disease, set against the foreign circumstances of frontier life, colonial medicine eventually came to compare itself, and later compete with, its professional parents. A common culture of medicine – sustained by the image of science as the universal agent of progress, and scientific medicine as its servant – became the hall mark of European empires throughout the world.[5]

Other historians have pursued this theme and argued that medicine, not a fixed entity but one often altered in various different geographical and historical contexts, was also 'refracted' in the colonial situation.[6] In the colonial situation, medicine was enacted through and by the State, and it was in this context that particular populations became the objects of medical knowledge.[7]

Psychiatry and colonialism

Where does psychiatry and its history in the colonies fit into all of this? As Roy Porter has argued, the nineteenth century was the period in which psychiatry was 'made'. It was also then that it was exported, and became an 'international enterprise'.[8] Like other medical and legal enterprises of this period, psychiatry was keen to make classifications of bodies in foreign places. Some of the histories of imperial or colonial medicine (and these words are often used to mean the same thing) perhaps suggest a reading of the 'colonial' setting where the predominant indigenous population was managed in and by white imperial institutional structures.[9] But what of white settler societies in the British dominions?[10] Nineteenth-century constructions of 'madness' and 'race' in these settings might even be more complicated than formerly supposed or imagined.

Until recently the colonial asylum has received minimal treatment by historians, despite the fact that it was in the new societies of America, and then younger colonial societies such as those in the four British dominions of Australia, New Zealand, Canada and South Africa, that the asylum – as an institution that became part of a fabric of welfare measures introduced by the State – began to develop a distinctive style. Nor have histories been comparative. In Australia a number of historians, including Stephen Garton and Mark Finnane, have explored the histories of madness and the asylum, including patterns of patient committal, and the ways in which the asylum's development was influenced by understandings of lunacy in the United Kingdom. Together with these studies there are histories of psychiatry and institutions in Australia and New Zealand, some of which consider asylum populations through readings of patient case-books.[11] There are no studies of madness which deal with either New Zealand or Australia as a whole.

Furthermore, no detailed comparison between asylums in Australia and New Zealand and their populations exists.[12] A comparative approach to asylum history would both underline the dynamics of colonization and also free this history from its usually parochial perspective, as Linda Bryder has suggested.[13] The relationship between 'colonial state policy' and 'lunacy policy' was important: they combined to produce and maintain colonial order.[14] The value of the comparative perspective where the colonial context is being examined is that 'comparison' is part of the very articulation of histories of colonialism.[15] It might also have the effect of producing patient-centered histories. Until recently the histories of the confined insane in colonies around the world in the nineteenth century have remained relatively hidden from investigation. This is in part because patient case-notes in case-books were often considered by historians to be sources of limited value for the history of psychiatry, despite their potential to be understood as productive of meanings around both madness *and* gender and 'race'.[16] For instance, Nancy Tomes has suggested that 'analysis of actual clinical records' might add much needed depth to the study of women and madness, which has largely focused on published sources.[17] In the colonial setting the case-notes both fulfilled legal and medical requirements which mimicked practices in Britain, and also fashioned new kinds of patients – patients who were particular to the colonial asylum.[18] It is for this reason that I argue that despite the relationship between metropolis and colony, the asylums in colonial settings may have had more in common with each other than historians have previously imagined or explored. Further exploration and analysis of the colonial asylum's patient population is crucial to an understanding of the development and acceptance of psychiatry in the colonies.

Writing about Australia and New Zealand and their shared histories, and the impact of social change on the incidence of mental illness, some historians see parallels in settler histories of population, gold rushes, rural prosperity and hardship, while the histories of indigenous–white contact, conflict and negotiation differ enormously, and migration patterns have differed in these two 'colonies'.[19] The inflections of ideas about madness 'at home' and the British asylum itself became crucial to the perceived role of the asylum in Australia and

New Zealand. In establishing the asylum on the colonial landscape the settlers were keen to reflect developments in Britain. Significant developments in medicine, legislation and administration which dealt with 'madness' occurred in nineteenth-century Britain, addressing the problem of how madness was to be contained, what kinds of women and men became asylum inmates and which inmates were considered appropriate asylum 'patients'.[20] These medical, legal and administrative developments which produced the asylum and its patients in Britain provided a model for the production of the asylum and its patients in the colonial settler societies of Australia and New Zealand which faced similar problems and established institutions modelled on those 'at home'. Doctors, and those who became superintendents of asylums in Australia, were trained in Britain.[21] Australia and New Zealand inherited British principles for the treatment of lunatics, and other aspects of British social policy.[22]

Yet different patient populations provoked different medical responses, and experienced medicine in different ways, in the colonial environment. The needs of the colonial population determined the responses of colonial administrators: for instance, in New Zealand, the 'very presence of Pakeha misery in the new colony ... constituted a challenge to the colonial dream'.[23] Can historians assume that the administrators of the colonial asylum had to alter their approach to lunacy, fashioned from the ideals of asylums 'at home', because they drew upon a different population? In making its 'mad' population the colonial asylum incorporated ideas about perceived threats to social harmony, and racial difference entered the discourse of classification, as did the problem of bodily difference in the form of physical debility and deformity. In their efforts to train 'lunatics' to be 'inmates' and then proper 'patients' the colonial asylums examined the questions of sexual and racial difference with more immediate anxiety than did asylums 'at home'. Megan Vaughan has claimed that 'colonial medical discourse was, without a doubt, preoccupied by difference'.[24] It was in the colonial setting that issues of gender, class and 'race', the 'differences' spoken about by Vaughan and others, were brought into sharp focus and became intrinsic to the question of madness. Certain interpretative gestures made in the texts examined in this paper were directly concerned with this creation of the problem of 'difference'. Cases of white male lunatics from the patient case-books of nineteenth-century Victoria, when juxtaposed with cases of Chinese men, show the ways in which psychiatric definitions and meanings were not immune to social influences, so that so-called 'objective and unchanging standards' of measuring lunacy were not employed.

[109]

Lunacy, laws and order in New Zealand and Victoria

The circumstances that led to the development of the asylum system in each of the Australian colonies differed from each other in terms of their approach to and characterization of the asylum.[25] From the earliest times in the establishment of institutions for the insane in Victoria (in the district known as Port Phillip until 1851) questions of who was a legitimate asylum inmate shaped the idea of the asylum. The distinction between 'prisoner' and 'lunatic' was important, as prior to the establishment of the space of the asylum some lunatics occupied the already crowded space in gaols. Before 1848 lunatics were detained in Port Phillip district gaols or sent to New South Wales to the Tarban Creek Lunatic Asylum, in accordance with the provisions of the 1843 Dangerous Lunatics Act.[26] This practice of confining lunatics in gaols, and transporting lunatics long distances to another colony, was increasingly seen to be inappropriate. The Lunacy Statute of 1867 in Victoria pronounced Yarra Bend an 'asylum' and provided for the establishment of Ararat and Beechworth asylums, which opened in the same year.[27] Yarra Bend had been operating in the Port Phillip district since 1848, first as a ward of Tarban Creek Asylum in New South Wales, and then from 1851 as Victoria's first institution for the insane. Kew Asylum followed in 1871. Official statistics show that the lunatic population increased rapidly from 1868.

In New Zealand, as in Victoria, there were early makeshift provisions for the reception of lunatics. By 1844 lunatics could be housed at Wellington Gaol and Auckland Hospital, and at other hospitals in the colony. The Lunatics Ordinance of 1846 – one of the first pieces of legislation enacted in New Zealand – suggested that specific provisions should be made for the insane; like the 1843 Act in place in Victoria, Australia, it emphasized the safe custody of the 'dangerously insane'.[28] New Zealand inherited a legislative influence from Australia where lunacy was concerned.[29] In fact it seems that various developments in the New Zealand colony parallelled those occurring in Victoria. As in Victoria, by 1868 in New Zealand the Lunatics Act was placing the asylum more firmly within the view of law. It was in 1854 that the first asylum for the confinement of all social classes and races was opened at Karori, near Wellington. As in Australia, the development of the asylum system in New Zealand was *ad hoc* and happened relatively quickly; there were eventually asylums of different shapes, sizes and qualities throughout the colony. Institutions were established at Otago and Canterbury in 1863, at Nelson in 1864, and Seaview Asylum opened in 1872.[30]

By the mid-nineteenth century asylums were perceived to be 'disorderly' spaces in colonial settings. An early report of a Royal Commission in New Zealand, prompted by the complaints of the asylum 'keeper' at Nelson lunatic asylum, Thomas Butler, offers hints of the concerns over sexual propriety in the institution.[31] Butler's complaints were directed at the matron of the institution. Some years earlier in Victoria, where a number of parliamentary committees and inquiries were established to examine the asylum, inmates were more clearly the cause of asylum disorder. A report of 1852 on the first asylum in Victoria, the Yarra Bend Asylum, included evidence from Eleanor Harkinson, the laundress, and her husband John. Certain 'filthy', 'vile', and 'sinful' 'practices' among asylum inmates preoccupied the Harkinsons. Eleanor had to place her foot against the door of her room to prevent the female lunatics from entering it, such was her fear of them; her husband John described the Yarra Bend as being 'no better than a brothel, or a low grog shop ... Because of the drinking, and because of the women having children'.[32]

Attempts to civilize, domesticate and regulate lunatic behaviour were common to nineteenth-century asylums; and attendant staff, matrons and 'keepers' were not immune to this domestic ideology. It seemed that the colonial asylum (while not entirely dissimilar in character to the asylum in Britain) was potentially a violent place, populated, as one commentator in the *Illustrated Melbourne Post* argued, by 'the worst of convicts, and brandy-mad diggers and others'.[33] Despite its similarities to asylums in Britain the asylum in Australia was often castigated with the use of the term 'colonial': just as there was an 'Australian' type of criminal ('and a most troublesome class they are') as one witness at a Royal Commission in the 1880s suggested, by implication there was a colonial type of 'lunatic'.[34]

Exactly who were the inmates in colonial asylums? Were they half-mad criminals and drunks? They were often persons whose situations threatened public order, even the 'decrepid old man named Jeremiah Bailey' who was found in the street 'in a dying state' in October of 1848 in Melbourne, and increasingly persons whose behaviour was seen to be 'dangerous', in the spirit of the earliest law regulating asylum committals, the Dangerous Lunatics Act of 1843.[35] In Auckland in 1842, Joseph Hale was apprehended 'wandering idle about the town' and taken into custody, causing the colonial surgeon to suggest that a 'proper asylum' was needed.[36]

The question of these 'others' is pivotal to this history. In the earliest period of the asylum in Australia the separations and distinctions being made within the category of 'lunatic' were keys to the subsequent development of the asylum on the social landscape. Sexual difference provided the first distinction among lunatics. W.D. Neil's account of the lunatic asylum at Castle Hill in New South Wales during the early years of the colony illuminates attitudes to women lunatics.[37] Female lunatics were in a minority and were neglected: in 1819 ten arrived at the new asylum 'nearly naked, with their clothing and bedding in a filthy state'. Accounts of their delusional identities as 'Queens, Princesses, Duchesses and Countesses' sit uneasily with descriptions of their physical condition; were these delusions characterized by men and borrowed from their own masculine imaginings of the asylum 'at home'? The female lunatic in early New South Wales was somehow disturbing. How she occupied space created some anxiety in the minds of the colony's authorities – even finding sufficient clothing for her proved difficult – and the very sight of her (self-)neglect and the sound of her delusions underlined this sense of how she filled institutional space.

Concern about female inmates was amplified as the asylum system expanded. Despite the fact that in both colonial Australia and New Zealand men were more vulnerable to apprehension by police and to asylum committal, mad women and femininity became representative of the 'disorder' inside the asylum.[38] Elsewhere I have argued that sexual difference was used as an organizing principle in the nineteenth-century asylum, and that increasingly it was the very question of 'difference' which came to cause anxiety among asylum administrators.[39]

The beginnings of the asylum in colonial Victoria, as it set itself apart from New South Wales, were crucial to the development of the category of the lunatic within the colonial state. In the early years of the colony there were fears that 'society had not settled down'. Medical Superintendent Robert Bowie could not establish the 'model asylum' in the early days at Yarra Bend because of a general social 'excitement' partly due to 'gold mania'. Inmates of asylums, it was felt, were often sufffering from this 'excitement', as historians have noted.[40] In both New Zealand and Australia, the impact of immigration to the colonies in the 1850s and 1860s meant the rapid expansion of the asylum system. Dr Edward Paley, inspector of asylums in Victoria between 1863 and 1883, commented that the conditions of colonial life produced 'a more than ordinary amount of insanity'. These conditions were characterized by Paley as 'the solitary life of shepherds, habits of intemperance and sudden reverses of fortune, especially among the mining population'.[41] Frederick Norton Manning of New South Wales agreed. The male patient was thus positioned within wider constructions of social unease and upheaval, anxiety and excitement. Men were often found wandering in the bush, described as having 'bush mania', a kind of 'madness' produced from the effects of isolation and desolation. Historians have to an extent perpetuated this positioning, and thus for Garton '[t]he typical Australian lunatic of the late nineteenth century was the maniacal labourer'.[42]

The 'pressures of the colonising life' had different impacts on men and women. If male insanity was in part shaped by notions of masculinity which emanated from empire (frontier life incorporated an 'ideal of manliness' and visions of escape and conquest), case-notes reveal that female insanity could be triggered by the experiences 'integral' to colonial life, such as 'separation and loss'.[43] And yet contemporary evaluations rarely took this view of female madness.[44] Compared to the male lunatic, the female lunatic posed darker concerns, which were enhanced by the medical understandings of her body already in circulation. The construction of the female lunatic patient as dangerous, disorderly and sexually unbounded in contemporary representations, such as published case-studies in medical journals, was pivotal to understandings about lunacy and the asylum. While historians have recognized that women were seen to have 'crossed the boundaries of acceptable feminine behaviour' in their 'madness', they have not always accorded as much significance to the role of gender, or sexual difference, within the classificatory systems of the asylum.[45] Yet the productive powers of the categories of class, 'race' and sex were used within asylums, both to classify patients and to produce meanings around 'madness'. Women and those who were poor or racially 'other', such as the Chinese, were accorded less power in the wider society, and were often more vulnerable to police surveillance than historians have shown. In the case of New Zealand, it seems Maori women and men became more susceptible to asylum committal in the early twentieth century.[46]

Anglo-American historians have argued that the asylum played a role in widening the conception of the nature of insanity, and that its popularity or perceived efficacy for the community meant that more and more kinds of disorderly bodies were confined by its walls.[47] Finnane has also argued that asylums became acceptable to the public because a 'reordering of people's relation to madness' had taken place; this 'reordering' was part of a wider project to define the appropriate 'body' or person for colonial society, a project which sometimes failed.[48]

During the nineteenth century the focus of this 'reordering' broadened, and perhaps shifted, from a concern about sexual difference within the asylum population to include other forms of difference, including racial difference. By the late 1860s in Victoria the range of patients in the asylum, including idiots (some of whom were children), imbeciles, epileptics, and particularly Chinese patients, caused anxiety to the asylum inspectors.[49] It was perceived that the situation was worse in Victoria than overseas in Britain: the Asylum Inspectors' Report for 1870 detailed the increase in numbers of the confined insane, commenting that 100 per cent of cases were in asylums in Victoria while many cases in Britain were dealt with by private institutions and poorhouses.[50] The news of Victoria's high number of the insane in asylums made its way to New Zealand. By 1888, the annual asylum inspectors' report in New Zealand commented on the range of patients in Victoria's asylums, explaining that the crisis of overcrowding was due in part to the 'incurable, noisy, excitable, dirty lunatics as well as idiots, dotards, and imbeciles'. The same report remarked that '[t]his description of the Victorian asylums is fairly applicable to those of New Zealand', but there were even fewer medical staff in New Zealand asylums.[51]

Developing categories of insanity or the asylum patient were represented by inspectors' reports. The problem for the medical world seemed to be one of power and influence: who had the power to both represent and, thus, control the asylum was a central theme in medical responses to the official inspection. In the battle to define the asylum, the inmates who caused the most anxiety were named as problematic and even utterly 'useless' to the asylum. Asylum inspectors' reports were not inquiries like select committees or royal commissions. They were designed as 'external' monitors of the world of the asylum and produced statistics for colonial governments. These reports indicate anxiety about the sick and infirm who were not 'productive' members of colonial society. Thus differences were monitored, and even constructed, through these reports which, like patient case-books, used descriptive conventions, or 'interpretative gestures', which kept 'otherness' in view.[52]

'Different' identities emerged in official reports, inquiries and in patient case-books from the latter part of the nineteenth century: the 'little Jewess' who was abused and had her eye cut; the 'quadroon' who 'appear[ed] to have negro blood in her veins'; 'Blackmug Billy' who was a 'tallish coon';[53] the 'Chinaman' who caused some disturbance and was implicated in the death of another male patient, and other 'deformed' or 'crippled' patients. At Ararat Asylum, in 1875, Louisa Kate Pink, described as a 'Creole', was admitted suffering from delusions. While there is no evidence that Louisa was treated badly, the very designation 'Creole' possibly contributed to her steady decline and eventual death in the asylum in 1883, as asylum efforts to transform patients were dependent upon perceptions of their usefulness within the social framework of nineteenth-century Victoria.[54] In New Zealand it was Pakeha men who identified with Maori belief systems, who were considered mad, and Maori women who were more likely to be labelled 'erotic' and promiscuous. Thus, in both places, racial differences became productive of meanings around madness.[55]

A failure to 'reorder'? Chinese in the asylum in Victoria

The inspectors' reports reveal increasing anxiety about racial difference in the asylum during the last decades of the nineteenth century in Victoria. That anxiety stemmed primarily from the presence of the Chinese. While they have been accorded a 'peripheral place' in white histories of Australia, stories about the Chinese thread their way through colonial pasts.[56] Chinese men became a presence on the colonial goldfields, inspired by the rush to California and by letters home from early emigrants to Australia. Despite the 'excitement' of the prospect finding gold, or perhaps because of it, their habit of migrating as single men left them vulnerable to loneliness, despair and, sometimes, illness and police surveillance.[57] They were tainted in the popular imagination with 'vice', especially gambling and opium-smoking.[58] Their status as lunatic asylum patients was particularly troubling. Interestingly, historians have shown that the Chinese communities in their camps on goldfields in Victoria generally looked after their own 'sick and destitute' quite effectively.[59] Mental breakdown, sometimes associated with the violation of local laws, was clearly more difficult for those camp communities to manage. It was perceived that Chinese men formed a sizeable and growing percentage of the inmates in Victoria's asylums in the 1870s.

The same concerns were held about the Chinese in other British colonies. In New Zealand, in 1871, the Chinese were perceived as 'unsettlers', or persons who were not 'permanent or desirable settlers'.[60] In British Columbia, Canada, in the 1890s, a ship 'full of Chinese patients' left for China amid concerns over 'foreign' insane, and the Chinese ward at the Provincial Lunatic Asylum (later Provincial Hospital for the Insane) was closed.[61] In Western Australia, an annual report of the asylum inspector in the 1890s pointed out that an increasing number of 'dark-blooded men' were being admitted.[62] The campaign to exclude Chinese from Victoria was at its height around 1880, reinforced by legislation restricting Chinese immigration in 1881.[63] The fears about Chinese began much earlier. They were subject to social, political and professional discrimination; they came to Victoria 'in search of a fortune in gold and found instead animosity, misunderstanding, abuse, assault, illness, incarceration and death'.[64] Kathryn Cronin has demonstrated that the Chinese were exploited on the pastoral and mining frontiers in Victoria, casualties of the racial ideology which underpinned the masculinist colonial 'adventure'.[65] In 1857 the colonists had acknowledged:

'We have got the Chinese among us', and set about 'keeping them well under the eye of the law'.[66]

Thus the perceived 'problem' of the 'Chinese patient' began with anxieties about Chinese migration.[67] Anxiety about immigration might be understood as an aspect of the attempt by colonists in Victoria to 'define who were or should be Victorians', just as the appropriate lunatic asylum inmate was being defined through medical and bureaucratic texts.[68] The Chinese were subject to the most abuse and criticism, including accusations of disease, addiction and sexual depravity. Medical journals also considered the problem of classifying kinds of patients, and 'race' was of special interest. The *Australian Medical Journal* first reported on the perceived problem and on the curiosity of the Chinese lunatic in 1865, around the same time as the Chinese Immigrants Statute, and there was a continuing medical interest in the bodily illnesses, especially diseases, of the Chinese.[69] The issue of miscegenation had already begun to raise fears in Victoria. A report in *Age* in 1869 about Chinese migration suggested that Chinese men should not 'form connections' with European women.[70] The 'half-caste' female caused special anxiety for the writer of this piece. Certainly, in the asylum case-books women described in this way were often designated as most difficult, their difference signalled through the use of particular language. There is a small number of cases of Chinese women in the case-books of the 1880s, including the case of Margaret Ah Lee who was brought by police to Kew Asylum in March 1887.[71]

Chinese male patients were represented in patient case-books as dangerous, or 'incoherent', or both. They were not 'feminized', and yet their bodies were marked as significantly different from the bodies of other male patients.[72] For instance, the 'Chinaman' referred to in the Kew Inquiry of 1876 was described in terms which reflected his difference from other asylum patients. At the point at which he is mentioned in the Minutes of Evidence, Kew Asylum is described as a place where 'all classes' of patient are sent. This Chinese patient was evidently a prisoner sent to gaol for 'stealing gold from some claim up the country' who somehow found his way inside the asylum, and by 1876 had been there for twelve months. His body attracted interest: he was described as 'a powerful man, very muscular', a 'violent man' (when interfered with) who wore 'heavy boots'. When asked if the 'Chinaman' spoke, the witness replied: 'No; he only says, "Too muchee fightum".' The speech of the Chinese patients was in this way made nonsensical.

Other Chinese patients were similarly 'incoherent'. They became curiosities: from the usual designation of their religion as 'Pagan' to the inscription of 'China', 'Canton' or 'Pekin' as their place of origin. Ah Lop, a Chinese male brought to Kew in January 1874 suffering from dementia, was 'quite demented' and 'given to pulling hair from head ... he is given to shouting at the top of his voice. Said to have murdered a man on the diggings: this is only hearsay. He is very insane ...'[73]. Ah Lang, brought to Kew in April 1874, was 'occasionally violent and quarrelsome' and 'rather dangerous'. His body posed a threat as he was 'well developed', but this did not prevent an examination of him: 'On examining the ears with a probe found both full of rubbish. The right containing a trousers button, boot nail about a dozen pieces of quartz ... and charred brown paper. The left ear containing rubbish of various kinds.'[74] Ah Shung was 'not to be trusted' and 'laughs and talks incoherently'. Ah Sin, potentially dangerous, excited, mischievous and sleepless, exhibited behaviour which was 'said to have been brought on by too much opium smoking'.[75] Ah Him was described as 'dangerous' despite being 'feeble and emaciated', and once again his incoherence as Chinese signified his difference; he was of 'immoral habits' and 'speaks no British'.[76] Cases of Chinese men who attempted cultural assimilation (for example, Ah See at Yarra Bend who played football but died in the asylum after a sporting injury, or Jimmy Ah John who battled 'intemperance' by joining the 'Blue Ribbon' movement) reveal that the most 'valiant' of efforts were only 'rewarded' in the asylum by misunderstanding.[77]

Cases of white men confined at Kew in the 1880s provide some interesting comparisons with cases of Chinese men. Dr Smith's belief that the monomaniac could and should be released from the asylum seems to have been practised in the case of Samuel Taylor, admitted in March 1880.[78] While he was 'said to be dangerous', this 60 year-old miner was 'sober and hard working', and a month after his admission he had become a 'good worker out of doors' and had lost his 'special delusions'; Taylor was discharged only two months after his admission.[79] Similarly, police admitted John Barry, aged thirty-two of East Brighton and suffering from 'Mania' and exhibiting 'constant low muttering and talking'. He made a steady improvement: he became 'good humoured', he worked in the garden, his facial expressions became 'more intelligent' and he expressed a desire to return home and to his work; he was finally discharged around six months after his admission. Joseph White suffered melancholia with delusions and shifted from illness to health, with a significant relapse in the process (marked by his refusal to work), but a year later was discharged.[80]

In contrast, in the 1880s a number of Chinese patients challenged conventional attempts to assess them, and a Chinese interpreter was called in.[81] In the cases of Ah Pee, Jimmy Ah John and Ah Fong the interpreter states: 'he is very insane'. Of Ah Pee the case-book notes that the interpreter's judgement mirrors what was already 'known' about this man: 'states he is very insane – which we are very able to judge by his actions'. Ah Fong's arrest by police near Daylesford, where he was 'wandering at large', brought him to Kew Asylum where the interpreter explained that he 'looks for his wife who calls him home China or elsewhere. Is incoherent on the point'. Jimmy Ah John was under the impression that his countrymen might try to kill him; this was enough to convince the interpreter of his insanity.[82] In Western Australia the Chinese patients were transferred to asylums with 'meagre information as to their mental state ... they [were] simply described as Chinese', leading Norman Megahey to speculate that Chinese patients may have been committed for reasons of 'expediency' rather than 'insanity'.[83]

Conclusion

Settler colonies created distinctive populations, and their newly established asylums reflected this. In colonial Victoria, the Chinese population became the object of both medical and legal knowledge. In the 1870s the asylum had become a crowded, unmanageable and, at times, ineffective institution. One signifier of its decline was its noisy population of Chinese, difficult to understand and disruptive of asylum and colonial communities. At the same time the very definitions of mental disease were still being fixed. By the 1880s in Victoria the condition of madness was still puzzling to medical men, despite the faith they had seemingly placed in the asylum system. Often talked about in symbolically spatial terms, such as through the notion of a 'borderland' or 'frontier', which conjured notions of a separate place or land called madness,[84] it was subject to scrutiny in abstract just as its sufferers were under constant surveillance within the space of the asylum and inside the texts that strove to represent it.

In this paper I have considered representations of Chinese patients in asylum case-books and asylum inspectors' reports within the context of anxieties about migration, miscegenation and racial difference, and madness in order to comment on the way the colonial asylum fashioned its population. The 'refraction' of imperial medicine, to borrow from Vaughan, effected practices of separation, distinction and classification within colonial asylums. Operating within a society which imagined itself as 'frontier', and with a definition of 'madness' as frontier-*like*, the asylum acted-out the frontier's divisions. At the close of the nineteenth century, and quite possibly beyond that moment, the 'ideal' asylum patient in the colonial state was still being invented. Further comparative work, which includes extensive studies of Australia and New Zealand, would perhaps show historians how this 'ideal' functioned, and thus not only how the asylum population was formed through the imperial discourses of law and medicine, but also how law and medicine contributed to articulations of racial and sexual difference in colonial settler societies.

Notes

1 Phrase from Kathryn Cronin, *Colonial Casualties: Chinese in Early Victoria* (Melbourne, Melbourne University Press, 1982).
2 Shula Marks, 'What Is Colonial About Colonial Medicine? And What Has Happened to Imperialism and Health?', *Social History of Medicine*, 10:2 (1997), 215; Lenore Manderson, *Sickness and the State: Health and Illness in Colonial Malaya, 1870–1940* (Cambridge, Cambridge University Press, 1996), p. 14.
3 Jock McCulloch, *Colonial Psychiatry and 'The African Mind'* (Cambridge and Melbourne, Cambridge University Press, 1995), p. 45.
4 Roy Macleod and Milton Lewis (eds), *Disease, Medicine and Empire: Perspectives on Western Medicine and the Experience of European Expansion* (London and New York, Routledge, 1988).
5 Macleod and Lewis, *Disease, Medicine and Empire*, p. 3.
6 Megan Vaughan, *Curing Their Ills: Colonial Power and African Illness*, (Cambridge, Polity Press, 1991), p. 8. See Also Mary-Ellen Kelm, *Colonizing Bodies: Aboriginal Health and Healing in British Columbia 1900–1950* (Vancouver, University of British Columbia Press, 1998), pp. 100–1.
7 David Arnold, *Colonizing the Body: State Medicine and Epidemic Disease in Nineteenth-Century India* (Berkeley and Los Angeles, University of California Press, 1993).
8 Roy Porter, 'History of Psychiatry in Britain', *History of Psychiatry*, 2 (1991), 279.
9 Waltraud Ernst, *Mad Tales From the Raj: The European Insane in British India, 1800–1858* (London and New York, Routledge, 1991); 'European Madness and Gender in Nineteenth-Century British India', *Social History of Medicine*, 9:3 (1996), 357–82.
10 Waltraud Ernst, 'The Social History of Pakeha Psychiatry in Nineteenth-Century New Zealand: Main Themes', in Linda Bryder (ed.) *A Healthy Country: Essays on the Social History of Medicine in New Zealand* (Wellington, Bridget Williams Books, 1991), pp. 65–84.
11 Stephen Garton, *Medicine and Madness: A Social History of Insanity in New South Wales, 1880–1940* (Kensington, NSW, University of New South Wales Press, 1988); Mark Finnane, 'Asylums, Families, and the State', *History Workshop*, 20 (1985), 134–48; Norman Megahey, 'More Than a Minor Nuisance: Insanity in Colonial Western Australia', in Charlie Fox (ed.), *Historical Refractions: Studies in Western Australian History*, xiv, (1993), 42–59, and Bronwyn Harman, 'Women and Insanity: The Fremantle Asylum in Western Australia, 1858–1908', in Penelope Hetherington and Phillipa Maddern (eds), *Sexuality and Gender in History: Selected Essays* (Nedlands, WA, University of Western Australia Press, 1993), pp. 167–81. On New Zealand, see Barbara Brookes, 'The Early Days of the Seacliff Asylum: The Admission and Treatment of Patients', in Rex Wright-St Clair (ed.), *Proceedings of the First New Zealand Conference on the History of New Zealand and Australian Medicine*, Waikato Hospital, Hamilton, New Zealand, 1987, pp. 172–76; Barbara Brookes, 'Women and Madness: A Case-Study of the Seacliff Asylum, 1890–1920', in Barbara Brookes, Charlotte Macdonald and Margaret Tennant (eds), *Women in History* (Wellington, Bridget Williams Books Ltd, 1992), vol. 2, pp. 129–47; Bronwyn Labrum, 'Looking Beyond the Asylum: Gender and the Process of Committal in Auckland, 1870–1910, *New Zealand Journal of History*, 26:2 (1992), 125–44. See Derek Dow's *Annotated Bibliography for the History of Medicine and Health in New Zealand* (Dunedin, Hocken Library, University of Otago, 1994).

12 Eric Cunningham-Dax wrote his contribution to the world-history of psychiatry in 1975; see 'Australia and New Zealand', in John G. Howells (ed.), *World History of Psychiatry* (London, Baillière Tindall, 1975), pp. 704–28.
13 Linda Bryder comments on the contribution of Ernst to her *A Healthy Country*, p. 3.
14 Ernst, 'The Social History of Pakeha Psychiatry', p. 67 and 83.
15 John Harley Warner, 'The History of Science and the Sciences of Medicine', *OSIRIS*, 10 (1995), 183–4.
16 Andrew Scull, *The Most Solitary of Afflictions: Madness and Society in Britain, 1700–1900* (New Haven, CT, Yale University Press, 1993), p. 360, n.74.
17 Nancy Tomes, 'Historical Perspectives on Women and Mental Illness', in Rima D. Apple (ed.), *Women, Health, and Medicine in America: A Historical Handbook* (New York and London, Garland Publishing, 1990), pp. 162, 170.
18 Sally Swartz, 'The Black Insane in the Cape, 1891–1920', *Journal of Southern African Studies*, 21 (1995), 399–415.
19 Cunningham-Dax, 'Australia and New Zealand', p. 726
20 Garton, *Medicine and Madness*, p. 12.
21 See Diana Dyason, 'The Medical Profession in Colonial Victoria', in Macleod and Lewis (eds), *Disease, Medicine and Empire*, pp. 194–216.
22 Garton, *Medicine and Madness*, p. 11, p. 14; see also Mark Finnane, *Insanity and the Insane in Post-Famine Ireland* (Totowa, London and New Jersey, Croom Helm, 1981), p. 87.
23 Ernst, 'The Social History of Pakeha Psychiatry', p. 67.
24 Vaughan, *Curing Their Ills*, p. 12.
25 Catharine Coleborne, 'Reading Madness: Bodily Difference and the Female Lunatic in Colonial Victoria, 1848–1888', unpublished Ph.D. thesis, La Trobe University, 1997, p. 7; A.S. Ellis, *Eloquent Testimony: The Story of the Mental Health Services in Western Australia 1830–1975* (Nedlands, University of Western Australia Press, 1984).
26 An Act to make provision for the safe custody of, and prevention of offenses by, persons dangerously insane; and for the care and maintenance of persons of unsound mind, known as Dangerous Lunatics Act, 7 Vic., No. 14, 1843.
27 An Act to Consolidate and Amend the Law relating to Lunatics, or Lunacy Statute, 31 Vic., No. 309 (amended in 1869 and 1878, 42 Vic., No. 628).
28 Ernst, 'The Social History of Pakeha Psychiatry', p. 68.
29 *Ibid.*, p. 74; and see p. 215 of Bryder's *A Healthy Country* for footnotes 38 and 39.
30 Warwick Brunton, 'The New Zealand Lunatic Asylum: Conception and Misconception', in Wright-St. Clair (ed.), *Conference on New Zealand and Australian Medicine*, pp. 158–9; L.K. Gluckman, *Tangiwai: A Medical History of Nineteenth-Century New Zealand* (Auckland, Whitcoulls Ltd, 1976), p. 110. See also Ernst, 'The Social History of Pakeha Psychiatry', p. 71.
31 'Report of the Royal Commission Appointed to Inquire into the Changes Made By Thomas Butler, Late Keeper, Nelson Lunatic Asylum', *Appendices to the Journals of the House of Representatives* (*AJHR*), New Zealand Parliament (Wellington, Government Printer, 1877), H.-34, p. 611.
32 See 'Report from the Select Committee of the Legislative Council on the Yarra Bend Lunatic Asylum, together with the Proceedings of the Committee, Minutes of Evidence and Appendix' *Victoria Parliamentary Papers* (VPP), 1852–53, vol. 2 (Melbourne, John Ferres, Government Printer, 1853). Eleanor Harkinson, Q. 240, p. 7; John Harkinson, Q. 230–1, p. 7.
33 'Yarra Bend Lunatic Asylum', *Illustrated Melbourne Post*, 25 June, 1862, p. 45.
34 'Royal Commission on Asylums for the Insane and the Inebriate. Reports together with minutes of evidence and Appendices', *VPP, 1884–87* (Melbourne, John Ferres, Government Printer), Minutes of Evidence, Q. 1597, pp. 72–3.
35 See *Argus*, 10 October 1848, p. 2.
36 As quoted by Brunton in 'The New Zealand Lunatic Asylum', p. 156, using a letter from the police magistrate to the colonial secretary.

37 W.D. Neil, *The Lunatic Asylum at Castle Hill* (Castle Hill, Dyas, 1992), p. 2.
38 See Labrum, 'Looking Beyond the Asylum', p. 143.
39 Coleborne, 'Reading Madness'.
40 'The Management of Lunatics', *Illustrated Melbourne Post*, 25 June 1862, p. 46; David Goodman, *Gold Seeking: Victoria and California in the 1850s* (Sydney, Allen & Unwin, 1994), p. 195.
41 *Australian Medical Journal*, 15 (1870), 151.
42 Stephen Garton, 'The Dimensions of Dementia', in Verity Burgmann and Jenny Lee (eds), *Constructing a Culture: A People's History of Australia Since 1788* (Melbourne, Penguin/McPhee Gribble, 1988), p. 67.
43 Penny Russell (ed.), *For Richer, For Poorer: Early Colonial Marriages* (Melbourne, Melbourne University Press, 1994), pp. 6, 9.
44 Jill Matthews, *Good and Mad Women: The Historical Construction of Femininity in Twentieth-Century Australia* (Sydney, Allen & Unwin, 1984).
45 Labrum, 'Looking Beyond the Asylum', p. 136.
46 *Ibid.*, p. 128.
47 Andrew Scull, *The Most Solitary of Afflictions: Madness and Society in Britain 1700–1900* (New Haven, CT, and London, Yale University Press, 1993), pp. 352–3; see chapter 7, 'The Social Production of Insanity'.
48 Finnane, 'Asylums, Families, and the State', p. 144.
49 C.R.D. Brothers, *Early Victorian Psychiatry 1835–1905* (Melbourne, A.C. Brooks, 1958), p. 109. It was 'race' that troubled state insane hospitals in mid-century America: Edward Jarvis, *Insanity and Idiocy in Massachusetts: Report of the Commission on Lunacy, 1855*, with a Critical Introduction by Gerald N. Grob, (Cambridge, MA, Harvard University Press, 1971), p. 56.
50 'Report of the Inspector of Asylums on the Hospitals for the Insane for the Year 1870', *VPP* (Melbourne, John Ferres, Government Printer, 1871), pp. 7–9.
51 'Report on Lunatic Asylums of the Colony for 1887', *AJHR*, New Zealand Parliament (Wellington, Government Printer, 1888), H.-8, p. 2.
52 Jann Matlock, *Scenes of Seduction: Prostitution, Hysteria, and Reading Difference in Nineteenth-Century France* (New York, Columbia University Press, 1994), pp. 140–1.
53 This description indicates that the inmate was an Aborigine. Only one male Aborigine was confined as a lunatic according to *Census of Victoria, 1871*, p. 21, and *Census of Victoria, 1881*, p. 109.
54 Louisa Kate Pink, 1 January, 1875, Victorian Public Record Series (VPRS) 7401/P1, Ararat Asylum, Unit 2, p. 73.
55 Labrum, 'Looking Beyond the Asylum', pp. 133, 135.
56 Cronin, *Colonial Casualties*, p. 1.
57 See *ibid.*, pp. 16–17; Goodman, *Gold Seeking*, p. 195.
58 Cronin, *Colonial Casualties*, p. 86.
59 *Ibid.*, p. 92.
60 'Report of the Chinese Immigration Committee' *AJHR*, New Zealand Parliament (Wellington, Government Printer, 1871) H-5, p. 20
61 Mary-Ellen Kelm, 'Women, Families and the Provincial Hospital for the Insane, British Columbia, 1905–1915', *Journal of Family History*, 19:2 (1994), 177–93, here at 184.
62 As cited by Megahey, 'More than a Minor Nuisance', p. 53.
63 Richard Broome, *The Victorians: Arriving* (Melbourne, Fairfax, Syme & Weldon Associates, 1984), p. 121; Chinese Act 1881, 45 Vic., No. 723; Chinese Immigration Restriction Act 1888, 52 Vic., No. 1005.
64 Edmond Chiu, 'Fart Din: The Plight of the Mentally Ill Chinese in Victoria, 1867 to 1879', *Medical Journal of Australia*, 1 (1977) 541–4, here at 544; 'Fart Din: More About the Plight of Mentally Ill Chinese in Victoria, 1867–1875', *Medical Journal of Australia*, 1 (1977), 594–7.
65 Cronin, *Colonial Casualties*, pp. 63–5.
66 *Constitution*, 22 June 1857, cited by Cronin, *Colonial Casualties*, p. 81.

67 See Andrew Markus, *Australian Race Relations* (Sydney, Allen & Unwin, 1994), pp. 59–72. Other studies of the Chinese in Australia include Morag Loh, *Sojourners and Settlers: Chinese in Victoria 1848–1985*, Victorian Government China Advisory Committee Sesquicentenary Publication, series editor, Joan Grant (Melbourne, Barradene Press, 1985); Morag Loh, 'Historical Overview of Chinese Migration', Working Papers on Migrant and Intercultural Studies, No. 12, December 1988; Peter Hanks and Andrew Perry (eds), *The Chinese in Australia* (Melbourne, Centre for Migrant and Intercultural Studies, Monash University, 1988).

68 Broome, *Victorians*, p. 120.

69 'Chinese Lunatics', *AMJ*, 10 (1865) 202–3; Chiu, 'The Raid of the Quack', *AMJ*, 20 (1875); Chiu, 'Fart Din', p. 541. Chinese Immigrants Statute 1865, 28 Vic. No. 259.

70 *Age*, 16 December, 1869, p. 3.

71 Margaret Ah Lee, 19 March 1887, VPRS 7397/P1, Unit 8, p. 88 p. 272.

72 For instance, Mrinalini Sinha, *Colonial Masculinity: The 'Manly Britishman' and the 'Effeminate Bengali' in the Late Nineteenth Century* (Manchester, Manchester University Press, 1995). Charlie Fox, 'Jumna Khan', in Jan Gothard (ed.) *Asian Orientations: Studies in Western Australian History*, 16 (1995), 53–68.

73 Ah Lop, 16 January, 1874, VPRS 7397/P1, Unit 2, p. 53.

74 Ah Lang, 22 April, 1874, VPRS 7397/P1, Unit 2, p. 130.

75 White male patients were often charged with intemperance, and occasionally with excessive tobacco smoking, as in the case of Alexander Fenton: 26 May, 1880, VPRS 7398/P1, Unit 7, p. 129.

76 Ah Shung, 6 March, 1875, VPRS 7397/P1 Unit 2, p. 89; Ah Sin, 26 March, 1875, *ibid.*, p. 104; Ah Him, 28 June 1878, *ibid.*, p. 149.

77 Chiu, 'Fart Din', p. 596; Jimmy Ah John, 7 May 1884, VPRS 7398/P1, Unit 7, p. 21.

78 Dr Patrick Smith, 'Hints on the Giving of Certificates of Lunacy', *AMJ*, 18 (1873), 360.

79 Samuel Taylor, 24 March 1880, VPRS 7398/P1, Unit 7, p. 110.

80 John Barry, 2 January, 1880, *ibid.*, p. 89; Joseph White, 7 January, 1880, *ibid.*, p. 91.

81 'Fart Din', p. 543.

82 Ah Pee, 16 August, 1883, VPRS 7398/P1, Unit 8, p. 204; Jimmy Ah John, 7 May, 1884, *ibid.*, p. 21; Ah Fong, 27 March 1886, *ibid.*, p. 289.

83 Megahey, 'More than a Minor Nuisance', p. 53, from the correspondence of the colonial secretary, 1896.

84 Dr Ball's speech, 'The Frontiers of Madness', *Age*, (Melbourne) 28 March, 1883, p. 3.

PART III

Justice, custom and the common law

Imperial hold over the workings of law in colonial
dominions was sometimes challenged as the
meaning of 'justice' was contested and refashioned.
The central theme here is conflict: of collision
between differing legalities and concepts of justice.
The focus is on legal principles and evidence, and
on narrative as imperial power.

CHAPTER EIGHT

Towards a 'taxonomy' for the common law: legal history and the recognition of Aboriginal customary law

Mark D. Walters

The common law is increasingly concerned about respecting the historical continuity of Aboriginal cultural and national identities, but on terms that also respect its own internal sense of continuity – the continuity of legal principle – and the result is a common-law doctrine of Aboriginal rights that might be seen to warp previously accepted understandings of legal history. Courts have recently affirmed that the law of Aboriginal rights is, and was, an 'intersocietal law', embracing norms derived from both native and settler systems, and from the customary practices that regulated their early relationships.[1] Present legal constructions of the initial contact between the common law and Aboriginal customary law must incorporate native and non-native legal and historical methodologies, a reconciliation that the courts are only just beginning to attempt.[2] It might be thought that the common law, informed by its imperial and colonial heritage, is incapable of adopting an appropriate cross-cultural outlook to perform this task. Setting its assumed content to the side, however, it is possible to identify within the common law a system of normative reasoning that shares with Aboriginal cultures some common assumptions about history. In the Western tradition, historians have tended to assume that relatively objective and linear historical realities can be identified through interpretations of written records in which the historian attempts both to keep his or her own cultural and historical perspective at a distance and to produce interpretations of history relevant to that particular cultural and historical position.[3] In contrast, Aboriginal conceptions of history are informed by oral traditions that are generally non-linear, and the goal is not to seek an objective truth detached from the present but to tell a story of the past in which the assumptions and aspirations of the teller and the listeners are more of an integral part.[4] At least in relation to *legal* history, common-law reasoning tends to resemble the native rather than the non-native conception of history:

judges tell stories of the legal past not to identify its historical reality but to derive rules and principles that have moral resonance and therefore normative force for those listening, i.e. the people whose lives today will be affected by the outcome of litigation.

Although the non-linear tendencies of common-law and Aboriginal conceptions of history suggest the existence of a methodological cornerstone upon which a truly 'intersocietal' legal edifice is being constructed, it must be said that construction of this edifice is still in its early stages; indeed, some basic points of design are still unsettled. Recent Australian and Canadian cases on the legal status of Aboriginal customary law confirm that judges have yet to fashion an adequate framework within which competing conceptions of history can be accommodated. The strained relationship between Aboriginal rights, the common law and history was described by Gummow J. in *Wik Peoples* v. *Queensland* in this way:

> There remains lacking ... any established taxonomy to regulate such uses of history in the formulation of legal norms ... Even if any such taxonomy were to be devised, it might then be said of it that it was but a rhetorical device devised to render past reality into a form useful to legally principled resolution of present conflicts.[5]

What is required, then, is an organizational system, or 'taxonomy', within which the distinct intellectual activities of 'legal' and 'historical' reasoning can be conducted simultaneously, legitimately and coherently from 'native' and 'non-native' perspectives. In light of its complexity and cross-cultural nature, this taxonomy will only emerge over time through on-going judicial and extra-judicial dialogue between native and non-native communities. This paper considers one aspect of this process, namely, the relationship between the common law and non-native conceptions of legal history, and how this relationship might fit into a larger 'taxonomy' for the common-law doctrine of Aboriginal rights and customs.

The judiciary remains uncertain about how, in constructing modern legal protections for Aboriginal cultures and customs, to respond to modern arguments about imperial and colonial *legal* history. Some judges purport to apply the 'time-honoured methodology of the common law' when considering the status of Aboriginal customary laws. Adopting this approach in her dissent in *Van der Peet*, McLachlin J. concluded that the 'golden thread' running through the history of Aboriginal–European relations is the common law's recognition of the ancestral laws and customs of Aboriginal peoples.[6] Similarly, Deane and Gaudron JJ. said in *Mabo* that a 'guiding principle' of common law throughout the British Empire was that indigenous rights under pre-existing native laws and customs were protected.[7] These statements can be defended as sound statements of legal history, but it must be admitted that they are not uncontroversial ones when judged by orthodox non-native historical methods.

The question, however, is whether statements of law like these need to be defended as sound statements of history, as defined by that orthodox view. It may be argued that their validity as statements of law depends upon different criteria of validity from those applicable to statements of history. The judicial assertion that the common law *did* protect Aboriginal customary law is, after all, only the first step in a legal argument according to which the common law (and, in Canada, the Constitution Act, 1982)[8] *does* protect certain Aboriginal customs today. Of course, if a modern judge were to say that the common law *did* recognize Aboriginal customs without offering *any* historical justification for that assertion, then it might be argued that the judge was simply concealing a political decision about modern rights behind a distorted view of the imperial and colonial legal past. If this argument has merit, then the whole idea of using imperial and colonial law – the very law that supported oppressive policies denying Aboriginal rights – to reconstruct a theory of Aboriginal rights fit for present sensibilities may be said to be intellectually dishonest. One might then conclude that the best course is to abandon common-law methodology altogether and, like the majority of the Supreme Court of Canada in *Van der Peet*, to construct from 'first principles'[9] a theory for the recognition of Aboriginal customary laws which is not dependaent upon their common-law continuity from the historical moment of their contact with the common law.

Without a sound 'taxonomy' for the common law, legal history and Aboriginal rights it is difficult to assess critically these competing approaches. To contribute to the development of such a 'taxonomy' it is necessary to begin by considering the various interpretative dimensions within which the law, both past and present, can be read. In light of my own cultural background, I will limit my comments to 'non-native' approaches to interpretation.

Competing interpretative perspectives for legal history and Aboriginal customs

In *The Ancient Constitution and the Feudal Law*, J.G.A. Pocock argued that only the insular 'common-law mind' could seriously have adopted the unhistorical view that English law in the seventeenth century consisted of immemorial custom derived from a Saxon constitution that pre-dated the Norman conquest.[10] In his view, common lawyers were concerned less with portraying legal history accurately than with providing a legal interpretation of history supportive of Parliament's struggle against Stuart abuses of the royal prerogative. This common-law tactic of the seventeenth century might be compared to efforts by common lawyers today to invoke the historical continuity of Aboriginal law at common law in support of modern Aboriginal claims: both may be argued to rely upon interpretations of legal history informed by modern values, concerns and moral assumptions. And, just as Pocock argued that the continuity of a pre-conquest constitution was legally superfluous given post-conquest limitations on the royal prerogative, so it could be argued that it is unnecessary to show common-law continuity of Aboriginal customs from the moment British sovereignty was asserted because any Aboriginal customs or rights that ought to be recognized today can be recognized through modern legal developments.

Locating the debate about common-law Aboriginal rights and history within this larger debate about the 'common-law mind' and historiography confirms that the challenges that Aboriginal claims present for non-native legal and historical methods involve a more general tension between the historical interpretation of law and the legal interpretation of history. In developing a 'taxonomy' for common-law Aboriginal rights and legal history, it is necessary to distinguish between these two interpretative perspectives.

Law can be conceptualized in several different dimensions. It exists in an empirical sense as a series of historical facts consisting of rules, orders and decisions, including (at common law) the decisions of judges in particular cases. To discover law in the empirical sense an attempt is made to read relevant legal materials literally to see what rules have been made: legal history is taken at face value, and under the doctrine of precedent (assuming no legislative intervention) the face of the legal past determines that of the legal present. Adopting this approach in the famous case of *Donoghue* v. *Stevenson*,[11] Lord Buckmaster looked to the duties of care in negligence law expressly recognized in past cases, and finding none to match the case at bar (a consumer's action against a manufacturer of a defective product) he concluded that the plaintiff had no cause of action. Lord Buckmaster was, however, in dissent. Lord Atkin for the majority read the past cases in a *normative* not an empirical light: he sought a 'general conception of relations giving rise to a duty of care of which the particular cases ... are but instances'.[12] He sought, in other words, an underlying theory explaining why particular decisions were made in the past and how analogous cases should be decided in the future. The 'general conception of relations' found – the duty to take care not to injure one's 'neighbour', or people who would likely be affected by one's conduct – liberated tort law from the narrow pigeon-holes of duty previously recognized. Thereafter, the 'neighbour' principle came to be seen as a normative backdrop for all activities.

If common-law history is read empirically, the identification of the 'neighbour' principle can be said to be the creation of a new legal rule. However, if common-law history is read, as Lord Atkin read it, in a normative light, then it can be said that the principle was inherent in the common law all along. Indeed, the latter approach is the orthodox common-law approach: law is not a set of historical facts, but a normative system. The common law is not (said Holmes) like 'the axioms and corollaries of a book of mathematics ... [rather] to know what it is, we must know what it has been, and what it tends to become'.[13] Legal and historical analyses are therefore conceptually detached.

The equivalent of a 'neighbour' principle can be identified for the common-law doctrine of Aboriginal rights. Read in an empirical sense, colonial and imperial legal history is ambiguous about, if not inimical to, the common-law status of native law and custom in Canada and Australia.[14] Read in a normative light – especially one that extends temporally and geographically throughout the British Empire – the many cases acknowledging the common-law continuity of the *lex loci* of newly acquired territories can be seen to derive from a very general normative principle, or doctrine, of continuity.[15] Simply put, the principle provides that judges acknowledged, recognized and/or applied as elements of British common law all local laws, customs, rights and institutions existing at the moment British sovereignty was asserted over a territory to the extent that they were not inconsistent with British conceptions of justice or morality, crown sovereignty, or valid legislation.[16]

This principle could *now* be used to explain why the common law *did* recognize native law and custom in Australia and Canada, but is the extension of the principle historically accurate? Did the common law *at the time* it was introduced into these colonial territories actually recognize native law and custom? In fact, some cases suggest that in 'settled' colonies occupied by non-European tribal societies the principle of continuity did not apply.[17] Can a legal assessment of legal history ignore these awkward historical precedents, adopt a more tolerant attitude toward Aboriginal cultures and customs, and rework the historical record to produce a different result more palatable to modern sensibilities? The empirical/normative models of interpretation require further refinement if a 'taxonomy' is to be developed to address this question.

A legal interpretation of common-law history must give weight to past cases, but each new case presents another opportunity to measure those cases against the normative background of the common law as a whole as interpreted in today's light. By this means, judges 'reformulate' the law to ensure consistency with 'common justice'[18] and 'the common law is kept in a constant state of adaptation and repair'.[19] Even when judges overturn past decisions, or correct 'ancient heresies', they are constrained by the common law itself: unlike legislators who may develop new laws 'founded purely upon policy' or on a 'utilitarian assessment' of society's needs, judges clarify and develop the law incrementally by analogy with existing cases.[20] This is not to say that judicial decision-making is not political or creative (it surely is), but only that in adopting a normative common-law perspective judges are constrained in their political, creative role by past law in ways in which legislators are not. In short, the dynamic nature of the common law permits the conclusion that past cases denying the common-law continuity of Aboriginal customs can be labelled as 'ancient heresies' and overruled as contrary to the true common-law position that ought to have been acknowledged at the time. But in light of the amount of time that has elapsed since the assertion of British sovereignty over places like Australia and Canada, and given the changing attitudes of non-native judges toward native cultures and customs, there is a real danger that this conclusion will appear contrived unless at least some historically based argument can be mustered in its support. It is therefore important to supplement the consideration of the dimensions of legal interpretation with a consideration of the various dimensions of historical interpretation.

A legal historian will be concerned to identify past law in its empirical sense and will strive to discover all relevant empirical data on particular legal points. But like the common lawyer, the legal historian will not be content with an empirical reading of these legal–historical data. Whereas the lawyer enlists the legal past in order to resolve present disputes, the historian seeks to understand the legal past in its full contemporary social, political and economic context.[21] For the historian, a reading of the legal past sympathetic to modern concerns is problematic, but for the lawyer it is not. The difficulty, however, is that the common law exists in any epoch both explicitly (the rules that were applied in actual cases) and implicitly (the rules that would have been applied had a relevant case been brought), and the legal historian may be just as concerned with identifying the latter as the former. In relation to issues that were not frequently litigated or conclusively resolved in the past – like the status of Aboriginal customary law – how should the resulting gaps and ambiguities in the empirically determined common-law history be interpreted? The historian and the lawyer will respond differently. The historian will seek to identify what the judicial response at the time would have been in light of the law as it was then understood.[22] The historian must therefore combine historical and legal methodologies: he or she must read the empirical legal data then in existence and attempt to fill the gaps or resolve the ambiguities by adopting the sort of normative judicial perspective then prevalent, minimizing the extent to which subsequent ideas about either judicial decision-making or substantive moral and political issues infiltrate and taint the analysis. In contrast, modern judges will not be concerned if present-day values inform their interpretation of the legal past; after all, their conclusions will be binding on living people as part of today's law, and they must be morally and politically defensible as such. Of course, judges must still give interpretations that 'fit', or are consistent with, the general structure of the legal system as a whole; revisions to the outward face of the common law must cohere with the overall framework of law as a social and political institution.[23]

In short, both historical and legal interpretations of past common-law gaps and ambiguities involve adopting a *normative* common-law perspective. In adopting that perspective the historian reads the legal past as a *secondary interpreter*, entering into the minds of judges of the relevant historical era in so far as possible. In contrast, the modern judge is a *primary interpreter*, guided only by his or her own judgment about the common law. It is now clear that whether the common-law principle of continuity explains the common-law continuity of Aboriginal customary law in Australia or Canada is a normative question that can be considered from either a primary (or modern judicial) perspective or a secondary (or legal–historical) perspective. Indeed, the central challenge for non-native legal and historical methodologies arising from the common-law doctrine of Aboriginal rights can be restated thus: in articulating legal norms relating to the common-law status of native law and custom, should judges be guided only by a primary interpretative perspective or must they also take into account the secondary interpretative perspective?

In general, can a primary interpreter disregard completely the conclusions reached by a secondary interpreter when attempting to fill gaps and resolve ambiguities in the common-law past? It depends upon the nature of the legal claim presently being made. Consider, for example, a claim concerning recent events, like a certain form of negligent conduct occurring last year. Assume that the first possible time that conduct of this nature could have been the subject of a negligence claim was the mid-nineteenth century (due to, say, technological developments). Assume as well that there is no reported case addressing this sort of claim but there is a leading case analogous to it which dates from the mid-nineteenth century, and that there is some doubt as to whether the common-law rule in this case extends to the facts in the case at bar. In these circumstances, it is consistent with common-law methodology for the primary interpreter – i.e. the judge hearing the case – to decide not to apply the mid-nineteenth century case on the basis of purely modern considerations and without any regard to how a mid-nineteenth-century judge would have dealt with the same issue. The primary interpreter can (within limits) restate the rule to make it more appropriate to present sensibilities and so that it coheres better with the many cases decided or statutes made since the mid-nineteenth century. A secondary interpreter – e.g. a legal historian – might say that the 'new' common-law rule developed by the primary interpreter is informed by modern moral or social factors or by cases decided since the relevant historical period, and as such would never have been adopted by a mid-nineteenth-century judge. However, the validity of this assessment of common-law history would not undermine the legitimacy of the primary interpreter's restatement of the common law as including the new rule. Indeed, the rule may only be 'new' for the secondary interpreter: the primary interpreter may rightly conclude that the common law, properly interpreted, always contained this rule.

The situation is more complicated, however, when the legal claim presently made relates to events of the more distant past. Consider, for example, a modern dispute about title to land in which one party relies upon a mid-nineteenth-century deed and the other party alleges that under common-law principles the deed was void. If at the time the deed was made the common law was unclear about this point and this ambiguity has not since been resolved (and assuming the action is not barred by a statute of limitations), it is arguable that the primary interpreter should be constrained in his or her articulation of the common law by the conclusions reached through a secondary interpretation of the legal past. Assume, for example, that the secondary interpretation reveals that a mid-nineteenth-century judge would definitely have articulated common-law rule x, but the primary interpreter concludes that, in a modern setting, common-law rule y is better. Assume as well that the deed is valid under rule x but void under rule y. In these circumstances, it seems intuitively problematic for the primary interpreter to adopt common-law rule y and declare the deed void. Adopting a different rule from the one that would have been adopted at the time appears to result in the retrospective nullification of a deed that was, when made, valid. In cases like these, the essence of the plaintiff's claim is not that present rights should be stripped away on account of present moral considerations; rather, the claim is that alleged present rights are, and always have been, qualified by certain other legally pre-existing rights.

The situation is further complicated if, in this hypothetical case, the secondary interpreter cannot say definitely what the mid-nineteenth-century judge would have said. Two variations of this scenario exist. First, the secondary interpreter's historical analysis might reveal that the mid-nineteenth century answer to the common-law question could have been either x or y (e.g., the reported cases go both ways). In this case, if the primary interpreter thinks y is the better common-law rule from today's perspective, it would seem legitimate to adopt rule y and hold the deed void because y was a possible rule at the time the deed was made. In this case, the choice between two historical interpretations is determined by wholly modern considerations. However, what would be the case if the secondary interpreter's historical research revealed that most of the reported cases tended to favour x and it was only in a few cases, dissenting judgments or academic commentaries that y was favoured? Again, if the primary interpreter concludes that y is the better common-law rule from today's perspective, then it may still be legitimate for the primary interpreter to adopt rule y and declare the deed void. This decision may be criticized as a retrospective nullification of an otherwise valid deed due to a distorted view of past law arising from an improper reading into the past of present-day ideas. However, this criticism can be avoided if the primary interpreter adopts, in the course of his or her primary interpretation, a secondary interpretative stance and offers an explanation why, from a mid-nineteenth-century perspective, y ought to have been acknowledged as the accepted common-law rule at the time the deed was made. In other words, the judge may be able to say that y is the better rule from both a modern and an historical perspective, even though many judges during the relevant historical period would (apparently) have disagreed. In cases like these, then, modern judicial analysis and historical analysis, though remaining within distinct conceptual spheres, overlap. The analysis is still a primary – or legal – one, but the secondary – or historical – argument is an important component.

This evolving 'taxonomy' can now be applied to the question of Aboriginal customary law. Are modern claims by Aboriginal peoples to the recognition of native customs relating to land or other matters like the 'deed' case above, or like the 'negligence' case? It is, of course, arguable that the legal status of Aboriginal customs today should not depend upon their historical legal status under colonial and imperial law. However, to argue that certain rights or customs ought now to form part of the law on account of today's moral and political sensibilities and regardless of previous case law is to formulate a political argument more suitable for lobbying legislators than persuading common-law judges. At least in the context of common-law adjudication it is, if possible, better to conceptualize Aboriginal rights' claims as claims not merely about what the law *ought* to be but also about what the law *is* and *has been*. As Wik confirms, the articulation of native rights as historically embedded in the common law permits the conclusion that the many legislative and executive instruments made during the colonial era and after must now be interpreted in light of a common-law context in which native law and custom were recognized. This conclusion is (from a non-native perspective) jurisprudentially difficult if native rights spring into legal existence decades or centuries after such instruments were made. Aboriginal claims seem to require some reconciliation of legal interpretations of history and historical interpretations of law, and therefore judges may have to have some regard to the views of 'secondary interpreters' in the course of developing their 'primary' interpretations.

In developing these secondary interpretations, what sort of empirical data ought judges use? The legal issues raised in most common-law cases can be examined from both primary and secondary normative perspectives because most cases involve events that transpired in the past. In a case involving events of a year ago a secondary interpreter today might conclude that the relevant legal rule is rule x on the basis that x would have been the rule applied by a judge a year ago; however, when applying the law today a judge might re-articulate that rule as being $x+1$ and apply it to resolve the dispute. This 'retrospective' application of newly discovered common-law principles is jurisprudentially problematic, but it is not the sort of methodological problem relating to history that is of central concern for this analysis. In the example given, the two points in time are relatively contemporaneous and so the application of a 'new' common-law rule to the parties is not grossly unfair even if, at the time the events arose leading to the litigation, this new rule was as yet only inherent in the common law. The result is not unfair because in average cases like this one the primary and secondary interpretative perspectives will usually lead to very similar statements of law since the empirical legal data analyzed will be more or less the same under both approaches and the moral, political and cultural assumptions underlying the judgment will not have shifted dramatically. However, as time between the relevant events and the resulting litigation increases, so does the possibility that primary and secondary perspectives will diverge in fundamental ways.

These observations assist in the identification of the empirical legal data that a secondary interpreter might consider when seeking a historical answer to the question of what legal status Aboriginal customary law had as of the moment British sovereignty was asserted over a colony. As stated, the objective is to subject the empirical legal data existing at this time to a normative common-law analysis, from the methodological and the moral outlook appropriate for judges of that time. The secondary interpreter would include within this data any analogous cases that had been decided prior to this date in relation to other colonial territories, but there will not be any cases on the legal implications for native customs of the assertion of sovereignty over that particular colony, since such cases could arise only after the assertion of sovereignty. However, it may be argued that the secondary interpreter should have reference to empirical legal data relating to the colony itself generated within a reasonable period of time after the relevant historical date. Since the objective is to construct a judicial response that would have been given in a case litigated following the initial assertion of sovereignty, reference to such data is legitimate. Furthermore, the secondary interpreter will have to consider *de facto* relations between natives, settlers and colonial/imperial officials which developed in that colony after the assertion of British sovereignty, for any common-law judge at the time would have attempted to render a decision that not only 'fitted' the existing legal structure but was also relevant to, applicable within and perhaps derivable from the larger socio-political context. Of course, the secondary interpreter will not reach too far forward in time when collecting empirical data as this would reduce the historical accuracy of the interpretation. Thus, some attempt must be made to distinguish between cases that are more or less contemporaneous with the assertion of British sovereignty and those that were decided sufficiently after the fact as to be, in themselves, legal interpretations that are 'historical' in a degree that exceeds the usual sense in which most common-law cases involve historical analyses.[24] As a rough guide to the sort of empirical legal data that might be regarded as legitimate, perhaps it can be said that any data generated within the period during which people who were living at the time sovereignty was asserted might have litigated the issue could be considered as sufficiently contemporaneous to the event as to reflect potential historical legal responses to that event. In these cases, the divergence between primary and secondary interpretative perspectives would not have been any greater than in the average common-law case, and, for our purposes, can therefore be disregarded. Using this rough guide, then, a secondary interpreter will include within the empirical data all cases, commentary or other relevant materials, including evidence of the socio-political context, generated within (say) fifty or sixty years of the assertion of British sovereignty.

The historical objective of the principle of continuity was to regulate, in as pragmatic and fair a manner as possible, the potentially chaotic circumstances attendant upon the absorption of a previously independent constitutional order within a larger imperial order during that period between the assertion of British sovereignty and a clear legislative statement from the Crown or Parliament about the status of local law.[25] It can be assumed that in light of the sort of empirical data mentioned above the principle of continuity could have been applied to explain the common-law status of Aboriginal customary laws in Canada and Australia as it was applied elsewhere in the Empire. This is *a* plausible secondary interpretation. In relation to Canada, the expansion of secondary analysis to include non-judicial sources (e.g. the well-entrenched Crown policy of respecting the continuity of Aboriginal title, customs and, indeed, self-government[26]), might lead a secondary interpreter to conclude that the common-law continuity argument was not only legally plausible at the time but that it fitted so well with *de facto* conditions that it must be regarded as the *best* secondary interpretation. Even in Australia, a full analysis of the historical context might suggest that acknowledgement of *de jure* continuity would not have been out of step with the *de facto* situation.[27] Of course, in taking sides and arguing for one interpretation over another, the secondary interpreter must be careful not to allow modern values to inform the choice. However, even if the secondary interpreter does side with one or other of several plausible historical explanations, it will remain open to the primary interpreter to make a different choice. The primary interpreter is charged with the task of declaring today's law, and may choose between competing plausible interpretations of legal history with a view to identifying that interpretation which presents the best legal interpretation of legal history from a modern legal perspective.

Conclusions: Canadian and Australian approaches to Aboriginal customs and imperial legal history

The interpretative models described above are deliberately abstract and artificial. In fact, judges shift back and forth between the empirical and normative interpretative perspectives, and they often blend primary and secondary interpretations of legal history. Most modern judges accept that an empirical reading of colonial and imperial legal history leads to conclusions that are, in today's light, unjust. Their responses, however, vary. In *Milirrpum*, Blackburn J. stated:

> If the approach is made to the question of the existence of a doctrine of communal native title, on the assumption that it may have been the law notwithstanding that no court applied or declared it, then it is reasonable to ask a question which is rather a historian's than a lawyer's question – 'Did people say or do anything which suggests that it was the

law?' To the lawyer the answer cannot be decisive whatever it is, but it need not be insignificant ... The problem is before the Court now, and can be dealt with as it ought to have been dealt with in, say, 1850, if it had arisen then.[28]

This statement represents a normative analysis from a primary perspective with a very strong secondary component. Blackburn J.'s conclusion, that it is impossible to say that the common law 'included, or now includes' a doctrine of native title in absence of executive or legislative recognition,[29] was overruled in *Mabo*, a case in which Brennan J. de-emphasized the secondary perspective and focused instead on the primary one (the common law can be 'modified to bring it into conformity with contemporary notions of justice and human rights').[30] While they accepted Brennan J.'s basic conclusion, that the common law *did* acknowledge native title upon the assertion of British sovereignty over Australia, Deane and Gaudron JJ. in *Mabo* premised their analysis on the assumption that there is no need to transpose backwards into common-law history modern moral and political values; in their view the conceptions of morality and justice that ought to have, and could have, informed judicial thinking during the relevant historical period also required respect for native customary law.[31] Their reinterpretation of the common law was therefore more squarely based upon a secondary view of the legal past, and may be more legally persuasive than Brennan J.'s as a result.

In Canada yet another approach may be observed. According to the 1996 *Van der Peet* case, Aboriginal customs are protected by section 35(1) of the Constitution Act 1982 if they originated in customs that were followed by their ancestors prior to contact with Europeans and are integral to their distinctive Aboriginal cultures.[32] This test was not developed through a normative analysis of common-law history at all, but was derived from first principles on the assumption that to require that modern Aboriginal rights have some historical legal status would be 'static and retrospective' and would 'perpetuat[e] the historical injustice' suffered by Aboriginal peoples at the hands of colonizers.[33] In short, the Supreme Court of Canada adopts an *empirical* reading of colonial and imperial legal history and concludes that it generally denied or restricted Aboriginal rights, but instead of subjecting the empirical legal data to a *normative* (re)interpretation, from either a *primary* or a *secondary* perspective, to determine if the common law as properly interpreted recognized a broader range of customs, the court concludes that the legal past is irredeemable and constructs a new basis for the recognition of Aboriginal customs that is not contingent on the idea that they gained a common-law foothold historically. Ironically, the effect of the new test is to narrow the range of common-law

Aboriginal customs that would have been recognized under a normative reading of the common-law past.

The common law is a discursive method that is simultaneously forward- and backward-looking, and the resolution of some modern legal problems requires attention to the state of the law in the past, and occasionally the best legal interpretation of that history is one that is informed by an appreciation of relevant historical interpretations of law. The common-law doctrine of Aboriginal rights is arguably one such case. It was not the purpose of this paper to suggest that Aboriginal claims today must have some historical legal foundation. In the end, there may be very compelling reasons for deciding to jettison the imperial and colonial legal past altogether and start again to construct an acceptable legal framework for the accommodation of Aboriginal cultures and customs. Indeed, the spectacle of modern judges constructing hypothetical colonial judicial views about the status of Aboriginal customs in order to buttress modern Aboriginal claims may be offensive to Aboriginal peoples today. On the other hand, it may be regarded as important to Aboriginal peoples to demonstrate that even in terms of 'settler' law, as it ought to have been applied, their ancestors had certain legal rights and that the historical denial of these rights by officials was unlawful. The purpose of this exercise was not to resolve that debate; rather, the objective was merely to suggest how non-native legal and historical methodologies might be recast to explain the common-law continuity of Aboriginal customs in an internally coherent manner. Without some idea of the orthodox non-native common-law position of Aboriginal customary law, the necessary dialogue between native and non-native communities, not to mention judicial efforts to develop new theories of Aboriginal rights from 'first principles', will proceed on mistaken assumptions about the legal past. Of course, how non-native legal and historical methodologies will combine with Aboriginal conceptions of law and history to produce an appropriate 'intersocietal' legal theory of Aboriginal rights remains to be seen.

Notes

1 R. v. Van der Peet [1996] 2 SCR 507, p. 547 quoting Brian Slattery, 'The Legal Basis of Aboriginal Title', in Frank Cassidy (ed.), Aboriginal Title in British Columbia: Delgamuukw v. The Queen, (1992), pp. 120–1).
2 R. v. Van der Peet [1996] 2 SCR 507, p. 547.
3 See in general R.G. Collingwood, The Idea of History (Oxford, Oxford University Press, 1946) and Edward Hallett Carr, What Is History? (New York, Random House, Inc., 1961).
4 Canada, Royal Commission on Aboriginal Peoples, Final Report (Ottawa, 1996), vol. I: Looking Forward, Looking Back, ch. 3, 'Conceptions of History'.
5 Wik Peoples v. Queensland (1996) 141 ALR 129 (H.C.), p. 231.
6 R. v. Van der Peet [1996] 2 SCR. 507, pp. 641–3.

7   *Mabo v. Queensland [No. 2]* (1992) 107 ALR. 1, p. 61.
8   Section 35(1) of the Constitution Act 1982 (being Schedule B to the Canada Act 1982 (UK) c. 11) entrenches 'existing aboriginal and treaty rights'.
9   *R. v. Van der Peet* [1996] 2 SCR 507, pp. 641–3 (McLachlin J. in dissent, describing the majority judgment).
10 J.G.A. Pocock, *The Ancient Constitution and the Feudal Law: A Study of English Historical Thought in the Seventeenth Century* (Cambridge, Cambridge University Press, 1957).
11 *M'Alister (or Donoghue) v. Stevenson*, [1932] AC. 562.
12 *Ibid.*, p. 580.
13 Oliver Wendell Holmes, Jr, *The Common Law* (New York, Dover Publications, 1991), p. 1.
14 Continuity was denied in Australia (*MacDonald v. Levy* (1833) 1 Legge 39 (N.S.W.S.C.); *R. v. Jack Congo Murrell* (1836) 1 Legge 72 (N.S.W.S.C.); *Cooper v. Stuart* (1889) 14 App. Cas. 286 (P.C.)), but cases go both ways in Canada (*Sheldon v. Ramsay* (1852) 9 U.C.Q.B. 105; *Connolly v. Woolrich* (1867) 17 R.J.R.Q. 75 (Que. S.C.)) and in New Zealand (*The Queen v. Symonds* (1847) [1840–1932] N.Z.P.C.C. 387; *Wi Parata v. Bishop of Wellington* (1877) 3 N.Z. Jur. (N.S.) 72).
15 See, in general, Brian Slattery, *Ancestral Lands, Alien Laws: Judicial Perspectives on Aboriginal Title*, Studies in Aboriginal Rights, No. 2 (Saskatoon, University of Saskatchewan Native Law Centre, 1983), p. 1; Paul McHugh, *The Maori Magna Carta: New Zealand Law and the Treaty of Waitangi* (Oxford, Oxford University Press, 1991), ch. 4.
16 *Calvin's Case* (1608) 7 Co. Rep. 1a, p. 17b; *Blankard v. Galdy* (1693) 4 Mod. 215, pp. 225–6, Holt K.B. 341, p. 342; *Anon.* (1722) 2 P.Wms. 75; *Campbell v. Hall* (1774) Lofft 655, p. 741.
17 E.g. *Cooper v. Stuart* (1889) 14 App. Cas. 286 (P.C.), and other cases summarized in *Milirrpum v. Nabalco Pty Ltd* (1971), 17 FLR 141 (N.T.S.C.).
18 *Woolwich Equitable Building Society v. I.R.C.* [1993] AC 70, pp. 171–2.
19 *Kleinwort Benson Ltd v. Lincoln City Council* [1998] 4 All England Reports 513, *per* Lord Goff at 535.
20 *Ibid.*, *per* Lord Hoffmann at 554
21 David H. Flaherty, 'Writing Canadian Legal History', in D.H. Flaherty (ed.), *Essays in the History of Canadian Law* (Toronto, Osgoode Society, 1981), pp. 4–12.
22 W.S. Holdsworth, *The Historians of Anglo-American Law* (New York, Columbia University Press, 1928), pp. 4 and 7; S.F.S. Milsom, 'Introduction', in Sir F. Pollock and F.M. Maitland, *The History of English Law, Before the Time of Edward I*, 2nd edn re-issue (Cambridge, Cambridge University Pres, 1968), pp. lxxii–lxxiii.
23 See, in general, Ronald Dworkin, *Law's Empire* (Cambridge, MA, Harvard University Press, 1986).
24 These subsequent cases may be useful to the historian as historical interpretations, but not as empirical data: Holdsworth, *Historians of Anglo-American Law*, p. 28.
25 Mark D. Walters, '"The Golden Thread of Continuity": Aboriginal Customs at Common Law and Under the Constitution Act, 1982' (1999), 44 McGill L.J. 711.
26 Mark D. Walters, 'The Continuity of Aboriginal Customs and Government Under British Imperial Constitutional Law as Applied in Colonial Canada, 1760–1860', unpublished D.Phil. thesis, Oxford University, 1995, Part Two.
27 Desmond Sweeney, 'Australia's Forgotten Legal Pluralism: The Western Australian Experience under Governor Hutt', unpublished paper delivered at the Joint Conference of the Australian and New Zealand Law and History Society and the Canadian Law and Society Association, Melbourne, 3–5 July 1998.
28 *Milirrpum v. Nabalco Pty Ltd* (1971) 17 FLR 141 (N.T.S.C.), p. 255.
29 *Ibid.*, p. 244.
30 *Mabo v. Queensland [No. 2]* (1992) 107 ALR 1, p. 19.
31 *Ibid.*, p. 61.
32 *R. v. Van der Peet* [1996] 2 SCR 507, pp. 554–7.
33 *R. v. Côté* [1996] 3 SCR 139, p. 175. See also *R. v. Adams* [1996] 3 SCR 101.

CHAPTER NINE

The problem of Aboriginal evidence in early colonial New South Wales
Nancy E. Wright

For the first ninety years after colonization, indigenous people in New South Wales were unable to give evidence in court. Only after the Evidence Further Amendment Act 1876 provided for a witness to make a declaration in lieu of an oath was testimony by Aboriginal people readily admissible in courts of law in New South Wales. Prior to 1876 testimony by Aboriginal people who had not converted to Christianity was routinely declared inadmissible because Aboriginal belief systems did not include the concepts of a 'Supreme Being' or a 'power which can punish or reward after death'.[1] Both were assumed necessary by imperial courts for an oath to function as a means to deter perjury. Initiatives from within colonial Australia to amend this aspect of the law of evidence, during the decade 1839–49, commonly referred to the harsh reality of frontier justice. For example, in 1841, Benjamin Hurst, a missionary, advised Superintendent La Trobe that unless provision was made to admit Aboriginal testimony, 'I [do not] see how they can be protected, or how justice can be done to them'.[2] Similarly, the Aborigines' Protection Society, in a statement to the Marquis of Normanby in July 1839, explained that the Aboriginal people 'have to cope with some of the most cruel and atrocious of our species, who carry on their system of oppression with almost perfect immunity so long as the Evidence of Native Witnesses is excluded from Our Courts'.[3] Letters and petitions addressed to government officials repeatedly identified the exclusion from evidence of testimony by Aboriginal people as an impediment to their access to justice.

Nevertheless the customary function of an oath as a deterrent to perjury was, from 1838 to 1876, routinely cited as an obstacle to amending the law of evidence in order to admit Aborigines' testimony or to allow a declaration in lieu of an oath. During this same period of time, however, the law of evidence was amended to make parties to actions competent to give testimony. Popular consensus, according to an anonymous editorial in the *Sydney Morning Herald* on 20 May 1865, 'acknowledged that the duty of a court of justice is to use every means of ascertaining the truth, leaving the danger of perjury to be met by the terrors of the law' in such cases. Despite this kind of popular argument that supported the reform of the law of evidence, the Supreme Court quashed convictions which were based in whole or in part on Aborigines' testimony. Such cases identify a point of resistance to law reform prior to 1876. This paper examines proposals, from 1838 to 1876, to amend the law of evidence and case law addressing the law of evidence. In addition it indicates the value of sources which extend beyond the customary definition of 'legal literature' to the study of colonial Australian legal history.

From 1805 to 1849 the inadmissibility of testimony by Aboriginal people was repeatedly framed as an impediment to justice that could be resolved only by means of legislation. In 1805 Judge-Advocate Richard Atkins argued, according to British common law, that Aboriginal people were 'incapable' of appearing before a criminal court, in his words, 'as Criminals or as Evidences'.[4] First, according to Atkins, their testimony could not be accepted as evidence according to the existing law because 'the evidence of Persons not bound by any moral or religious Tye can never be considered or construed as legal evidence'.[5] Second, they could not (because of their ignorance either of the English language or of the law) 'when brought to Trial, plead Guilty or not Guilty to an indictment, the meaning and tendency of which they must be totally ignorant of'.[6] Atkins asserted that Aboriginal people were 'within the Pale of H.M. protection' because, from the moment of settlement, they became British subjects.[7] The tenor of his statements, however, makes clear that he had little concern for the fact that as a result of the law of evidence Aboriginal people were, in Bruce Kercher's words, 'subjects without enforceable rights'.[8]

This is the issue that needs to be addressed when evaluating the implications of cases which came before the Supreme Court of NSW before 1876, such as *R. v. Fitzpatrick and Colville* (1824), in which Forbes C.J. asserted that 'the best evidence' for the charge was not available because of the inadmissibility of testimony by an Aboriginal witness.[9] In this case Bullwaddy, an Aboriginal man, witnessed Fitzpatrick killing a shepherd named Bentley and reported that information to a constable.[10] Colville, who was also indicted but subsequently acquitted of the murder, and another man, Sears, offered corroborative testimony to the facts of the case. Nevertheless, the guilt of Fitzpatrick was, in the words of Forbes C.J., 'presumptive, and ... without taking into consideration his confession, it does not completely bring home the Guilt of Murder to his charge – the confession is qualified, by the affirming of the prisoner, that he killed the deceased ... by accident and without knowing at the time he had killed him'.[11] As a result, Forbes C.J. respited Fitzpatrick after his conviction for murder in order to allow Governor Brisbane to consider the case, in Forbes's words, 'divested [of] those restraints which the strict rules of evidence imposed upon the Court at the trial, and with that light which the evidence or statement of Bullwaddy will in all probability throw upon it'.[12] Brisbane reported to Forbes his decision, based upon Bullwaddy's testimony, against exercising the prerogative of mercy on Fitzpatrick's behalf: Bullwaddy, Brisbane recounted,

> gave a clear and distinct account of the murder of Bentley which removed every doubt in my mind of Fitzpatrick having committed a cool and deliberate murder on the unfortunate Bentley. This link in the chain of evidence I felt necessary to fortifying my mind as to the [guilt] of the Prisoner, which Bullwaddy's testimony has completely turned against him ... .[13]

The case of *R. v. Fitzpatrick and Colville* reveals that the testimony of an Aboriginal witness was, on occasion, not only taken into account but received as persuasive and credible in extrajudicial circumstances. This case demonstrates that responsible jurists and governors acted on their knowledge of the conditions of frontier justice in order to exercise legal reasoning and discretionary powers within the bounds of justice.[14] The admission of the testimony of Aboriginal witnesses in extrajudicial circumstances, however, did not construe it as legal evidence. Instead it was weighed as corroborating information upon the discretion of the governor in his capacity to exercise the royal prerogative of mercy. As a result it did nothing to implement and exercise the rights of Aboriginal people as British subjects.[15]

The inadmissibility of testimony by Aboriginal people asserted by the judge-advocate in 1805 was frequently addressed from 1838 to 1849 but remained unremedied by legislation in NSW. In 1839 Burton J. of the Supreme Court of NSW described the reasons why an Aborigine's testimony could be inadmissible more accurately than Atkins had: Burton J. specified that an Aborigine's testimony was inadmissible only 'where a proposed witness has been found ignorant of a Supreme Being and a future State'.[16] Burton J. acknowledged that this defect of the law could be remedied by means of an Act. Burton had drafted a Bill 'for the amelioration and protection of the Aboriginal Natives of this colony ...' in 1838 that made provision for all Aboriginal people to testify upon avowing to tell the truth.[17] It did, however, specify (as Milliss notes) that 'reasonable' objections could be made to the credibility of Aboriginal witnesses before admitting their testimony – a provision that extends beyond the customary responsibility of a jury to determine the credibility of a witness's testimony.[18] Burton's Draft Bill inaugurated the decade when the subject of the admissibility of Aborigines' testimony was most frequently addressed by jurists and legislators.

Within months of the trial of seven men involved in a massacre at Myall Creek, the NSW Legislative Council in 1839 passed An Act to allow the Aboriginal Natives of New South Wales to be received as Competent Witnesses in Criminal Cases.[19] Despite support for amending the law of evidence within the Colonial Office, the Act was disallowed by the colonial secretary on the advice of the law officers who objected that 'To admit in a Criminal case the evidence of a witness acknowledged to be ignorant of the existence of a God or a future state would be contrary to the principles of British jurisprudence'.[20] The fact that the Act did not specify the weight to be given to evidence admitted by a witness who could not take an oath was identified as a flaw that prevented its confirmation. Subsequently, in 1843, imperial legislation allowed unsworn evidence to be given by, in its words, 'Tribes of barbarous and uncivilized peoples, destitute of knowledge of God and religious belief'. However, this Act 'to authorize the Legislatures of certain of Her Majesty's Colonies to pass Laws for the Admission in certain cases, of unsworn Testimony in Civil and Criminal Proceedings'[21] did not lead to new statutes on evidence in NSW. Instead, as legal historian Alex Castles has noted, efforts by government officials to introduce legislation to that effect were obstructed: 'In 1844, the Council rejected a Bill supported by Governor Gipps on the admission of Aboriginal evidence.'[22]

The same obstructive response occurred in 1849 when 'the Council refused to adopt a proposed law along the lines of those already in force in the western colonies'.[23] The 1849 Bill which proposed to admit Aborigines' evidence in criminal proceedings, as the anthropologist A.P. Elkin has argued, was intended to prevent clashes between whites and Aborigines in marginal regions.[24] Such legislative efforts to reform one aspect of the law of evidence, described by Mr Justice Knox as the 'rule in all civilized countries that testimony in Courts of Justice should only be given by persons who made some appeal to the divinity',[25] were unsuccessful in NSW prior to the Evidence Act of 1876. According to section 3 of that Act, a judge could direct a witness by whom the obligation of an oath was not understood 'to tell the truth, the whole truth, and nothing but the truth'.

Yet important decisions based on the requirement of an oath were made by jurists in the 1870s prior to the amendment of the law. The requirement of an oath did not exclude all Aborigines from giving testimony in courts of law. In *R. v. Lewis* (1872) Stephen C.J. ruled that an

Aborigine was competent as a witness because he had knowledge of a God who would make him happy if he was good and punish him if he was wicked. The ruling established that it was unnecessary to inquire into the grounds of the witness's belief in his responsibility to a Supreme Being. If the belief existed, the witness's testimony was admissible. Such a ruling was not, however, universally applied. An understanding of the obligation of an oath was the criterion used to quash a conviction for murder in *R. v. Paddy* (1876). On appeal to the Supreme Court Sir James Martin C.J. rejected the evidence of two Aborigines who did not hold beliefs that satisfied the rule that 'a witness cannot give evidence on oath unless he believes in a future state of reward and punishment'. This decision in 1876 reiterates the opinion of the judge-advocate in 1805.

Discussion of English reform after 1849

What the preceding brief survey reveals is the failure, during the decade 1839–49, of legislative efforts to amend the rule of evidence requiring a witness to be competent to take an oath. Subsequently the subject largely lapsed in NSW legislation until it re-emerged successfully in 1876. Significant in this re-emergence were discussions of English law reform and case law brought to the attention of the public in NSW newspapers.

Law reform undertaken in the 1860s in order to rationalize the law of evidence was well received in colonial New South Wales. An article entitled 'The Law of Evidence' printed in the *Sydney Mail* on 20 May 1865, when three Bills for the reform of the law of evidence were before the House of Commons, drew to readers' attention how impediments to justice had previously been remedied:

> Under the old practice, two maxims had ingrained themselves into the whole system of procedure. One was, that none but thoroughly disinterested testimony should be listened to; the other, that no man should be compelled to criminate himself. The first maxim excluded not only persons under accusation in criminal or quasi-criminal investigations, but every party to a civil suit, and every witness who had the remotest pecuniary interest in the question ... [But] it shut out in most cases the evidence of those who were best acquainted with the facts, and in many cases caused a total failure of justice. The one argument in its favour was, that it saved courts of justice, to a certain extent, from the scandal of frequent perjury. By successive steps, Lord Denman and Lord Brougham succeeded in demolishing the old principle, and it is now acknowledged that the duty of a court of justice is to use every means of ascertaining the truth, leaving the danger of perjury to be met by the terrors of the law.

The editorial argued that changes to the law of evidence needed to be continued, in particular by enabling one accused of adultery to testify on her or his own behalf in divorce proceedings. The predicament of an innocent man unjustly accused, the author argued, in any rational evaluation of the law of evidence, should outweigh the emphasis that, according to custom, was placed on the possibility of perjury. Where was the logic, the author asked, in assuming that 'the temptation to perjury would be so great that it would be better to let justice halt for want of evidence than to put a witness into the box who might be induced to ... falsehood'.[26]

The drive to reform rules of law that excluded statements of some witnesses from evidence, so forcefully expressed in this article in the *Sydney Mail*, did not recall to the writer or legislators the subject of Aboriginal witnesses that had drawn comment in preceding decades. When commenting on *R. v. Fitzpatrick and Colville* (1824), four decades earlier, Forbes C.J. argued that 'interest' was a more valid criterion than an oath to determine the admissibility of testimony. Forbes C.J., who considered Bullwaddy's testimony crucial to a decision against granting a reprieve, identified 'several defects' in legislation about the law of evidence; in particular, when considering the rule that excluded the testimony of a witness who could not take an oath, he proposed: 'Why is not competency confined to interest, and credibility left in all cases to the jury?'[27] In England by 1865 legal reform set aside 'interest' as a criterion of a witness's competence, the factor that decades previously had seemed to Forbes C.J. a more valid reason for excluding testimony from evidence than an inability to take a judicial oath. The fact that the inadmissibility of Aborigines' testimony did not draw comment in discussion of other reforms of the law of evidence in the 1860s is surprising, as I will explain next, because the argument that the exclusion of testimony by Aboriginal witnesses was an impediment to the Crown's prosecution of the celebrated murder case *R. v. Wilkes* was kept alive in newspapers long after the case had been decided in 1858. In fact the press now played a major role in securing reform.

The Wilkes case

Sydney newspapers kept the issue of reform before the public with reports of the Wilkes trial, outraged editorials about a delayed announcement to the prisoner of his reprieve and reports of angry debates in the Legislative Assembly. Although Wilkes was brought to trial for the murder of his eldest son, the press informed the public that his wife and another young son had also been killed. The *Sydney Morning Herald* on 20 April 1858 recounted all the details of what they

described as the 'very extraordinary circumstances connected with the
fearful tragedy ... [in] which the death of the young lad Wilkes forms
but a melancholy incident':

> In the month of March or April, 1855, the wife and two sons of the
> prisoner, a shepherd, who was then residing at a place called Deep Creek,
> near Casino, were foully and most mysteriously murdered ... He was
> confined in the lock-up; and, after some weeks' incarceration, he charged
> a person of the name of Lynch with the murder of his family, having
> received, as he said, an intimation of the fact in a vision, in which his
> wife and children assured him that Lynch was their murderer. The
> person was arrested, but not a tittle of evidence could be adduced against
> him, and he was discharged ... He was more than once arrested and set
> at liberty for want of evidence to sustain a case against him; so reckless
> did he become under the impression that he had nothing to fear from
> human interference, that he even petitioned the Legislative Assembly to
> be indemnified for the injury he had sustained in the loss of property,
> alleged by him to have been stolen by the murderers of his family. The
> matter was referred to a select committee, and Wilkes was examined, but
> his evidence was so full of glaring inconsistencies and contradictions
> of former statements, that suspicion stronger than ever fell upon him as
> the perpetrator of the atrocities he sought to convict another of ... [T]he
> Government have succeeded, after great delay and expense, in obtaining
> such additional evidence as to justify them in putting Wilkes finally
> upon his trial.

Reports of the trial in the *Sydney Morning Herald* and *The Empire* on
23 April, when Wilkes was pronounced guilty, share all the characteristics of broadside ballads and other popular genres concerning
murders. On 28 April *The Empire* ran an editorial that, in order to
advance an argument against capital punishment, criticized the
reliance of the prosecution upon circumstantial evidence:

> The murderer generally endeavours to evade detection and punishment
> by committing his awful crime in secret. Nothing but an inference from
> circumstances amounting to a presumption of guilt is available to bring
> him to justice. To require direct evidence against him would, in most
> cases, amount to a guarantee of im[m]unity. A conviction, therefore,
> must in the nature of things depend upon a chain of circumstances reach-
> ing from the crime committed to the person accused. And this chain has
> sometimes appeared to be so strong and complete as to justify the saying,
> that circumstantial evidence is better than positive proof.

But the chain can have defective links, wrote the editors of *The Empire:*

> These are supplied by the logical subtlety of the prosecuting counsel in
> conjunction with the imagination of the jury, the abhorrent character of
> the accusation, and the suspicious position of the presumed criminal at

the bar. A bias unfavourable to the prisoner is thus produced in the strongest minds, while the less reflecting ... feel disposed to hurry him at once from the dock to the scaffold. ...

It was necessary, therefore, continued the editorial, 'to pause before we execute the terrible sentence of death' for '[i]f a mistake is committed ... it is a mistake which admits of no rectification, and which makes the avengers of murder the worst of murderers themselves'. These considerations, concluded *The Empire*, furnished the 'strongest of all reasons for the abolition of capital punishments'.

This theme – that circumstantial evidence was not sufficient to satisfy the standard of proof – was taken up in the Legislative Assembly after Wilkes was granted his reprieve on 2 June. Debates in the Assembly on 5 June ostensibly addressed the delay with which the reprieve was communicated rather than the exercise of the royal prerogative of mercy on Wilkes's behalf. Many members articulated their reprehension of those responsible for 'torturing' Wilkes by postponing an announcement of the reprieve in order, they assumed, to extract a confession of his guilt from the condemned man. Debate, however, directed attention repeatedly to questions of evidence first raised in *The Empire*'s editorial.

Mr Faucett addressed 'the value of circumstantial evidence':

[He] believed that no evidence could be more conclusive than this, and none bring home guilt more conclusively to the perpetrator than this would do. Let it be remembered that there must be laid before the courts and jury a train of circumstances, not merely consistent with the guilt of the accused, but utterly inconsistent with his innocence of the crime, and they would at once appreciate its value, and say that not even direct evidence could be better or more conclusive. In the case of direct evidence, for instance, a man might swear that he saw a murder committed, but the evidence resting upon the testimony of one person, a doubt might be cast upon it and he might not be believed; whereas in the case of circumstantial evidence they had a number of persons deposing to a series of connected facts, that left no possibility of mistake or doubt, or of unbelief.[28]

Mr Hay intervened to clarify the function of circumstantial evidence:

Circumstantial evidence was quite as good as any direct evidence, and it was quite consistent with the observations of all the most eminent men of the law that such evidence was more valuable than any other. If they were never to carry out the extreme penalty of the law, except in cases where the evidence was direct, then the very worst class of criminals would escape; for, whilst they who committed murders, that verged almost upon manslaughter, in the presence of a witness, would suffer death, they who planned their murders in cold blood, and executed them only at times when no human eye could behold them, would go free and scatheless.[29]

These extracts indicate clear concern about the law of evidence, particularly the relation of circumstantial evidence to the standard of proof and the exercise of legal reasoning. These aspects of the law of evidence continued to circulate in a column in the *Sydney Morning Herald* on 7 June. A column titled 'Notes of the Week' commented on two matters: the assertion that 'we *have* seen men acquitted when the chain of circumstances appeared fully as strong' as in the Wilkes case, and that this 'sudden reprieve has caused a great sensation'. This article commenting on debate in the Legislative Assembly described as erroneous some conclusions drawn about circumstantial evidence and advocated protecting the royal prerogative of mercy.[30] Like other articles commenting on the trial, this editorial juxtaposed discussion of the legal reasoning, based on circumstantial evidence, with sensationalized accounts of Wilkes's reprieve.

This dichotomy of reason and sensation was addressed in an entirely different manner in Charles De Boos's writings about *R. v. Wilkes* (1858) in the 1860s. De Boos was the parliamentary reporter for the *Sydney Morning Herald* when the Legislative Assembly discussed Wilkes's reprieve and the nature of the evidence against him. De Boos, however, did not return to the debates or the reports and editorials about the trial in his writings about the Wilkes case. Instead he turned to the report of the Select Committee of Inquiry that had first brought Wilkes under scrutiny. The investigation of Wilkes for murdering his son was recorded in a 'Blue Book' produced by the Government Printer in 1857.[31] The *Second Progress Report from The Select Committee on 'Administration of Justice and Conduct of Official Business in Country Districts'*[32] is an example of a standard Blue Book, a government publication that included administrative reports and the proceedings of the legislative and executive bodies. This Select Committee of Inquiry, as the Blue Book documents, heard the petition of Wilkes relating to an accusation of police incompetence. Wilkes filed this petition in order, he claimed, to secure redress of specific grievances resulting from the investigation of the murder of his wife and two of his children. His testimony and the circumstantial evidence, however, in due course made the Select Committee suspect Wilkes of the crime. The Select Committee learned that mysterious and unsolved murders had occurred previously where Wilkes had lived; in fact, Wilkes was implicated in three unsolved murders and in the deaths of his two daughters by poisoning. Investigation of his responsibility for his daughters' deaths had been initiated by police, but Wilkes was not tried. The Select Committee's report recommended the further investigation of Wilkes that resulted in his conviction for the murder of one of his sons.[33]

The report of the Select Committee in 1857 became the basis of two further works by Charles De Boos. The historical novel *Fifty Years Ago: An Australian Tale* included plots and characters that adapted the circumstances of Wilkes's murderous acts. Gordon & Gotch, Sydney, published that novel, first in a series of fourteen pamphlets, then as a single volume in 1867. Subsequently, *Fifty Years Ago* was serialized by the *Australian Journal*, Melbourne, from April 1869 to February 1870 before being published in 1906 by the NSW Bookstall Company in a posthumously revised and abridged edition titled *Settlers and Savages*.[34] Prior to the serialization of *Fifty Years Ago*, De Boos 'revisited' the scene of Wilkes's crimes in a true-crime serial, titled *The Romance of the Blue Books: Pursued by Fate*, published by the *Sydney Mail* from 30 May to 4 July 1868. De Boos's dissemination of information about the Wilkes case from the official publication produced by the Government Printer provides insight into ideas about the law of evidence circulating widely in NSW in the 1860s.

The testimony given by Wilkes before the Select Committee in 1857, De Boos astutely recognized, contained subject matter well suited to literature. And, perhaps, this should not seem surprising when one considers the extensive writing about the relation of literature and law, particularly the law of evidence, in the nineteenth century. 'In the history of the common law', Alexander Welsh has explained, 'rules of evidence and treatises on the subject burgeoned in the later eighteenth century when, for one thing, the sharp increase in the number of published law reports made modern adjectival law possible'.[35] Jeremy Bentham and, later, James Fitzjames Stephen, among others, used narrative or the metaphor of a narrative 'chain of circumstances' as the model of reasoning from effect to cause when evaluating direct and indirect evidence. In his *Rationale of Evidence*, first printed in 1827, Bentham addressed 'the relationship between the world of fact, the world of fiction and our modes of apprehending both; [and] the institution of the oath as an instrument and as a symbol of both coercion and abuse of power by the forces of unreason …'.[36] These issues, illustrated by Wilkes's statements to the Select Committee and other direct evidence deemed inadmissible at his subsequent trial, were themes of De Boos's narratives.

In the original 1857 report of the Select Committee, Wilkes's assertions strike the reader as a well-crafted yarn and, on occasion, as a tall tale. When examined on 22 January by the Select Committee, he stated to the members what he had previously communicated to his gaolers in a written statement – that he had seen and conversed with his dead wife and children while in gaol. Wilkes asserted to the chairman that 'my wife and four children appeared to me on that night, in company

of an assembly of angels' to reveal their murderer's name and to excul-
pate Wilkes.[37] The Select Committee, not surprisingly, focused on the
probability and credibility of Wilkes's assertions. The content of the
report investigating Wilkes's petition, printed in 1857, led to Wilkes's
indictment for the murder of one of his sons.

There was a market in England for a sensationalist novel based on
the story of Wilkes and the murders he had committed. De Boos's treatment of the subject, however, entirely departed from the norms of sensationalism in order to address the subjects of frontier justice and the
need to reform the law of evidence – subjects that concerned legislators
in NSW from 1839 to 1849. The theme that binds the four books of
Fifty Years Ago together is the need to renounce a code of revenge that
had been used to rectify wrongs in the colony around the first decade
of the nineteenth century. The narrative showed how the developing
role of the colonial police and the law made it necessary to foreswear
vengeance in order to secure justice. The circumstances of the murder
of Wilkes's wife and children, recounted in the *Second Progress Report
of the Select Committee*, provide the framing tale of *Fifty Years Ago*,
with one significant exception. Whereas Wilkes, who blamed alter-
nately another shepherd and some Aborigines, had, in fact, murdered
his family, in De Boos's novel, George Maxwell, the father, is innocent.
George and his surviving son swear to avenge their family. Each of the
four books comprising the novel provides another illustration of how
vengeance circumvents, rather than implements, justice.

The law of evidence is also addressed in the third book of the novel
in which a murder is not resolved because the authorities cannot admit
the testimony of some Aborigines. This plot alludes to a defect in the
system of justice in colonial Australia illustrated by the Wilkes case.
The *Second Progress Report of the Select Committee* noted that direct
evidence implicating Wilkes was inadmissible because the Aborigines
who witnessed Wilkes threatening his wife were unable to take an oath
and, as a result, were unable to offer relevant testimony in a court of
law. The local magistrate had explained that a translator had taken an
oath in order to report the testimony of some Aborigines who had
intervened, the day prior to the murder, when they witnessed Wilkes
threatening his wife with an axe. This information, the police magistrate acknowledged to the Select Committee, although corroborated by
circumstantial evidence, could not be recorded as evidence.[38] De Boos
refers to this information in order to address the consequences of a
judicial oath as the criterion for the admissibility of testimony and the
need for law reform.

The rule that excluded Aborigines as witnesses, De Boos noted, had
nothing to do with their knowledge, reliability or competence. De Boos

questioned the emphasis placed on an oath as a means to deter perjury in a manner similar to Bentham and James Fitzjames Stephen, who argued that 'a consideration of the degree to which circumstances corroborate each other, and of the intrinsic probability of the matter sworn to, is a far better test of truth than any oath can possibly be'.[39] The results of this defect in the law of evidence were emphasized in De Boos's true-crime serial *Pursued by Fate*, which accurately explained that Wilkes had previously escaped conviction for the murder of his daughters because of similar rules. In both of the works based on the Wilkes case, De Boos explained to his readers the law of evidence in relation to questions of law and questions of fact. This is most evident when the authorial narrator of *Pursued by Fate* asks the reader to consider Wilkes's motives for narrating such a religious tale and confirming it when being examined by the Select Committee.

The narrator insists that readers take into account the effects of narratives told by a petitioner before a Select Committee and a witness in a court of law. He asks readers to consider one response that Wilkes might have intended to produce by narrating his vision. As a result of Wilkes's vision, the narrator advised, a reader might easily, but mistakenly, assume that 'A man like this could hardly be the murderer of his wife and children – I mean a man who could write in so religious a spirit. One would think not'.[40] In order to expose Wilkes's intentions, De Boos comments directly upon the effects produced by the narrative. He reveals the fallibility of the assumption that religious belief – belief in a Supreme Being and an afterlife – will ensure truthfulness or prevent perjury. De Boos encourages his readers to appreciate that religious belief did not prevent Wilkes from attempting to deceive the Select Committee and for that reason, by analogy, religious belief should not be the criterion of a witness's competence.

In addition, De Boos advises the reader about evaluating the credibility and probability of narratives that cannot be confirmed by circumstantial evidence. The narrator functions like a judge who, Twining explains in *Theories of Evidence*, in Bentham's analysis of evidence 'is to assess the probative force of the relevant evidence in terms of the degree of persuasion that it produces in his mind'.[41] When De Boos includes a sensational passage of Wilkes's testimony, such as the vision, he frames the murderer's statement with circumstantial evidence and thereby requires the reader to judge whether circumstances corroborate the witness's statements. Rather than evoking the sensationalism of the testimony reported in the 1857 Blue Book, De Boos inquires dispassionately into motivation, circumstances and probability. He conducts his narrative in a manner similar to that of many nineteenth-century prosecutors and judges who, Alexander Welsh explains, theorized 'for the jury about probability and drawing inferences'.[42] De Boos asked his readers to examine critically the role of narrative in constructing the semblance of truth. He approaches this topic indirectly by casting himself in the role of the reader rather than that of the author. He explains that he had recently been searching through an old volume of the *Votes and Proceedings of New South Wales*

> for traces of a political matter which at that time engrossed public attention [i.e. the Wilkes case]. In turning over the leaves, a passage in print accidentally caught my eye. I read that passage as well as several others which followed. I became interested, and read on and on until I made myself acquainted with the whole circumstances of the case detailed. The whole thing seemed to me so extraordinary that I could not rest satisfied until I had followed the matter up to its ending ... I think the story will be found interesting. I am sure it has a moral, which I would wish to be better recognised than it is.[43]

It is important to appreciate that De Boos did not indulge in the moralizing sentiments of popular evangelical literature. Instead the 'moral' or lesson to which he directs attention concerns the law – that is, how the law of evidence should guide a reader's evaluation of a narrative, such as a witness's testimony. The narrator's insistence upon the importance of the reader viewing 'the whole circumstances of the case' recalls Bentham's arguments about the relative value of circumstantial evidence and testimony. Bentham, Welsh notes, 'posits that circumstantial evidence has the important capacity to assimilate "a mixture of truth and falsehood" from direct testimony or partial confession'.[44] Although circumstantial evidence could be the means to establish a 'particular truth' from a falsehood, Bentham also commented on its function 'when the whole narrative is viewed together, in a general point of view'.[45] The authorial narrator's commentary in *Pursued by Fate* assigns as the role of the reader the task of judging probability and exercising judgment, tasks relevant to the weighing of evidence.

Conclusion

De Boos's works alluding to *R. v. Wilkes* (1858) indicate his knowledge of utilitarian and legislative arguments about reform of the law of evidence. His narratives written in the 1860s, unlike parliamentary reports about the Wilkes case in the 1850s, enabled him to function as a popular agent of the law who disseminated information about the law of evidence and utilitarian arguments for its reform, issues that had lapsed from legislators' attention. His writings based on the Wilkes case invoke the arguments of legislators from 1838 to 1849 who addressed the subject of the inadmissibility of testimony by Aborigines as a defect in the law of evidence and the administration of justice in the colony. The coincidence of the conclusions reached by De Boos in the 1860s with those of legislators in the 1840s identifies the intervening decade as the period in which the inadmissibility of Aborigines' testimony lapsed as a subject of popular and legislative discussion. Paul Tennant's assertion (made in reference to Canada) is also true of New South Wales: 'public concern in Britain over the treatment of aboriginal peoples was declining'[46] in the 1850s – a fact reflected in both colonies by the silence of legislators and reform groups, such as the Aborigines' Protection Society, on the subject of law reform necessary to admit Aborigines' testimony as evidence. The *Second Progress Report of the Select Committee* in 1857 took note of the inadmissibility of direct testimony by Aborigines but did not make a recommendation on the subject. This omission characterizes not simply the attitudes of the liberal members of the Government who served on the Select Committee but those of other members of the Government who failed to raise the subject in the Legislative Assembly, when discussing the circumstantial evidence used to convict Wilkes. De Boos, in addressing this subject of Aborigines' testimony in his two works published in the late 1860s, acted as a popular agent advocating law reform. Through Sydney newspapers, De Boos revived the subject of law reform for a wide, popular readership and, through the power of narrative, contributed to the legislative reform which was finally achieved in 1867. De Boos's writings, both his fictionalized account of the Wilkes case in the novel *Fifty Years Ago* and his true-crime serial *Pursued by Fate*, complement more conventional sources for the study of the legal history of colonial NSW.

Notes

1 Sir James Martin C.J., *The Queen* v. *Paddy* (1876), 14 SCR (NSW) 440.
2 Hurst to La Trobe, 22 July 1841, Bonwick Transcripts, Box 54, Mitchell Library Sydney (hereafter ML).
3 *Historical Records of Australia* (hereafter *HRA*), Ser. I, vol. 20, p. 304.
4 'Judge-Advocate Atkins' Opinion on the Treatment of Natives', *HRA*, Ser. I, vol. 5, p. 504. See Alex C. Castles, *An Australian Legal History* (Sydney, Law Book Company, 1982), pp. 532–3.
5 'Judge-Advocate Atkins' Opinion', p. 502.
6 *Ibid.*, p. 503.
7 *Ibid.* Bruce Kercher, *Debt, Seduction and Other Disasters: The Birth of Civil Law in Convict New South Wales* (Sydney, Federation Press, 1996), p. 86, explains that the doctrine of *terra nullius* meant Aborigines should have been able to enforce their rights in the colony's Court of Civil Jurisdiction.
8 Bruce Kercher, *An Unruly Child: A History of Law in Australia* (Sydney, Allen & Unwin, 1995), p. 17.
9 Forbes C.J. to Governor Brisbane, 24 June 1824, Chief Justice's Letter Book, Archives Office of New South Wales, 4/6651, p. 1. All quotations from the case of *R. v. Fitz-*

patrick and Colville and from correspondence regarding it are cited from Bruce Kercher, *Decisions of the Superior Courts of New South Wales, 1788–1899* (Sydney, Division of Law, Macquarie University, 1999). Available at: www.law.mq.edu.au/scnsw

10 See the report of the case in the *Sydney Gazette*, 24 June 1824.

11 Forbes C.J. to Governor Brisbane, 24 June 1824, Chief Justice's Letter Book, Archives Office of New South Wales, 4/6651, p. 1.

12 Forbes C.J. to Governor Brisbane, *ibid.*

13 Brisbane to Forbes, 24 June 1824, Archives Office of New South Wales, 4/6651, p. 2.

14 Forbes in relation to this case questioned the wisdom of one of the icons of the common law tradition, Coke. Forbes to Wilmot Horton, 14 August 1824 (Catton Papers, Australian Joint Copying Project (hereafter AJCP), reel M791). *Ibid.*

15 Saxe Bannister, attorney general, just two months prior to *R.* v. *Fitzpatrick and Colville* coming before Forbes C.J., wrote to the Colonial Office to recommend that an Act of Parliament be drawn up to remedy the fact that Aborigines were denied justice because they could not take an oath. See 'Bannister to Under Secretary Horton, 16 August 1824', *HRA*, Ser. IV, vol. 1, pp. 554–5. John Ferry, 'An Examination of the Various Aboriginal Evidence Bills of New South Wales, South Australia and Western Australia in the Period 1839–1849 as well as an Analysis of the Racial Attitudes which Were Espoused During the Controversies', unpublished BA Honours thesis, University of New England, 1980, p. 10.

16 'Burton to Labouchere, 17 August 1839', *HRA*, Ser. I, vol. 20, p. 305.

17 Ferry 'An Examination', pp. 80–1.

18 See Burton, Draft Bill 'for the amelioration and protection of the Aboriginal Natives of this Colony ...', EC Minutes and Memoranda 1838 (1), which he forwarded to Governor Gipps who did not proceed further with it. See Roger Milliss, *Waterloo Creek: The Australia Day Massacre of 1838, George Gipps and the British Conquest of New South Wales* (Sydney, University of NSW, 1994), p. 261 and p. 825 n.69.

19 For the original Bill and debate on the Bill, see *Sydney Morning Herald*, 13 and 20 September 1839. See also Milliss, *Waterloo Creek*, p. 686; and Castles, *Australian Legal History*, p. 533, who explains that the NSW Act (3 Vic. No. 16) specified that Aborigines would be permitted to give evidence with the making of affirmations rather than on oath.

20 'Campbell and Wilde to Russell', 27 July 1840, *HRA*, Ser. I, vol. 20, p. 756; Ferry, 'An Examination', p. 101; Minute of James Stephen to Lord John Russell, 9 September 1840, written on despatch of George Grey to Lord John Russell, 4 June 1840, c.o. 201/304 (AJCP, reel 330), f. 245, and Minute of James Stephen to Lord John Russell, 8 April 1841, written on despatch of Hutt to Russell, 19 August 1840, c.o. 18/25 (AJCP, reel 428), ff. 289–92.

21 6 and 7 Vic. xxii.

22 Castles, *Australian Legal History*, p. 535

23 *Ibid.*

24 A.P. Elkin, 'Aboriginal Evidence and Justice in North Australia,' *Oceania*, 17:3 (1947), 191. Cf. Milliss, *Waterloo Creek*, pp. 724–5, and Ferry, 'An Examination', pp. 125–6.

25 In *R.* v. *Lewis*, NSW Supreme Court, F.C. *The Australian Digest, 1825–1933*, vol. 8, col. 161.

26 *Sydney Mail*, 20 May 1865.

27 Forbes to Wilmot Horton, 14 August 1824 (Catton Papers, AJCP, reel M791), quoted from Kercher's annotation of *R.* v. *Fitzpatrick and Colville* (1824).

28 'Legislative Assembly', *Sydney Morning Herald*, 5 June 1858.

29 *Ibid.*

30 'Notes of the Week, Saturday, 5th June 1858': *Sydney Morning Herald*, 7 June 1858. This column was reprinted on 10 June 1858.

31 See R.B. Pugh, *The Records of the Colonial and Dominions Offices* (London, HMSO, 1964), pp. 40–3, on specifications established by the Colonial Office for Blue Books.

32 This Blue Book is indexed in D.H. Borchardt, ed., *Checklist of Royal Commissions,*

Select Committees of Parliament and Boards of Inquiry, Part IV: *New South Wales 1855–1960*, La Trobe University Library Publications No. 7 (Melbourne, La Trobe University, 1975), p. 6.

33 *Second Progress Report of the Select Commitee*, pp. 16, 28–9 and 34.

34 On *Settlers and Savages* see J.J. Healy, 'The Treatment of the Aborigine in Early Australian Fiction, 1840–1870', *Australian Literary Studies*, 5 (1972), 233–53.

35 Alexander Welsh, *Strong Representations: Narrative and Circumstantial Evidence in England* (Baltimore, MD, Johns Hopkins University Press, 1992), pp. 10–11.

36 William Twining, *Theories of Evidence: Bentham and Wigmore* (London, Weidenfeld & Nicolson, 1985), p. 19.

37 *Second Progress Report*, p. 27

38 *Ibid.*, p. 23.

39 James Fitzjames Stephen, *A History of the Criminal Law of England*, 3 vols (New York, Franklin, [1883] 1964), vol. 1, p. 401.

40 'Pursued by Fate', *Sydney Mail*, 13 June 1868.

41 Twining, *Theories of Evidence*, p. 53.

42 Welsh, *Strong Representations*, p. 25.

43 'Pursued by Fate', *Sydney Mail*, 30 May 1868.

44 Welsh, *Strong Representations*, p. 39.

45 Jeremy Bentham, *Rationale of Judicial Evidence*, ed. J.S. Mill, 5 vols (London, Hunt & Clarke, 1827), vol. 3, pp. 9–10.

46 Paul Tennant, 'Aboriginal Rights and the Canadian Legal System: The West Coast Anomaly', in John McLaren, Hamar Foster and Chet Orloff (eds), *Law for the Elephant, Law for the Beaver: Essays in the Legal History of the North American West* (Regina, Canadian Plains Research Centre, University of Regina, 1992), p. 109.

CHAPTER TEN

Assuming judicial control:
George Brown's narrative defence of the
'New Britain raid'

Helen Gardner

Colonization was not a simple inevitable force in the Pacific Islands in the nineteenth century. In many cases the establishment of imperial power over a region was debated by Europeans with links to an island group – traders, missionaries, scientists and administrators. In these debates the narratives of imperial control mingled with calls for the recognition of indigenous rights and land ownership. Missionaries in the nineteenth century had a particularly complex relationship to colonization. While many laboured in as yet uncolonized lands, they often did so in a milieu fraught by hostilities between settlers, traders, explorers and Islanders. In the latter part of the nineteenth century missionaries in the Pacific frequently courted imperial intervention despite some reluctance to intervene in affairs of the state.[1]

One missionary stepped well beyond the boundaries of his spiritual jurisdiction to assume judicial control over the heathen Islanders to whom he was ministering. In 1878, while establishing a Methodist mission on the islands of the Bismarck Archipelago off mainland Papua New Guinea, George Brown orchestrated an attack on a number of villages whose inhabitants had participated in the killing and consumption of four mission teachers. There were no deaths among the expeditionary force, but there were heavy losses among the villagers deemed guilty of the crime. Brown's first reports to his father-in-law in New Zealand cited 80–100 deaths.[2] In his journal, Brown wrote that one village leader, or 'big man', reported forty-seven dead from his district alone, some of whom had been killed outright while others died as a result of their wounds.[3] These figures were significantly revised by Brown in his autobiography, where he claimed that no more than ten people died, though the death toll was unconfirmed and remained a disputed point in the debate.

The raid was an unprecedented event in the history of evangelical missions in the Pacific and caused great controversy among colonial

Christians. Forced to respond to an act that was both unchristian and illegal, Methodists in the Australian colonies debated the actions based on the primary version of the events, which was Brown's published account. In Methodist debates and in Brown's account, Islanders were portrayed as 'savage' and uncontrollable, a characterization more commonly found in popular depictions of indigenous people. Debates over Brown's raid centred on 'native' morality and 'native' law and the rights of missionaries over the people in their mission fields. While other Europeans could demand the right to free passage in uncolonized lands and the right to defend person and property in the face of 'native' attack, this did not automatically extend to the missionary. Many people in the colonies held that Brown had acted improperly.

Rarely have the boundaries between Christian mission and imperial power been as blurred as they were in Brown's attack on Tolai villages in 1878.[4] The actions occurred under the uncertain jurisdiction of early colonial law in the Bismarck Archipelago, six years prior to the formal annexation of the region by Germany. Legally, Brown was answerable to the High Commissioner of the Western Pacific, Arthur G. Gordon, who was also the governor of Fiji. Gordon was empowered by the Western Pacific Order in Council to try civil and criminal matters and deport British subjects (only) from one part of the Pacific to another. This order had been enacted in 1877, largely to control the labour trade then supplying workers for plantations in Fiji and Queensland. The act covered most of the Micronesian islands, the Solomon Islands, the Bismarck Archipelago and 'all other islands in the Western Pacific not being ... within the jurisdiction of any civilised power'.[5] Nearly eighteen months after the raid Brown was charged with manslaughter by the Gordon administration in Fiji, although the charges were eventually dropped over a conflict of juridical administration.

During May and June of 1878 Brown locked himself in his study at Port Hunter on the Duke of York Islands and wrote letters to many of his colleagues detailing his response to the deaths of the teachers. The version that Brown wrote to his superior, Benjamin Chapman, for publication was a compelling narrative defending his actions. After writing his account of the events Brown acknowledged to his father-in-law in New Zealand that he had greatly exceeded his brief as a missionary and that he must 'be properly under judicial investigation and for that I am quite prepared now'.[6]

The correlation between narrative and power has been the subject of some recent academic discussion. White suggests that by describing events in a narrative, actions are retrospectively shaped to a particular 'politicosocial order'.[7] In relation to colonization, Said argues that the representation of events is in itself an act of power: 'The capacity to represent, portray, characterise, and depict is not easily available to just any member of just any society; moreover, the "what" and 'how' in the representation of "things", while allowing for considerable individual freedom, are circumscribed and socially regulated.[8] Brown was not explicit in his claim for judicial authority in his letter for publication; this was assumed and implied thorough the plotting of the events as a tale of crime and punishment.[9] His narrative defended his raid through a particularly harsh characterization of those villagers decreed guilty. In a distinct shift from many of Brown's other texts, in which Islanders were portrayed as intelligent moral beings, those who killed the teachers were depicted as unbounded savages who were pacified purely as a result of Brown's intervention.

The following extracts from Brown's narrative of events have been taken from the letter to Benjamin Chapman that was subsequently published in Methodist weeklies and the *Sydney Morning Herald*.[10] Following a preamble on the good effects of the raid, the tale opens in Brown's study:

> On April 8th ... as I was sitting in the study at night ... a native came to the window and said 'I have just heard that the New Britain natives have murdered Sailasa and some teachers.' ... I felt assured there was some truth in it knowing as I did that Sailasa and some of the teachers had planned a journey inland [confirmation of the killings was received the next day].

Brown drew the reader into his version of events by setting the tale in the first person and opening with the shocking moment when he received the news. He established his legal relationship to the deaths by translating the messenger's verb as 'murdered', thus describing the perpetrators as criminals. Yet in his corresponding journal entry Brown chose the verb 'killed' to record the deaths of the teachers and wrote a more dispassionate account, in the events of which he played no part: 'a report had come from New Britain that four of the teachers had been killed by the bush natives'.[11]

Such is the horror of the opening of the published narrative that all of the subsequent events appear to have been a response. The rest of the tale fell into place as Brown sought to find and punish those deemed guilty of the crime.

> I started next day and reached Kabakada on the following one, April 11 ... We soon heard the many horrible accounts of their death [*sic*], which made our blood boil as we heard them, and I could see by the compressed lips of the teachers, and their significant, sullen silence, that their feelings were so deeply moved that they were no longer master of their passions.

Brown consistently claimed that he conducted the raid in order to avert the threat of uncontrollable passions erupting between the Christian teachers from Samoa and Fiji and the heathen villagers of New Britain. In his investigation of counter-insurgency rhetoric and Indian historiography, Guha identified a series of metaphors of natural phenomena used in the description of peasant revolts: 'They break out like thunder storms, heave like earthquakes, spread like wildfire, infect like epidemics'.[12] Brown required little evidence that the teachers' anger was about to be 'unleashed': indeed they demonstrated their passions through their 'silence' and 'compressed lips', a significant deviation from more common descriptions of savage displays as noisy outbursts. In his autobiography Brown claimed that amid the 'passions' of the teachers and the wailing grief of the widows 'some one must keep cool and I prayed for strength to enable me to do so'.[13] By placing reason and duty against emotion Brown reasserted his English self as responsible for the uncontrolled 'native', whether Christian Fijian or heathen Tolai.

At this point Taleli makes his first appearance in the narrative. A big-man from a village near Kabakada, he was known to the teachers stationed in the region as an ally. Modern oral histories claim that Taleli offered the teachers safe passage on their proposed route, but then sent a secret message – in the form of a leaf and shell money – to villagers along the path to attack and kill them.[14] The shell money in the region was called *tambu*, although Brown consistently referred to it in his texts by the Duke of York name *diwara* (now *divara*). Taleli looms large in descriptions of the events of 1878. He is recollected in local histories as the most accomplished fighter on the northeast coast of the Gazelle Peninsula and as an outstanding trader who was in charge of the markets of the region.[15] Yet it would appear that Brown was ignorant of the power relations of the region, for he makes no mention of Taleli prior to the killing of the teachers.

The published account then continues with a point-by-point justification for Brown's decision to attack.

Let me try to explain to you the position in which I was placed ...

1. There was the fact that the teachers themselves were actually preparing to go, they all said that life was no longer safe in any of the towns, nor was the mission work practicable if these murderers were not punished.

2. The few whites here also assured me that unless something was done, their lives also were no longer safe. They volunteered their help and urged immediate action ...

3. My own convictions also were that unless these murders were punished, they would soon be followed by others. I felt that punishment was necessary, not so much to avenge the deaths of the native minister and teachers as to protect the lives of those who remained ...

> I therefore determined to enlist the sympathies and help of all the
> well-disposed natives on our side ...

These points were taken from a detailed entry in Brown's journal. Yet
that journal entry is entirely in the past tense and appears to have been
written simultaneously with the narrative following the conclusion
of hostilities.

On the first point Brown had added in his journal that he 'might of
course have positively forbidden them [the teachers] to go and under
such pressure they would probably have stayed but they would lose all
hope and interest in our work'. The flip side of 'native eruption' was
'native despondency'. Enervated and emasculated 'natives' were held
to be as difficult to rouse as their passion was to contain. Islander
responses were commonly portrayed as a pendulum that swung
beyond the correct boundaries of the European character. Yet Brown's
capacity to stop the teachers from retaliating was clearly detrimental
to his case, and he dropped this point from his published narrative.
There is evidence, however, against Brown's assertion that the teachers would have acted regardless of his involvement. In 1879 Captain
Purvis of the British warship *Danë* investigated the events for the
Gordon administration in Fiji. He conducted an interview with Ratu
Livai Volavola, who was stationed at Nodup at the time of the initial
deaths and who was present when Brown arrived at Naukukidi's house
in Kabakada.[16] Ratu Livai assured Purvis that he 'did not hear that the
teachers had determined beforehand on an Expedition, whether the
Rev. Brown went or not'. Samuela Ului also reported that 'the teachers
had made no previous arrangements for revenging the deaths of their
fellow workers but were guided entirely by the Rev. Brown'.[17]

In relation to the second and third points, Brown had little evidence
that further attacks were being planned on mission or trading stations.
Indeed this was unlikely, for traders and teachers lived in villages
under the protection of big-men who viewed their guests as a means of
increasing their shell-money holdings. It is difficult to imagine that
these big-men would endanger their investments.

In order to represent the killings as 'criminal', Brown was required
to establish a motive. In his autobiography Brown acknowledged that
Taleli was angry at any movement of goods along the trading lines to
which he had exclusive rights.[18] Modern local histories agree with this
detail: by moving inland of their own volition the teachers were
threatening the trade routes between coast and interior.[19] Indeed Brown
had already been warned that such a trip would be dangerous. Three
months before the raid he wrote to Fredrick Langham in Fiji that he
planned a trip to the inland regions of the Peninsula 'whether the
natives like it or not ... Hitherto they have prevented any whiteman

[*sic*] from going out of the coast districts but we mean just to go and ask them about it afterwards'.[20] The demand for free passage in uncolonized lands had long been present in many European legal systems. Fitzpatrick's analysis of the sixteenth-century Spanish jurist Vitoria's claim for free passage suggests that while indigenous dominion was acknowledged any resistance to free passage was met by the 'natural right' to pursue the 'full extent of conquest and dispossession'.[21] Brown's refusal to recognize the political geography of the Tolai landscape was, in effect, the same claim for free passage. Thus he played down the question of a motive, knowing that any discussion of trade routes might welcome the ambiguous charge of trespass. In his narrative for publication he merely noted: 'The murder of Sailasa and the teachers was not in any way connected with their position as Christian teachers ... They were killed simply because they were foreigners and the natives wanted to eat them.'

Cannibalism as a motive had a ghoulish attraction, and there is a little doubt that body parts were consumed by a number of villagers allied with Taleli. Yet it was a difficult characterization, for it could be used by Brown's detractors as an argument that these Islanders were, by nature, unreasoning or incapable of acting morally. This might have placed the Tolai closer to the medical category of 'insane', thus altering the terms of their punishment *and* challenging Brown's raid as an attack on those who could not be held responsible for their actions. By 1878 colonial and metropolitan courts had long been using insanity as a defence in a range of trials, including those for murder, unlawful detention, disputed wills and theft.[22]

Most of the Europeans in the region participated in the raid, along with a number of Tolai from some of the villages where the Christian teachers had been stationed. The narrative made much of these alliances:

> The towns [Nodup, Malakuna and Matupit], however, where they [the teachers] were stationed, spoke of the murder[s], as an insult and an injury to them, and were quite prepared to resent it if we would help them. I then went up to see Bulilalai, a noted chief in this part of the island ... I wished to secure his help if possible, but if not, at least to be certain that he would not oppose us ... [The raiding party had split in two, but Brown's group was halted by an alliance forged between Bulilalai and Taleli that usurped the agreement between Bulilalai and Brown.] On the hills we could see by the smoke that our party from Blanche Bay were successful ... all the houses that were seen were burnt and about twenty of the murderers were killed ... [Some days later a further attack was made on the Blanche Bay village of Diwaon.][23]

The alliances were central to Brown's defence. Tactically alert to their importance, Brown implied that they were formed from a mutual sense of repugnance for the initial killings. But he was aware that the motives of the allied villagers might have differed from his own. This point was repeated only in letters to personal friends:

> I saw the evil of making it appear to be a war of mission and whites against natives and so made it a war of mission whites and good natives against a set of murderers. The plan succeeded well especially as they saw that we were in earnest about it and so many joined us for the sake of the plunder and they were not disappointed.[24]

Powell, a visiting adventurer–scientist who had joined Brown in the raid and afterwards wrote his own account, noted: 'There was much taboo [shell money] found and many curiosities in the huts, which were taken as spoils of war.'[25] Brown made no comment on looting in the narrative for publication, yet his texts vary considerably on this issue. In his correspondence Brown noted that 'our native allies paid themselves so well from the murderers [sic] towns that they asked for no pay from me saying they were quite satisfied'.[26] In a journal entry, however, he wrote that at the conclusion of hostilities he 'paid Tolituru, Tobula and Tokoropa for their help in the war'.[27] The suggestion that the allied villagers acted for personal gain would have reflected badly on the raid and created an unsavoury portrait of Brown as the head of a mercenary force. Yet here Brown was probably acting within accepted Tolai practices of warfare for, as Brown's ethnology demonstrated, alliances for warfare were made through the promise that shell money would be paid to those who participated.

If Brown failed to note his payment to the allied villages, he readily represented the shell money paid to him by villagers who participated in the cannibalism. The suggestion that the payment was compensation was central to his defence in his published narrative.

> On Sunday 21st (next day), I sent out and tried to secure the bones of the murdered teachers, and succeeded in getting some belonging to Sailasa and Timote ... On Monday two towns sent in some diwara [shell money] as a peace offering for having joined in the cannibalism.

In the ceremonies held to reconcile the warring parties Brown returned most of the shell money that was offered along with a 'substantial present far exceeding in value that of the *diwara* which they had given as payment'. The exchange implied that the villagers were 'paying' for their crime and making restitution. Yet in Brown's description of Tolai peacemaking in his ethnology, he described the exchange of *diwara* at the conclusion of hostilities not as the payment by a vanquished party but as a means to restore a balance between the enemies. The deaths were counted and money was paid for each one; 'according to this curious arrangement, the party which had killed the most of the enemy would have to pay the most money when peace was declared, as payment for each man killed'.[28] While Brown was correct in his claim that reconciliation was effected 'according to their own customs', he failed to provide an adequate description of them. Instead he implied that his return payment of *diwara* was an expression of his own largesse and not an acknowledgment that he had caused the greater number of deaths. The *nassa callosa* shell, which was strung together then coiled in large rolls, differed from European money on several key points.[29] Brown noted in other texts that *diwara* or trade items were given as 'payment' for fright, anger and murder, and as an acknowledgement of compliments.[30] Powell acknowledged that the payment of shell money for murder did not readily 'fit' the English legal system: 'This request for payment may sound strange to civilised ears, and seem a somewhat savage way of compensating for murder, but in reality it is not so to those who understand these natives.'[31]

Brown implied that the shell money was offered freely by the villagers. In his letter to Commodore Wilson of the British navy Brown made this point explicitly, insisting that the villagers 'voluntarily brought presents of native money and begged to be forgiven'.[32] His journal, however, recorded that he had demanded shell money. From the unpunished villages, such as Raluana and Baravonu, the payment of 30 fathoms averted an attack. From Diwaon and Keravia, Brown demanded 50 fathoms as payment and punishment for not responding to his first request.[33]

The entire tale concluded with these words:

> I honestly believe that the plan I adopted was the best, and was, in fact, the only one which could save the Mission and many of our lives. It is true that many lives have been lost; but the present and future good of thousands will far outbalance that ... Ours was an honourably conducted war in conjunction with the natives themselves, and one which was forced upon us to save our own lives, and to prevent a recurrence of any such barbarities ... There is not a native in the group who does not acknowledge that we did right and that no other resource was left us.

Brown was selective in his narrative of the raid. He emphasized some points, elided others and allowed certain key details to be muddied and confused. The happy conclusion to the tale was a powerful argument for Brown's actions. In a version that could not be easily reconciled with other texts, Brown simplified the events to imply that the villages deemed culpable accepted their guilt and paid money as atonement, thus justifying his attack and suggesting the peace would be long lasting.[34]

In mid-June 1878 the German barque *Johan Ceasar* took the news of the raid from the Bismarck Archipelago to the colonies through letters from Brown to Arthur Gordon in Fiji, to Benjamin Chapman in Sydney and to Wallis, Brown's missionary father-in-law, in New Zealand. Brown also informed his influential friends and his Methodist colleagues in Fiji and Samoa.[35] The *Johan Ceasar* berthed in Sydney in mid-September breaking the news to the Australian colonies. The *Sydney Morning Herald* immediately published a version of the events detailing the deaths of the teachers but glossing over the subsequent raid. It was concluded that Brown's response was defensible given the 'whetted appetite' of Taleli and the possibility that the 'kindled fire' of native passions would be spread. Overall, Brown's action was considered to be a 'sharp and salutary' lesson to the local inhabitants.[36] The *Herald*'s editorial that followed, however, used a geographically determinist argument to condemn Brown's attempt to establish the mission inland: 'it has always been the case that the mountain tribes are fiercer than those on the coast, more backward in civilisation, more difficult to subdue'. The news of the raid appeared soon after reports that the Italian explorer D'Albertis had attacked villagers in the Fly River region of mainland New Guinea. The editor upheld the explorer's right when 'engaged in peaceful exploration to protect himself when attacked', but concluded that Brown had made a 'serious blunder', and that 'Christian missionaries undermine their own special force when they bear the sword'.[37]

First accounts by the Methodist press gave similar versions to those in the secular broadsheets, though with more emphasis on the Islanders' consumption of the teachers: 'The poor fellows were quickly dispatched, and their remains cooked and eaten at a native feast amid the most barbarous ceremonies.' Again Islanders were characterized by metaphors of natural destruction:

> The news spread among the natives like wildfire ... The whole mission was in imminent danger ... The natives were generally clamorous and insolent. The Rev. G. Brown deemed immediate aggression the truest defense. Accordingly the whites, teachers, and natives were organised and severe punishment inflicted on the cannibals, who at length sued for peace. Since then the mission work has gone on as usual.[38]

Surprisingly, the vanquished villagers also used a metaphor of natural disaster when they described the raid as 'an earthquake and not a fight'.[39] Indeed, in his ethnology Brown depicted fighting in the region as a circumscribed act performed on village boundaries after prayer and rituals. Protagonists took care not to expose themselves and most fights concluded after the death of one or two.[40] It is not merely ironic that the New Britain villagers used a metaphor of natural disaster to describe the events: it also showed the flexibility of Brown's defence. The metaphor of the 'earthquake' did not establish a tension in

Brown's account and suggest that perhaps he was not always acting within Tolai law; instead it implied Tolai naiveté and their inability to properly separate metaphor from reality.

The editorial that appeared in the *Spectator* a week after the first report struggled to defend an action that was undoubtedly 'without precedent in missionary history'. The editor finally settled on a defence based on Brown's paternal relationship to the Fijian and Samoan teachers – 'he had led them into peril'. The editorial concluded with an allegory that reinterpreted the events in 'terms which we can better understand':

> Suppose some midnight the Mission Secretary of Sydney discovered an assassin in his house bent on taking his children's lives. It is certain that on the highest Christian principles he would knock the ruffian down, and, if gentle dissuasives were not sufficient to shelter the lives dependent upon him, would knock the man's brains out.[41]

This allegory completely reframed the events. The 'assassin in the house' implied an attack on the mission station, yet this did not occur. The teachers were killed in a region far from any Christian village. 'The house', in this representation, was Brown's entire mission field and the allegory assumed both spiritual and legal jurisdiction over the region.

The Australian Methodist Missionary Society Board called an extraordinary meeting about the raid. Present was the carpenter, McGrath, who had participated in the attack and who insisted that the mission and other European residents had been in great danger. Following McGrath's report and the reading of Brown's narrative, the Board announced its findings, beginning with an acknowledgement of its receipt of a

> letter from Rev. George Brown dated June 26th communicating the intelligence that on April last, Rev. Sailasa Naukudi [*sic*], and Peni Luvu Livai Naboro and Timoci, had been treacherously murdered and eaten by the natives of the interior of New Britain and that he, with the assistance of others had adopted measures for the prevention of further outrages.

The wording is significant. Brown's response was merely 'the adoption of measures for the prevention of further outrages'. By comparison, the Tolai acted as savage criminals when they 'treacherously murdered' the teachers. However, the Board deeply regretted that Brown seemed to have no option than to attack in order to protect the mission workers.[42] Brown's narrative was then released to the press. The Methodist weeklies, the *Advocate* and the *Spectator*, published it verbatim and also regretted that 'no other course seemed to be open, which would ensure the safety of himself and of the large number of persons belonging to the mission party'.[43] The only daily broadsheet to print the account in full was the *Sydney Morning Herald*, a paper with strong ties to the evangelical movement in Sydney.[44] The preamble to the published accounts included a defence of the missionary based on McGrath's testimony.

Not all were convinced that Brown's narrative was a sufficient defence for a Christian missionary. The Melbourne *Age* made editorial comment on the events based on a succinct rendition that began 'Four natives connected with the mission were murdered and eaten by the tribes inland'. The analysis that followed condemned the teachers as trespassers and invaders: 'The fact that the four men were strangers, and, to the tribe attacking them, intruders upon their domain, may have something to do with it; but of this our information is not good enough to provenance.' The article continued in a particularly sardonic tone:

> The drum ecclesiastic was beaten and traders and friendly natives both roused in the cause ... the unhappy natives, he observes, made but slight and ineffectual resistance, their weapons being powerless against Christian arguments in the shape of bullets ... having murdered six for one the civilised and religious enterprise concluded with satisfaction to its promoters.[45]

Brown's response to the *Age* was a telling comment on the components of his identity: 'Does this gentleman really condemn me for this?' he wrote in his autobiography. 'Does he think that in becoming missionaries we cease to be men and above all cease to feel and act as Christian Englishmen?' Brown felt that by killing and consuming the teachers the Tolai had offended an accepted order based on the proper relationship betwen the native and 'the Christian Englishman'. Yet the tension in Brown's response can be read in the angry words that followed: 'Does he think that it would have been more becoming for us to sneak away like cowards to our shelter, and leave a few white men and one white lady to the tender mercies of a lot of cannibals who had just tasted blood and were thirsting for more?' In the corpus of Brown's texts, this flight of penny-fiction melodrama would probably rank as the least edifying. His writing more commonly argued against racist portrayals of Islanders. On this occasion, however, he ignored the tempering demands of his Christian faith and slipped into a narrative characterized by the 'natural' right of the moral Englishman over the immoral 'native'.

The Annual Methodist Conference formally considered Brown's actions in February 1879. Benjamin Chapman made the case for Brown using the narrative, as well as letters from traders and a favourable report from a German man of war. In the debate that followed, only one motion argued for Brown's recall and censure. Formerly a missionary to Fiji, William Moore insisted that missionaries went to the field 'sacrificially', and 'if the work could not be done without the sacrifice of life it was proof that the field was not ripe for such work'. Moore felt that Brown had allied himself too closely to the traders and that, at best, the raid had been a 'fearful mistake'. All the motions that followed disagreed with Moore's analysis. Woolnough's motion was a review of the case from the published correspondence, which he followed by 'pointing out the law in reference to cases of this kind'.

> it fully appears to us that in the judgment of the natives themselves, Mr Brown has administered justice without seeking revenge; and whilst we still cherish the utmost confidence in Mr Brown ... [we] now solemnly affirm that we can never sanction the use of military measure in our missionary enterprises.

Woolnough's ambivalent amendment was passed with a large majority.[46] His legal argument was discussed further in the *Weekly Advocate*: where he claimed that Brown's status as an Englishman did not negate his right to respond to the 'rude unwritten code of law that prevails in New Britain'. The self-confessed guilt of the Tolai people justified the 'scant justice ... that was meted out to them'.[47] Clearly Brown's narrative had convinced his colleagues who, while uneasy about the raid, were soothed by the success of the action and the suggestion that punishment had been administered to the guilty who acknowledged their wrongdoing.

The Gordon administration was less readily convinced. In November 1879, as Brown was returning to the Bismarck Archipelago following a severe illness, he was charged with manslaughter. Aware that the charges were forthcoming, Chapman and others Methodist leaders accompanied Brown to Fiji. Brown's raid had increased the tension between the Gordon administration and the influential Methodist mission. Of the Reverend Langham, head of the Fijian mission, Gordon complained privately that he held 'very much the position of one of the political bishops of the Middle Ages'.[48] In public, however, Gordon treated the missionaries diplomatically in acknowledgment of their considerable power. On arrival in Fiji, Brown was invited to dinner with Gordon at Government House. The following day the results from the British naval investigation were submitted and were favourable to Brown. Methodists in Fiji later claimed it was chief judicial commissioner (also attorney general), Gorrie, who had pushed for Brown's prosecution. The summons for manslaughter arrived while Gordon was interviewing Chapman on the raid, making the case *sub judice* and removing it from the high commisioner's jurisdiction.

Brown's colleague Fison launched a newspaper campaign suggesting that Gordon and Gorrie were in disagreement on the matter and that the jurisdiction was unclear. At a brief interview between Brown and Gordon, from which Gorrie was absent, Gordon admitted to the missionary that the evidence and depositions would not have led him to seek criminal prosecution and he hoped the trial would 'free him from all imputation of criminality'.[49] In the light of the tension between the judiciary and the office of the high commissioner, Gorrie bowed to Gordon's authority and did not proceed with the prosecution. The trail was essentially an address by Gorrie on the finer points of the legal issues raised by the affair. At the conclusion of the proceedings Brown was 'free to depart'.[50]

Brown's published narrative was not only primary to his defence: it was the *only* circulated version of the events. Powell's account was published some years later. The investigations by the German and English navies were conducted with European residents or the Samoan or Fijian teachers; language problems precluded the interviewing of the Taleli or others from the villages that had been attacked by the raiding parties. In the absence of any conflicting evidence, and given the great difficulty of obtaining such, it would appear that the Methodist Church and the administration in Fiji were constrained in their efforts to respond to the issue. In these circumstances Brown was able to construct a narrative around the popular view of the relationship between the erupting Islander and the controlled European. It was a recognizable tale of 'native' crime and metropolitan punishment.

Brown's conclusion, that the two sides were reconciled through the self-confessed guilt of the culpable Tolai, was an unexpected outcome that retrospectively imbued the entire narrative with the idea that both European and Islander agreed that justice had been done. This was the strongest argument in Brown's favour. However, while Brown claimed that the events occurred under a shared moral and legal code, there was considerable ambiguity on several key points. Brown's implication that shell money was offered as compensation for the deaths of the teachers was especially dubious. It would appear from Brown's ethnology that at the conclusion of hostilities shell money had been paid for individual deaths. Therefore Brown's return offer of a present 'far exceeding in value that of the *diwara* which they had given in payment' acknowledged that he had caused more fatalities, thus allowing the reconciliation between the Christian and heathen parties.

Yet the question remains: how could Brown reconcile his faith with his actions in the light of so many Tolai deaths? The answer, I believe, lies in his response to the vehement attack on him by the *Age*, when he wrote: 'Does he think that in becoming Christians we cease to be men, much less Christian Englishmen?' Brown's belief in the legacy of his English Protestant history was essentially a claim for English rights over those of the 'native'. This assumption, that he was exercising the natural rights of a Christian Englishman, permeated his narrative. His colleagues publicly accepted his arguments, although there was some private disquiet. Indeed there was significant debate over the issue, for the assumption of a 'natural' right based on race could not be legally or theologically defended. Brown's raid was interesting precisely because it was an aberration in the history of evangelical mission. In order to justify this departure from his Christian ethics and the English legal system, Brown needed a careful and powerful defence. He achieved this through his compelling narrative.

Notes

1 B. Stanley, *The Bible and the Flag* (Leicester, Apollos, 1990), ch. 1; N. Gunson, *Messengers of Grace* (Melbourne, Oxford University Press, 1978), ch. 15; Gunson, 'Missionary Interest in British Expansion in the South Pacific in the Nineteenth Century', *Journal of Religious History*, 3 (1965), 310; Gunson, 'The Theology of Imperialism and the Missionary History of the Pacific', *Journal of Religious History*, 5 (1965), 256–65.
2 Brown to Wallis, 2 July 1878 (Mitchell Library, Sydney: George Brown Papers (hereafter ML)).
3 Brown, journal, 11 May 1878 (ML).
4 The collective noun 'Tolai' postdates Brown's residence in the region. I use it here for the sake of convenience and because it has become the chosen name for those on the Gazelle Peninsula of New Britain.
5 'Western Pacific Order in Council, 1877' in J. Whittaker, N.G. Gash, J.F. Hookey and R.J. Lacey (eds), *Documents and Readings in New Guinea History* (Queensland, Jacaranda Press, 1975), pp. 499–501. See also J. K. Chapman, *The Career of Arthur Hamilton Gordon* (Toronto, Toronto University Press, 1964), pp. 265–304.
6 Brown to Wallis, 2 July 1878 (ML).
7 H. White, *The Content of the Form: Narrative Discourse and Historical Representation* (Baltimore, MD, Johns Hopkins University Press, 1990), pp. 11–12.
8 E. Said, *Culture and Imperialism* (London, Vintage, 1994), p. 95.
9 Roland Barthes suggests that there is a series of narrative sequences familiar to the reader who then grasps the 'logical succession of actions as a nominal whole'; see 'Structural Analysis of Narratives', in S. Sontag (ed.), *A Roland Barthes Reader* (London, Vintage, 1993), p. 273.
10 Brown to Chapman, 26 June 1878 (ML); *Sydney Morning Herald*, 20 September 1878; *Weekly Advocate*, 21 September 1878; *Spectator* (Melbourne), 27 September 1878.
11 Brown, journal, 8 April 1878 (ML).
12 R. Guha, 'The Prose of Counter-Insurgency', in R. Guha (ed.), *Subaltern Studies II* (Delhi, Oxford University Press, 1983), p. 2.
13 G. Brown, *George Brown, D.D.: Pioneer Missionary and Explorer, an Autobiography* (London, Hodder & Stoughton, 1908), p. 254.
14 H. Schütte, 'The Six Day War of 1878 in the Bismarck Archipelago', *Journal of Pacific History*, 24 (1989), 3.
15 *Ibid.*, 41.
16 For the teachers' names I have followed N. Threlfall, *One Hundred Years in the Islands: The Methodst United Church in the New Guinea Islands Region 1875-1975* (Rabual, Tok Save Press, 1975), pp. 249–69.
17 Report of Captain Purvis of the *Danë*, 21 September 1879 (ML).
18 Brown, *Autobiography*, p. 256.

19 K. Neumann, *Not the Way it Really Was* (Honolulu, University of Hawaii Press, 1992), pp. 81–2.
20 Brown to Langham, 8 November 1877 (ML).
21 P. Fitzpatrick, 'Terminal Legality: Imperialism and the (De)Composition of Legal Culture', in this volume.
22 C. Coleborne, 'Reading Madness: Bodily Difference and the Female Lunatic Patient in the History of the Asylum in Colonial Victoria, 1848–1888', Ph.D. thesis, La Trobe University, Melbourne, pp. 69–73.
23 Brown to Chapman, 26 June 1878 (ML); *Sydney Morning Herald*, 20 September 1878; *Weekly Advocate*, 21 September 1878; *Spectator*, 27 September 1878.
24 Brown to Buddle, 2 July 1878 (ML).
25 W. Powell, *Wanderings in a Wild Country* (London, Samson Low, Marston, Searle & Rivington, 1883), p. 142.
26 Brown to Wallis, 2 July 1878 (ML).
27 Brown to Langham, 8 November 1877 (ML).
28 G. Brown, *Melanesians and Polynesians* (New York, Benjamin Blom, [1910] 1972), p. 257.
29 On the literature of the shell money of the Bismarck Archipelago, see F. Errington and D. Gewertz, *Articulating Change in the 'Last Unknown'* (Boulder, CO, Westview Press, 1995), pp. 54–6.
30 Brown, *Melanesians and Polynesians*, pp. 251–8, 292–301.
31 Powell, *Wanderings in a Wild Country*, pp. 126–7.
32 Brown to Commodore Wilson, 9 September 1879 (ML).
33 Brown, Journal, 21 April 1878 (ML).
34 White argues, in *The Content of the Form* (p. 52), that the conclusion of a narrative links it to the beginning, and that the entire tale is retrospectively endowed with a particular flavour and meaning.
35 Brown, Letterbook, June 1878 (ML).
36 *Sydney Morning Herald*, 14 September 1878.
37 *Sydney Morning Herald*, 18 September 1878.
38 *Spectator*, 20 September 1878.
39 *Weekly Advocate*, 21 September 1878; *Sydney Morning Herald*, 21 September 1878; *Spectator*, 27 September 1878.
40 Brown, *Melanesians and Polynesians*, pp. 152–5.
41 *Spectator*, 27 September 1878.
42 'Methodist Church of Australasia: Department of Overseas Mission Papers', in Whittaker *et al.* (eds), *Documents and Readings in New Guinea History*, p. 424.
43 *Weekly Advocate*, quoted in *Spectator*, 27 September 1878.
44 The *Sydney Morning Herald* published the narrative over 21 and 22 September 1878.
45 *Age*, 27 September 1878.
46 *Weekly Advocate*, 22 February 1879.
47 *Weekly Advocate*, 1 March 1879.
48 A.G. Gordon, quoted in J.K. Chapman, *The Career of Arthur Hamilton Gordon, First Lord Stanmore* (Toronto, University of Toronto Press, 1964), p. 197.
49 Brown, *Autobiography*, p. 308.
50 *Ibid.*, pp. 309–10.

PART IV

Land, sovereignty and imperial frontiers

Land and its acquisition was central to the
nineteenth-century imperial project. Here we pick
up themes from the first section and explore and
analyze specific historical instances where law and
history intersect, challenging European paradigms
of sovereignty and fairness from the perspective of
indigenous rights.

CHAPTER ELEVEN

The fate of Maori land rights in early colonial New Zealand: the limits of the Treaty of Waitangi and the doctrine of Aboriginal title

Ann Parsonson

Indigenous land rights in early colonial New Zealand, it is sometimes assumed, were afforded rather greater recognition than those in other countries colonized by the British. After all, in New Zealand Maori had the benefit of a bilingual treaty with the Crown, the Treaty of Waitangi, which (in both Maori and English texts) afforded them strong guarantees. One of the best-known judgments on indigenous land rights, *R. v. Symonds*, also dates from this period. Only seven years after the signing of the Treaty, it was held in the Supreme Court of New Zealand that the Treaty had not in fact been necessary to protect Maori land rights, because 'the Native title' was protected in any case at common law.[1] Paul McHugh argued convincingly some years ago that the doctrine of Aboriginal title had thus been successfully transferred to New Zealand: the common law presumed the continuity of indigenous property rights upon the Crown's assumption of territorial sovereignty.[2] Maori land rights might seem to have been doubly protected.

It is clear, however, that even these protections were not enough. From the beginning there were ominous signs foreshadowing the Government's sustained assault on Maori rights which was under way by the 1860s, with war, land confiscations and the establishment of a Land Court whose job was to extinguish customary title, to ensure that Maori held their land from the Crown and to facilitate land purchase. The main thrust of the policies of the new Government was to secure favourable conditions for British settlement, and inevitably it began to limit Maori land rights. It is easier, however, to identify blatant breaches of Maori land rights, such as confiscation or fraudulent purchases, than to recognize policies which undermined them more subtly in that they were based on a worldview quite different from that of the indigenous people. It has taken the proceedings of the bicultural and bilingual Waitangi Tribunal, charged since 1985 with investigating historical grievances, to draw attention to the kinds of assumptions that underlay the Government's Maori land policies, and to hold those assumptions up to scrutiny.

In particular, the Tribunal has drawn attention in recent years to the importance of recognizing the cultural gap in a matter as central to the early Maori–Pakeha interface as land transactions, and of giving equal weight in considering such transactions to the Maori worldview, the Maori value system, laws and policies.[3] The settler tendency to dismiss aspects of Maori culture of which they were ignorant, or which they did not understand, it is suggested, has lingered to the present, and still affects the way in which the history of Maori–Pakeha interaction is interpreted. It also affects attitudes to expressions of Maori autonomy, which historically have always raised Crown hackles. The Waitangi Tribunal has not shrunk from emphasizing the centrality of this issue to the claims brought before it. The determination of the Crown to control the arrangements for the acquisition and management of land exemplified British impatience of Maori authority, and of any real dialogue with Maori on matters of huge concern to them.

The Treaty of Waitangi (the particular focus of the Tribunal in its elucidation of Maori rights) was evidence enough that the British foresaw the need for protocols between themselves and Maori as they stood poised on the brink of a colonizing venture. Such protocols between governments and indigenes, it is argued, ought properly 'to ensure good order, harmony, and peace', and to respect Aboriginal autonomy – the 'inherent right of all peoples in their native countries'. It follows that 'on the colonisation of inhabited countries, sovereignty, in the sense of absolute power, cannot be vested in only one of the parties'. In New Zealand, 'sovereignty was constrained ... by the need to respect Maori authority'.[4]

If such arguments are held to proceed from a purely modern understanding of the respective rights and duties of governments and indigenous peoples, it may equally be insisted that even the written record (culturally so important to Westerners) shows that Maori calls for autonomy and Maori opposition to government policies are generations' old; and that to highlight the worldview, values and beliefs that underlie such insistence on indigenous rights is less to enjoy the advantage of hindsight than to afford the indigenous culture the same respect, in constructions of the past, as is taken for granted by the power culture.

Surveyed in this light, early colonial land policy in New Zealand seems culture-specific indeed. From the outset the Government controlled the definitions of indigenous land rights, the debate on their nature and extent, and the legislation and policy determining the recognition and extinguishment of rights. The limitation of Maori land rights began with the Crown's introduction of feudalism to New Zealand, based on the early decision that land titles in the colony must derive from Crown grant: it was evident in the first piece of legislation passed in New Zealand that directly affected Maori land rights, the Land Claims Ordinance 1841, which established a crucial legislative precedent in New Zealand. The Ordinance provided that all titles to land claimed by virtue of pre-Annexation purchases or conveyances from Maori were null and void; it enacted the Crown's sole right of pre-emption and provided for a Commission to investigate claims. But it also spelt out the extent to which Maori rights were to be recognized: 'all unappropriated lands within the ... Colony ... subject however to the rightful and necessary occupation and use thereof by the aboriginal inhabitants of the said Colony, are and remain Crown or Domain Lands of Her Majesty ...'.[5]

This provision was not lightly written: it was based on Secretary of State Lord John Russell's December 1840 instructions to Governor Hobson, which laid down that the lands of 'private persons' (that is, settlers) should at once be identified, as also should lands retained by Maori. Then the Crown demesne, that is, the rest of the lands, should be surveyed, sold and settled. Hobson's formal Instructions and the Charter for erecting New Zealand as a colony in its own right provided both for protection of Maori in the 'occupation and enjoyment' (as English law would have it) of their lands, and for the division and survey of the entire colony into counties, hundreds, towns and parishes.[6] It may seem, indeed, that the British – in employing their own legal terms – enjoyed the luxury of both maintaining the discourse of recognition of Maori rights and simultaneously reading them down. If this was the extent to which the tribes' 'private rights of land ownership' survived the Crown's acquisition of sovereignty under the doctrine of Aboriginal title, the common law might seem to have afforded limited protection indeed.

The dangers of the British capture of definitions of Maori rights became very evident by the mid-1840s. In 1846 Governor Grey was instructed that government officials were to decide the extent of lands to which natives 'claim[ed] either a proprietary or possessory title'; a land court was to decide whether such claims were valid, and proof of validity was to depend on actual occupation, use and enjoyment, 'either as places of abode, or for tillage, or for the growth of crops, or for the depasturing of cattle, or otherwise ... by means of labour expended thereon'.[7]

Thus the British assumed the right both to require Maori to supply proof of their title and to decide – by reference to the agricultural economy of imperial power – the bases on which title would be determined. For if Maori could be confined to a series of delineated villages surrounded by cultivated fields – rather than moving seasonally to harvest a range of resources within their descent-group territories – large tracts could be released for British settlement. Governor Grey, as is well known, departed from the letter of his instructions, for the opposition that they aroused among Maori, missionaries, and nervous settlers was not lost on him. But their spirit continued to permeate government policy.

If customary hunting and gathering rights deemed inimical to British interests were to be circumscribed, there were other rights too which were a headache to the Government – in particular the right of Maori to enter into various kinds of leasing arrangements directly with settlers. Government discussions about leasing in the 1840s and 1850s reveal both a striking carelessness of Maori interests and considerable concern about the extent and nature of Maori rights. For the fact was that Maori were entering into their own transactions with Pakeha in 1840 – post-Treaty – as they had in the years before 1840. Lieutenant-Governor Hobson (as he then was) was worried particularly about the Auckland area, where he had decided to establish the capital, and where he discovered that the practice of 'leasing' for long terms was 'most universal'. Twice during 1840 Hobson raised the issue with Governor Gipps of New South Wales, fearing that the practice might produce 'most mischievous consequences'.[8]

Gipps agreed that the 'evil', as he put it, must be dealt with, and a law passed to put an end to such leases. But he also seems to have accepted Hobson's opinion that 'those lands are the property of tribes, and the parties holding them ... continue to occupy and cultivate them as tenants under the chief'.[9] Surely there was a major contradiction here? Gipps, unsurprisingly, brushed it aside, taking refuge in the view that Maori, lacking an individual property right, could not convey any such interest – whether by sale or lease – to others. This principle, he suggested, should be the basis of any new law. In other words, the only way to deal with the exercise of inconvenient indigenous property rights, in Gipps's view, was to rule them out of order on the grounds that they were incompatible with English land law.

The British reaction to this correspondence was, perhaps, predictable. Lord John Russell, the secretary of state, instructed Hobson in August 1841 to pass a law immediately which declared European leases 'from the natives' invalid.[10] But even before he received copies of the Gipps–Hobson correspondence, Lord Russell had already written to Hobson urging him to legislate to declare 'the absolute invalidity of any conveyance, or contract, or will, for the disposal of land by any native chief or chiefs' to a European; and to forbid a European from acquiring land, 'or interest in land', in this way.[11] Hobson's new Land

Claims Ordinance, repealing the earlier New South Wales Ordinance on which it was closely modelled, was reworded accordingly.

Government determination to prevent leasing was evident in a later ordinance, the Native Land Purchase Ordinance 1846, which laid down penalties for settlers who dealt directly with Maori, buying land, or agreeing to 'purchase ... the right' to cut timber, or depasture sheep or cattle, or to use or occupy any land not Crown-granted.[12] And in the Constitution Act 1852, any transactions with Maori other than those conducted by the Crown, whether purchases, or acceptances of 'any release or extinguishment' of their rights in any land 'belonging to, or used or occupied by [the natives] in common as tribes or communities', were deemed unlawful. Nor were any conveyances or agreements to convey or transfer land either in perpetuity or 'by way of lease or occupancy' valid, unless made with the Crown.[13]

Why, then, did this matter so much to the Government? Despite the justifications offered in the preamble of the Native Land Purchase Ordinance – that private contracts between Maori and non-Maori would endanger the peace of the colony because of uncertainties about title and the meaning of contracts – the answer is very clear. As Donald McLean, the chief land purchase commissioner, explained – with extraordinary candour: 'leasing lands from the natives threatened a most serious evil on the prospects of the Colony, as they would not of course alienate any of their lands to the Crown if such a system was permitted to exist'.[14] But there was still a protective imperative: it was the Government's duty, according to McLean, to ensure that Maori did not become 'idle' while living on the proceeds of rents.[15] Thus the rhetoric of the civilizing mission was pressed into service for colonial ends; what was a legitimate source of income for a colonial gentleman was a ticket to social degradation for Maori.

The Wairarapa region posed a particular problem for the Government in the 1840s: some forty or fifty settlers had driven herds of sheep and cattle there, at a time when there seemed little hope of Crown purchases of the land, and had made their own arrangements with Ngati Kahungunu–Rangitane. No major disputes arose over a period of six years – until newcomers offering Maori higher payments tempted some to accommodate them too; and during that time the arrangements, according to one settler, were

> observed as faithfully as tho' sanctioned by law, the Natives know us as their Tenants, bound to them, if not legally, at least in integrity and good faith, and themselves under the same obligation to recognize our rights to the privileges guaranteed to us by their several agreements in all cases ...[16]

When attempts were made to negotiate the purchase of the land (by F.D. Bell for the New Zealand Company in 1847 and by H.T. Kemp for the Crown in 1848), strong Maori opposition was encountered, and Bell's appeal to Governor Grey for help produced some typically Grey-ish threats directed at the chiefs: 'if you will not conclude such an arrangement, then I shall desire the Europeans to depart from your land and shall put an end to the arrangements at present existing'.[17] The stockholders were considered to have their uses in that they accustomed Maori to their presence, and to the financial benefits they brought, but when the Government was ready Maori were informed in no uncertain terms that the honeymoon was over, and that they could no longer collect rents from settlers in defiance of the law.

The Government, in short, was determined to deny Maori the right to manage their land on their own account. The question is, why did neither the Treaty nor the common law protect that right? The acknowledgment in the Treaty of *te tino rangatiratanga o o ratou w[h]enua* – 'the unqualified exercise of their chieftainship over their lands' – the Tribunal has found, 'carries with it all the incidents of tribal communalism and paramountcy'. But the treaty's English text guaranteed simply 'full exclusive and undisturbed possession of their Lands'.[18] Later the Privy Council, in *Nireaha Tamaki* v. *Baker*, would advise that the 1841 Land Claims Ordinance, to the extent that it recognized the 'rightful and necessary occupation' of Maori, was a 'legislative recognition' of the rights guaranteed in Article 2 of the Treaty.[19] At least one commentator has vigorously challenged this interpretation, stating that it 'was nothing of the sort'.[20] And the Judicial Committee did not consider such recognition to extend very far: it did not create a legal right in the 'Native occupiers'.

What, then, of the doctrine of Aboriginal title? Should it not have protected the Maori right to lease their lands? On the face of it, evidently not. Aboriginal rights – as clearly stated in *Mabo* – can only be possessed by indigenous people, and are 'not ... assignable outside the overall native system'.[21] The common law could give no recognition to the rights of an 'alienee' where those rights depended on native custom.[22] Thus it might seem that the early legislation, nullifying title which settlers might claim by virtue of any kind of transaction with Maori, merely restated the common law position.

Conversely, it might be argued that the passing of legislation indicates that prohibitions on private transactions were a policy matter, rather than 'a consequence of the application of English law'; or at least that there was some doubt at the time as to whether private transactions would be valid under colonial law.[23] The Gipps–Hobson–Russell discussions, in this context, are interesting. Clearly, legislation was felt to be necessary to prohibit leasing, though it was directed at non-Maori rather than Maori, and did not explicitly extinguish Maori rights. Did this reflect some British discomfort about extinguishing native 'territorial rights' that were at the time being exercised: perhaps some political – if not legal – recognition that the 'overall native system' was expanding to include non-indigenes? Since the common law allows that native practices, customs and traditions will change over time, British doubts might seem not unreasonable.

In *R. v. Symonds*, however, the judges did not consider this to be an issue. Chapman J. drew a neat line in his discussion of native title, characterizing it as purely pre-contact. Native title, in his well-known words, was 'entitled to be respected', and could not be extinguished without indigenous consent. 'All the enjoyments' that Maori had from the land before contact with Westerners were thus secured to them, 'and as much more as the opportunity of selling portions, useless to themselves, affords'.[24] Chapman J. thus failed to consider the possibility that Maori might 'use' their lands by installing non-Maori on them who would benefit their communities in various ways. The new kinds of transactions which had developed between Maori and settler in some regions in the crucial contact years both before and after the Crown's proclamations of sovereignty were written out of the script.

If indigenous rights were to be respected, then, the British were to determine exactly how far they were to be respected. In New Zealand, indigenous people were offered two alternatives: they could subsist, or they could sell land. They could not be landlords, which would be to step outside the roles allotted to them in a colonized society.

The limits of contemporary British conceptualization of Maori land rights seem even more striking in light of recent findings by the Waitangi Tribunal on pre-Treaty transactions in the Muriwhenua (far northern) region. The Tribunal – drawing both on understandings conveyed by the Muriwhenua *hapu*, and on its members' cross-cultural experience – has argued that these transactions, which to Pakeha were purchases of land, had a quite different character to Maori, 'rather like a lease but nothing like a sale'.[25] In terms of their own value system, Maori interpreted such transactions as a 'social contract' rather than a property conveyance. Their whole starting-point was different from that of Westerners: their focus was on bringing outsiders into the *hapu* to strengthen the *hapu*, allocating land to them – rather than alienating it – and forming a mutually beneficial relationship. While the Tribunal's findings relate to a specific group of transactions in one area, their message is unmistakable: indigenous interpretations of cross-cultural dealings must be sought out by those competent to do so, and respected.

It may also be argued that in 1840 Maori did not adopt a Western view of such transactions overnight. We must ask, for instance, whether Maori entering into 'leases' in the Auckland area in 1840 distinguished those transactions from 'sales' – only a handful – that they conducted with government agents at the same time, for which they were paid in a mixture of money and goods. The fact that the process of government purchase in the area was initially less than rigorous – characterized for instance by failure to provide all articles listed as part of the payment at one time, or to mark out and survey the boundaries – cannot have helped Maori differentiate these transactions.[26] In 1842 Ngati Paoa were still staying, when they visited Auckland to trade, on sections owned by settlers; clearly they did not consider that settlers had established exclusive rights to the land.[27]

Further south, in Taranaki, where there was a large settler influx in 1841–43, a monocultural lens is equally inadequate for viewing Maori–Pakeha transactions. This was a region where, in the wake of an early New Zealand Company 'purchase', British settlers contested the land with the local Te Ati Awa people. Governor FitzRoy ignored the recommendation of the land claims commissioner to grant extensive lands to the Company, and instead secured a small block of land round the new town of New Plymouth.

In the wake of this decision, various Te Ati Awa *hapu* formed relationships with those of the settlers who decided to remain on lands north of New Plymouth which they had selected, even though the Crown could not guarantee their title. As occupants of Te Ati Awa land, these settlers – though living close to an organized Pakeha community with its own mores – were clearly considered to have entered into a social compact with their hosts. Josiah Flight and his partner Devenish were among those whom one of the Puketapu leaders, Te Whaitere Katatore, sought to retain on Puketapu lands in 1844: 'There are some 7 or 8 that live at Puketapu who behaved very quietly', he told Governor FitzRoy in 1844; 'I don't want to part with them'.[28] Yet he was also determined not to part with the land. In the years that followed, Flight and Devenish found themselves part of the community; and if at times they felt exploited – their bullocks and cart requisitioned to cart Puketapu wheat, Katatore's wheat stacked in Flight's rickyard for threshing, his bread brought for baking in the oven – clearly they accommodated themselves to Puketapu expectations. In 1848 they were living with their neighbours on friendly terms, and they begged the New Zealand Company's agent F.D. Bell – temporarily charged with land negotiations in the area – not to stir up trouble by trying to buy their land![29]

There was, in other words, a dynamic to Maori–Pakeha relations on the ground quite different from what might be deduced from the uncompromising tone of contemporary government correspondence on land purchase, which reflected a preoccupation with extinguishing customary title over lands near New Plymouth, and with moving Maori off lands that were considered desirable for the settlers. Even after Crown purchases began in earnest in Taranaki, from the mid-1840s, this kind of relationship did not disappear. When large blocks were purchased, lands were set aside for Maori for their own use: the native reserves which were to be the basis for their future. In Taranaki, Maori began to lease some of their reserves to settlers, and thus to enter into relationships which involved rights and responsibilities on both sides. The authorities, however, moved quickly to stop such transactions. In 1854 the provincial superintendent, concerned that the province might be called on to maintain lessees in possession, drafted a public notice stating that agreements for the purchase or leasing of native reserves, 'being the property of tribes or communities', were illegal and void under the 1852 Constitution Act, and liable to penalties under the Native Land Purchase Ordinance.[30] And the local land purchase sub-commissioner, who had seen nothing wrong with the leases, and wrote anxiously to his superior for support, earned a sharp rap on the knuckles from Chief Land Purchase Commissioner Donald McLean: 'I have strenuously opposed such transactions in all parts of the Island', wrote McLean;' if we let the natives lease their reserves we will never get them to sell any good land'.[31]

Following the publication of the superintendent's notice in the *Gazette* at the end of 1854, Richard Brown, a local trader whose wife was Te Ati Awa, was prosecuted under the 1846 Ordinance for depasturing his sheep on the Moturoa Reserve in the Grey Block. Brown, defending himself in the case, argued that the 1846 Ordinance did not apply, as the native title in the block had been extinguished by purchase, and the reserves were 'virtually comprised in a grant from the Crown'.[32] The provincial solicitor suggested, however, that native title subsisted in the reserves, just as it had previously in the whole block. As it was a collective title, the purpose of the Government's prohibition on leasing was a protective one. The role of the Crown, he said – paraphrasing the preamble of the 1846 Ordinance – was to stand between Maori and settler, to make sure the consent of all Maori involved in any transaction was obtained, and thus prevent disputes.[33] So casual was the Crown about its protective responsibilities, however, that the commissioner of crown lands – who also appeared – was unable to say whether the reserve was vested in trustees, or whether a Crown grant had been issued for it – or for any native reserve in the province.[34] The resident magistrate, his hands tied in that the court was debarred from deciding questions of title, imposed the minimum fine on Brown (regretting that he couldn't fine him less), on the grounds that the land was in common occupancy.

The case highlighted the ambiguous status of native reserves, and the disempowerment of Maori. Both arose from the land purchase policy established by Governor George Grey in the mid-1840s, as he piously resumed the Crown's right of pre-emption in the wake of Governor FitzRoy's waiver policy.[35] Grey's loud insistence on the protective rationale of pre-emption (backed by the Supreme Court in R. v. Symonds), would ring very hollow for the iwi who felt the full force of Grey's determination to purchase large tracts – particularly Ngai Tahu in the South Island who lost nearly all their lands by 1860, and whose 'requests' for reserves were often rejected by Crown officials.[36]

Grey's policy was based on the systematic extinguishment of customary title, control by Crown officials of the size and location of Native Reserves created at the time of purchase, denial of Maori control and management of the reserves, and recognition only of a Maori right to 'use and occupy'. Grey's purchase agents had been instructed that the reserves should be registered *within* a tract where purchase had extinguished the 'native title'. This would mean, of course, that Maori could not subsequently claim the protection of the courts for their customary title. Nor did Grey intend to issue Crown grants to Maori for their reserves, which were to be communally held; technically, the reserves remained Crown land.[37]

As a government minister explained in a matter of fact way to the Legislative Council later, native reserves 'did not belong to the Natives'.[38] This also meant that there was no legal protection for Maori reserves as such. This was highlighted much later, in the judgment in R. v. Fitzherbert (1872), when Maori sought to repeal a Crown grant of a section of reserved land to a third party. On that occasion the chief justice, reviewing early legislation, stated: 'It appears ... that the creation of Native reserves was not one of the objects specially provided for in the statutes, charter, instructions, and ordinances by or under which the management and disposal of the demesne lands of the Crown was regulated'.[39] Therefore, even though Crown officials acted as if they believed the lands were legally set apart as reserves, in fact the Crown was not bound to hold the lands in trust as reserves.

In any case, the extinguishment of the title meant that the Crown could control the reserves.[40] And when the new settler Parliament began to pass legislation, one of its early statutes was the Native Reserves Act 1856 which provided for the management of the reserves by commissioners appointed by the Government, who had the power to sell, lease or exchange the land, and to spend the proceeds on behalf of and for the benefit of Maori.[41] There was no provision for Maori to take any part in matters relating to the control of the land; or for the commissioners to consult Maori once their land had been placed under the Act. Well over a century later, thousands of acres of reserved land throughout New Zealand, set aside at different times and under different circumstances, remained under the administration of the Maori trustee, while the Maori owners were still excluded from any share in the administration of their own lands.[42]

Thus the Government took steps to ensure that Maori did not control the lands they kept – either before or after sale. Given that the reserves Maori were able to keep were small, it was the prohibition on leasing customary lands that perhaps had the more dramatic impact – both on Maori participation in the new economy, and on their relationship with their Pakeha neighbours. For Maori, leasing (as they understood it) was an ideal arrangement which could have had long-term benefits.

We get a glimpse in nineteenth-century Maori accounts of the value of such arrangements to communities. At Te Kopua, on the Waipa river – an area where the Queen's writ did not run prior to the British invasion (1863) – it was decided to charge rent after the chief Te Toenga of Ngati Maniapoto returned from Sydney where he had become familiar with grazing leases. The Wesleyan missionary Thomas Buddle agreed to pay rent, and gave three cows; the people reared them and eventually had fifty; 'some were stock from the three and the others were for yearly payments of rent'.[43] Later missionaries grazed sheep as well as cattle, and the payments were divided among the various *hapu* who had rights to the land. The fact that cattle given in payment might be given names underlines the fact that such transactions were not seen as simply commercial. The names of the animals – also passed on in oral histories – reinforced the association of the people with the land and with Pakeha whom they allowed to live there, who also found a place in the histories because their payments recorded recognition of the rights of those in whose communities they lived.

In short, leasing arrangements were acculturated; they reflected hapu association with and control of the land. This raises interesting questions, in light of *Mabo* and *Wik*. If, to Maori, such arrangements involved the incorporation of Westerners into their community, rather than any alienation or appropriation of land; if they saw no inconsistency between their own continued access to the land, and the exercise of rights by a newcomer in their midst, why should their arrangements have been summarily deemed unlawful according to English law?[44] For it is clear that – in a variety of contexts – non-indigenous people were being folded into Maori communities on Maori terms, and were acknowledging Maori law.[45]

Hapu-initiated and controlled arrangements highlight the gulf between Maori concepts of the nature of their relations with settlers and British concepts. The Government, for its part, neither consulted with Maori about its policies, nor explained them. It assumed the right to act on the basis of inappropriate legal theory that the radical title was vested in the Crown; it failed to agree the doctrine of tenure with Maori (despite its huge implications for their rights), and passed its legislation in a small distant chamber. In its recent Muriwhenua and Taranaki reports, the Waitangi Tribunal has condemned this lack of government consultation with Maori on all aspects of its land policies. In the far north, the Government had interpreted pre-Treaty transactions to suit itself – as both extinguishing Maori title and failing to convey the land to the purchaser – leaving the Government free to keep such lands as it chose not to grant to settlers. Thousands of acres of Muriwhenua land which had not even been sold in the first place, as Maori saw it, were thus confiscated.

In post-Treaty Taranaki, the high-handed conduct of purchase negotiations, the low prices paid, the small reserves allocated and the Crown's retention of control over them were bad enough; but underlying all these was a fundamental failure on the part of the Government to acknowledge Maori autonomy and authority over their lands, and to treat with Maori 'as they equals that they were'. Instead, it was presumed that the Government would determine arrangements for land acquisition unilaterally, and the result – in a region where the main settlements of Te Ati Awa were on coastal lands coveted by the settlers – was sustained pressure applied by government purchase agents, increasing tension within the close-knit yet autonomous Te Ati Awa communities north of New Plymouth, and eventual hostilities among themselves. 'From the outset', the Tribunal concluded,

> governors would not meet with the Maori leadership to agree upon the terms on which north Taranaki might be settled. Such was required by the Treaty, in our view. It was also plain good manners and common sense to treat with the leaders of a place before entering on it.[46]

This is to stand the usual assumptions about the rights of a colonizing power on their head. But the alternative, as is evidenced by the experience of Te Ati Awa in the early colonial period, was an unpleasant series of government manipulations and attempted manipulations of various tribal leaders in a desperate attempt to secure offers and counter-offers of land. In the process, cross-cultural relations in Taranaki were also soured. Te Ati Awa leaders were labelled either friend or enemy, co-operative or unco-operative, depending on whether or not they were perceived to be willing to sell land. Some potentially influential friends of the settlers were lost in this way – most notably Wiremu Kingi Te Rangitake of Waitara, the greatest chief among Te Ati Awa at this time. Yet it is clear that such leaders were not anti-Pakeha, but only anti the government attitudes they perceived towards themselves and the apparently implacable determination to secure their land. Wiremu Kingi, cornered as he visited New Plymouth by a settler who (in his own words) 'attacked' him about selling land, burst out that he wished there was no land at all 'that he might hear no more about it'.[47]

But in the end the governor denied Kingi's right to protect the interests of the large Te Ati Awa community at Waitara from a handful of their relatives who wished to try to push a sale through, and sent British troops to occupy the land. War broke out, and during the next decade spread throughout central New Zealand. At this crucial time in New Zealand history neither the treaty nor the doctrine of aboriginal title came to the rescue of Maori. As the Government prepared to confiscate land from Maori, Crown lawyers skirted the guarantees in article 2 of the treaty – the article that has always mattered most to Maori – emphasizing variously, the Crown's sovereign rights under article 1, and the constitutional authority of the New Zealand legislature to pass laws affecting Maori property rights.[48] And in this crucial context the doctrine of Aboriginal title was ignored altogether. Only fifteen years after the landmark judgment in *R. v. Symonds* had been delivered, it was passed over by the attorney-general and his staff as they considered the nature and extent of Maori land rights in post-Annexation New Zealand. Even more surprising is a comment at the same time by former Chief Justice William Martin, who had given judgment in *R. v. Symonds*. 'No Native', he wrote 'can, in any way, enforce any right of ownership or occupation of land, held by the Native Tenure, in the Courts of the Colony.'[49] This remarkable statement underlines the limits of the *R. v. Symonds* decision: evidently Martin did not consider Maori had justiciable legal rights. The groundwork for the denial of customary and treaty rights in the courts was in this way laid in the early 1860s as the Government honed its justifications for military intervention and the confiscation of Maori land.

The disadvantages under which Maori were placed by the Crown in the 1840s, in respect of free exercise of their land rights, were to have long-term economic, social and political consequences. In the years after the Treaty, Maori were denied both permission to keep lands they wished to keep and recognition of their right to sell and lease freely. The issue of direct Maori leasing, in particular, lays bare the essential conflict of interest between indigenous people and colonizers, for it may be argued that exercise of a right which in effect allowed Maori to control the speed of settlement, the price of land and the nature of their relationships with settlers was so deeply at odds with the colonizing imperative and the perceived role of a colonizing state that the government saw no alternative but to curb it.

In the 1860s, the circumstances of the *raupatu* (war, military occupation and land confiscation) that followed emphasized the passing of control on the ground from Maori to colonizers. The basis of relationships between Maori and Pakeha who settled on their land was shattered. The arrival of soldiers, the destruction of villages, the building of military fortifications, and the confiscation proclamations all conveyed in unmistakable terms a message until then quietly tucked away in legislation and in policy documents, or evident in the demeanour of individual Crown purchase agents: that Maori law was to be ignored. Maori and their *interests* were to be protected – and the Government had laid a long paper-trail that bore witness to its determination to discharge its humanitarian obligations – but Maori *rights* were rather less pressing.

It is not surprising, therefore, that Justice Durie, chairperson of the Waitangi Tribunal, has recently suggested that the English introduced their own law in defiance of Maori law, and ignored the fact that in Maori legal tenure there was already a radical title in this country.[50] We have, perhaps, been too slow and tentative in recognizing that the basis of indigenous land rights was as valid as that of English rights – and that steamrollering Maori rights on the grounds that they were inconvenient to colonizers, and incompatible with *their* law, was indefensible.

Notes

I wish to thank The Honourable Justice Durie (chairperson of the Waitangi Tribunal), Denese L. Henare (Law Commission), Professor Gordon Orr (Waitangi Tribunal), and Mr G. Leane (School of Law, University of Canterbury), for very helpful discussions on aspects of this paper. Richard Boast (Law Faculty, Victoria University of Wellington) and Dr Barry Rigby (Waitangi Tribunal) kindly commented on a draft.

1 (1847) [1840–1932] N.Z.P.C.C. 387 (SC).
2 P.G. McHugh, 'The Aboriginal Rights of the New Zealand Maori at Common Law', D.Phil. thesis, University of Cambridge, 1987, p. 220.
3 *Muriwhenua Land Report, Wai 45: Waitangi Tribunal Report 1997* (Wellington, GP Publications, 1997), pp. 1–5.
4 *The Taranaki Report (Kaupapa Tuatahi), Wai 143: Waitangi Tribunal Report 1996*, (Wellington, GP Publications, 1996), pp. 17, 20. By Article 1 of the Treaty Maori ceded 'sovereignty' to the Queen; in the Maori text, however, 'sovereignty' was translated as *kawanatanga* (governance, or 'government over the land'). In Professor Sir Hugh Kawharu's words, 'there could be no possibility of the Maori signatories having any understanding of government in the sense of "sovereignty", i.e. any understanding on the basis of experience or cultural precedent': I.H. Kawharu (ed.), *Waitangi: Maori and Pakeha Perspectives of the Treaty of Waitangi* (Auckland, Oxford University Press, 1989), p. 319.

5 Land Claims Ordinance, 4 Vic. No. 2 (NSW Act 4 Vic. No. 7 repealed).
6 As it happened, the fledgling Government was quite unable to embark on survey on such a massive scale at that time. See Russell to Hobson, 9 December 1840, in *Irish University Press Series of British Parliamentary Papers* (hereafter *IUP–BPP*), *Colonies: New Zealand* (Shannon, Irish University Press, 1970), vol. 3, p. 152; also encl. 1 (Charter for Erecting the Colony of NZ), p. 154, and encl. 3, p. 161.
7 Grey to Grey, 23 December 1846, in *IUP–BPP, Colonies: New Zealand*, vol. 5, pp. 524–5, 540–1.
8 Hobson to Gipps, 25 October 1840; enclosed in Gipps to Russell, 5 March 1841, *IUP–BPP, Colonies: New Zealand*, vol. 3, p. 438.
9 Hobson to Gipps, 17 February 1841, and Gipps to Hobson, 6 March 1841, *ibid.*, p. 439.
10 Russell to Hobson, 3 August 1841, *ibid.*, p. 440.
11 Russell to Hobson, 28 January 1841, *ibid.*, p. 174.
12 *The Ordinances of the Legislative Council of New Zealand and of the Legislative Council of the Province of New Munster, 1841–1853* (Wellington, Government Printer, 1871).
13 *The Statutes: Revised Edition*, vol. XI: *14 & 15 Victoria to 16 & 17 Victoria: A.D. 1851–1853* (London, Eyre & Spottiswoode, 1877).
14 McLean to Cooper, 12 July 1854, Donald McLean, Letterbook, Private Correspondence, 1854–57, Alexander Turnbull Library, Wellington.
15 McLean to the Colonial Secretary, 5 February 1854, *Appendices to the Journals of the House of Representatives (AJHR)*, 1861, C No.1, p. 264.
16 W.H. Donald to William Mein Smith and others, 1 October 1850, New Munster Series 8 (Colonial Secretary, Inwards Correspondence), 50/1054, National Archives.
17 According to Bagnall, the effect of the threat was negligible, for Grey's letter was intercepted in the Wairapapa and destroyed: A.G. Bagnall, *Wairarapa: An Historical Excursion* (Masterton, Hedley's Bookshop for the Masterton Lands Trust, 1976), p. 84.
18 *Report of the Waitangi Tribunal on The Orakei Claim (Wai 9)* (Wellington, Waitangi Tribunal, 1987), p. 135; see Kawharu (ed.), *Waitangi*, pp. 316–20.
19 (1900–1) [1840–1932] N.Z.P.C.C. 371 at 373.
20 D.V. Williams, 'The Queen v. Symonds Reconsidered', *Victoria University of Wellington Law Review*, 19 (1989), 393.
21 *Mabo v. Queensland (No. 2) (1992)* 175 CLR 1 at 110 per Deane and Gaudron JJ.
22 *Ibid.* at 59 per Brennan J. Delgamuukw is less dogmatic: though lands held pursuant to Aboriginal title are held to be 'inalienable to third parties', it is emphasized that uses of land held by Aboriginal title do not need to be confined to aspects of Aboriginal practices which are 'integral to distinctive Aboriginal cultures'. *Delgamuukw* v. *British Columbia*, CNLR [1998] 1 at 58–9 per Lamer C.J.
23 See Kent McNeil's interesting arguments – and his comments on inconsistency in imperial practice: K. McNeil, *Common Law Aboriginal Title* (Oxford, Clarendon Press, 1989), pp. 221–35. The overall case, however, was dismissed in *Mabo*.
24 (1847) [1840–1932] N.Z.P.C.C. 387 at 390–1
25 *Muriwhenua Land Report*, p. 73. The claimants explained that the term used in their area for land allocations to those they wished to bring into the *hapu* – *tuku whenua* – was used by missionaries in their land deeds with the quite different meaning of 'sale'.
26 See for instance [Colonial Secretary] to Chief Protector, 1 February 1842, and 8 June 1842, 1A 4/27, National Archives, Wellington.
27 Colonial Secretary to Protector of Aborigines, 4 February 1842, 1A 4/271.
28 'Minutes of Meeting, Saturday 3 August 1844 ...', Donald McLean Papers, Folder 1, Alexander Turnbull Library, Wellington.
29 Bell to Wakefield, 15 April 1848, New Zealand Company Papers, Series 105/7, No. 9/48, National Archives, Wellington.
30 The notice was eventually published in the *New Zealand Government Gazette for the Province of New Plymouth*, 4 November 1854.

31 McLean to Cooper, 12 July 1854, Donald McLean Letter Book, Private Correspondence, 1854–57, Alexander Turnbull Library, Wellington.
32 Reported in the *Taranaki Herald*, 16 May 1855. The Native Land Purchase Ordinance provided for penalties to be imposed on those who, without a Government license, used or occupied land 'not comprised within a Grant from the Crown'. The English text of the Grey Block deed, after reciting the boundaries of the purchase, states that the governor 'agrees to reserve for us certain lands within the boundaries which have been herein set forth and surrendered altogether to him'.
33 Reported in the *Taranaki Herald*, 2 May 1855.
34 The Moturoa Reserve was 200 acres in total. The first Crown grant for part of the land was issued in 1862; others were not ordered to be issued till 1887.
35 FitzRoy had adopted the policy – without opposition from the Colonial Office – in order to distance the Crown from land purchase. He was aware that Maori were already seeing the Crown's exercise of its right of pre-emption as inimical to, rather than protective of, their rights.
36 The Ngai Tahu Claim against the Crown arising from these purchases, first articulated in 1849, would be carried by the tribe through succeeding generations, until it was finally settled in 1998.
37 Grey to Grey, 15 May 1848, *IUP–BPP, Colonies: New Zealand*, vol. 6: *Further Papers Relative to the Affairs of New Zealand* (July 1849), pp. 22–6.
38 F. Whitaker, *New Zealand Parliamentary Debates*, 3 July 1856.
39 *R. v. Fitzherbert and Others* (1872) C.A. 143 at 170.
40 This was clarified much later in *Te Poho Mokoare* v. *Davy and the Public Trustee* (1896) S.C. NZLR 14, in which Prendergast C.J. (an unlikely judge!) distinguished the status of two reserves connected with two different purchases of Taranaki land (one in 1853 and one in 1854) on the basis of his interpretation of the wording of the deeds. The judge stated that the reserve before the court in the first case (Purakau) was not excepted from the sale by Maori, but the reserve in the second case (Paraiti) was included in 'sacred places' excepted from sale; 'consequently the Native title was not then extinguished, and never has been extinguished' (p. 536).
41 The Native Reserves Act 1856, *The Statutes of New Zealand*.
42 In 1920 all native reserves were transferred from the public trustee to the native trustee, whose Office was established by statute. As both the terms of leases and the rents of reserved land over generations were controlled by statute – very much to the detriment of Maori owners – this state of affairs became the subject of vocal protest in recent years, and the Government finally embarked on a series of measures to restore control of the lands to Maori.
43 Evidence of Thomas Hughes, 26 April 1888, Maori Land Court Minute Books, Otorohanga Book 3, Kopua–Pirongia–Kawhia, pp. 145–6. See also evidence of Hauauru, 24 April 1888, *ibid.*.
44 It may be noted that, on the face of it, leases by Maori would not fail tests for Aboriginal title outlined in *Delgamuukw* by Lamer C.J., that lands held pursuant to Aboriginal title 'cannot be used in a manner that is irreconcilable with the nature of the claimants' attachment to those lands'; nor can land be put to uses that would threaten the relationship of an Aboriginal community with its land. It is interesting that the judge, who insists on the requirement of exclusive occupation of Aboriginal lands at sovereignty, nevertheless considers the possibility that joint title could arise from shared exclusivity, noting that 'shared exclusive possession is the right to exclude others except those with whom possession is shared' – in other words, the retention of control over the lands was important to demonstrating exclusivity. He confined himself, however, to consideration of joint title shared between two or more Aboriginal nations: *Delgamuukw* v. *British Columbia*, CNLR [1998] 1 at 62–3 and 73–4 per Lamer C.J.
45 Cf. Brennan J.'s evident assumption in *Mabo* that a non-indigenous person would not acknowledge indigenous laws or observe their customs, and could not therefore acquire from them 'a right or interest possessed as a native title': *Mabo* v. *Queensland* (No. 2) (1992) 175 CLR 1 at 60.

46 *The Taranaki Report/Kaupapa Tuatahi*, p. 55. See also pp. 21, 56.
47 J. G. Cooke to D. McLean, 17 January 1849, McLean Papers, MS 32, Folder 226 (14) Alexander Turnbull Library, Wellington.
48 F.D. Fenton, Right of Government to Take Lands Compulsorily from Aboriginal Natives, 28 November 1862, encl. in Grey to Newcastle, 24 February 1863, *AJHR*, 1863, E No. 3, s.1, pp. 13–16; F. Whitaker, 21 February 1863, enclosure in Grey to Newcastle, 24 February 1863, C.O. 209/172, pp. 163–4.
49 Observations on the Proposal to take Native Lands under an Act of the Assembly, enclosure in Martin to W. Fox, 16 November 1863, enclosure in Grey to Newcastle, 6 January 1864, No.9, C.O. 209/178, p. 163 (35).
50 E. T. Durie, 'Will the Settlers Settle? Cultural Conciliation and Law', F.W. Guest Memorial Lecture 1996, *Otago Law Review*, 8:4 (1996), 461–2.

CHAPTER TWELVE

'Because it does not make sense': sovereignty's power in the case of *Delgamuukw* v. *The Queen* 1997

John Borrows

'Because it does not make sense to speak of a burden on the underlying title before that title existed, aboriginal title crystallized at the time sovereignty was asserted', the Supreme Court of Canada declared in its historic judgment of *Delgamuukw* v. *The Queen* in 1997.[1] Sovereignty is pretty powerful stuff: its mere assertion by one nation is said to bring another's land rights to a 'definite and permanent form'.[2] Its simple conjuring is held to change an ancient people's relationship with its land; a society under its spell is ostensibly transformed. Use and occupation are found to be extinguished, infringed or made subject to another's designs. How can lands possessed for centuries by aboriginal peoples be undermined by another nation's assertion of sovereignty? What alchemy transmutes the base of aboriginal possession into the golden bedrock of Crown title?

This chapter analyzes the Supreme Court's decision in *Delgamuukw* and argues that the Court's unreflective acceptance of Crown sovereignty perpetuates 'the historical injustice suffered by aboriginal peoples at the hands of the colonizers who failed to respect the distinctive cultures of pre-existing aboriginal societies'.[3] This danger flows from the case despite its extraordinarily progressive attempt to recognize and facilitate indigenous legal pluralism within Canada. Despite its positive features, there are many ways the case's treatment of sovereignty negatively influences indigenous peoples' ability to question the taking of their lands. The Court negatively uses sovereignty to define the terrain on which aboriginal peoples must operate if they are going to dispute the Crown's actions in Canadian courts.

The claim

The Supreme Court of Canada's decision in *Delgamuukw* considered the Gitksan and Wet'suwet'en peoples' claim to Aboriginal title and self-government over approximately 58,000 square kilometers of land in (what is now called) northwestern British Columbia.[4] Both nations have lived in this area as 'distinct people' for a 'long, long time prior to [British assertions of] sovereignty'.[5] For millennia, their histories tell of their organization into Houses and Clans in which hereditary chiefs are responsible for the allocation, administration and control of traditional lands. Within these Houses chiefs pass on important histories, songs, crests, lands, rank and property from one generation to the next. The passage of these legal, political, social and economic entitlements is performed and witnessed in their Feasts. Gitksan and Wet'suwet'en Feasts substantiate the territories' relationships as a hosting House will serve food, distribute gifts, announce the House's successors to the names of deceased chiefs, describe the territory, raise totem poles and tell the oral history of the House. Chiefs from other Houses witness the actions of the Feast, and at the end of the proceedings validate the decisions and declarations of the Host House. As such, the Feast is an important 'institution through which the people governed themselves', and confirms the relationship between each House and its territories.[6] As the trial judge Chief Justice McEachern observed:

> The spiritual connection of the Houses with their territory is most noticeably maintained in the feast hall, where, by telling and re-telling their stories, and by identifying their territories, and by providing food and other contributions to the feast from their territories, they remind themselves over and over again of the sacred connection that they have with their lands.[7]

The first known European to contact the Gitksan and Wet'suwet'en peoples was William Brown, a Hudson's Bay Company trader who established a fort on Lake Babine in 1822. He described these people as 'men of property' and 'possessors of lands' who regulated access to their territory through a 'structure of nobles or chiefs, commoners, kinship arrangements of some kind and priority relating to the trapping of beaver in the vicinity of the villages'. Writing in his journal in 1823 Brown observed that the chiefs 'have certain tracts of country, which they claim an exclusive right to and will not allow any other person to hunt upon them'. In this connection the trial judge accepted the evidence of Professor Arthur Ray who related how the first Europeans to reach the middle and upper Skeena river area in the 1820s discovered that the indigenous people

> were settled in a number of relatively large villages. The people subsisted largely off their fisheries that, with about two months of work per year, allowed them to meet most of their food needs. Summer villages were located beside their fisheries. Large game and fur bearers were hunted on

surrounding, and sometimes, on more distant lands ... [In addition] 'hunting territories were held by 'nobles' on behalf of the lineages they represented and these native leaders closely regulated the hunting of valued species. The various villages were linked into a regional exchange network. Indigenous commodities and European trade goods circulated within and between villages by feasting, trading and gambling activities.[8]

This and other evidence persuaded the trial judge that aboriginal people had 'been present in parts of the territory, if not from time immemorial, at least for an uncertain, long time before the commencement of the historical period'.[9] Significantly, in terms of evaluating the Supreme Court's attempt to avoid the risk of 'perpetuating historical injustices that aboriginal people suffered at the hands of the colonizers', the period of Gitksan and Wet'suwet'en presence in the area was for 'a long, long time prior to sovereignty'.[10]

However, despite finding an historic and contemporary aboriginal presence in the areas claimed, McEachern C.J., in a much criticized judgment, dismissed the Gitksan and Wet'suwet'en's claims to ownership and jurisdiction.[11] This occurred through the recitation of the dogma 'that aboriginal rights, arising by operation of law, are non-proprietary rights of occupation for residence and aboriginal user which are extinguishable at the pleasure of the Sovereign'. As such, he 'was not satisfied that they owned the territory in its entirety in any sense that would be recognized by law'. McEachern's judgment rested upon the mystical 'proposition that ... aboriginal rights are ... dependent on the good will of the Sovereign', and 'existed at the pleasure of the Crown, and could be extinguished by unilateral act'. As a result, he held that 'aboriginal rights to land had been extinguished ... because of certain colonial enactments which demonstrated an intention to manage Crown lands in a way which was inconsistent with their continued existence'. He continued: the 'law never recognized that the settlement of new lands depended upon the consent of the Indians'; he therefore held that 'the Crown with full knowledge of the local situation fully intended to settle the colony and to grant titles and tenures unburdened by any aboriginal interests'. Furthermore, he 'rejected the ... claim for a right of self-government, relying on both the sovereignty of the Crown at common law, and [what he considered to be] the relative paucity of evidence regarding an established governance structure' among the people.[12] By relying on assertions of British sovereignty to diminish and dispossess Gitksan and Wet'suwet'en rights to land, McEachern C.J. employed discursive practices that recognized prior aboriginal presence on the land, but denied this fact any attendant legal protection.

The Gitksan and Wet'suwet'en appealed this decision to the British Columbia Court of Appeal. In a 3–2 decision this Court's invocation of

British sovereignty upheld the trial judge's rejection of Gitksan and Wet'suwet'en claims to ownership and jurisdiction, though the Court recognized lesser aboriginal sustenance rights. In dealing with the claim to ownership Macfarlane J.A., writing for the majority, stated: 'I think the trial judge properly applied correct legal principles in his consideration of the plaintiff's claim to ownership.' Thus, McEachern's finding that aboriginal land rights were non-proprietary in nature and a burden on the Crown's underlying interest was left undisturbed by the Court of Appeal. Furthermore, in upholding the trial judge's decision concerning jurisdiction, Macfarlane wrote:

> I think that the trial judge was correct in his view that when the Crown imposed English law on all the inhabitants of the colony, and in particular, when British Columbia entered Confederation, the Indians became subject to the legislative authority in Canada. The division of governmental powers between Canada and the Provinces left no room for a third order of government.[13]

When British Columbia entered confederation in 1871 Indians composed a majority of the people within the province, yet did not participate in the province's creation.[14] Most continued to live within their own governments on their lands as they had done for centuries, with little regard for British assertions of sovereignty. As was stated by former United States Supreme Court Justice John Marshall:

> It is difficult to comprehend the proposition that the inhabitants of the globe could have rightful original claims of dominion over the inhabitants of the other, or over the lands they occupied; or that the discovery of either by the other should give the discoverer rights in the country discovered which annulled the pre-existing rights of its ancient possessions.[15]

It should be asked: how, then, under such circumstances, did the Indians become 'subject to the legislative authority of Canada', as the Court of Appeal suggests? Is it because they 'became a conquered people, not by force of arms, for that was not necessary, but by an invading culture and a relentless energy with which they would not, or could not compete', as McEachern suggested? Or did this subjection come about by the assertion of British sovereignty through unjust and discriminatory laws?

In 1881, ten years after union, Indians were still the majority population in British Columbia: there were 28,704 Indians, 4,195 Chinese and 19,069 settlers of European origin.[16] Yet in 1872, a year after union, when the Indian population was closer to 40,000, and the settler population was smaller still, one of the new province's first legislative acts was to remove voting rights from the Indians.[17] The new provincial Government was the successor to the old colonial Government of British

Columbia, and continued to uphold laws that denied Indians' fee simple title   to pre-empted lands taken up through settlement, a right freely granted to non-Aboriginal people in the province. Furthermore, this Government only allowed for the surveying of extremely small reserves for Indians, and would not recognize any aboriginal title to land. When aboriginal peoples in British Columbia tried to dispute this mistreatment, the province responded by further diminishing their land and political rights, and the Federal Government eventually followed suit by amending the Indian Act and making it all but illegal to raise these matters before the courts.[18]

'Taking the perspective of the aboriginal people themselves on the meaning of the rights at stake', as the Supreme Court itself proposed in *R. v. Sparrow*, it should be asked whether the authority of an imposed, obstructionist and unrepresentative Government should be recognized as legally infringing or extinguishing any 'aboriginal legislative or other jurisdiction' which aboriginal people possess.[19] In these circumstances, is the assertion of British sovereignty over aboriginal peoples in British Columbia, as *R. v. Van der Peet* asks, a 'morally and politically defensible conception of aboriginal rights'? Does the decision, as *R. v. Cote* cautions, 'perpetuate historical injustice suffered by aboriginal peoples at the hands of the colonizers'?[20] Is *Delgamuukw v. The Queen* consistent with the Court's own standard of upholding the 'noble and prospective purpose of the Constitutional entrenchment of aboriginal and treaty rights in the Constitution'?[21] If assertions of sovereignty operate to undermine the prior legal authority of Aboriginal peoples, should we question, as the Australian High Court asked in *Mabo v. Queensland*, whether 'an unjust and discriminatory doctrine of that kind can any longer be accepted'?[22]

Having failed to persuade the lower courts to recognize aboriginal ownership and jurisdiction in their territories, the Gitksan and the Wet'suwet'en appealed their case to the Supreme Court of Canada. In its decision the Supreme Court did not substantially depart from the previous courts' reliance on assertions of British sovereignty in grounding its discussion of aboriginal title. It found that '[a]boriginal title is a burden on the Crown's underlying title'. Furthermore, it did not recognize or affirm Gitksan and Wet'suwet'en ownership or jurisdiction over their territories. This result does not substantially depart from Canada's colonial heritage. To examine how Crown sovereignty infuses the Court's understanding of Aboriginal title, a closer reading of the case is in order. A full understanding of the judgment requires that the Court's own words be thoroughly scrutinized.

The issues before the Supreme Court in *Delgamuukw* were:

- Do the pleadings preclude the Court from entertaining claims for aboriginal title and self-government?
- What is the ability of this Court to interfere with the factual findings made by the trial judge?
- What is the content of aboriginal title, how is it protected by s. 35(1) of the Constitution Act 1982 and what is required for its proof?
- Has a claim to self-government been made out by the appellants?
- Did the province have the power to extinguish aboriginal rights after 1871, either under its own jurisdiction or through the operation of s. 88 of the Indian Act?[23]

Pleadings

In some respects, the issues in the *Delgamuukw* case show Canada to be a place (much like medieval England) with a bewildering diversity of legal systems, a broad array of cultures, containing a variety of bodies of law. From the maritimes to the mountains there are laws of the Mik'Maq, Mohawk, Cree, Ojibway, Okanagan, Salish, Haida, Nisga'a, Gitksan and Wet'suwet'en, etc. Canada and the common law is the story of the colony's attempted expansion at the expense of these indigenous legal jurisdictions.[24] To accomplish this extension, contemporary pleadings perform a role similar to the ancient forms of action, as parties present written statements of factual and legal issues they believe the court can resolve. They serve a consolidating function that extends the common law's jurisdiction at the expense of indigenous legal systems. While today's pleadings are infinitely more flexible than mediaeval forms of action, if a party does not frame the case properly, a court may refuse to resolve the issue before it by declaring a defect in the pleadings. The discipline this uniformity imposes on litigants allows for the extension of Crown sovereignty through the centralized control of access to justice.

Pleadings are a 'necessary passport to gain entry to the common law courts'.[25] Acquiring such a visa is obligatory in disputing the justice of Crown dealings with aboriginal peoples – because the Crown does not recognize legal claims brought in any other way. There is something deeply troubling about having to recognize Crown assertions of sovereignty in framing a case to dispute the effect of these assertions. This difficulty is apparent in the *Delgamuukw* case as the Supreme Court did not consider the specific merits of the Gitksan and Wet'suwet'en claims because of a defect in that party's pleadings. In effect, the Court found that these peoples' passport papers were out of order. They were not permitted to cross the border separating Gitksan–Wet'suwet'en legal systems and the common law because they had not followed proper procedures.

The Court's frontier patrol of 'the borders of the Canadian legal imagination' is effective in further extending Canadian sovereignty over aboriginal territories.[26] The Gitksan and Wet'suwet'en's pleadings 'originally advanced 51 individual claims on their own behalf and on behalf of their house for ownership and jurisdiction over 133 distinct territories'.[27] The Court found that there were two changes in these pleadings from the trial to the appeal: the first was that claims for ownership and jurisdiction were replaced with claims for aboriginal title and self-government; the second was that the individual claims by each House were amalgamated into two communal claims, one advanced on behalf of each nation. The Court found that the first change concerning the substitution of aboriginal title and self-government was 'just and appropriate' in the circumstances because the trial judge allowed 'a de facto amendment to permit a claim for aboriginal rights other than ownership and jurisdiction'.[28] The Court upheld the trial judge's ruling because 'it was made against the backdrop of considerable legal uncertainty surrounding the nature and content of aboriginal rights'.[29] However, the Court rejected the second change concerning the amalgamation of individual into collective claims because 'the collective claims were simply not in issue at trial'.[30]

This seems rather formalistic and inflexible given that the Court recognized 'considerable weight' in the argument that 'the collective and individual claims are related' because 'the territory claimed by each nation is merely the sum of the individual claims of each house'. It appears as if the form of action which the Gitksan and Wet'suwet'en plead must be exact, even 'against the backdrop of considerable legal uncertainty'. The Court's approach supports F.R. Maitland's observation that 'the forms of action we have buried, but they still rule us from their graves'.[31] As such, the Court 'reluctantly' concluded that the province had suffered some prejudice because the plaintiff's change 'denied them the opportunity to know the appellant's case'. It is interesting to note that in this historic case which considers the wholesale territorial dispossession of two entire aboriginal peoples, the ratio of the case turns on the Court's finding that the province suffered prejudice in considering this issue. Given the imbalance in the parties' financial and political resources, and the century-long denial of aboriginal land and political rights in British Columbia, this sleight of hand is remarkable. Sovereignty's extension is careful not to prejudice the Crown. In order to allow the province a better opportunity to know the plaintiff's case, the court ordered a new trial.

Evidence

Canadian sovereignty is also extended over aboriginal peoples when courts receive and interpret 'factual' evidence from aboriginal litigants. For millennia aboriginal peoples created, controlled and changed their own worlds through the power of language, stories and songs. These words 'did not merely represent meaning, they possessed the power to change reality itself' as indigenous languages and cultures shaped their legal, economic and political structures, and the socio-cultural relationships upon which they were built.[32] Many of these narratives were considered private property. The restriction on their presentation and interpretation helped to ensure that the authority to adjudicate and create meaning remained within aboriginal societies. When aboriginal narratives are given to another culture to authoritatively judge their factual authenticity and meaning, aboriginal people lose some of their power of self-definition and determination.

What constitutes a *fact* is largely contingent on the language and culture out of which that information arises. The person who decides what a 'fact' is defines it from within the matrix of relationships he or she shares with others.[33] Non-Aboriginal judges do not usually share the same language and relationships as aboriginal peoples. Variations between these groups help encode 'facts' with meanings that differ with each culture. Therefore, the cultural specificity of what constitutes a fact in a given culture may make it difficult for a person from a different culture to concur. This creates an enormous risk of non-recognition and misunderstanding when one culture submits its 'facts' to another for their interpretation.[34]

In litigation this problem is especially acute, as factual determinations can vary significantly between judicial interpreters, according to the judge's language, cultural orientation and experiential background. In such circumstances, common-law judges have had an especially difficult time understanding and acknowledging the meanings aboriginal people give to the facts they present.[35] In *Delgamuukw*, the Supreme Court's extension of the laws of evidence to accommodate aboriginal traditions and histories is meant to counteract these difficulties. The Court wrote that in 'cases involving aboriginal rights, appellate intervention is ... warranted by the failure of a trial court to appreciate the evidentiary difficulties inherent in adjudicating aboriginal claims when, first, applying the rules of evidence and, second, interpreting the evidence before it'.[36] These difficulties in applying aboriginal evidence prompted the Court to direct judges to 'adapt the laws of evidence so that the aboriginal perspective on their practices, customs and traditions and on their relationship with the land, are given equal weight'.[37]

They further wrote that oral histories should receive 'independent weight' and be 'placed on an equal footing with the types of historical evidence that courts are familiar with'.[38] The Court justified this more liberal approach to aboriginal evidence by noting that to do otherwise would 'impose an impossible burden of proof on aboriginal peoples, and render nugatory any rights they have' because 'most aboriginal societies did not keep written records'.[39]

However, the Court's progressive instruction to adapt the laws of evidence to incorporate aboriginal factual perspectives does not undo the spell of Crown assertions of sovereignty. Aboriginal title and sovereignty are still diminished, despite the Court's extraordinarily fair and generous approach. For indigenous peoples, the language and culture of law is not their own: legal interpretation of aboriginal traditions and history is centralized and administered by non-aboriginal people.[40] Aboriginal people barely participate in the administration of this system, and are certainly not in positions of control. Furthermore, the evidence they present must not 'strain the Canadian constitutional and legal structure'.[41] The justification for this approach is that aboriginal rights must be 'reconciled' with the 'assertion of Crown sovereignty over Canadian territory'.[42] Once again, Crown sovereignty is the standard against which aboriginal rights must be measured. It disciplines and defines the terrain on which aboriginal people must operate if they are going to dispute the actions of Canadian governments in Canadian courts.

Content, protection and proof of Aboriginal title

As it did in its discussion of pleadings and evidence, the Supreme Court drew heavily on British assertions of sovereignty in defining the content, protection and proof of aboriginal title. Once again, the Court's reliance on sovereignty's curious magic led it to further diminish aboriginal interests. Their invocation of sovereignty over distant and distinct peoples is their justification for impairing aboriginal possessions; it is the standard against which aboriginal legal interests must be measured. The Court's approach should be contrasted with statements made in 1888 by the Gitksan and Wet'suwet'en's neighbours, the Nisga'a, who said:

> what we don't like about the Government is their saying this: 'We will give you this much land'. How can they give it when it is our own? We cannot understand it. They have never fought and conquered our people and taken the land in that way, and yet they say now that they will give us so much land – our own land. These chiefs do not talk foolishly, they know the land is their own; our forefathers for generations and generations past had their land here, all around us; chiefs had their own hunting

grounds, their salmon streams, and places where they got their berries; it has always been so. It is not only during the last four or five years that we have seen the land; we have always seen and owned it; it is no new thing, it has been ours for generations. If we had only seen it for twenty years and claimed it as our own, it would have been foolish, but it has been ours for thousands of years. If any strange person came here and saw the land for twenty years and claimed it, he would be foolish. We have always got our living from the land ...[43]

As this statement demonstrates, aboriginal people in British Columbia have a hard time understanding how Crown assertions of sovereignty gave other people any entitlements to their land. To them 'it does not make sense' to speak of aboriginal title being a 'burden' on the Crown's 'underlying title'. 'Because it does not make sense to speak of a burden on the underlying title before that title existed',[44] aboriginal people wonder how it 'makes sense' that Crown title 'crystallized at the time sovereignty was asserted'. The Court might as well speak of magic crystals being sprinkled on the land as a justification for the diminishment of aboriginal occupation and possession. It does not make sense that one could secure a legal entitlement to land over another, merely through raw assertion. As Chief Justice Marshall once observed, it is an 'extravagant and absurd idea'.[45] It is even less a 'morally and politically defensible' position when this assertion has not been a neutral and noble statement, but has benefited the Crown to the detriment of the land's original inhabitants. Crown title simply does not make sense to aboriginal people.

The Court recognizes that its past decisions have not made much sense of aboriginal title. It observes that 'there has never been a definitive statement ... on the content of aboriginal title'.[46] It also states that its terminology has not been 'particularly helpful' and that 'the courts have been less than forthcoming'.[47] The Supreme Court's recent contribution to clearing up this confusion is to characterize aboriginal title as *sui generis*.[48] It finds that 'aboriginal title has been described as sui generis in order to distinguish it from "normal" proprietary interests'.[49] While many aboriginal people would agree that a legal doctrine which diminishes aboriginal occupants of ancient territories is 'abnormal', the Court cast its difference in another light. It held that aboriginal title is

sui generis in the sense that its characteristics cannot be completely explained by reference to either the common law rules of real property or to the rules of property found in aboriginal legal systems. As with other aboriginal rights, aboriginal title must be understood by reference to both common law and aboriginal perspectives. [...] The idea that aboriginal title is sui generis is the unifying principle underlying the various dimensions of that title.[50]

While the court's *sui generis* delineation of aboriginal rights by reference to aboriginal perspectives is preferable to having them defined solely through a reliance on the common law, these perspectives still have to be reconciled with British assertions of sovereignty.[51] This might not have been troubling had the Court recognized that reconciliation could not diminish aboriginal legal and political rights without aboriginal authorization. However, the Court did not take this path. It chose to find that the 'reconciliation of aboriginal prior occupation with the assertion of the sovereignty of the Crown' displaces the fuller pre-existent rights of the land's original occupants. The Court noted that

> because ... distinctive aboriginal societies exist within, and are a part of, a broader social, political and economic community, over which the Crown is sovereign, there are circumstances in which, in order to pursue objectives of compelling and substantial importance to that community as a whole (taking account of the fact that aboriginal societies are part of that community), some limitation of those rights will be justifiable. Aboriginal rights are a necessary part of that reconciliation of aboriginal societies with the broader political community of which they are a part; limits placed on those rights are, where the objectives furthered by those limits are of sufficient importance to the broader community as a whole, equally a necessary part of that reconciliation.[52]

The Court's approach to reconciliation forcibly includes non-treaty aboriginal peoples within Canadian society and subjects them to an alien sovereignty, even though most never consented to such an arrangement. This inclusion subordinates aboriginal sovereignty, and limits the uses to which their land can be put. The implications of this approach deeply undermine original aboriginal entitlements – and this occurs on no other grounds but self-assertion! The conjuring of Crown assertions of sovereignty in this manner validates the appropriation of aboriginal land for non-aboriginal people. It sanctions the colonization of British Columbia and directs aboriginal peoples to reconcile their perspectives with this diminution of their rights. The Court's invocation of Crown assertions, behind a cloak of sovereignty, endorses the infringement of aboriginal rights in furtherance of legislative objectives which are 'compelling and substantial', to the 'European colonizers'. As such, the Court writes:

> In the wake of Gladstone, the range of legislative objectives that can justify the infringement of aboriginal title is fairly broad. Most of these objectives can be traced to the reconciliation of the prior occupation of North America by aboriginal peoples with the assertion of Crown sovereignty, which entails the recognition that 'distinctive aboriginal societies exist within, and are a part of a broader social, political and economic community.

[200]

Justice Lamer continued:

> In my opinion the development of agriculture, forestry, mining, and hydro-electric power, the general economic development of the interior of British Columbia, protection of the environment or endangered species, the building of infrastructure and the settlement of foreign populations to support those aims, are the kinds of objectives that are consistent with this purpose and, in principle, can justify the infringement of aboriginal title.[53]

Words, as bare assertions, are pulled out of the air to justify a basic tenet of colonialism: the settlement of foreign populations to support the expansion of non-indigenous societies. To paraphase Joseph Conrad, colonization is not a pretty thing, when you look into it. In reconciling Crown assertions of sovereignty with ancient rights stemming from aboriginal occupation, the Court labels colonization an 'infringement' (as if the interference with another nation's independent legal rights were a minor imposition – at the fringes of the parties' relationship). Calling colonization 'infringement' is an understatement of immense proportions. While these 'infringements' must be 'consistent with the special fiduciary relationship between the Crown and aboriginal peoples', the effect of the Court's holding is to make Aboriginal land rights subject to the 'colonizer's' objectives.[54]

Furthermore, the Court's test for the proof of aboriginal title demonstrates how this interest in land is defined by reference to assertions of Crown sovereignty. Non-aboriginal sovereignty permeates the criteria aboriginal groups must satisfy 'to make out a claim for aboriginal title'. For example, in order to establish title, aboriginal people have to prove that:

- the land must have been occupied prior to sovereignty;
- if present occupation is relied on as proof of occupation pre-sovereignty, there must be a continuity between present and pre-sovereignty occupation;
- at sovereignty occupation must have been exclusive.[55]

Why should aboriginal groups have to bear the burden of proving their title, and the Crown be presumed to possess it through bare words? Could the Crown establish occupation of land prior to sovereignty? Could the Crown show continuity of occupation between present and pre-sovereignty occupation? Could the Crown show that at sovereignty its occupation was exclusive? The Court's mantra of Crown sovereignty is repeated over and over again as the measuring rod for the proof of aboriginal title. This sceptre is waved at each stage of the Court's test to ensure that proof of aboriginal occupancy reconciles prior aboriginal occupation of North America with the assertion of

Crown sovereignty. Why should the aboriginal group have to bear the burden of reconciliation by proving their occupation of land? After all, the Crown is the subsequent claimant. Why should the Crown not have to prove its land claims? The Court's acceptance of assertions of Crown sovereignty ensures that the Crown does not have to meet this burden, that it is not held to the same strict legal standard as aboriginal peoples in proving its claims. This double standard is deeply discriminatory and unjust because it holds aboriginal people to a higher standard in proving title, a standard that the Crown itself could not meet. The Crown does not have to meet any tests of occupation and exclusivity. It gains its title through mere assertion, as the Court states: 'Because it does not make sense to speak of a burden on the underlying title before that title existed, aboriginal title crystallized at the time sovereignty was asserted.'[56] Justice Brennan's statement is profound. Whatever the justification advanced in earlier days for relieving the Crown of this burden, an unjust and discriminatory doctrine of this kind can no longer be accepted.

The claim to self-government

In its brief – two-paragraph – examination of self-government, the Court once again revealed the effects of its unreflective acceptance of the final sovereignty of the Crown on its comprehension of the issues before it. After relying on assertions of Crown sovereignty to ground Crown rights throughout the judgment, the Court did not extend to aboriginal peoples equally generous treatment concerning the effects of aboriginal sovereignty. Relying on its earlier judgment in R. v. Pamajewon,[57] the Court reasserted that aboriginal 'rights to self-government, if they existed, cannot be framed in excessively general terms'.[58] The contrast in the Court's treatment of Crown and aboriginal sovereignty could not be more striking. The Court was quite willing to frame Crown rights to self-government in the most excessive and general of terms – simple utterances were sufficient to grant the Crown the widest possible range of entitlements to others' ancient rights. On the other hand, detailed evidence concerning Gitksan and Wet'suwet'en sovereignty (houses, clans, chiefs, feasts, crests, poles, laws, etc.) over specific people and territory was too broad to 'lay down the legal principles to guide future litigation'.[59] As a result the Court held that the advancement of the aboriginal right to self-government, in the supposedly very broad terms in the case before it, was not cognizable under s. 35(1) of the Constitution. Is the Crown's assertion of broad rights of Crown sovereignty any more cognizable given its unexamined extension and unquestioned acceptance by the Court in this case? Where, in this treatment, is 'equality before the law'?

Given that aboriginal people in British Columbia were not conquered and never agreed to diminish their governmental rights, Aboriginal sovereignty should be placed on at least the same, if not a greater, footing as Crown sovereignty. The implications of the assertion of Crown sovereignty need to be more carefully scrutinized to assess the legality and justice of the non-consensual colonization of British Columbia. Without such an examination, the unequal treatment of aboriginal and Crown sovereignty perpetuates historical injustices and therefore fails to respect the distinctive cultures of pre-existing aboriginal societies in contemporary Canadian society.

Extinguishment of Aboriginal rights

The final section of the judgment dealt with arguments concerning the potential extinguishment of aboriginal rights. In considering this issue, the Court continued its unreflective treatment of Crown sovereignty when it noted that section 91(24) of the Constitution Act 1867 vests the Federal Government with the exclusive power to legislate in relation to 'Indians and lands reserved for Indians'. The Court interpreted this power as 'encompass[ing] within it the exclusive power to extinguish aboriginal rights, including aboriginal title'.[60]

The Court's ascription to the federal Crown of a right to terminate ancient indigenous entitlements once again demonstrates the detrimental effect that unquestioned Crown sovereignty can have over aboriginal people. As the Court wrote: 'jurisdiction to accept surrenders lies with the federal government. The same can be said of extinguishment ... the jurisdiction to extinguish lies with the federal government'.[61] This is a one-sided treatment of the issue. In commenting on the power of extinguishment the Court did not mention aboriginal people possessing the jurisdiction to participate in this regard – though that would be more consistent with their status as original occupants of the land, and more in harmony with the idea that it is they who would have to consent to any alteration of their legal status. Thus, while the Court in this case finds that the provinces cannot exercise these powers of extinguishment, this does not mean that the assertion of sovereignty cannot dispossess aboriginal peoples of their ancient rights. This can be done, as long as it is done by the proper manifestation of the Crown, which in this instance is the federal Government.

Conclusion

The Court's decision in *Delgamuukw* is suffused with the Court's acceptance of a subsequent claimant's non-consensual assertion to a prior owner's land. The Court concluded its judgment in *Delgamuukw* by observing: 'Ultimately, it is through negotiated settlements, with good faith and give and take on all sides, reinforced by the judgments of this court, that we will achieve what I stated in Van der Peet ... to be a basic purpose of s. 35(1) – "the reconcliation of the pre-existence of aboriginal societies with the sovereignty of the Crown". Lets face it, we are all here to stay.'[62]

In saying that 'we are all here to stay' the Court did not imply where 'here' is. However, it is clear that if 'here' is principally defined in relation to a reconciliation with magical assertions of Crown sovereignty, 'here' will never be a place where aboriginal peoples have underlying title and a sphere of overriding sovereignty. It may be instructive to remember the statement of the Gitksan chiefs from Gitwangak in 1884 on this issue: 'In making this claim, we would appeal to your sense of justice and right. We would remind you that is the duty of the Government to uphold the just claims of all peaceable and law abiding persons such as we have proved ourselves to be.' The Gitksan chiefs 'hold these lands by the best of all titles. We have received them as a gift from the Creator to our Grandmothers and Grandfathers, and we believe that we cannot be deprived of them by anything short of direct injustice.'[63]

Notes

This is a revised and abridged version of an article published as 'Sovereignty's Alchemy' in the *Osgoode Hall Law Journal* (1999).

1 *Delagamuukw* v. *The Queen* [1998] 1 CNLR 14 para. 145, per Lamer.
2 Definition of *crystallize* found in Funk and Wagnalls, *Standard College Dictionary* (Toronto, Fitzhenry & Whiteside, 1974), p. 325.
3 *R.* v. *Cote*, (1996) 138 DLR 4th 385, para. 53.
4 The Wet'suwet'en are an Athabaskan-speaking people, and the Gitksan are associated with the Tsimshian language group. Their territories are located in or near villages sites on the Skeena, Babine and Bulkley Rivers in British Columbia. See *R.* v. *Delgamuukw*, para 30, per Lambert; Gisday Wa and Delgam Uukw, *The Spirit in the Land* (Gabriola, BC, Reflections, 1992).
5 *Delagamuukw* v. *British Columbia* (1991) 79 DLR 4th 185 at 278, 282.
6 Antonia Mills, *Eagle Down in Our Law: Witsuwit'en Law, Feasts, and Land Claims* (Vancouver, University of British Columbia Press, 1995).
7 *Delgamuukw* v. *the Queen* [1993] 1 WWR 97 p. 240, per Lambert J.A.; quoting McEachern.
8 Arthur Ray, Trial 202, p. 13387, Report, Exhibit 960, p. 27; see also Arthur Ray, 'Fur Trade History and the Gitksan and Wet'suwet'en Comprehensive Claim: Men of Property and the Exercise of Title', in Kerry Abel and Jean Friesen (eds), *Aboriginal Resource Use in Canada: Historical and Legal Aspects* (Winnipeg, University of Manitoba Press, 1991).
9 See note 5: p. 204, per McEachern.
10 Arthur Ray, Exhibit 964–5, 1(87).
11 See Dara Culhane, *The Pleasure of the Crown* (Vancouver, Talon Books, 1998); Ardythe Wilson and Don Monet, *Colonialism on Trial* (Philadephia, PA, New Society Publishers, 1992); Leslie Hall Pinder, *The Carriers of No: After the Land Claims*

Trial (Vancouver, Lazara Press, 1991); Julie Cruickshank, 'Invention of Anthropology in British Columbia's Supreme Court: Oral Tradition and Evidence in Delgamuukw v. B.C.' *B.C. Studies*, 95, special issue (1992), 25; Robin Fisher, 'Judging History: Reflections on the Reasons for Judgment in Delgamuukw v. BC', *B.C. Studies*, 95, special issue (1992), 43; Joel Fortune, 'Construing Delgamuukw: Legal Arguments, Historical Argumentation and the Philosophy of History', *Faculty of Law Review* (University of Toronto), 51 (1993), 80; Mark Walters, 'British Imperial Constitutional Law and Aboriginal Rights: A Comment on Delgamuukw v. BC', *Queen's Law Journal*, 17 (1993), 350; Natalie Oman, 'Sharing Horizons: A Paradigm for Political Accomodation in Intercultural Settings', Ph.D. thesis, McGill University, 1997.

12 *Delgamuukw*, see note 1: per Lamer: paras 17 and 23; 24; 23; 24; and 20.

13 For commentary on the jurisdictional aspect of this judgment, see Bob Freedman, 'The Space for Aboriginal Self-Government in British Columbia: The Effect of the Decision of the British Columbia Court of Appeal in Delgamuukw v. British Columbia', *University of British Columbia Law Review*, 28 (1994), 49, para. 171.

14 Cole Harris, *The Resettlement of British Columbia* (Vancouver, University of British Columbia Press, 1997)

15 *Worcester* v. *Georgia* 31 U.S. (6 Pet.) 515, 8 L.Ed. 483 (U.S.S.C.).

16 Harris, *Resettlement*, pp. 136–160.

17 Figures projected from Wilson Duff, *The Indian History of British Columbia*, vol. 1: *The Impact of the White Man* (Victoria, Provincial Museum of British Columbia, 1965), p. 42; Qualification and Registration of Voters Amendment Act 1872, s. 13.

18 See Paul Tennant, *Aboriginal Peoples and Politics: The Indian Law Question in British Columbia, 1849–1989* (Vancouver, University of British Columbia Press, 1990), pp. 96–114.

19 *Sparrow* v. *the Queen* (1990) 70 DLR 4th 385 p. 411.

20 *R.* v. *Van der Peet* [1996] 4 C.N.L.R. 177 para. 42; *R.* v. *Cote* (1996) 138 DLR 4th 385 para. 53.

21 *Ibid.*

22 Brennan J., in *Mabo* v. *Queensland* (1992) 175 CLR 1 (H.C.) p. 42

23 *Delgamuukw*, see note 1: para. 72, per Lamer.

24 Macklem, 'First Nations' Self-Government and the Borders of the Canadian Legal Imagination', *McGill Law Journal*, 36 (1991), 382.

25 F.W. Maitland, *The Forms of Action at Common Law* (Cambridge, Cambridge University Press, 1958), p. 2.

26 Macklem, 'First Nations' Self-Government', 382.

27 *Delgamuukw*, see note 1: para. 73, per Lamer.

28 *Ibid.*, paras 75–6.

29 *Ibid.*

30 *Ibid.*

31 Maitland, Forms of Action, p. 2.

32 Penny Petrone, *Native Literature in Canada: From Oral Tradition to the Present* (Toronto, University of Toronto Press, 1990), pp. 9–12.

33 Pinder, *The Carriers of No*; Ludwig Wittgenstein, *Philosophical Investigations*, trans. G.E.M. Anscombe, 3rd edn, (New York, Macmillan Publishing Co., 1958), pp. 154, 155. Understanding the meaning of a fact is 'knowing how to go on'; Martin Heidegger, *Being and Time*, trans. John Macquarrie and Edward Robinson (New York, Harper & Row, 1962), p. 157.

34 Charles Taylor, 'Understanding and Ethnocentricity', in *Philosophy and the Human Sciences, vol. 2, Philosophical Papers* (Cambridge, Cambridge University Press, 1985), pp. 119, 121.

35 Richard Rorty, 'On Ethnocentrism: A Reply to Clifford Geertz', *Michigan Quarterly Review*, 25 (1986), 115; Abdullahi Ahmed An-Na'im, 'Problems of Universal Cultural Legitimacy for Human Rights', in A. An-Na'im and Francis Deng (eds), *Human Rights in Africa* (Washington, Brookings Institute, 1990); Richard Devlin, 'Justice or Just Us?', *Provincial Court Judges Journal*, 4 (1996), 20; Louise Mandell, 'Native Culture on Trial', in Sheilah Martin and Kathleen Mahoney (eds), *Equality and Judicial*

Neutrality (Toronto, Carswell, 1987), p. 358; Joan Ryan and Bernard Ominayak, 'The Cultural Effects of Judicial Bias', in ibid., p. 346; Robin Ridington, 'Cultures in Conflict: The Problem of Discourse', in W.H. New (ed.), *Native Writers and Canadian Writing* (Vancouver, University of British Columbia Press, 1990), p. 273.

36 *Delgamuukw*, see note 1: para. 86, per Lamer.
37 *Ibid.*, para. 84.
38 *Ibid.*, para. 87.
39 *Ibid.*, para. 80.
40 There are only sixteen Aboriginal judges in Canada, none of whom sit on an appellate court.
41 *Delgamuukw*, see note 1: para. 82.
42 *Ibid.*, paras 82, 81 and 87.
43 David McKay, *Calder* v. *A.G.B.C.* (1973) 34 DLR (3d) 145 (S.C.C.).
44 *Delgamuukw*, see note 1.
45 *Worcester* v. *Georgia* (1932) 31 U.S. (6 Pet.) 515 8 L.Ed. 483.
46 *Delgamuukw*, see note 1: para. 116.
47 *Ibid.*, paras 112 and 117, per Lamer.
48 John Borrows and Len Rotman, 'The Sui Generis Nature of Aboriginal Rights: Does it Make a Difference?', *Alberta Law Review*, 36 (1997), 9.
49 *Delgamuukw*, see note 1: para. 112.
50 *Ibid.*, paras 112 and 113, per Lamer.
51 For a discussion of this principle, see John Borrows, 'With or Without You: First Nations' Law' (in Canada), *McGill Law Journal*, 41 (1996), 629.
52 *Ibid.*, para. 161, quoting *R.* v. *Gladstone* (1996) 137 DLR (4th) 528 para 72.
53 *Delgamuukw*, see note 1: paras 161, 153, 165, per Lamer.
54 *Ibid.*, para. 162.
55 *Ibid.*
56 *Delgamuukw*, see note 1.
57 (1996) 138 D.L.R. (4th) 204 (S.C.C.).
58 *Delgammukw*, see note 1: para. 170.
59 *Ibid.*
60 *Delgamuukw*, see note 1: para. 173.
61 *Ibid.*, para. 172.
62 *Ibid.*, para. 186.
63 Wilson and Monet, *Colonialism on Trial*, p. 1.

CHAPTER THIRTEEN

Land, conveyancing reform and the problem of the married woman in colonial Australia

Hilary Golder and Diane Kirkby

Land and its acquisition was at the heart of Australia's colonial history: land was the defining feature of settler colonialism. As historian Humphrey McQueen has pointed out, 'just how important land was in the formation of the political and social consciousness of the Australian people [is] demonstrated by recounting some of the pro-longed battles [the colonists] waged in order to establish a "yeomanry"'.[1]

Those battles were won when urban middle-class legislators responded to the call to 'unlock the lands'. Consequently the years between 1860 and the 1880s saw an intensification of settlement in rural regions which had a devastating impact on the indigenous populations.[2] McQueen claims that 'in order to appreciate the intensity of feeling that "land" can generate' among European colonizers, 'it is essential to realise the mythical, indeed, religious qualities with which it can be endowed'.[3] It is impossible, he claims, to overestimate the impact of industrialization on the agricultural communities of the British Isles which bore the brunt of its worst features. It was they, the labouring poor, the displaced artisans, the Scottish crofters and the Irish peasants, who formed the diaspora which became the immigrant population to the Australian colonies. Their hunger for independence coincided with a capitalist enterprise focused on proprietorship in land.

Democratization of land ownership among the non-indigenous inhabitants was therefore a defining concern of Australian liberalism in the mid-nineteenth century. Politicians boasted that colonial land was 'as much an article of trade as a bale of goods', making explicit comparisons with Britain where too much of this valuable commodity was corralled in large estates.[4] Popular access to Crown land was supposedly guaranteed by a series of 'free selection before survey' acts, which promised to cover 'our fertile plains with the happy homes of a race of peasant freeholders'.[5] This proved to be a mirage, but population growth would stimulate suburban subdivision and happy-home building in the coastal cities, Melbourne and Sydney especially.

There was always a tension within colonial liberalism between the social conservatism of the colonial vision of *settlement* and the capitalist imperative to commodify land, to promote a free and often speculative market. The free selection acts were quickly followed by conveyancing reforms, pioneered by the public servant R.R. Torrens in South Australia, which made land transactions cheaper and simpler for struggling smallholders and speculative subdividers alike. Yet the market in land for settlers was hampered by the limitations the law imposed on married women's economic agency, on a married woman's capacity to buy and sell property.

The complications of coverture

The Australian colonies had inherited the common-law doctrine of coverture, which could only restrict the free trade in land. At marriage a woman surrendered her legal and economic identity to the husband beneath whose 'wing, protection and cover she performs everything'.[6] Her personal property and leasehold lands passed to him, although he acquired only a life interest in her freeholds and there were limitations imposed on his power to alienate them without her consent.[7] According to historian Lee Holcombe, the husband was thus constituted as the guardian of the property for the benefit of succeeding generations.[8] This locates the husband's property rights as well as the wife's disabilities within what Michel Foucault has called the 'deployment of alliance, a system of marriage, of fixation and development of kinship ties, of transmission of names and possessions'.[9] Land was locked into lineage in ways which restricted the agency of husbands as well as of wives.

The same comment applies to the wife's 'compensatory' common-law right of dower. If she was widowed, she was entitled to a life interest in one-third of her husband's freehold lands, and her maintenance was thus enforced irrespective of the wishes of her husband or his heirs. Dower was a particular irritant to free traders because the right attached not only to the lands held by a husband at his death but to lands held during the marriage. A widow might, therefore, have a legitimate claim on real estate which had passed out of her family many years before and been sold again several times. Her continuing interest was justified only by her role in the 'alliance system' – as the mother of children who might have inherited those lands. Such an ambush of unsuspecting land buyers, the undermining of present enjoyment by past obligations, did not sit well with the idea of land as a mere commodity. No wonder colonial purchasers developed a 'great horror of dower'.[10]

Criticisms of coverture were current throughout the common-law world. They were 'made in England', but they had a particular resonance in the mobile migrant societies of settler colonies, in this case Australia, where the fictional availability of land was an incentive to migration. The Australian colonists therefore tried various tactics to circumvent coverture without actually confronting the issue head on. In the early part of the nineteenth century the New South Wales Court of Civil Jurisdiction simply 'bent the rules' so that married women might hold property, even land.[11]

Australians also imported solutions developed in England. When New South Wales, for example, acquired a Supreme Court with an equitable jurisdiction in 1814, it became possible for colonial wives to enjoy a 'separate estate' under a marriage settlement.[12] Such settlements were enforceable in equity and overrode a husband's common-law rights. At first, however, they seem to have been reserved for the families of wealthy colonists.[13] After all, the device had been perfected in seventeenth-century England to allow rich fathers to settle property, including land, on their marrying daughters and secure it from the interference of their sons-in-law. That property was vested in trustees who had to manage it for the wife's 'separate use' and often for the benefit of her future children. In its classic form the marriage settlement was another aspect of the 'deployment of alliance' described by Foucault, in that it regulated the property relations of families of origin and families of marriage. While a settlement might guarantee wives some independent income from their lands, it was not designed primarily to facilitate their sale. Indeed many settlements included a specific 'restraint on anticipation' or 'restraint on alienation'.

Eventually the equitable concept of 'separate use' proved to be extremely flexible, and later reformers, including Torrens, would exploit its potential in order to solve the 'problem of the married woman'. But in the early nineteenth century the traditional marriage settlement did not seem to promise liberation for Australian land markets. To soften the effects of coverture, therefore, the colonies chose to adapt the English legal device known as 'levying a fine', which briefly reinvented the married woman as a consenting adult. This adaptation began with a proclamation by Governor Macquarie in 1819. This enabled wives in New South Wales and Van Diemen's Land to agree to the barring of their dower rights or to the sale of lands which they brought to the marriage. A woman had to acknowledge before the judges-advocate of those territories that she consented 'freely and voluntarily and not for Fear or by Reason of any Threats and Menaces'.[14]

The Australian colonies also adopted the English Dower Act of 1833, which did not wait for wives to volunteer, but initiated the gradual extinction of dower rights by allowing men married after a certain date to bar those rights without their wives' concurrence. In 1850 New South Wales gave the story a new twist by legislating to disallow the dower rights of the long-lost English wife who turned up (like a character from a Wilkie Collins novel) to disturb the buyers of her immigrant husband's Australian lands. Meanwhile colonial wives continued to surrender dower rights, where these survived, or to consent to land sales as successive statutes made the 1819 procedures for 'taking their acknowledgments' more widely available, to rural as well as urban women.[15]

The demands of the early land market thus allowed wives a temporary legal existence, although they were always treated as property holders in need of special protection. Even in the 1850s wives still had to be interviewed apart from their husbands to make sure that they were not being coerced or tricked into any sale. The interview may have been either a farce or a formality, but the assumptions embedded in these procedures retained the power to frustrate reformers when they claimed that married women's disabilities were simply out-of-date and out-of-place in the colonies. They discovered that the idea of the wife as a member of a protected species did not survive in mid-nineteenth-century Australia only as an embarrassing remnant of feudalism: protection was being revitalized and acclimatized as well as contested.

In practical terms the problem of the land-holding wife in the Australian colonies was quite a minor issue: the number of women and acres involved was not that significant. Yet the colonial emphasis on freeing up the land market, which gathered momentum in the decade after the goldrushes, did raise questions about the need for married women's property reform in Australia. Logically that emphasis should have promoted the reform project by lending it both urgency and respectability. There was also the precedent of legislation passed in several US jurisdictions.[16] Instead, colonial legislators found other ways of eroding married women's disabilities, without addressing the wider issues of married women's property reform and thus daring to detonate a dangerous sexual politics.[17]

They took as their starting-point the conveyancing reforms initiated by Torrens in South Australia in 1858. These were adopted in all eastern colonies by 1862, almost simultaneously with the free selection acts, and were taken up by Western Australia in 1874. Torrens's reforms were designed to make land as marketable as that 'bale of goods'. Parliaments later tinkered with Torrens's innovations to accommodate the *possibility* of the married woman owning land while representing that possibility as reassuringly rare. Change to the married woman's legal status was, thereby, safely contained. Indeed the alterations made seemed so marginal that they often went through parliaments without really being debated. Married women and their land were being 'smuggled' into the Torrens system for practical purposes, and in every colony where the Torrens system was adopted these refinements of Torrens's reforms preceded married women's property acts, often by several years. It thus seems quite likely that this piecemeal pragmatism held up more general married women's property legislation in the Australian colonies because it loosened the land plank in the reformers' platform. It was harder to invoke the familiar rhetoric of 'unlocking the land' if the 'locks', constituted by married women's disabilities, had been quietly picked. What is of interest here is the process by which the adoption of the Torrens system facilitated colonial married women's holdings of real property while the doctrine of coverture was maintained.

Torrens's conveyancing reforms

To promote his conveyancing reforms, Torrens argued that colonial land transactions were unnecessarily complicated by the dependent nature of land titles in English law. A buyer was obliged to research the history of the relevant title, working back through a chain of deeds to make sure that the vendor had the right to sell and to identify any lurking competing interests in the land. The process was costly, time-consuming and possibly inconclusive. The title validated by this chain of deeds was 'no stronger than its weakest link. Each transaction add[ed] a fresh link, increasing the *perplexity and risk of loss*'.[18]

Torrens argued that registration should *create* title. He proposed to provide each landowner with a single document, the certificate of title, which would be indefeasible and on the public record. Once a colony adopted his reforms, all new grants of Crown land would be made in duplicate, one copy (the certificate of title) being given to the grantee and the other bound into the Torrens Register. Torrens also provided that existing landowners could apply to bring their properties into his system by submitting all available 'instruments of title' for examination. And he made it clear that a certificate would be issued when the landowner's title was substantially good even if it was not technically perfect. This opportunity to cure 'infirmities' in an applicant's title was especially appealing since many early colonists had taken a rather casual approach to conveyancing. The clear incentives to entering the Torrens system were the indefeasibility of title, except in cases of outright fraud, and the relative simplicity of land transaction within that system. A prospective buyer had only to consult the Register to find the undisputed 'registered proprietor' of the relevant land. Torrens also promised that dealings such as mortgages would be recorded on the certificate of title so that every circumstance that might affect the property could be seen 'at a glance'[19]

This summary exaggerates the simplicity of the new regime, as Torrens himself tended to do when he was selling his reforms. In fact his South Australian model legislation had to be amended three times in the years 1858–61 and other colonies also needed to re-tool the system. But Torrens's essentials had an obvious appeal to the liberals who were beginning to dominate colonial politics. The promise of quicker, cheaper conveyancing fitted the expectations of widespread land ownership which those liberals had encouraged. And his reforms were, in Bruce Kercher's words, 'Australia's legal gift to bourgeois land owning'.[20] They perfected the commodification of land in colonial Australia and embodied an essentially individualistic concept of land ownership. For example, Torrens originally planned that, every time a parcel of land changed hands, the new owner would be issued with a fresh certificate. His title – the masculinity of the owner was assumed – could thus be presented as pristine, not just indefeasible but somehow ahistorical. It was Torrens's boast that there was no need to 'look behind the Register'. It seems appropriate to speculate that this had a particular appeal in colonial societies where all land holding was based on Aboriginal dispossession and the erosion of very different understandings of land tenure.

However, Torrens admitted that titles could not wholly be divorced from their historical and social context: they might be 'encumbered', and encumbrances, such as dower, had to be notified on the certificate. Dower was a relatively minor irritant which South Australia and Victoria, for example, effectively legislated out of the Torrens system.[21] But how would that system accommodate the full complexity of coverture, and how would it register the 'relational' rights and disabilities created by marriage? Were the demands of kinship, embedded in the doctrine of coverture, at all compatible with Torrens's reforms? Other questions were raised by the long history of evasions of coverture. How would the system accommodate the equitable reconstruction of property relations between husband and wife and the development of devices such as the marriage settlement?

These questions were not really addressed, let alone answered in South Australia's first Real Property Act in 1858.[22] Torrens himself was so far from being a radical on married women's property reform that he barely recognized the possibility of the wife as a registered proprietor. He did, however, consider the marriage of a woman who already held a certificate of title. How would his system register the husband's life interest and the wife's dormant rights in the land which she brought to the marriage? Torrens's first solution seemed to reduce the bride to a cipher; it was the husband who had to notify the registrar general that the marriage had taken place, and the two men then dealt with the transmission of the woman's title. He was 'entitled to be registered as proprietor' of the land because her interest had become 'by law vested' in him.[23] She was not to worry her little head about the fact that her rights were not visible. At least one critic, Mr Baker MLC, wondered if this registration would actually obliterate those rights and give her husband unfettered powers which the common law had not guaranteed.[24]

This claim seemed to invest the certificate of title with almost magical properties, but perhaps Torrens's own promotion of his reforms had encouraged this tendency. He contested Baker's reading of the 1858 Act and eventually produced the 'clarifying' concept of co-proprietorship. Section 77 of the Real Property Act of 1861 seemed to retrieve some agency for the land-owning bride, because it required a written statement from her before her husband would be registered as co-proprietor. (Such registration would be unnecessary if the land was 'held for her separate use'.) But what exactly was co-proprietorship? The contemporary commentator A.P. Canaway warned that the word was 'not quite plain in meaning' and decided that 'the registration of a husband as co-proprietor seems merely to be the appropriate method of completing his title to what the common law gives him'[25] In other words section 77 represented a marriage of convenience between Torrens and the common law, a way of expressing a traditional relationship.

However, the revised South Australian legislation did open up possibilities for remaking that relationship in pursuit of a freer land market. Lawyers often complained that Torrens's legislation, before and after the amendments of 1858–61, was riddled with ambiguities and inconsistencies. And these were imported into other colonies as they adopted South Australian models. But perhaps it was those ambiguities which allowed the men who administered the Torrens system some room for manoeuvre, some opportunities for constituting a wife as an agent capable of holding and selling land.

After the silence of his original 1858 Real Property Act, Torrens explicitly recognized that there were circumstances in which a wife would be issued with a certificate of title. In particular he provided that a husband could transfer land to his wife (and she could reciprocate). Again devices such as postnuptial settlements had already been developed to allow such transactions and subvert the common law's insistence that the husband and wife were one person. What Torrens provided was a simpler, cheaper and publicly recorded means of allowing couples to transfer assets.

Such transfers were useful in the colonial context because the nomadic work patterns of many Australian men made for some 'semi-detached' marriages.[26] It made sense for the wives left behind to have some independent resources. This kind of asset shifting could also insulate the families of businessmen against periodic economic crises, as the husband's creditors could not touch land which was registered in the wife's name. Or could they? Even in Queensland, which administered the Torrens system more strictly than other colonies, it appears that the insolvency jurisdiction allowed couples some leeway. When a husband went bankrupt, and his wife held land under the Real Property Act, the trustees appointed to administer his estate did not enforce that husband's common-law rights and claim the rents and profits back for his estate.[27] So Torrens had at least facilitated the kind of asset shifting or asset 'parking' which allowed families to salvage something from their economic wreckage.

This was a sympathetic scenario, with the wife acting as domestic saviour. But the issue of a certificate of title to a married woman raised more controversial questions. Could that certificate's magic transform her into a property-owning individual and did it wholly extinguish her husband's common-law rights? Did a simple inter-spousal transfer subvert the natural order of things and authorize her to dispose of 'her' land? In Queensland, at least, the Supreme Court answered 'No'. In 1883 the acting chief justice ruled that such a transfer did *not* give the registered wife 'a different right to what [she] had at common law'.[28] But while the judgment restricted changes to the traditional construction of property relations between husband and wife, this case and others suggested that Torrens had encouraged an expectation of change in the Queensland population.

The solution to these perplexities lay in the equitable doctrine of 'separate use', which would allow a wife to both hold and dispose of land. The architects of the Torrens system were thus able to build on the liberal construction of this doctrine by English and Australian judges. This was despite the fact that the classic marriage settlement, which vested property in trustees, worked against the transparency of Torrens's title. Trusts were always a problem since the logic of the new system demanded that the *legal* ownership of the trustees be registered, which left the beneficiary, the wife, in a kind of limbo. Her interest in the land was certainly not apparent 'at a glance'.[29]

However, the classic settlement was being rewritten in ways that made trustees redundant, which was fortunate because the bustling businessmen of colonial Australia were increasingly reluctant to act as trustees. In 1862 Torrens claimed that 'we do away with that artificial structure completely, and a man simply says in plain language what he wants done'.[30] In Torrens's scenario the man – presumably a father or husband – was still the actor and speaker while the woman was a passive recipient. But he did imply that the plain language of 'separate use' enabled wives not simply to retain independent ownership of land which they brought to a marriage, but to acquire and dispose of land, without the intervention of trustees, after marriage. In this he was perhaps a little optimistic because crucial precedents were not established until the mid-1860s.[31] But the gradual refinement of the doctrine of separate use was opening up a space for the land-holding and land-trading wife.

The administrators of the Torrens system, including those in Queensland, were encouraged to devise formulae for the transfer of land to a wife for her separate use. Such formulae were equally useful to the anxious father, the fond husband and the complete stranger who wanted to sell his land to a married woman. And they were well publicized. In Victoria, for example, the form of words was included in the commissioner of titles's Advice under the Transfer of Land Statute of 1866. The great value of these arrangements was their simplicity and transparency. The necessary forms were printed, the clerks at the Land Titles Office provided advice and, once the 'separate use' certificate of title was issued, it was on the public record.

This visibility reduced the uncertainty which could deter people from dealing with a married woman. The economically active wife, who was often a partner in one of those semi-detached marriages, inhabited an uncertain world. Many colonial wives ran smallholdings and dairies, for example, which were regarded as their property. In such cases the common law was not so much circumvented as ignored. The courts were increasingly tolerant of this attitude and might construe the husband's tacit consent as an unwritten settlement of the property for her separate use.[32] The various Real Property Acts improved on this slightly surreal solution by providing the land-owning wife with a powerful piece of paper. Unless her certificate of title included a restraint on alienation (which was not advised by the Victorian commissioner of titles) that wife could dispose of the land 'in the same manner as any other proprietor'.[33] That, at least, was the opinion of Victorian commentators.

Victoria's innovations

The Victorian legislation went much further than this. Like other colonies, Victoria followed the South Australian Real Property Act of 1861 and allowed for the registration of husband and wife as co-proprietors when a female land-owner married. But its 1866 Transfer of

Land Statute teased out the implications of this procedure. The solution crafted by Torrens raised two questions – who was to initiate the registration and what would happen if the application to register the husband was never made? Canaway notes, rather disapprovingly, that the South Australian model might *possibly* leave the initiative with the wife.[34] Victoria seemed to seize on this possibility. Section 108 of the Victorian Act made it clear that there could be no registration of a husband without an application from his wife, and that until she did apply she was 'deemed to [be] the sole and absolute proprietor' of the land. When it came to dealing with that land she kept the legal and economic identity of a single woman. This raised the possibility of her deploying this identity to acquire and dispose of other land.

The push to 'disencumber' the Victorian land market thus conjured up the anomaly of an unmarried–married woman, a figure who usually struck terror into the minds of legislators and was calculated to send married women's property debates spiralling out of control.[35] Opponents of reform often represented economic independence, that is a wife's involvement with people and profits outside the private sphere, as a kind of infidelity. The discussion was implicitly, sometimes explicitly, sexualized as legislators shied away from the possibility of 'uncovering' the married woman. What, therefore, would they make of a woman who was so independent that she refused her husband's rightful registration as a co-proprietor?

Curiously, she seems to have crept into Victoria without alarming anyone, perhaps because very few legislators were aware of her arrival. The 1866 Act was a major revision of the legislation which established the Torrens system in Victoria in 1862. The relevant Bill was drawn up by Commissioner of Titles John Carter, and even the Minister who took charge of it in the Legislative Council admitted he could not follow all its complex provisions.[36] This was not a Married Women's Property Bill and it was never presented as a 'women's issue'. Indeed the clauses relating to wives were simply a minor part of the omnibus Bill and were hurried through without debate. The whole exercise suggests that changes in married women's rights were achievable when the attention of Members of Parliament was focused on the manly question of the land market.

Carter was a Torrens enthusiast, but also a lawyer who could not resist the chance to improve the original model. Yet his reforms were also problematic. Why did he experiment with section 108 when the 'separate use' provisions seemed sufficient to bring married women and their holdings into the Torrens system? Perhaps Carter felt that too many Victorian women were marrying without securing property to their separate use and that the existing arrangements for registering co-proprietorship were ambiguous. His solution was certainly tidier; it ensured that a bride's land was always saleable and was consistent with the political imperative of freeing up the land market.

For Carter, like Torrens, the married woman was almost certainly a marginal figure and changes to her property rights were simply minor housekeeping of the Torrens system. This may explain inconsistencies in his legislation. Section 108 conflicted with the assumptions implicit in section 61, which still provided special arrangements – special protections – for the married female vendor. A'Beckett's commentary on the legislation suggests even that section 61 *implied* that she needed her husband's concurrence in order to sell.[37] Two versions of 'the wife' therefore co-existed uneasily in Carter's reforms. While section 108 constituted the married woman as a remarkably free agent, section 61 kept her in protective custody. In practice the confused sexual politics of the legislation did not seem to matter because the commissioner of titles privileged section 108. It was his legislation after all. And, almost inadvertently, he had constituted the wife as an independent land-owner.

In many ways the 1866 Transfer of Land Statute was the married woman's perfect property reform because parliament scarcely noticed it. Legal commentators did, however, pursue its implications. A'Beckett argued that 'curious complications may arise from [the wife's] perfect dominion under the statute and ignored existence under the general law'.[38] Perhaps this is why Victoria was the first colony, by several years, to pass married women's property legislation. In 1870 the Victorian colonial Parliament took a very conservative Married Women's Property Act, which had just been passed in England, and amended it to cover real estate. Significantly this was done 'at the fag end of the session'[39] and almost without debate, suggesting that thoroughgoing married women's property reform was only possible when legislators were not fully engaging with the issues.

In Victoria, changes to the Torrens system did not obviate the need for more general legislation on married women's property. Indeed Carter's cavalier attitude to coverture may have dragged the Victorian Parliament into unusually radical reform. In the neighbouring colony of New South Wales, however, more circumspect changes to that system served to hold up the progress of married women's property reform. New South Wales actually passed a Married Women's Property Act as early as 1879, but it did not wholly cover real estate.[40] That reform was not achieved until 1893 and the lack of urgency may be explained in part by amendments to the colony's Real Property Act in 1878. These clarified the position of the wife holding land for her separate use, and the Torrens Register for New South Wales shows a small number of wives independently acquiring and selling land long before 1893.

Clearly the relationship between Torrens's reforms and the married women's property issue was complex and was negotiated differently in different colonies. In Western Australia, for example, there were hints that an easy-going administration of the Torrens system reduced the perceived need for general married women's property legislation,[41] whereas a much stricter regime in Queensland perhaps helped to convince an unenthusiastic parliament in 1890 that such general legislation was overdue. There was, however, one common element in these colonial experiences. It appears that Torrens's reforms were always the dominant partner in the relationship, influencing the timing and scope of married women's property reform. And while changes in married women's rights might be achieved under Torrens's 'wing, protection and cover', this had the effect of hiding the feminist implications of those changes and muffling debate on the economic autonomy of wives.

Land-owning was not the primary objective of most women migrating to the Australian colonies in the nineteenth century, but the realities of the colonial experience meant that marriage was often their destiny and land-owning became the consequence. 'Settlement' and the yeoman ideal depended on families owning and running family farms, so that wives were necessary to the process of 'unlocking the lands'.[42] However, while the work of wives and mothers drove colonialism forward, a married woman's legal status simultaneously conflicted with the colonial project because her legal disabilities put a brake on it. This was 'the problem of the married woman' that Torrens's conveyancing reforms tangentially addressed. While Australian legal scholars have recognized the innovativeness of Torrens's system for land titles, the implications for married women's property rights and therefore the connections between conveyancing reform and colonialism, have never been explored.

Notes

1 Humphrey McQueen, *A New Britannia*, rev. edn (Melbourne, Penguin Books, 1986), p. 156
2 H. Goodall, *Invasion to Embassy: Land in Aboriginal Politics in NSW, 1770–1972* (Sydney, Allen & Unwin/Black Books, 1996), part 2: 'Regaining the Land,1860–1900'; R. Gollan, *Radical and Working Class Politics: A Study of South-Eastern Australia 1850–1910*, (Melbourne, Melbourne University Press, 1960), ch. 2: 'Independence on the Land', pp. 33–49; S. Roberts, *A History of Land Settlement in Australia 1788–1920* (London, Macmillan, 1924, reissued 1968), pp. 236–58; D. Baker, 'Origins of the Robertson Land Acts', *Historical Studies, Selected Articles*, first series (1967), pp. 103–26.
3 McQueen, *New Britannia*, p. 153.
4 A. Stephen, 'Parliament', *Sydney Morning Herald*, 28 August 1857.
5 Robertson evidence, Select Committee on the State of Agriculture, *Votes and Proceedings of the Legislative Council of New South Wales*, vol. 2, p. 299.
6 Blackstone's summary of 'coverture' quoted in L. Holcombe, *Wives and Property:*

Reform of the Married Women's Property Law in Nineteenth-Century England (Oxford, Martin Robertson, 1983), p. 25.

7 A husband might sell the land but, if his wife survived him, her rights in that land would revive to the detriment of any purchaser. See A.C. Millard and G.W. Millard, *The Law of Real Property in NSW* (Sydney, Law Book Co., 1905), p. 240.

8 Holcombe, *Wives and Property*, p. 20.

9 M. Foucault, *The History of Sexuality*, trans. R. Hurley (Harmondsworth, Penguin, 1981), vol. 1, p. 106.

10 Salter evidence, Royal Commission into the Real Property Acts, *Votes and Proceedings of the Legislative Assembly of NSW (VPLA NSW)*, 1879–80, vol. 5, p. 1130; on dower in the Australian colonies see Andrew Buck, '"A Blot on the Certificate": Dower and Women's Property Rights in Colonial New South Wales', *Australian Journal of Law and Society*, 4 (1987), 87–102.

11 B. Kercher, *An Unruly Child: A History of Law in Australia* (Sydney, Allen & Unwin, 1995), p. 50.

12 J.M. Bennet, *A History of the Supreme Court of New South Wales* (Sydney, Law Book Co., 1974), p. 94.

13 E.g. Marriage Settlement of Frances Riley, *General Register of Deeds*, vol. 11, No. 654 (Land Titles Office of NSW).

14 *Sydney Gazette*, 6 March 1819. For the device of levying a fine, see Holcombe, *Wives and Property*, pp. 20–1, and R.E. Kemp, *Principles of the Law of Real Property in NSW* (Sydney, Law Book Co., 1903), pp. 291–5.

15 See for example the Deeds Registration Act, 3 Vic. No.8.

16 See Carole Shammas, 'Re-Assessing the Married Women's Property Acts', *Journal of Women's History*, 6:1 (1994), 9–30; Norma Basch, *In the Eyes of the Law: Women, Marriage and Property in 19th Century New York* (Ithaca, NY, Cornell University Press, 1982); Constance Backhouse, 'Married Women's Property Law in Nineteenth-Century Canada', *Law and History Review*, 6:2 (1988), 212–57; Lori Chambers, *Married Women and Property Law in Victorian Ontario* (Toronto, Osgoode Society for Canadian Legal History–University of Toronto Press, 1997); for a discussion of the implications of the US reforms for Canadian reforms, see Philip Girard and Rebecca Veinott, 'Married Women's Law in Nova Scotia 1850–1910', in Janet Guildford and Suzanne Morton (eds), *Separate Spheres: Women's Worlds in the Nineteenth Century Maritimes* (Fredericton, Acadiensis Press, 1994).

17 The implications of married women's property reform for the marriage contract, and the anxiety which they created among colonial politicians is discussed in Hilary Golder and Diane Kirkby, 'Unmarrying Wives: Divorce and Married Women's Property Reform in Colonial Australia,' paper presented to the Australian Historical Association Conference, Hobart, 1999.

18 R.R. Torrens, *The South Australian System of Conveyancing by Registration of Title* (Adelaide, Register and Observer General Printing Office, 1859), p. 9.

19 Torrens evidence, Select Committee on the Registration and Preservation of Records, *VPLA NSW*, 1858, vol. 2, p. 11. See also R. Crundwell, H. Golder and R. Wood, *From Parchments to Passwords: A History of the Land Titles Office of NSW* (Sydney, Hale & Iremonger, 1995), pp. 31–5.

20 Kercher, *Unruly Child*, p. 130.

21 Burton evidence, Royal Commission into the Real Property Acts, *VPLA NSW*, 1879–80, vol. 5, p. 973.

22 21 Vic. No. 15. This legislation was revised/superseded by the Real Property Law Amendment Act of 1858 (22 Vic. No. 16), the Real Property Act of 1860 (23 and 24 Vic. No. 11) and the Real Property Act of 1861 (24 and 25 Vic. No. 22).

23 21 Vic. No. 15, Form N (Declaration of Owner Taking by Transmission)

24 Speech by Baker, *South Australian Parliamentary Debates, 1857–58*, pp. 762–3.

25 A. P. Canaway, *The Real Property Act (NSW)* (Sydney, Maxwell, 1887), pp. 57–8.

26 See Shirley Fisher on the family economy in Patricia Grimshaw, (ed.), *Families in Colonial Australia* (Sydney, Allen & Unwin, 1982), pp. 153–62.

27 Speech by Thynne, *Queensland Parliamentary Debates*, vol. 56 (1889), p. 20.

28 *Burke* v. *Fox*, in *Brisbane Courier*, 'Reports', 19 September 1883. The situation in Queensland was more clear-cut than in other colonies because the Real Property Act of 1861 (25 Vic. No. 14) included a proviso (s. 30) that 'the powers and authorities of the husband of any married woman shall in no wise be altered or abridged' by the issue of a certificate. This proviso had been devised but then rejected by Torrens in South Australia.

29 For attempts to resolve this problem, see T. A'Beckett, *The Transfer of Land Statute (Victoria)* (Melbourne, F.F. Balliere, 1867), pp. 5–6; Canaway, Real Property Act (NSW, p. 51.

30 Torrens evidence, Select Committee on the Land Titles Bill, *VPLA NSW, 1862*, vol. 4, p. 1165.

31 Kemp, *Principles of the Law of Real Property in NSW*, pp. 283–4.

32 *Smith* v. *Hall*, VLR 9 at 231. For English precedents, see Holcombe, *Wives and Property*, ch. 3.

33 A'Beckett, *Transfer of Land*, pp. 39, 98–9.

34 Canaway, *Real Property Act (NSW)*, p. 57.

35 Explored in Golder and Kirkby, 'Unmarrying wives'.

36 Speech by Hervey, *Victorian Parliamentary Debates, 1864–65*, vol. 11, p. 877.

37 A'Beckett, *Transfer of Land*, p. 99.

38 *Ibid.*, p. 41.

39 Speech by Anderson, *Victorian Parliamentary Debates, 1870*, vol. 11, p. 507.

40 The act allowed wives to invest their earnings in land but did not, for example, deal with land brought to the marriage or inherited after it.

41 Speech by De Hamel, *Western Australia Parliamentary Debates*, series 2, vol. 2, p. 376.

42 For the importance of families in the selection of land and a fuller exploration of the work of wives, see various chapters in Grimshaw, *Families in Colonial Australia*.

CHAPTER FOURTEEN

The construction of property rights on imperial frontiers: the case of the New Zealand Native Land Purchase Ordinance of 1846

John C. Weaver

During the past 200 years, individualized property rights over land – embodying exclusive use, transferability and heritability – have been refined to increase a land-owner's absolute authority. The discussion of events in New Zealand that follows depicts the law as a commanding artifact that failed initially to provide just steps for individualizing title. Exploration of the law's one-sided instrumentality, however, entails an awareness of complexity. Three complications surface in this account. First, the problems posed by the economic interaction of two peoples with alien attitudes on land use and value were not immediately solvable in any neat way. The New Zealand evidence suggests that unregulated associations incited friction. Second, the law contained a sea of possibilities. Third, economic self-interest and ideas about the proper course of colonization fragmented the colonists; therefore, distinct European communities of interest attached themselves to disparate legal doctrines.

European squatters routinely initiated transformations in property rights. They forced colonial governments to introduce land laws that inevitably affected the indigenous peoples. A number of European land-hunters – often graziers – forfeited the prized attribute of full property rights when they peremptorily occupied pastures in North America, Australia, South Africa and New Zealand. Their shallow common-law possessory rights propagated inferior – but recognized and saleable – property interests. Many who grasped these imperfect interests subsequently strained to enlarge their rights: the greater the property rights, the greater the asset value. European newcomers battled their way from raw squatting to authorized usufruct, to leasing, to freehold.[1]

The chronicle for New Zealand begins with the Anglo-American legal doctrine that prohibited direct land transactions negotiated between individual colonists and first peoples. It had been a principle of British overseas expansion, enforced since the Restoration, that no valid title to land could be acquired except through the Crown. This can be labelled the *doctrine of the jealous sovereign*. From time to time, officers of the Crown upheld it by prohibiting direct land dealings between individual colonizers and first peoples.

This ban on direct sales between indigenous peoples and settlers, though defied by European settlers on New World frontiers, provides a key to understanding land secessions by first peoples, because it weakened their negotiating position.[2] During the first half of the nineteenth century, the British Crown and the American Republic maintained ambitious plans for New World lands, and combated squatters.[3] Seeking cheap land, such individuals had no quarrel with the concept of a root title, but if they could not get a good title cheaply many would take something less, and would work to augment their rights. Thus the ban on direct dealing made these land-hunters fairweather partners for indigenous peoples, because they could not grant the graziers security of tenure.

Governments and squatters on several colonial frontiers conducted their disputes by marshalling European artifacts: contracts, the common law, and statutes.[4] Many indigenous peoples later discovered 'the portentous significance of pieces of paper'.[5] Governments could initiate ordinances and statutes, and administer their application by force where necessary and feasible. Circumstances determined exactly how authorities applied statute law to address the challenge of squatters.[6] In jurisdictions with self-government, land occupiers might choose to carry their demands for property rights through the democratic processes. In Crown colonies, the politics of land allocation, which was exercised through petitions, stressed loyalty, character and productivity.[7]

Contests for choice territory in New Zealand were intricate. Formative events in the acquisition and allocation of the islands' best land occurred from 1840 to 1865, and involved the doctrine of the jealous sovereign, possessory occupation and the adaptation of Maori to a market economy. As best they could, the squatting colonizers capitalized on contracts made directly with indigenous chiefs.[8]

Among the first peoples who negotiated with colonizers during the nineteenth century, Maori participated more fully in private land dealings than did many others: they 'sold' land directly to Pakeha before the British assumption of sovereignty by the Treaty of Waitangi (1840), and granted usufructuary rights to a number of Pakeha tenants in subsequent years. Two factors constrained the doctrine of the jealous sovereign in New Zealand, and promoted insubordinate conduct: the insecurity of British authority; and the land-hunters' economic utility. Another way of looking at matters is to suggest that the doctrine of the jealous sovereign presumed a 'Hobbesian' society 'in need' of a centralist legal system with powers of enforcement. However, in the absence of a strong government, land-hunters established a thriving 'Lockian' sphere of private arrangements with Maori chiefs. This state of affairs temporarily suited the wishes of some Pakeha and Maori. Reference to the contrasting realms of Hobbes and Locke is pertinent to debates in law and economics about the possibilities of 'order without law'.[9] To demonstrate that formal judicial processes may burden certain businesses, a few economists and legal scholars have searched for economic activities governed by norms rather than laws. Land dealings outside the law in New Zealand offer a further opportunity to see whether people have been able to establish satisfactory agreements without a government-managed system.

The heyday of Maori land-use agreements, from 1842 to about 1860, provides examples of economic exchanges free from the cost of a Crown grant, and from the expenses of surveying and registering.[10] However, the prohibited agreements to use land held by indigenous peoples were fraught with conflicts. There were disputes over the price of usufruct, the number and identity of parties to the agreement and the boundaries of the territory involved. Graziers knew the relative costs, risks, and benefits. Until they could secure a more complete set of property rights, they worked within an illicit land-use system in which they attempted to establish 'order without law'. Many New Zealand pastoralists tried to work out disputes with Maori and Pakeha neighbours; however, they faced conflicts with parties from each community. The pastoralists' land system outside the law was inherently unstable. As a remote part of an international capitalist economy, Maori usufruct agreements were discounted as assets, and that fact added to their *ad hoc* quality. For Europeans, informal agreements were bound to be expedients, not ends in themselves.

Direct dealings between Maori and European land-hunters flourished in defiance of prohibitions that culminated in a punitive ordinance of 1846. The Treaty of Waitangi conformed to Anglo-American doctrines on the status of most indigenous peoples and to the doctrine of the jealous sovereign that such peoples could not be allowed to initiate a root title for property. The more visibly sedentary and politically organized first peoples on common-law frontiers were *usually* accorded legal interests as occupants.

In the nineteenth century, the substantive question about the theory of rights of *most* first peoples was not about whether they had rights with respect to land – but whether they had established *possession of particular areas*. At times in the early 1840s, at least until 1845, administrators in the Colonial Office glanced ruefully back to 1840, wishing that parts of New Zealand – for example, portions of the South

Island – had been declared *terra nullius*, like Australia where the British denied that Aboriginal people had any possessory occupation. As late as 1848, the New Zealand Company, which wanted land cheaply, insisted that in order for Maori to have a possessory right there 'must be a real mixing of soil and labour'.[11] Instead, local colonial officials conceded, by at least 1846, that Maori were in unqualified possession of all of the North and South Islands.

Some officers of the Crown in London and New Zealand regretted an apparent recognition of sweeping rights to Maori. These rights *almost* allowed a Lockian world of land-use agreements between newcomers and Maori chiefs. From the British imperial perspective, the treaty precluded this world of contracts, because it entrenched two legal concepts that upheld the doctrine of the jealous sovereign, and later assisted the Crown's acquisition of land. First, the Crown claimed sovereignty. That provided authority to enact ordinances and statutes affecting land questions. Second, the treaty asserted the Crown's right of pre-emption – the right to purchase land before other parties. The full importance of these two precepts was perhaps transparent only to a handful of jurists and Colonial Office personnel. Yet, when combined and manipulated, sovereignty and pre-emption had the potential to consummate many land sales from Maori to the Crown, but a complication vexed the Crown's land-purchasing missions throughout the 1840s. Crown purchases were compromised by private arrangements between colonizers and Maori chiefs.

How could land transactions between Maori and newcomers proliferate if banned? The answer appears in Lieutenant-Governor William Hobson's cry of dismay in 1841 when he encountered Pakeha renting land from Maori chiefs. Hobson asked the attorney general of New South Wales to advise as to how he might suppress such dealings. Familiar with squatting on Crown land in New South Wales the attorney general failed to grasp the intricacy of Hobson's question. Consequently, he recommended that Hobson initiate trespassing proceedings. But the Crown did not possess the land in question, Maori did. There could be no trespass action by the Crown.[12]

Hobson reacted by promulgating an ordinance that declared illegal any direct transactions in land, whether sales, leases, rentals, or gifts. This measure attempted to put teeth into the doctrine of the jealous sovereign and British interpretation of the power of Crown pre-emption found in the treaty. It made proscribed transactions unenforceable in law.[13] This denial of rights would so inconvenience buyers and tenants, it was hoped, that they would forsake these forbidden practices. The ordinance did increase risks for squatting graziers, because trespassing rivals could not be ejected through a prompt and inexpensive legal process that made use of justices of the peace. Removal would require an action in the Supreme Court over disputed property interests. However, frontier reality, replete with security considerations, ordained that illegal rental had some practical force. If Maori chiefs accepted that a tenant was a worthy neighbour who paid a fair rent, then they might uphold the terms of the agreement and bar other graziers. Then, again, they might not.

Grazier John Yule of the Manawatu river alleged in 1846 that the arrival of another stockman prompted Maori to re-open their agreement with him. When Yule declined to renegotiate, Maori 'watched when [his] Cattle strayed beyond the boundary lines and immediately hunted them till the Cattle became wild as deer'.[14] The opportunity cost facing early New Zealand graziers involved a decision about whether wool profits might offset, among other things, the costs of defending an unrecognized property right or the loss of stock which strayed over vague boundaries. Graziers had little choice really in regions where the Crown had trouble buying land, and where some of it went to the New Zealand Company. From roughly 1842 to about 1850, illegal Maori rental arrangements – so-called leases – presented realistic opportunities for pastoral enterprise. Ambitious graziers had to work out arrangements with chiefs, but from the beginning stockmen encountered territorial disputes and collective ownership issues in their dealings with Maori landlords.[15] These matters complicated agreements and prompted a few graziers to explore ways of avoiding friction. For example, one of the earliest graziers on the Canterbury Plains, William Deans, assumed in 1843 that prospects were attractive in that region because the Maori population was small and less threatening than around Wellington.[16]

The decision to deal directly with Maori may have been easy for some graziers who, like Deans, found receptive landlords, but most tenant-graziers remained vulnerable to what they branded as unpredictable actions by Maori. Graziers' tenure under so-called 'Maori leases' was not only insecure because of an ordinance that denied their legality, but because Maori held land collectively. Traditional Maori tenure provided a weak warranty for the graziers' tenure, because there were disputes among Maori themselves about the boundaries of the territory in question.[17] Deans, who had compensated one chief, encountered hostility from another over which lands were covered by that compensation.[18] Tenants confronted uncertainty respecting duration of tenure, precise boundaries, annual rent and the identity and number of landlords who might claim payments. Nevertheless, Pakeha payments for rent – as well as for labour, produce and cartage – nurtured patrons among Maori.

In the common law, moreover, the agreements and evidence of occupancy built legal interests that were valid against other Pakeha land-hunters, although not against the Crown. But there were grave defects in the relationship between Maori landlords and Pakeha tenants. Some tenants contributed to instability, for they had not bargained in good faith. A number of graziers scorned the prospect of Maori chiefs enduring as landlords. By the late 1840s and early 1850s, they looked to improve their tenure by conniving with colonial officers to advance Crown purchases from Maori, and then grazing with the benefit of a Crown license. Some tenants also behaved irresponsibly toward their Maori neighbours and trespassed on land excluded from agreements.[19]

Land-use agreements possibly numbered in the hundreds by 1846. In the far north and around Auckland, they protected timber cutting and quarrying.[20] In southern parts of North Island and on the South Island, they protected sheep runs. At the townsite of New Plymouth, colonists contracted so-called 'leases' until such time as the Crown and Maori had settled purchase disputes. Occupants employed these township leases to protect their interests as late as August 1851.[21] The term 'lease', although used by colonists who entered into arrangements with Maori, may not have denoted well-defined compacts recorded on paper. Some understandings began as informal verbal agreements between Maori chiefs and colonists. In the Wairarapa, for example, it appears that early rental agreements consisted of giving a chief something valuable, like a horse, and then a £12 payment for one year's use of the land.[22] Documents soon emerged as more colonists arrived, because so-called leases could deter other Pakeha from trespassing. It is difficult to estimate the gross sums involved annually in rentals, but two observations are firm. Rents rose as chiefs became acquainted with a cash economy, and the graziers had little choice but to meet the new demands, even if understandings had been negotiated for ten or twenty years. Existing agreements were also exposed to *ad hoc* renegotiations when additional Maori claimants arrived at a station and insisted on a share in the rents. Wise graziers loosened purse strings on demand, but adjustments reinforced the graziers' willingness to regard Maori leases as an inferior expedient.[23] Without the security represented by root titles, maps, well-defined property instruments and registration systems, order was frayed.

A few agreement documents survive, and their formality indicates the occupants' desire to hold a record. Pakeha employed interpreters to draft agreements in Maori, and Government Interpreter R.J. Deighton confessed in September 1848 to drawing up contracts.[24] Opinions about the legality of Maori leases were sought in the early 1840s.[25] Unable to settle on land for which he held New Zealand Company land orders,

Joseph Greenwood in 1843 asked a certain Mr Halswell in Wellington whether 'natives were allowed to lease land that was not taken by the New Zealand Co.'.[26] By the end of the decade, queries like this had escalated into a professional sideline for Wellington lawyers. Solicitor Charles Cator held clients' leases and in 1847 attempted to use them as evidence of occupation to secure government grazing licenses.[27] Another Wellington solicitor, John King, advised Wairarapa squatter W.H. Donald on Maori leasing issues as late as 1854.[28] The care exercised over legal form appears to have been undertaken to protect graziers against encroachment by rival stockmen and to establish a claim should the land be purchased by the Crown. During the early 1840s, a set of provisional understandings between the graziers and the Government emerged as the former spread their operations to accessible pastures in the Wairarapa Valley, the Rangitikei region, the Kaikoura and Banks peninsulas, the Canterbury Plains and the Otago district. Pastoral squatting burgeoned under the auspices of Maori leases, but the Lockian world of contracts remained imperfect. The parties maintained fundamentally different ideas about land tenure and landlordship. There was insufficient community cohesion – within and across racial lines – to support an informal system, for that depended on the norms of a close-knit community.[29]

After Hobson's ordinance of 1841, the Government made no move against leasing until 1846. Colonial officials silently accepted Maori leases for several reasons. Hobson's death, in 1842, removed an implacable foe of direct land dealings. His successor, Captain Robert FitzRoy, inexperienced with property issues, faced Maori rebellion, and forceful remonstrations made him fear for the colony's survival. As well, there were now troops in the colony, and they required the supplies that squatting graziers could furnish.[30] Therefore, FitzRoy relaxed the 1841 ban by granting the Crown's right of pre-emption to individuals who petitioned for privileges to negotiate with Maori. His subordinate in Wellington, Major Mathew Richmond, permitted well-financed graziers to established sheep stations on South Island and in the Wairarapa Valley with the consent of Maori.[31] From 1843 to 1846, graziers protected their ventures by contracts with chiefs and letters of consent from colonial officers who formally approved of a few leases. In October 1845, Superintendent Richmond even sent a circular to Wairarapa chiefs 'reminding you to keep strictly to your Agreements about land demanding no more than is in the Book [Agreement]'.[32] The native protector at Port Levy told a grazier in April 1845 that 'the natives have a perfect right to do as they please with their land same as any landed proprietor in England can do as he pleases with his estate'.[33]

During this interlude when limited leasing had official consent, the doctrine of the jealous sovereign lay idle in New Zealand, although it stirred in London. The secretary of state for the colonies recalled FitzRoy and charged his successor George Grey with the task of restoring orthodoxy. Grey hastened to put backbone into New Zealand affairs. His attorney general prepared a new ordinance to check the progress of Maori leases. 'An Ordinance to Provide for the Prevention, by Summary proceeding, of Unauthorised Purchases and Leases of Land' – popularly known as the Native Land Purchase Ordinance – was gazetted in December 1846.[34] It imposed a fine of £5–£100, to be recovered in a summary way, on anyone found contracting to use Maori land.

Almost immediately, missionaries protested to Grey.[35] They worried about the status of the land they occupied, and about Maori reaction to a measure suppressing budding economic relations. Grey promised to apply the law sparingly, to punish only disreputable leasees. In reply to the protestations of the Reverend Robert Maunsell, Colonial Secretary S.E. Grimstone suggested that the law would 'prevent runaway convicts, criminals flying from justice and other dissolute characters from spreading themselves over this country, and under the pretence of holding leases from the Natives occupying portions of land where there are no officers of justice'. Maunsell was told that the Crown wanted to stop 'parties from obtaining pretended leases of large tracts of land which they do not require for their own uses, but intend to sublet at a large profit'. The Crown would not disrupt 'occupations properly conducted'.[36] The permissive allowance of leasing from 1843 to 1846 had flaws, but policy was compromised by uneven application.

In addition to individual objections to the ordinance, there was a petition filled with partisan insights into the state of relations between Maori and the Pakeha colonists. Signed by 183 inhabitants of Auckland, it attacked the ordinance and the colony's Government. Some citizens wanted an elected body to restrict the governor's authority, and the ordinance contributed an exhibit for their claims of authoritarian high-handedness. Their petition advanced a half-dozen objections to the ordinance. Several complaints appealed to a defence of rights. The first rights defended were those of Maori, although Maori did not – in the eyes of the protestors – have racial equality. Petitioners stated that they could not 'but fear the consequences of so direct and unnecessary an encroachment on the rights of a suspicious and easily excited people'. Those who prepared the petition knew that many tenants on Maori land mistrusted their hosts, and they knew, too, that the Government worried about Maori rebellion. Property rights were esteemed by those who drafted the petition. They knew that graziers on Crown land in New South Wales had been tenants at the pleasure of the governor, but recently had succeeded in their campaign for leases in preference to licenses that permitted grazing. The petition implied that investors might shun New Zealand in favour of New South Wales. A contract with Maori, the petition implied, might outfit an investor with greater security than a governor's permission to squat. At least, they argued, it might offer investors an equivalent to the pastoral leases in New South Wales. The argument was vague, perhaps spurious, but the business community of Auckland knew something important: Maori leases bought vital goodwill from people who outnumbered Pakehas ten-to-one.

The Auckland petition announced that practical people wanted to come to terms with Maori and feared rash intervention by a weak Government. By taking itself too seriously in attempting to act on presumed powers the Government could throttle enterprise. It may have been proper, at one time, the petitioners wrote, to discourage direct transactions between Maori and Pakeha, but nothing could now prevent increasing associations. Should the Government diligently prosecute offenders, 'it would annihilate the greater part of the present whaling, timber, cattle, and trading stations, from which have been derived at least three fourths of all articles of export'. An appeal to rights again entered the brief when petitioners denounced the power of prosecution. They insisted that the laying of an information by an aggrieved individual before a justice of the peace exemplified English liberty by minimizing the authority of the Government, but to empower officers of the Crown to lay information besieged liberty. 'By this Ordinance especially numbers are placed entirely at the mercy of any person appointed by the Governor, a state of affairs which your petitioners humbly believe to be inconsistent with the liberty usually enjoyed by British subjects.' The ordinance emerged amid the contemporary growth in the prosecutorial powers of local governments in the United Kingdom, the British colonies and the United States. The petition was in tune with international critiques of mounting police authority..[37] It concluded with a demand for representative institutions.[38]

By enforcing the ordinance, the Government would have alienated Maori and many of the colony's business people. It could not risk damaging its relations with either. In his covering despatch to the colonial office, which he enclosed with the petition, Grey defended his actions and pulled his hand out of a hornet's nest by indicating how judiciously he intended to administer this measure. Illegal transactions, he claimed, had to be brought under control to expedite the settlement of land disputes among Maori themselves, disputes which he intimated were inflamed by jealousy over rental payments. As late as the end of 1846, he naively hoped the chiefs would agree to register their claims;

checking the spread of leases, he suggested, could advance the cause of a rational land system. Nothing in Grey's optimistic despatches about land questions in this period suggest that he intended the ordinance as a weapon to coerce Maori to sell land to the Crown, by denying them capital from rental income, and thus constraining them to surrender occupation. He believed – as Hobson had done – that informal transactions could only exacerbate friction between Pakehas and Maori, and he felt obliged to control inter-communal land dealings. But simultaneously he had to neutralize critics, and thus he promised a tactful application of the ordinance.[39]

To guide discretion, Grey drew a momentous distinction between current leases and those in contemplation. 'The Government do not propose', he wrote,

> unless under extraordinary circumstances to attempt to dispossess any persons already in possession of depasturing or timber stations, but on the contrary to secure to them all such advantages as it may be found expedient from circumstances of this country to attach to the right arising from preoccupancy.

Grey recognized a right attached to 'preoccupancy', but the ordinance was levelled at *any* direct land dealings. Would those prosecuted as examples abide the hair-splitting duplicity that allowed neighbours to escape fines? When Grey's Government determined, in 1848, to use the ordinance in the Wairarapa Valley to force sales of land to the Crown, the governor hoped

> that it may not be necessary to resort to a measure which the Government could only adopt with the utmost reluctance, and the results of which, whatever their particular character, could not fail to involve the most serious injury if not the entire ruin of the squatters concerned.[40]

The boundary between discretion and preference was becoming blurred. Moreover, the cunningly conceived and wholly indecent new function of the ordinance expressed a rank abuse of law to the detriment of an indigenous people.

While intended by 1848 to weaken selected Maori landlords, the ordinance was still administered with a discretion that usually respected the interests of parties who held Maori leases. The colonial secretary expressed the official position in 1850 when advising a Wanganui magistrate. The magistrate could not, he instructed, use the ordinance to eject just anyone: power was reserved to execute a matter of policy, or 'to prevent some evil which would bear upon the relations between Natives and Europeans. No one but a person appointed for the purpose by the Government can act in the matter; and in each case specific instructions would probably be issued'.[41] Discriminatory restraint fostered confusion.

Problems also ripened because a number of local colonial officers winked and allowed graziers to enter into new agreements with Maori. This practice flourished outrageously in Hawke's Bay.

When Maori leases negotiated after the ordinance were challenged by rival graziers, officials indicated that the occupants were in possession and it would harm the economy to prosecute them. The trick for squatters after 1846 was to arrange a Maori lease, put stock on the land, and find a compliant commissioner of Crown lands to file unofficial paperwork that could later reinforce a claim for a license to graze on this new Crown land.[42] All this had to be done before intrusive and legalistic officials could intervene. Hard- and soft-line officials disputed how to enforce the ordinance, but from 1846 to 1860 Grey's indulgent policy and its manipulation by local officials compounded land issues. In Hawke's Bay, the flexibility that Grey had in mind – lubricated by self-interested Crown officers – contributed to a rising debate about whether the ordinance of 1846 should be uniformly enforced or cancelled. For a while, defenders thought that it assisted the Crown with pre-emptive land purchases, but uneven application, at the heart of Grey's policy, bothered a number of colonists.

Confusion about the ordinance derived from a major restraint built into it. To critics who claimed the Government's power of prosecution violated English liberty, Grey countered that the ordinance specified that 'no person shall be convicted of any offence named in it except on the information of the Surveyor General or some other officer duly authorized in that behalf'. Between 1846 and 1850, the Crown appointed only three officers in the southern district or New Munster: T.H. FitzGerald, the government surveyor at Wellington; Donald McLean, the inspector of police at New Plymouth; and John Tinline, the magistrates' clerk at Nelson. In 1848, the colonial secretary for New Munster proposed empowering the 'officers and non-commissioned officers of the Armed Police force to lay information under the Native Land Purchase Ordinance'.[43] It never happened. In 1850, the resident magistrate for Otago requested authority to lay information; however, Lieutenant-Governor Edward Eyre rejected the petition. He was reluctant to empower people, 'especially at so great a distance from head quarters, where the Government cannot know what is passing'.[44]

The first three officials empowered to lay information had disparate understandings of their role. Tinline was out of his depth. In 1848, under pressure, he improperly applied the ordinance to prosecute a squatter on property belonging to the New Zealand Company.[45] FitzGerald's activities seem unremarkable until 1860 when he championed a rigorous enforcement. It was Donald McLean who best appreciated Grey's clever policy of equivocation. Essentially the chief land-buyer for the Crown from roughly 1848 into the mid-1850s, McLean integrated the ordinance with his negotiations to get Maori to part with their land.[46] The ordinance became a tool for securing land for the Crown and for himself.

How could this have happened? From 1844 to 1848, the Crown's toleration of Maori leases advanced the interdependence of some chiefs with graziers. Mutual benefit eventually assisted the Crown with land purchases in the Wairarapa and at Hawke's Bay from around 1848 to 1855, because it made Maori vulnerable to the threatened prosecution of Pakeha lessees. Beginning in late 1848, Maori landlords in the Wairarapa were made to believe that they should sell to the Crown or else face a drying-up of rental payments because their Pakeha partners would be prosecuted and driven from the valley. This threat of economic sanctions required the co-operation of a few graziers. The Crown made it clear to graziers that they would not suffer if they colluded. The graziers accepted.[47] An invidious tactic for securing land in the Wairarapa evolved from economic interdependence and the ordinance's provisions for prosecution. The path from the drafting of the ordinance to its status as a tool for land acquisition was indirect. At first, the Crown's fear of Maori and the opposition of influential colonists restrained prosecutions under the ordinance. By the late 1840s, the Government in New Munster felt more secure; by the early 1850s, the ordinance assumed its role as a land-acquisition instrument.

Until 1851, the Crown restricted the prosecutorial apparatus. Then, with the demise of the New Zealand Company, which held pre-emptive land rights, the colonial Government understood precisely the scope of Crown lands on South Island, and lands it might acquire on North Island. These considerations prompted an increase in government officers empowered to lay information under the ordinance.[48] Most of the lightly settled South Island had been purchased from Maori in a few transactions during the 1840s and early 1850s, and the ordinance of 1846 removed squatters from what the Crown claimed as its domain. Some Pakehas on South Island insisted that they held Maori leases; but this appeal incited prosecutions under the ordinance. Several Otago graziers devised a dodge: 'that the natives should nominally be graziers, taking charge of the settlers' cattle, employing the stock-owners and their servants as shepherds and stockmen'.[49] Walter Mantell, the Crown's agent sent to tidy up a land purchase in the region, alleged that there were so many Maori leases and such determination to defy the Government that he could exhaust himself trying to stamp out the practice. Prosecution under the ordinance would irritate the squatters 'without suppressing the offence'.[50] Eventually, the Crown made arrangements with the graziers, usually granting them grazing rights away from prime settlement areas.

As noted, on the North Island the ordinance evolved into a land-purchasing instrument whose potential was recognized when the government devised its strategy for buying land in the Wairarapa valley where Donald McLean influenced the application of the ordinance. When McLean and his enemies argued over how best to sever land from Maori, they primarily disputed the extractive possibilities of the ordinance. McLean applied it selectively to intimidate Maori chiefs into selling to the Crown; he used it also to pressure selected graziers into speaking well of land sales when meeting with Maori neighbours. By the late 1850s, these tactics had lost their punch and Maori chiefs were refusing to sell. Critics proposed, as a new measure, the legalization of private land transactions between Maori and colonizers through a land court which would individualize Maori collective title to provide the basis for the property rights desired by Pakeha. The slowdown in purchases and the granting of responsible government led to radical land-acquisition doctrines that consigned the Crown to a diminished role in land purchasing until the late nineteenth century.[51]

In 1848, McLean had brandished threats of prosecution in the Wairarapa to present to the chiefs an exaggerated case that, if they refused to sell to the Crown, all white settlers could be driven from the valley, with painful consequences for the economic well-being and security of Maori. In late 1850, he applied this tactic during the first of many purchasing expeditions to Hawke's Bay.[52] The Wairarapa was home to entrenched graziers, but squatters at Hawke's Bay were still arriving. McLean threatened to prosecute newcomers, but on the side he struck agreements: if holders of Maori leases agreed to advocate Crown purchases to their Maori landlords – or at least not stand in the way – then they would later receive Crown grazing licenses. McLean negotiated a partnership with a leading squatter. As an imperial governor, Grey had stumbled onto discretionary prosecution to keep alive the doctrine of the jealous sovereign while deflecting opposition. As a frontier agent, McLean manipulated the practice of discretionary prosecution in order to acquire land for the Crown and for a clique of graziers who showered him with opportunities. By the 1850s, as the master practitioner of a land-buying technique, McLean could articulate a brilliant analysis of the land issues and the ordinance's role.

Existing Maori leases, and the likelihood of more, McLean believed, undermined the Crown's ability to purchase land cheaply from Maori. He knew, too, that enjoyment of land under Maori leases allowed lessees time to make improvements to the lands so that 'the price at which the public will have to purchase them will be greatly in excess of what has hitherto been paid'. The Crown could buy the land from Maori, but settlers would be deterred from purchasing this land from the Crown because the prior Pakeha occupant would claim compensation for improvements. Thus, parties who defied the ordinance could improve their way into prolonged occupation. As McLean expressed it, 'the sanctioning of such proceedings will give one section of the public a most undue advantage over those who are restrained by obedience to the laws from taking possession of lands until they become Crown property'.[53]

McLean contended, too, that Maori would never come to respect English law when 'they find that those laws are not respected by the Pakehas themselves'.[54] McLean certainly did not want to harm the grazing interests by punishing all graziers who operated with Maori leases. He moved against them in a sequence of actions. As more parties were authorized to lay information, he preferred to stay on the sidelines and direct operations. Someone else would lay information, usually where Crown purchases were being negotiated. For bargaining purposes, McLean may have wished to sustain his reputation as a friend of Maori. During the interval between the laying of an information before a magistrate and a court proceeding, McLean looked for government direction as to which transgressors 'should be more vigorously proceeded against'.[55] While government officials preached to Maori about how English law had to be respected, the judicial system was being manipulated by land-hunting colonists. Some Maori recognized the situation, and reached unflattering conclusions.[56]

By the late 1850s, the irregular application of the Native Land Purchase Ordinance incited criticism, especially in the Hawke's Bay region where intricate land dealings embittered a few graziers who had been fined, or upset others who wanted the Government to declare their Maori leases valid in order to ward off rival graziers.[57] Former government surveyor T.H. FitzGerald, the superintendent of Hawke's Bay province in 1860, denounced the ragged way the law was applied, reporting that local officials favoured a coterie of Hawke's Bay graziers. Some of the fortunate few owned freehold estates and grazed sheep or cattle on adjacent Maori land, and paid a rent – supposedly to compensate Maori for trespass. This rationalization was a pretence for Maori lessees, who included Donald McLean and his brother Alexander. FitzGerald demanded consistency, arguing that it mattered not if Maori lands were rented by newcomers or by established gentlemen. The damage to respect for the law would be the same under either circumstance. The payments – not their origin – were the evil. FitzGerald denounced the discrimination in prosecutions as a convenience to the favoured few.[58]

FitzGerald's stance briefly prevailed. In May 1860, the governor authorized all police in the province to lay information; in December

1860, FitzGerald warned in the province's *Government gazette* that he was going to enforce the ordinance strictly.[59] He had already moved in November against Donald McLean's brother 'for Depasturing sheep and cattle on Native Lands'.[60] If Alexander McLean did not like it, wrote FitzGerald, he could appeal the fine all the way to the Privy Council.[61] This prosecution struck at the favouritism permitted by a discretionary application of the ordinance. In addition to irritating a clique, the campaign against leases stirred up Maori chiefs who protested that the leases constituted a reasonable *modus vivendi*, whereas prosecutions threatened to undercut their revenue. These chiefs requested Crown titles to their land, so that they could legally let it to Pakeha tenants. By allowing them to do this, they wrote, 'the grass will be thrown open by our bringing it out from the dark place where it is lying'.[62] An interesting argument, it overlooked practical issues about who precisely would have authority to collect rents for specific locales; a reliable rental market would have required a land-registration system. By this time, the days of the ordinance were numbered. From 1858 to 1865, North Island politicians debated how settlers could best secure more Maori land. Maori resistance to sales to the Crown increased greatly: Crown purchasing faltered, and the impatient favoured direct transactions. For them, the pivotal challenge was how to individualize title to Maori land, how to transform collective rights into personal property rights. A land court was created to accomplish the transformation. The act of 1865 which finalized this process rescinded the ordinance of 1846.[63]

Maori leases and the counter-stroke of the ordinance of 1846 exemplified the tangles over property rights that cropped up on several frontiers. In North America, Australia and South Africa, there were intricate and distinctive histories of land acquisition and allocation; in general, colonizing governments drafted laws about land, only to have to bend them to accommodate pressure from squatters. The ordinance of 1846 was one such manipulated law. It emerged from the doctrine of the jealous sovereign that applied to Anglo-American frontiers, and which promised an intelligible starting-point for rational projects of colonization. It attracted idealists who sought a humane pace to contacts between first peoples and colonizers; it was agreeable to certain colonizers who desired absolute dominion over the New World land they wished to exploit, and who therefore craved root titles; it originated in established legal theory. But the doctrine of the jealous sovereign faltered in New Zealand. Graziers who pursued the use-value and the exchange-value of frontier lands founded property interest by direct dealing with indigenous peoples in defiance of the doctrine of the jealous sovereign.

Informality left too many unresolved particulars. A history of Maori leases discloses the conditions that work against 'order without law'. Homogeneous communities that might support common norms were lacking; and too often there was a dearth of genuine trust and good faith. While graziers spurned the jealous sovereign and made agreements with Maori chiefs, they generally treated these transactions as temporary: graziers esteemed the documents as levers to help them in the next campaign for property rights. As well, the collective property rights of Maori proved difficult to convert to individual property rights. On the one hand, unfettered direct negotiations between first peoples and colonizers furnished no sound foundation for a land-tenure system. On the other hand, government regulation became abused. The ordinance of 1846 originated to stop leasing in order to reaffirm Crown sovereignty and restrain land prices. Like numerous control measures on other frontiers, differential enforcement led to cynical disregard, profitable favouritism and cancellation of the law.

If Hobson's mission to annex New Zealand had been motivated in part by a desire to check the friction and exploitation likely to ensue from an invasion of land jobbers, then it wildly miscarried. The intertwined history of Maori leases and the ordinance of 1846 identifies the paradox of an imperial annexation of territory that was justified on the basis of its intention to protect an indigenous people. The history of the ordinance also unfolds a cautionary tale about how prohibitory statutes with powers of prosecution can foster hypocrisy and discriminatory practice. The ordinance's history describes, too, a balancing act as a Government with jurisdiction over a settlement frontier attempted to assert sovereignty, maintain respect for the law and exercise pragmatism. The ordinance's history describes one instance – among many – of how, in recent history, collective property rights have been redefined as individual and absolute. Finally, aspects of the history of the ordinance reveal how, in one colony, some property rights were taken from an indigenous people and assigned to Europeans. At the time these events occurred, more equitable outcomes were improbable.

Notes

1 For example Australia, as described in John C. Weaver, 'Beyond the Fatal Shore: Pastoral Squatting and the Occupation of Australia, 1826–1852', *American Historical Review*, 101 (1996), 981–1007
2 For an account of the history of Crown pre-emption, as that history was applied to New Zealand, see National Library of New Zealand, Turnbull Library, MS 0842, Address of Governor Sir George Gipps to the Legislative Council, 9 July 1840. For the United States, Thomas Donaldson, *The Public Domain: Its History with Statistics* (Washington, Government Printing Officer, 1884), pp. 158, 240. For defiance and illicit direct land dealing, see Thomas Perkins Abernethy, *Western Lands and the*

American Revolution (New York, Russell & Russell, 1959), pp. 260–2. The Supreme Court of New Zealand followed the chain of American decisions in *McIntosh* v. *Symonds*, a ruling that affirmed Crown pre-emption for New Zealand. See *New Zealand Government Gazette (Auckland)*, 7:11 (1847), 63–6.

3 For the United States see Roy M. Robbins, *Our Landed Heritage: The Public Domain, 1776–1936* (Princeton, NJ, Princeton University Press, 1942); Malcolm Rohrbough, *The Land Office Business: The Settlement and Administration of American Public Lands* (Belmont, 1990). For Australia see Peter Burroughs, *Britain and Australia: A Study in Imperial Relations and Crown Lands Administration* (Oxford, Clarendon Press, 1967); Sharon Morgan, *Land Settlement in Early Tasmania: Creating An Antipodean England* (Cambridge, Cambridge University Press, 1992). For Upper Canada, see David T. Moorman, 'The "First Business of Government": The Land Granting Administration of Upper Canada', Ph.D. thesis, University of Ottawa, 1997.

4 Robert Gordon, 'Paradoxical Property', in John Brewer and Susan Staves (eds), *Early Modern Conceptions of Property* (New York, Routledge, 1996), pp. 95–110.

5 Peter Gow, 'Land, People, and Paper in Western Amazonia', in Eric Hirsch and Michael O'Hanlon (eds), *The Anthropology of Landscape: Perspectives on Place and Space* (Cambridge, Cambridge University Press, 1995), p. 59.

6 Rohrbough, *Law Office Business*, pp. xv, 51, 110, 183–4; Daniel Feller, *The Public Lands in Jacksonian Politics* (Madison, University of Wisconsin Press, 1984), pp. 16–17, 128.

7 Tom Brooking, *Lands For the People? The Highland Clearances and the Colonisation of New Zealand: A Biography of John McKenzie* (Dunedin, University of Otago Press, 1996), pp. 67–130; J.M. Powell, *The Public Lands of Australia Felix: Settlement and Land Appraisal in Victoria with Special Reference to the Western Plains* (Melbourne, Oxford University Press, 1970), pp. 51–4, 66–7, 89–98, 105–18.

8 For illegal dealings west of the Appalachians, see Jack Mack Faragher, *Daniel Boone: The Life and Legend of an American Pioneer* (New York, Henry Holt, 1992), pp. 81–125; Donald Berthrong, 'Cattlemen on the Cheyenne – Arapabo Reservation, 1883–1885', *Arizona and the West*, 13 (1971), 5–32.

9 Robert Ellickson, *Order Without Law: How Neighbours Settle Disputes* (Cambridge, Cambridge University Press, 1991).

10 Douglas W. Allen, 'What Are Transaction Costs?', *Research in Law and Economics*, 14 (1991), 1–18. Allen argues that transaction costs are the costs of establishing and maintaining property rights.

11 National Archives, Wellington (hereafter NA), NZC 102/18, Despatches from the Secretary to the Principal Agent, 21/48, T.C. Harington to W. Wakefield, 12 November 1847.

12 NA, G36/1, Governor's Papers, Despatches of Lieutenant-Governor William Hobson, Hobson to Sir George Gipps, 16 February 1841.

13 4 Vic. No. 2. An Ordinance to Repeal within the said Colony a certain Act of the Governor and Council of New South Wales [9 June 1841].

14 NA, IA (Internal Affairs), 1/46, Colonial Secretary, Incoming Letters, 46/1703, John Yule to the Superintendent of the Southern District, 26 October 1846.

15 For similar complications in the United States see Berthrong, 'Cattlemen', 19–26.

16 Gordon Ogilvie, *Pioneers of the Plains: The Deans of Canterbury* (Christchurch, Shoal Bay Press, 1996), pp. 36–40.

17 A.G. Bagnell, *Wairarapa: An Historical Excursion* (Masterton, Hedley's Bookshop for the Masterton Lands Trust, 1979), pp. 69–91.

18 Ogilvie, *Pioneers of the plains*, pp. 43–4.

19 NA, NM 8/12, 46/495, Translation of a Letter from Na Hamiora Pakaiahi (Samuel Pakaiahi) to the Governor, Port Nicholson, 14 August 1846.

20 See for example 'A Return of the Applications for Licenses to Occupy Government or Native Lands since 16 November 1846', *New Zealand Government Gazette (Auckland)*, 7:23 (1847), 125. Reports similar to this one appeared in subsequent issues.

21 NA, NM 8/49, 51/1173, Henry King, Resident Magistrate at New Plymouth, to Alfred Domett, 24 August 1851.
22 Bagnell, *Wairarapa*, p. 56.
23 Jeanine Graham, *Frederick Weld* (Auckland: Auckland University Press, 1983), pp. 7–19.
24 NA, NM 8/33, 48/1092, R.J. Deighton to the Colonial Secretary, 28 September 1848.
25 The term 'lease' is not necessarily appropriate for these agreements. It was the term used by many Europeans at the time, and for good reason: it implied a degree of legitimacy and lent solidity to the transactions. For the sake of convenience, the term will be used without quotation marks in the remainder of this account.
26 Turnbull Library, Joseph Hugh Greenwood, Dairy, MS 4882, 13 January 1843.
27 NA, NM 10/7, Entry Book of Outward Letters of Lieutenant-Governor of New Munster, 19 March–21 October 1847, unnumbered, S.E. Grimstone, Acting Secretary, to Charles Cator, Solicitor, 6 August 1847; NM 5/1, General Outward Correspondence from the Lieutenant-Governor of New Munster, July 1847–February 1853, 56/47, Grimstone to Cator, 21 September 1847.
28 NA, LS W 2/3, 54/153, John King to W.H. Donald, 8 June 1854.
29 A.G. Bagnall, *Wairarapa*, pp. 90–7.
30 *Ibid.*, p. 136.
31 NA, NM 10/3, unnumbered, S. E. Grimstone to the Police Magistrate, Nelson, 22 August 1845; Mathew Richmond to Mr Dean, Putaringamota, Middle Island, 23 August 1845; Grimstone to the Resident Magistrate, Akaroa, 22 May 1847.
32 NA, MA-W (Maori Affairs for Wellington), 1/1, unnumbered, Circular: Friends of the Inhabitants of Wairarapa, October 1845 [translation from Maori].
33 Turnbull, MS 4882, Joseph Greenwood, Diary, 1841–47, 13 April 1846.
34 For the legislative course of the ordinance see *New Zealand Government Gazette (Auckland)*, 4:20 (1846), 100.
35 10 Vic. No.19; *New Zealand Government Gazette*, 6:22 (1846), 180.
36 NA, IA 4/3, Colonial Secretary to Reverend Robert Maunsell, 18 December 1846.
37 Douglas Hay, 'Using the Criminal Law, 1750–1850: Policing, Private Prosecution, and the State', in Douglas Hay and Francis Snyder, *Policing and Prosecution in Britain, 1750–1850* (Oxford, Clarendon Press, 1989), pp. 4–52.
38 NA, G30/11, Duplicate Despatches and Enclosures from Grey to the Secretary of State for the Colonies, October–December 1846, no.137, Grey to Gladstone, 28 November 1846, enclosure: Memorial from 183 of the Inhabitants of Auckland against the Native Land Purchase Ordinance (no. 19, session 7).
39 NA, G25/2, Outward Despatches, 1845–47, no. 136, Grey to the Secretary of State for the Colonies, 27 November 1846.
40 NA, NM 10/9, Letterbook of the Lieutenant-Governor of New Munster, 1848–49, 48/1102, Domett to Kemp, 12 October 1848.
41 NM 10/10, 50/774, S.E. Grimstone, for the Colonial Secretary, to the Resident Magistrate, Wanganui, 12 October 1850.
42 NA, LS-NA 1/2, 57/46, Copy of Statement of Mr R. Collins about a Run Application.
43 NA, IA (Internal Affairs), 4/254, 48/2416, Incoming Reference, Colonial Secretary to Commissioner of Crown Lands, 10 November 1848.
44 NA, NM 10/10, 50/567, Alfred Domett to the Resident Magistrate, Otago, 13 October 1850.
45 NA, SSD (Superintendent for the Southern District), 1/1, unnumbered, Francis Jollie to Mathew Richmond, 3 March 1848.
46 NA, NM 10/10, 49/824, Alfred Domett to Donald McLean, 29 September 1849. Domett conveyed the Government's instructions for the purchase of land in the Wairarapa Valley, warning him not to harm the squatters.
47 NA, NZC 3/9, Principal Agent's Despatches, 27/1848, pp. 393–455. Francis Dillon Bell to J. C. Harington, Secretary of the New Zealand Company, 31 December 1848. Dillon Bell describes the plan which was accepted by the Executive Council of New Munster. The squatters met to discuss their fate, and resolved to agree to help the Government make the purchases. See NZC 3/9, 27/1848, enclosure: Minutes of the

Meeting of the Squatters Resident in the Wairarapa Valley Held on Tuesday the 14th November 1848 at Captain Smith's Station. The final orders to put the plan into action were given to Donald McLean in September 1849. See NA, NM 10/10, 49/824, Alfred Domett to McLean, 29 September 1849.

48 NA, LS-N 1/1, unnumbered, George Grey to Mathew Richmond, 24 February 1851 (copy). *New Zealand Government Gazette (New Munster)*, 3:8 (1850), 38; 4:5 (1851), 25; 4:21 (1851), 112; 4:24 (1851), 151; 4:25 (1851), 155; 4:26 (1851), 159.

49 Turnbull Library, MS 1308, Walter Mantell, Letterbook on Native Claims and Native Affairs in General, Mantell to the Colonial Secretary, 18 August 1853. This practice appeared in Indian Territory, Berthrong, 'Cattlemen', 7.

50 Turnbull Library, MS 1308, Walter Mantell, Letterbook on Native Claims and Native Affairs in General, Mantell to the Colonial Secretary, 18 August 1853.

51 For the revival of Crown purchasing see Brooking, *Lands For the People*, pp. 131–56.

52 J.G. Wilson, *History of Hawke's Bay* (Wellington, A.H. & A.W. Reed, 1976), pp. 192–5.

53 NA, LS 1/1a, 55/29, McLean to Alfred Domett, 29 March 1855.

54 *Ibid.*

55 NA, LS NA (Lands and Surveys, Napier), 1/1a, 55/29, Donald McLean to Domett, 29 March 1855.

56 NA, NM 8/54, 52/499, Te Harawiri Tatari to McLean, 12 April 1852 (translation).

57 NA, LS W (Lands and Surveys, Wellington), 2/5, 56/54, W.B. Rhodes to Francis Dillon Bell, 26 February 1856; 56/57, William Fitzherbert, Provincial Secretary, to Bell, 27 February 1856.

58 T.H. FitzGerald to the Colonial Secretary, 3 June 1859; Henry John Tancred, for the Colonial Secretary, to FitzGerald, 22 June 1859, printed in *Government Gazette (Province of Hawke's Bay)*, 1:5 (1859), 14.

59 *Government Gazette (Province of Hawke's Bay)*, 1:33 (1860), 182–4.

60 Turnbull Library, Donald McLean Papers, MS 32, folder 954, Summons to the Defendant upon an Information or Complaint, 27 November 1860.

61 Turnbull Library, Donald McLean Papers, MS 32, folder 954, T.H. FitzGerald to Alexander McLean, n.d.

62 Na Tareha, Na Renata Tamakihikurangi, Na Karaitana, Na Te Wirihana Toatoa to the Provincial Council of Hawke's Bay, *Government Gazette (Province of Hawke's Bay)*, 2:37 (1861), 1–3.

63 29 Vic. No. 71. An Act to Amend and Consolidate the Laws Relating to Lands in the Colony in which the Proprietary Customs still Exist and to Provide for the Ascertainment of the Titles to such Lands and for the Regulating the Descent thereof and Other Purposes [1865].

PART V

Colonialism's legacy

Colonialism lives on in settler societies and other so-called 'postcolonial' states, in continuing conflict over natural resources, in the construction of national histories, in the daily reconstitution of gender and 'race', in the ongoing challenge to the veracity of indigenous evidence in courtrooms. Here the very concept of *history* is problematized, as law and history work together in native title cases, as themes of exclusion, justice and legal principle are once again explored for their contemporary significance in today's law.

CHAPTER FIFTEEN

International law – recolonizing the Third World? Law and conflicts over water in the Krishna River Basin

Radha D'Souza

Drawing from a critique of different schools of thought in Marxist legal studies, Allan Hunt proposes a constitutive theory of law that sees legal relations as one constituent of social relations.[1] In this theory, the distinctive feature of legal relations is that they constitute social relations by calling into existence social actors (natural and corporate) as 'legal subjects'. However, law cannot create social relations *ab initio*, and social relations must exist first before legal relationship can emerge. In colonial–imperialist situations colonial law was a tool of social engineering used by imperial governments to transform society. Through administrative fiats, state regulation and statute law, colonial law tried to rebuild both production and production relations by calling into existence legal categories that were alien. In colonial situations ruptures with history, together with the imposition of a colonial political economy, made stabilization of local social relations difficult. The result was often the creation of a legal system that internalized the contradictions of a colonial economy as integral and structural features of law in colonial societies. In such a legal system, the indigenous and the 'Western', the traditional and the modern, operated as a total system, one reinforcing the other to maintain a permanent schism in law that may have a role in consolidating relations of imperialism–subordination even when, later, the political relations underwent radical transformation. Indeed, it is possible to argue that the schisms internalized in the legal systems enabled new forms of imperial relations to emerge after the old forms of political colonialism ended.

This paper attempts to locate the role of law within debates on the imperialist nature of world political economy after international law, through the UN Charter, formally ended colonialism at the end of the Second World War. In India, after Independence in August 1947, law continued to be seen as an instrument of 'development' that would transform society. Indian legal studies, however, has repeatedly drawn attention to the colonial nature of law in independent India and its failure to emerge as a catalyst for far-reaching social change.[2] Referring to changes in law that have attempted such social transformation, Dhavan contends: 'Empirical assessment and intuitive assessment both suggested that something quite different was happening "out there". The legal system as a social reality reflected and reproduced social realities not affected, or even moderated, by the proposed change.'[3]

What follows is an attempt, first, to examine legal and institutional structures created by British colonization in relation to water,[4] a key resource in social production, and the contradictions it created in society both for the colonial Government and the population in the Krishna River Basin in the Deccan Peninsula of southern India. The Krishna Basin is the second largest river in India. Originating in the western Ghats at an altitude of 1,337 meters, the river travels a distance of about 1,400 km through the most arid and drought-prone regions in peninsular south India to join the Bay of Bengal, draining an area of 258,000 km. Several tributaries form large interstate rivers in their own right. The Krishna is a rain-fed river with wide variations in rainfall – 3,000 mm at the western Ghats in Maharashtra to 450 mm in the arid Deccan plateau of Karnataka. The river flows through three states: Maharashtra, where the river has its source, which shares 28.8 per cent of the Basin; Karnataka, the middle riparian state, which shares 43.8 per cent of the Basin; and Andhra Pradesh, the lower riparian state, which shares 29.4 per cent of the Basin. Agriculture is the predominant economic activity in the basin, and throughout its history irrigation has been the backbone of economic activity and water use: it dominates the Basin's social history, including the history of colonialism, imperialism and neo-colonialism.[5]

Next I examine how international and national law and institutions combine in maintaining the structures put in place by colonization in relation to water, and draw parallels between the dilemmas of the British colonial Government and later the World Bank and the federal Government in the post-Independence period. Contemporary debates on water often see conflicts over water in dichotomous terms such as 'modern versus traditional', 'big dams' versus 'tank irrigation', 'anti-development' versus 'pro-development'.[6] An understanding of the historical legal processes extends our understanding to the ways in which law can maintain the dichotomous and conflictual relations over water in a state of irresolution.

Then I consider the sources of different types of conflict in relation to water, and argue that the processes which keep the issue of water locked into these conflicts are equally important.

The colonial era

Systems of water management and control in the pre-colonial period were shaped by constraints imposed by a monsoon ecology. Treating the village as a basic social unit enabled the holistic integration of land relations, land management, cropping patterns, cultivation rights, and required collective responsibility for common services with water distribution and management.[7] At the time of British colonial intervention, the predominant 'irrigation technology' in the Basin was a combination of channels, tanks and wells.[8] The Krishna Basin fell under British domination over a period of 100 years from the middle of the eighteenth century onwards. During the early phases of colonization legal developments in India were embroiled in intense jurisdictional conflicts arising out of tensions between the Crown, the East India Company, the native rulers, the native population, the shareholders of the East India Company and European rivalries over colonies.[9]

From the 1750s to the 1850s, the company attempted to improve its financial profitability and rate of return through revenue. Atomizing the production process into distinct components and making each of these a source of revenue could enhance the overall returns to the company. Laws, policies and institutions fragmented production into three broad areas – land, labour and water – and proceeded to tax each of these components. Atomization did not occur through commodification processes as in capitalist countries, but for more efficient revenue collection. A legal framework that made this possible evolved over time.

Land relations in the Deccan Peninsula were regulated largely through the Ryotwari Acts.[10] Generally, under the traditional *ryotwari* system of land tenure prevalent in the Deccan, village lands were allocated to individual cultivator-tenants by the village community. With the Ryotwari Acts this system was adopted in a truncated form by the colonial State usurping the community's role in the traditional system and interpolating itself as 'The Community' through black-letter positive law. In place of the village community assigning lands for cultivation to individual villagers, the colonial State entered into individual tenancy agreements with the cultivators. This opened up the possibility of introducing from English common law such concepts of proprietary rights over land as mortgage, sale and alienation of land, and tenancy rights such as tenants-at-will. Land revenue became payable to the colonial state in return for rights of cultivation.

The Indian Easements Act 1882 introduced riparian rights by public law. Under this Act, prescriptive easement rights could be claimed between private persons but not against government. The law further gave the state rights to regulate, collect, retain and distribute waters of rivers' streams, channels and any public irrigation work. The right of cultivators to irrigate their fields from waters of rivers and channels was not considered an easement right.

If the land laws were a truncated form of Indian customary laws, the water laws were truncated English customary laws. Taking control over hundreds of thousands of tanks and channels over a vast area comprising different political and ecological conditions was not easy. The most important legal categories called into existence to enable imposition of water levies, maintenance of works, construction of new works, management of water generally and to transform social relations over water were the categories 'major' and 'minor'.

Generally speaking, irrigation works that serviced more than 300–500 acres were treated as 'major' works. These works were government-maintained and a higher cess was levied on them. The others were considered unprofitable for the colonial state to handle and were left to the peasants to manage in the traditional way with lower cess. 'Major' works were constructed by the newly established Department of Public Works and the 'minor' works were left to the cultivators. Repair and maintenance of 'major' works was the State's responsibility.[11]

Through such fragmented legal categories it became possible to undertake new works or improvements on old works by inviting private-sector investment in 'major' works, by increasing water-rates and pushing for water-intensive cash and commercial crops for markets. 'Minor' irrigation works could continue to support a part of the economy that could not be absorbed by colonial interests. The foundations of a water law, one part of which linked Indian agriculture to the vicissitudes of world markets and European capitalism and the other that supported a subsistence economy not absorbed by imperial interests, came into existence.

The political consolidation which took place over such a prolonged period was not uniform over the Basin area. Different arrangements were made at different times with different indigenous rulers. Broadly, there were three types of political arrangement. Parts of the region were governed directly, first by the East India Company and later by the Crown, and were known as 'British Presidencies'; parts were 'agency states' where local princes ruled as agents of the Crown; and others were the 'Princely States', protectorates of the Crown, that were in theory independent. In a top-down enforcement of law, these differences in political structure meant that the institutional and administrative mechanisms varied from region to region. In the 'British Presidencies', legal institutions, courts, policies, subordinate legislation and social institutions to give effect to the laws were manned and developed by the Indian Civil Service, the backbone of colonial administration. In the

[246]

other areas, though laws were introduced due to British insistence, the administrative and institutional mechanisms were manned by local administrators who interpreted the laws with a 'traditional' bias. That there are serious disparities between the regions under directly ruled and indirectly ruled parts of the Basin is generally accepted.[12] How much of it can be attributed to the administrative and institutional differences in colonial law and institutions requires more investigation.

The Ryotwari Acts and the Indian Easements Act 1882, and the designation of the individual as the unit for taxation, were far-reaching top-down changes that laid the foundations of a colonial legal system that attempted through fiat of law to change social relations over land, water and the village community. The far-reaching changes failed to expand the production base so as to enable a complete transformation of social relations.[13] Instead, repeated famines became an endemic feature of colonial rule. Abandonment of land from cultivation due to excessive taxation and the depopulation of entire villages that followed are recorded in the reports of the Famine Commission 1879 and the Indian Irrigation Commission 1901–3.

In the Krishna Basin, the first large project to be undertaken was the Kurnool–Cudappah Canal System. The project was modelled after the Cauvery Delta Canal system that had existed since the second century AD. Faced with a financial crunch following the First War of Independence in 1857, the colonial Government, in 1859, empowered a private company, the Madras Irrigation and Canal Company, to raise up to £2 million in the capital markets and guaranteed a return of 5 per cent on capital up to £1 million. The project faced excessive cost over-runs and returns were far below what was required to make the projects viable. By 1881, the colonial Government, faced with the 'blunders of private irrigation enterprise' amounting to £3.7 million abandoned the idea of private enterprise in irrigation.[14]

In the areas where canal irrigation was extended the result was not very lucrative. High taxes, poor infrastructure, market fluctuations and problems of salination and water-logging required subsidies, tax-cuts and incentives that made the rate of return elusive.[15]

Two factors distinguish the Indian colonial situation from classical European capitalism. The first relates to technology. In peninsular India, water rather than land was the critical component of agriculture. The British did not possess superior technologies that could transform Indian agriculture in any radical way. The second relates to what Harvey calls the 'spatial fix'.[16] The spatial expansion of European capitalism through colonization helped stabilize capitalist production and social relations in Europe. Such 'spatial-fix' options were not available in colonial India to stabilize social crises arising from the far-reaching changes in agriculture. As the legal changes were top–down, rather than emerging from social relations, no social classes existed to use the law to further their interests.

Colonial rulers faced a dilemma: a more equitable revenue policy and democratic water management could improve the productive capacity of the region, but would reduce the rate of return from irrigation projects. Maintaining the rate of return threatened to destroy the productive base of the economy and create social instability.[17] The predicament is one that is by its very nature irresolvable, yet one on which the legal edifice came to be constructed.

'Solutions' to the crisis continued to be based on the existing legal categories of 'major' and 'minor'. Successive Famine and Irrigation Commissions built upon it two further categories: 'productive' and 'protective' works. A categorization based on the size of the work now included functions. 'Protective' works were those undertaken as measures of famine relief, which were not required to yield any fixed rate of return. 'Productive' works were expected to yield a fixed rate of return. Eligibility for subsidies, fiscal incentives, rates of cess, levies and taxes followed the categorization. Different institutional mechanisms and policy frameworks evolved for the two types of work.

In the absence of 'spatial-fix' options, the legal framework that emerged enabled the stabilization of colonial rule by giving the system flexibility. In times of economic and fiscal crisis the state machinery could be mobilized to encourage 'major', or 'productive', works, and expand 'modern' agriculture. In times of social and political crisis the state machinery could be mobilized to encourage 'minor', or 'protective', works and give relief to subsistence cultivators. The productive base of society was locked into a permanent state of irresolution that became the essence of a state of 'under-development'.

Period of transition: general framework of the law

It is useful to see the period 1914–45 as one of transition from a unilateral colonial form of imperialism under British hegemony to a multilateral imperialism under the leadership of the United States of America and the dominance of monopolistic capital.[18] The political events that enabled that transition to occur, especially the two world wars and the events preceding and following them are well known. Perhaps less well known are the legal and institutional changes brought about in India in this period that transformed the mode of governance from a central executive authority to a more rule-based legally and constitutionally oriented government, with the corresponding institutions of governance.

Five distinct developments in law and policy at the time need to be read together. First, as capitalism became transnational and monopolistic, new international non-governmental organizations such as the International Telecommunications Union (1865), the Universal Postal Union (1874), among others, emerged to create the rules, norms and standards for capital. Between 1840 and 1919 it is estimated that 400 permanent private organizations were established.[19] Colonial governments recognized these organizations, facilitating the norms and standards to be extended to colonies.

Second, European rivalries called for a greater role for international law. Though formed to keep the peace, the League of Nations became increasingly involved in economic and trade issues and setting up international organizations that could lay down the rules for the capitalist game worldwide.[20] India's active participation in such organizations had implications for the development of law.

Third, a weakened Britain and the European rivalries strengthened Indian elites, the industrialists, the civil servants and the emergent 'modern' farmers – in two ways. The British needed to find allies within India, and the Indian elite could choose between competing sources for capital and technology. The result was the emergence of a decisive leadership that could forge a united opposition against colonial rule.[21] War improved the economic position and enabled the leadership to trade off support for British war efforts against political independence at the end of the war.

Fourth, from around 1914, constitutional reforms became the central theme of governance in India. The Government of India Acts of 1919 and 1935 were the precursors of the Constitution of Independent India. It is now generally accepted that the 1935 Act forms the framework of the Constitution of Independent India, adopted in 1950.[22]

Fifth, as a prime British colony, India was involved as a founding member in international organizations such as the United Nations, the International Labour Organization and the Bretton Wood Institution since their inception.

These five factors taken together shaped constitutional developments within India, developments that centred around two broad issues. The first related to the drawing of territorial boundaries for the nation–state called India within a federal polity. It included creating a federal constitutional structure and a representative forum to deal with the other 584 autonomous 'Princely States'. The Chamber of Princes was created in 1921 to deal with the Princely States as a bloc.[23] The Government of India Act of 1919 provided for the creation and devolution of powers to the provinces even while retaining the unitary character of the constitution. The Government of India Act of 1935 attempted unsuccessfully to integrate the 'Princely States' into a federal India. The Act also created provincial autonomy with elected provincial governments. The Constituent Assembly that debated and finalized the Constitution of Independent India was set up under the Cabinet Mission Proposals by the British Government in consultation with Indian political leadership. It provided for representation of the Chamber of Princes in the Constituent Assembly and the unification of India into a federal structure.[24]

The second issue related to the division of powers between federal and state governments. For the first time the Government of India Act of 1919 classified subjects into *provincial* and *central*. Defence, external relations, currency, coinage copyright, public service commission and residuary subjects were with the central Government. The remaining subjects were within the jurisdiction of provinces. Provincial subjects were further classified into 'reserved' and 'transferred'. 'Reserved' subjects were under provincial jurisdiction, but the central Government could intervene if necessary. The Government of India Act 1935 removed the distinction between 'reserved' and 'transferred' subjects and streamlined the division of subjects into federal, provincial and concurrent jurisdictions. Subjects of importance to finance capital such as banking, insurance, incorporation of companies, taxation, customs and excise, patents and copyrights, transport and communications were federal subjects. The constitution after Independence retained this division of powers. Subjects critical to finance capital or the 'modern' sector remained with central Government, the rest with state governments.

Period of transition: water in the legal framework
Several important legal and institutional changes enabled colonial state enterprise in 'productive' water-works to be opened to international finance capital. The constitutional changes progressively 'decentralized' water. Under the Government of India Act 1919 water, 'including water supplies, irrigation and canals, drainage and embankments, water storage and water power', was under provincial governments but 'subject to legislation by the Indian Legislature with regard to matters of inter-provincial concern or affecting the relations of a province with any other territory'. Besides, water was a 'reserved' subject and the central Government could intervene if required. The Government of India Act 1935 further 'decentralized' water. 'Water, that is to say, water supplies, irrigation and canals, drainage and embankments water storage and water power', was a provincial subject. The Act provided the machinery for the resolution of inter-state disputes.[25]

Once again the assumption that legal changes will bring about changes in social production prevailed. Having legislated to 'decentralize' authority over water large – scale investments in water and power projects were expected to follow. Earlier, the recommendations of the Famine and the Indian Irrigation Commissions of 1879 and 1901–03, respectively, suggested expansion of irrigation works, both 'productive' and 'protective', 'major' and 'minor', in a sustained effort to prevent famine and improve agricultural production. The enabling legal changes were, however,frustrated by the international economic situation.

In the Krishna Basin, a number of major works, such as the Anjanapur Project on the Kumudvati river, the Bhadra Anicut on the Bhadra river, the Gokak Nala system and the extensions on the older Dharma Canal systems undertaken on the recommendation of the Famine and Irrigation Commissions.[26] The transfer of water as a provincial subject facilitated the raising of loans in overseas financial markets for projects. Money was, however, slow in coming because of the troubles experienced by overseas financial markets at that time. By the 1930s there was a reversal of investment in irrigation, so that between 1931 to 1940 outlay on major irrigation works declined. Construction of major irrigation works was halted and many approved projects languished for lack of finance. Faced with the failure of the major–productive sector, efforts switched once again to reviving tank irrigation.[27]

In the Constituent Assembly, there were intense jurisdictional disputes on control over water.[28] The states viewed water in conjunction with agriculture and forests, both state subjects. The centre saw power and large multi-purpose inter-state river valley projects as an important element of the industrialization that was to follow Independence. This was especially important as industry became a central subject when its control 'was declared by Parliament to be expedient in public interest'.[29] Under the Constitution of Independent India, 'water, that is to say', water supplies, irrigation and canals, drainage and embankments, water storage and water power, subject to the provision of entry 56 of List I', continued to be a state subject as in the earlier Government of India Act 1935, but with a rider: entry 56 of List I (central list) includes the 'regulation and development of inter-state rivers and river valleys to the extent to which such regulation and development under the control of the Union is declared by Parliament to be expedient in public interest'.

The constitutional framework entrenched one part of water-management, the 'major' and 'productive' works, into international capital and investments and another part, the 'minor' and 'protective' works, into a struggling subsistence economy, thereby deepening the historical schism discussed above.

International institutions and international law

In the post-independence period two factors brought about far-reaching changes in relation to water: the emergence of international institutions and national planning. During this period generally, and especially after 1968, the World Bank became extensively involved in India's agricultural sector, especially the water sector.[30] The World Bank was formed in 1944, and India became a member in 1945. The World Bank started lending operations in June 1946. India gained Independence on 15 August 1947. The first World Bank team visited India to survey the economic conditions in December 1948, and in 1950 the first stage of a loan for the large river–valley project, the Damodar Valley Corporation, was funded. This corporation was modelled on the Tennessee Valley Authority.[31] The dates are significant. Though the World Bank remained focused primarily on European reconstruction until the 1960s when the focus shifted to Third World 'development', because of India's historically pre-eminent position in the capitalist–colonial relationship the institutional mechanisms for integrating India into the post-war new world order had commenced some time before Independence, thus maintaining a smooth continuum into the post-independence period.

The World Bank and the International Monetary Fund were at the heart of the international law that emerged as part of the UN system at the end of the Second World War. International law under the UN system shifted the emphasis from the politics of the colonial era to economics. Formal equality of states made it possible to reduce the economic relations between the colonizing and colonized states to contractual obligations rather than political ones. While nation–states contribute 10 per cent of the capital base of the World Bank, 90 per cent is raised from private capital markets.[32] In the new era of multilateral imperialism, institutions like the World Bank were able to co-ordinate and channel transnational investments.

For nearly a century, from 1865 to 1965, the criteria for state investment in irrigation projects were determined by the 'financial productivity test' first set out in policy guidelines and later formalized in 1897 by the Select Committee on Indian Public Works of the House of Commons. Under this policy 'productive' works were to yield a fixed rate of return, generally of 5–6 per cent in the colonial period; the rate was reduced to 3.4 per cent in 1949.[33] Neither the role of irrigation in colonization nor the laws and policy framework were questioned. Reduction in the rate of return facilitated the expansion of large works and the involvement of the World Bank and other developmental agencies, as the Government of India undertook more projects whereas the World Bank's lending criteria remained as before.

By the late 1960s, the 'rate of return' approach was termed too 'colonial' by an increasing body of 'experts' who advocated shifting the criteria to those of 'benefit–cost'. Under the new criteria projections of non-monetary social benefits were included to make the rate of return more ambiguous, thereby facilitating the further involvement of international developmental agencies. It exacerbated the minor–major, market–subsistence economy dichotomies in agriculture. By contributing a part of the investments, international institutions could ensure that national resources were mobilized to support large projects.[34] The underlying assumption of international development assistance was that the projects would increase productivity to a critical point where, after repaying interest on international capital domestic accumulation of capital could occur. As in the colonial period, such an outcome required the complete transformation of social relations, risking serious social instability.

Planning in India

The legal status of the Planning Commission has always been ambiguous. In theory it is a body that advises the central Government on planned economic development. In practice the Planning Commission is the forum where 'who-gets-what' is effectively decided. The planning process involves states putting up project-proposals for approval and the approval is generally followed by federal financial support. The federal Government negotiates with international agencies and is the nodal point for co-ordinating international finance capital with state projects and undertakings.

The planning process dovetailed with the international development assistance process. It enabled a 'project' to be isolated from its social and political context and the parcelling of it for sale to finance capital internationally. International agencies in turn could limit their lending to formal contractual terms that involved a specific amount of capital and target date for completion. As Bhambri puts it: 'This project approach allowed the Bank in its selection and rejection of projects, a considerable say in the guidelines for economic development of recipient countries.'[35] However, neither process would have been possible without the laws and institutions that were put in place first during the colonial period and later during the transition period.

The increase in the number of projects that the World Bank and the planning process together facilitated in the post-independence period did not transform social relations of production in relation to water in any fundamental way.[36] The contradictory nature of colonial law, and its role in removing water-management from the hands of cultivators and creating a large irrigation bureaucracy ensured that institutions and organizations with a clear interest in water were slow to emerge. This created a 'lag' between project development and the growth of water-management institutions.

Since the 1970s, the World Bank has been seriously concerned about the 'under-performance' of irrigation projects. The attention of the Bank shifted increasingly to organizational and management issues. In the 1970s it promoted the notion of 'command area development',[37] an idea based on extensive changes in administrative and bureaucratic structures. The Bank funded a major initiative to review the functioning of eighty-five projects under the National Water Management Project;[38] later it comprehensively reviewed the irrigation sector and recommended extensive reform including market-oriented water pricing, water-users' organizations and legal reform.[39]

In line with international law under the UN system, institutions like the World Bank sought to remain 'purely' financial institutions, but the sticky issue of 'adequate rate of return' that had plagued water projects since colonial times continued to visit the World Bank, forcing it to become involved in social, political and institutional issues.

Whereas the international expansion of finance capital had, since the mid-1960s, prompted the expansion of the 'productive' sector, the agrarian crisis in the 1960s,[40] the peasant protests in the 1970s,[41] the ecological 'crisis',[42] the 'debt' crisis, and the movements against displacement of people,[43] all increased the social costs of expansion and prompted critics to advocate for 'minor' and 'protective' irrigation.[44] The colonial legal framework still served its purpose in stabilizing the essentially colonial nature of the contradictions and stunting the development of cohesive social relations over water.

'Winners'? 'Losers'?

The sources of conflicts over water in the Krishna Basin can be traced to the 'winners' and the 'losers' in large projects, and the consequent pressures on legal and constitutional mechanisms as evidenced by inter-state conflicts. Together, the conflicts have prevented the emergence of a unified conception of water resources' management situated in the wider context of economic independence and resistance to imperialism.

Recent development literature has highlighted movements arising from the large-scale dislocation wrought by river valley projects.[45] In the colonial era similar movements merged into the broader coalition that emerged against colonial rule.[46] Deepening schisms in social relations imposed by colonial legal relations frustrate the emergence of a broad-based anti-imperialist coalition in the independent India.

[254]

Struggles around rehabilitation, compensation and livelihood have called attention to the World Bank's lack of 'social responsibility'. The World Bank has twice withdrawn but later returned to financing the Upper Krishna Project, the largest project pending in the Krishna Basin, due to unsatisfactory implementation of the rehabilitation schemes. The Karnataka Government maintains that it can only do what is possible.[47] Such disputes have in turn pushed up the costs of projects, increased time over-runs and delayed returns on investments.[48]

Farmers using water from established large projects, the 'winners', have been at the forefront of movements against the General Agreements of Trade and Tariffs (GATT) under the World Trade Organization as they have been the focus of pressure from Western governments to remove agricultural subsidies and open domestic markets to foreign competition.[49] Though not directly connected to water, such movements raise issues about the conditions under which 'productive' works can become truly productive.[50] Free- and open-market relations in land, water, electricity and fertilizers push up the costs, and can survive only under conditions of assured markets and prices for agricultural products. Ironically both the World Bank and the World Trade Organization are sister organizations arising from the Bretton Wood agreements having similar status in international law.[51]

Inter-state conflicts

The scramble for projects in the post-Independence period created serious disputes between the three states of Andhra Pradesh, Karnataka and Maharashtra that led to the dispute being referred by the Government of India to a Tribunal constituted under the Inter-State River Disputes Act 1956.[52] The states impugned the legality and validity of pre-Independence agreements on inter-state water sharing, claiming that those settlements were imposed by a colonial regime, that they were discriminatory to the erstwhile 'Princely States' and not binding in a free and independent India to which those States had acceded. Interestingly the states did not pursue this claim. Instead, they agreed that the issues need not be decided; indeed they agreed that the colonial agreements should be superseded and that the Tribunal should determine the dispute on legal principles of equitable allocation.

In determining equitable allocation, the Tribunal relied heavily on the decisions of US courts where the social and historical contexts of the dispute were very different. The Tribunal also relied on the principles settled by the International Law Association, the International Law Commission and other UN bodies in river-water disputes that had divorced the rules from historical and political contexts in order to find 'universally' applicable laws. Essentially, the principles involved prioritizing uses. Two recognized principles were applied – existing uses were to be protected and water for irrigation given priority over water for power. Regions under the erstwhile 'Princely States' were more dependent on tank irrigation than where areas under direct British rule, where large projects were already in place.[53] Protecting prior uses meant that states with large projects obtained more water than those dependent on tank irrigation.

The Tribunal followed the categories of major–minor, productive–protective in prioritizing allocation. It departed, however, from the existing definition of 'major'–'minor' based on investment and instead based it on the quantum of water used by the projects. This further consolidated the categories on a less flexible basis.

Though priority status was also given to 'protective' works in drought-prone areas, as they were of small scale, the total allocation of water on that count also was small. The decision of the Tribunal was based on the project proposals of the states. The more fundamental issues of whether a basin could be segregated into 'drought-prone' and 'non-drought-prone' regions and how 'drought-prone' was to be defined never arose. The structure of federal–state financial relations meant, if the states did not bid for big projects, they could not get money. Determination of the inter-state dispute by the Tribunal cleared the way for the further expansion of projects. The Tribunal was, however, unable to put in place an authority to monitor the enforcement of the award because of constitutional constraints on jurisdiction over water.[54] In the meantime multi-purpose projects have brought in their wake new conflicts between Karnataka and Andhra Pradesh arising out of conflict of interests in power generation and irrigation uses.[55]

Conclusion

These conflicts over water emphasize core features that have persisted in pre- and post-Independence India. Efforts by colonial and, later, international and federal law and institutions to bring about radical transformation in relation to water have remained trapped in contradictions. Like earlier colonial administrations, international developmental organizations like the World Bank face similar dilemmas – for example the social transformation needed to make water projects profitable could create political instability, and managing political stability has adverse financial implications. The continuities suggest that colonial law may not be a *legacy* of the past but a living instrument for the reproduction of imperial international relations.

Notes

I am grateful to Professor Richard Le Heron, Professor Jane Kelsey and Dr Gordon Winder for their suggestions. This paper draws from my Ph.D. fieldwork in India supported by the NZ Asia Research Fund and the Auckland University Graduate Research Fund.

1 A. Hunt, *Explorations in Law and Society: Toward A Constitutive Theory of Law* (New York, Routledge, 1993).
2 See U. Baxi, *The Crisis of the Indian Legal System: Alternatives in Development Law* (Delhi, Vikas Publishing, 1982).
3 R. Dhavan, 'Jurisprudence and Sociology of Modern Indian Law', in M. Galanter (ed.), *Law and Society in Modern India* (Bombay, Oxford University Press, 1989), pp. xxiii–xxiv.
4 The generic term 'water' in legal and environmental studies is used interchangeably with 'irrigation'.
5 B.K. Narayan, *Bachawat Award and After: Krishna Basin Projects In Karnataka* (Mumbai, Himalaya Publishing, 1996); T.S. Shomashekhara Reddy, 'Development Impact in Krishna River Basin: Conflicts and Alternatives', *Water Nepal*, 4:1 (1994), 237–46.
6 See e.g. W.F. Fisher (ed.), *Toward Sustainable Development: Struggling Over India's Narmada River* (New York, M.E. Sharpe, 1995).
7 N. Sengupta, 'Field Systems, Property Reform and Indigenous Irrigation', paper delivered at the conference 'The Heyday of Colonial Rule, 1830s–1914', Leiden, 1985; N. Sengupta, 'Irrigation: Traditional and Modern', *Economic and Political Weekly*, XX:45–7 (1985), 1919–38; N. Sengupta, 'Colonial Impact On Agriculture: A Systems View', paper delivered at the conference 'Comparative Studies of Rural Transformation in Asia', Delhi, 1986; S. Singh, *Taming the Waters: The Political Economy of Large Dams in India* (Delhi, Oxford University Press, 1997); M.S. Vani, *Role of Panchayat Institutions in Irrigation Management: Law and Policy* (New Delhi, Indian Law Institute, 1992).
8 B.N. Chaturvedi, 'The Origin and Development of Tank Irrigation in Peninsular India', *The Deccan Geographer*, 6 (1968), 57–85; Sengupta, 'Irrigation: Traditional and Modern'.
9 For developments in law during the early colonial period, see A.B. Keith, *A Constitutional History of India: 1600–1935*, 2nd edn (Allahabad, Central Book Depot, 1961).
10 The Act was brought into force in different areas at different times. For an account of land relations in the 'Princely State' of Hyderabad, see P. Rukhsana, 'Land and Revenue System in Hyderabad–Karnataka Region Under Nizam's Rule', paper delivered at the Seminar on the Hyderabad–Karnataka region 'Economy: Problems and Prospects', Gulbarga, 1994.
11 Vani, *Role of Panchayat Institutions*.
12 For differences in regional development between the erstwhile 'Princely State' of Hyderabad and other parts of the State of Karnataka, see A. Aziz and S. Krishna (eds), *Regional Development: Problems and Policy Measures* (New Delhi, Concept Publishing Company, 1996).
13 On the 'colonial mode of production', see H. Alavi, 'India and the Colonial Mode of Production', *Economic and Political Weekly*, special issue (1975), 1235–62. Also see Sengupta, 'Colonial Impact'.
14 Vani, *Role of Panchayat Institutions*, p. 43.
15 G.N. Rao, 'Transition from Subsistence to Commercialised Agriculture: A Study of Krishna District of Andhra, c. 1850–1900' *Economic and Political Weekly* XX:25–6 (1985), A60–9.

16 D. Harvey, 'The Geopolitics of Capitalism', in D. Gregory and J. Urry (eds), *Social Relations and Spatial Structures* (New York, St. Martin's Press, 1985), pp. 128–63.

17 Bolding *et al.* draw parallels between the 'problems' of colonial irrigation and those of the present day in their paper on 'protective works' in the Nira Left Bank Canal, in the Krishna Basin: A. Bolding, P.P. Mollinga and K. Van Straaten, 'Modules for Modernisation: Colonial Irrigation in India and the Technological Dimension of Agrarian Change', *Journal of Development Studies*, 31 (1995), 805–44. On similar dilemmas of colonial law and land, see D. Washbrook, 'Law, State And Agrarian Society in Colonial India', in Yash Ghai, Robin Luckham and Francis Snyder (eds), *The Political Economy of Law* (Bombay, Oxford University Press, 1987).

18 Bagchi attributes this to the stunting of the growth of market relations under colonial rule: A.K. Bagchi, 'Foreign Capital and Economic Development in India: A Schematic View', in Kathleen Gough and Hari P. Sharma (eds), *Imperialism and Revolution in South Asia* (New York, Monthly Review Press, 1973), pp. 43–76. Also see Alavi, 'India', and R. Harshe, *Twentieth Century Imperialism: Shifting Contours and Changing Conceptions* (New Delhi, Sage Publications, 1997).

19 B.S. Chimni, *International Law and World Order: A Critique of Contemporary Approaches*, vol. 1 (New Delhi, Sage Publications, 1993).

20 On international organizations under the League of Nations and the UN systems, see D.W. Bowett, *The Law of International Institutions* (New Delhi, Universal Book Traders, 1964). For developments in international law in the context of colonialism and imperialism, see Chimni, *International Law*.

21 Bagchi, 'Foreign Capital'.

22 For details of the Union and the state list, and for comparisons between the 1935 and 1947 constitutions, see *The Framing of India's Constitution: Select Documents*, ed. S. Shiva Rao, vols. 2 and 5 (New Delhi, Indian Institute of Public Administration, 1967).

23 John Hurd II, 'The Influence of British Policy on Industrial Development in the Princely States of India, 1890–1933', *Indian Economic and Social History Review*, XII:4 (1975) 409–24.

24 Rao, *The Framing of India's Constitution*.

25 B.R. Chauhan, *Settlement of International and Inter-State Water Disputes in India* (Bombay, Indian Law Institute/N.M. Tripathi, 1992)

26 K. Puttaswamaiah, *Economic Development of Karnataka: A Treatise in Continuity and Change*, vol. I (New Delhi, IBH Publishing, 1980).

27 D. Rothermund, 'The Great Depression and British Financial Policy in India, 1929–34', *Indian Economic and Social History Review*, XVIII:1 (1981–82) 1–17. About this time power production became a contender for water resources because of the expansion of industries during the world wars; this added a new dimension to water conflicts.

28 See R. D'Souza, 'The Legal Process and Limits of Environmental Legislation in India', *F.I.L Working Papers*, No. 7 (Oslo, University of Oslo, 1995), pp. 44–6. Also see Rao, *The Framing of India's Constitution*.

29 Under the Industries (Development and Regulation) Act 1951, most major industries became a central subject.

30 C.P. Bhambhri, *World Bank and India* (New Delhi, Vikas, 1980); K. Sarwar Lateef (ed.), *The Evolving Role of the World Bank: Helping Meet the Challenge of Development* (Washington, DC, World Bank). *India: Irrigation Sector Review*, Vol. I. (India, 1991). SRA, 9518–IN; *The World Bank in India* (New Delhi, World Bank, 1993). S.N. Jain, A. Jacob and S. Jain's *Inter-State Water Disputes in India: Suggestions for Reform in Law* (New Delhi, Indian Law Institute/Bombay, N.M. Tripathi, 1971) mentions that in the mid-1950s the Government of India considered setting up a Minor Irrigation Corporation with the assistance of the US Agency for International Development (US AID) out of PL 480 Funds. Curiously this was never pursued.

31 The first loan was for a railway project, in 1949. See Bhambhri, *World Bank and India*.

32 On international law and the legality of economic coercion in international rela-

tions, see B.S. Brown, *The United States and the Politicization of the World Bank* (London, Kegan Paul, 1992).

33 *Report of the Committee on Pricing of Irrigtion Water* (New Delhi, Planning Commission, Government of India, 1992). See also: N. Rath, 'The Current Method of Choosing Irrigation Projects in India: A Review'; N.V. Sovani, 'Economic Yardsticks for Irrigation Projects: Review and Perspective'; V.K. Srinivasan, 'Return from Investment: An Area of Increasing Concern'; all three papers delivered at the seminar 'The Role of Irrigation in the Development of India's Agriculture', 1976.

34 On the political economy of large dams in India, see Singh, *Taming the Waters.*

35 Bhambhri, *World Bank And India.*

36 According to Singh, *Taming the Waters*, 1,554 large dams were constructed in India by 1979, most of them after Independence.

37 V.S. Gopalakrishnan, 'Organization for Command Area Administration in India', *Indian Journal of Public Administration*, 19:2 (1973), 177–86; R. Wade, 'The World Bank and India's Irrigation Sector', *Journal of Development Studies*, 18:2 (1982) 171–84.

38 See, e.g., *Final Evaluation Report Under National Water Management Project – 1: Evaluation of Schemes in Karnataka and Sathanur Scheme in Tamil Nadu – Volume 1 Main Report* (Colombo, International Irrigation Management Institute, 1995); and World Bank, *India.*

39 World Bank, *India.*

40 See R. Sau, 'India's Economic Crisis' in S.A. Shah (ed.) *India: Degradation and Development*, vol. I (Secundrabad, M. Venkatarangaiya Foundation, 1982), p. 192.

41 For protests movements in the state of Andhra Pradesh, see K. Balagopal, *Probings in the Politcal Economy of Agrarian Classes and Conflicts*, (ed.) G. Hargopal, (Hyderabad, Perspectives, 1988), p. 230.

42 See Singh, *Taming the Waters*, ch. 5.

43 See E.G. Thukral (ed.), *Big Dams, Displaced People: Rivers of Sorrow, Rivers of Change* (New Delhi, Sage Publications, 1992).

44 In the state of Maharashtra, 'minor' and 'protective' works were undertaken in the 1970s as part of famine-relief work under the Employment Guarantee Scheme.

45 Fisher, *Toward Sustainable Develoment*; Thukral, *Big Dams.*

46 See F. Ahmad, 'Popular People's Movements in Water Resources Management and the Role of Law', in Chhatrapati Singh (ed.), *Water Law in India* (New Delhi, Indian Law Institute, 1992).

47 On resettlement and rehabilitation of project-displaced people in the Upper Krishna Project, see M.V. Nadkarni, Syed Ajmal Pasha and K.V Govinda Raju, *Monitoring and Concurrent Evaluation: Report on Resettlement and Rehabilitation of Project Displaced Families in Upper Krishna Project (Almatti Dam Area)* (Bangalore, Institute for Social and Economic Change, 1997).

48 On developmental conflicts in the Narmada Valley, see Fisher, *Toward Sustainable Development.*

49 In Karnataka the Karnataka Rajya Raitha Sangha and in Maharashtra the Shetkari Sanghatna are examples of movements of farmers largely dependent on irrigation water.

50 On market-oriented water-pricing reforms, see recommendations in the *Report of the Committee on Pricing of Irrigation Water.*

51 Other social movements include environmental movements in the Malaprabha and Ghataprabha sub-basins; and there are movements against water-logging and salination and self-help movements in drought areas involving communitarian water projects. See Thukral, *Big Dams*, and, Ahmad, 'Popular People's Movements'.

52 *The Report of The Krishna Water Disputes Tribunal with the Decision* (New Delhi, Krishna Water Disputes Tribunal, 1973); *Further Report of the Krishna Water Disputes Tribunal* (New Delhi, Krishna Water Disputes Tribunal, 1976).

53 For comparative perspectives, see P. Devasena Naidu, 'Growth Rates of Irrigation – A Case Study of Andhra Pradesh and Karnataka', *Southern Economist*, 20 (1982), 17–19.

54 The Inter-State River Disputes Act 1956 was amended after this award to give he Tribunal power to constitute an authority to monitor its awards.
55 'Alamatti Talks Fail as Karnataka Rejects AP Plea', *The Hindu*, 10 August 1996; 'Govt Takes Tough Stand on Alamatti Dam', *The Hindu*, 11 August 1996; 'Jurala Project Row Deepens', *The Hindu*, 11 August 1996; 'River Waters Run Deep', *The Hindu*, 12 August 1996; 'Patel Govt Mishandled Alamatti Issue', *The Hindu*, 14 August 1996.

CHAPTER SIXTEEN

Historians and native title: the question of evidence

Christine Choo

Since the 1992 *Mabo* decision and the passing of the Commonwealth Native Title Act in 1993 historians have become increasingly involved in the native title process. Not only are historians being engaged to gather and organize historical information to assist in the preparation of native title claims both by the applicants and by the respondents, but they have been called as expert witnesses in claims that have reached the Federal Court of Australia. Historical evidence has become significant as applicants are required to show evidence of *continued use and occupation* of the land under claim.

Historians and lawyers are not accustomed to working together, and there are many lessons to be learnt on both sides. Historians must learn the language and the requirements of lawyers and the courts; they must also learn to adapt their writing styles and the ways they present their material for the courts. More importantly, historians' conception, analysis and presentation of historical evidence have come into the spotlight, particularly in the legal context.[1] Lawyers and judges, on the other hand, must learn about the different ways in which historians deal with questions of evidence and how they present their opinions based on historical evidence.

Drawing on the successive decisions in *Delgamuukw* v. *British Columbia* which provide precedents on this matter, I examine the ways in which historians have been used as expert witnesses in two native title claims in Australia – the *Yorta Yorta Aboriginal Community* v. *State of Victoria & Others* and *Ben Ward & Others* v. *State of Western Australia & Others* (East Kimberley).[2] I offer critical comment on these processes, their implications for historical research on native title claims and the questions they raise for historians in general. These arguments emerge in the context of the development of Australian jurisprudence, which signals an acknowledgment of the particular rights of native title applicants. However, implicit in the Australian

[261]

legal system, which is based in the British model, is the assumed superiority of that system over other jurisdictions, including customary law of indigenous and other (migrant) Australians from different cultural, social and legal backgrounds.

Mabo *and native title*

The *Mabo* decision is of deep significance to the legal, political and social life of Australia, and constitutes a critical moment in our history as a nation. In 1992, ten years after Eddie Mabo and four other Torres Strait Islanders who inhabited the Murray Islands began action for a declaration of native title over their traditional lands, the High Court of Australia decided in *Mabo v. Queensland (No. 2)* (hereafter *Mabo No. 2*)[3] that the Meriam people were entitled as against the whole world to the possession, occupation, use and enjoyment of (most of) the land of the Murray Islands in the Torres Strait. The court concluded that while the content of native title was to be determined according to the traditional laws and customs of the title-holders, there were certain common characteristics in all native title. These are that native title

- is inalienable other than by surrender to the Crown or according to traditional laws and customs;
- is a legal right which can be protected by legal action;
- may be possessed by a community or group depending on the content of the traditional laws and customs;
- is not frozen as at the time of European occupation.

Brennan J., Deane and Gaudron J.J. and Toohey J., set out the elements of proof which must be satisfied in a claim of native title. These are that

1 there must be an identifiable Aboriginal community or group;

2 the Aboriginal group must have a traditional connection with or occupation of the land that it claims, under the laws and customs of the group in question;

3 there must be substantial maintenance of the connection with or occupation of the land in question by the Aboriginal group in question from the time of Crown sovereignty to the present.

Evidence required for proof of native title

Proving native title in the courts of Australia is a process that is still in early stages of development; with two major decisions, appeals in the High Court of Australia, and a number of other cases being heard in the

Federal Court. The onus of proving the elements of native title remains the responsibility of the applicant, and the standard of proof is the civil standard of the balance of probabilities. The Native Title Act which governs all native title litigation also contains guidance on the evidentiary process and how the litigation should be conducted.[4] Of particular interest is the instruction that the proceedings in the Federal Court 'must take into account cultural and customary concerns of Aboriginal peoples and Torres Strait Islanders' (s. 82(2)) and that the Court is not bound by technicalities, legal forms or rules of evidence (s. 82(3)).

In *Mason v. Tritton* Kirby J. stated that in order to prove native title one of the elements that must be satisfied is that the clan or group applying for native title must show that it has continued to acknowledge the laws and to observe the customs 'as based on the traditions of that clan or group', and that such evidence 'would establish that the "traditional connection with the land has been substantially maintained"'.[5] Among the details which could be brought together as evidence for the group's continued use and occupation of the land, and therefore proof of native title, are the following (though this list is not exhaustive):

- residence on the land;
- maintenance of a nomadic way of life on the land;
- hunting, gathering and obtaining sustenance from the land;
- bearing and rearing children on the land;
- building and using shelter;
- holding ceremonies and conducting traditional Law Business;
- using materials derived from the land, for example, stones, ochres, minerals;
- caring for the land and particular sites of significance on the land;
- maintenance of knowledge about the land and about individuals' and the community's connections with the land;
- recognition of particular connections with specific sites on the land.

In native title proceedings the rules of evidence applied must take into account 'the particular evidentiary difficulties faced by Aboriginal people in presenting such claims for adjudication and the evidence adduced must be interpreted in the same spirit, consistent with the judicial power vested in the Court under the Constitution'. Lee J. went on to highlight this point:

> Of particular importance in that regard is the disadvantage faced by Aboriginal people as participants in a trial system structured for, and by, a literate society when they have no written records and depend upon oral histories and accounts, often localized in nature ... In this proceeding the principal opponent to the claims of the applicants is the Crown in the

right of the State and in the right of the Territory. If it is accepted that the Crown is presumed to have had knowledge of relevant circumstances and events concerning the burden of native title on its land at material times and to have access to all relevant resources, there can be no suggestion of unfairness in a trial process in which Aboriginal applicants are permitted to present their case through use of oral histories and by reference to received knowledge.[6]

In native title cases, as in other jurisdictions, the 'best evidence' principle applies, that is that the parties in the proceedings must seek out and present the best evidence to support their arguments in court. In Australia, the oral evidence of the applicants and other Aboriginal people with direct knowledge of the aplicants' genealogy, culture and society, how these have been expressed and practised in the past and are being practised at present, and how they are to be transmitted to future generations, is of vital significance and should be taken as best evidence. In *Ejai* v. *Commonwealth* Owen J. of the Supreme Court of Western Australia stressed the importance of cultural sensitivity in the proceedings when he stated that the courts

> ... must be alive to the fact that in Aboriginal culture, notions of property and association may take a different form to that with which Western cultures are familiar.
>
> The courts must also recognise that there are elements of Aboriginal culture and spirituality about which there is much sensitivity. It is not always easy for law men and women to disclose details of sensitive matters in an open forum where the information is available to persons to whom disclosure would otherwise be prohibited.
>
> In claims touching on native title the best evidence lies in the hearts and minds of the people most intimately connected to Aboriginal culture, namely the Aboriginal people themselves. Expert evidence from anthropologists and others is of significance and due regard must, and will, be afforded to it. However, it seems to me that the full story lies in the hearts and minds of the people. It is from there that it must be extracted. This is not always easy, particularly from a people whose primary language might not be English and who, historically, have depended on oral rather than written recording of tradition.[7]

Besides the evidence given by the applicants themselves as witnesses in the court proceedings, expert anthropologists, archaeologists, geographers, cartographers, linguists, oral historians, historians and other specialists may be called as witnesses by the applicants or the respondents in the case. The expert is usually asked to give an opinion in response to a brief from the solicitors working for a particular party. Experts' reports may be used internally as briefing documents to the solicitors, or they may be presented to the court as evidence. The expert witness, whose written report is tabled in court, is examined and may be cross-examined by lawyers for all respondents. The evidence of expert witnesses, speaking from the strength of their particular areas of professional expertise, is provided primarily to assist the court and the trial judge to make a determination on whether or not native title exists.[8]

The use of evidence of 'experts' and oral evidence in native title cases

Historians have an important contribution to make in the presentation of evidence in the native title litigation process. Expert historical evidence amounts to more than the production for the court of a collection of uncontested objects called 'facts' or a chronology. The very process of historical research, including the identification of relevant material and report writing, entails a level of interpretation which is implicit in the presentation of the historian's opinion. This is something often overlooked in the judicial treatment of expert evidence from historians.

It is helpful to examine the use of historical evidence in a number of specific cases. As the law on the determination of native title is in its infancy in Australia I look to other countries, Canada for instance, with a developed case law jurisprudence for precedents. In the 1991 precedent case of *Delgamuukw & Others* v. *British Columbia*, heard in the Supreme Court of British Columbia, Canada, fifty one hereditary chiefs representing sub-groups of Aboriginal peoples claimed tracts of land in British Columbia on behalf of themselves and their people. The trial judge, McEachern, then chief justice of British Columbia, dismissed the Delgamuukw claim for a declaration of ownership, the right to govern and for damages. This decision was appealed by the fifty-one hereditary chiefs, and in June 1993 a decision was made to allow the case to proceed to the British Columbia Court of Appeal. Among the grounds on which the Delgamuukw people appealed the original decision of McEachern C.J., were that the trial judge

- ignored or rejected, without reason, the evidence of a historian with respect to pre-contact Gitksan and Wet'suwet'en land ownership, self-government and trade;
- rejected the entire body of the applicants' oral histories as evidence of detailed history of land ownership, use or occupation and said that they could not provide direct evidence of the fact in issue except in a few cases where they could constitute the confirmatory proof of early presence in the territory;
- rejected the evidence of the anthropologists called by the plaintiffs.

[265]

The treatment of the evidence of both the applicants and some of the expert witnesses was questioned. While oral evidence and the expert evidence were admitted in court, the most significant question was the weight given to this evidence by the trial judge, and what reasons he gave to justify his decisions regarding the credence he gave to the evidence.[9]

The appeal against the *Delgamuukw* decision was then heard in the Supreme Court of Canada, which is equivalent to the High Court of Australia. In December 1997 the Supreme Court held that the appeal was to be allowed in part, and a new trial was ordered. Chief Justice Lamer with three of the five justices of the Supreme Court concurring, found among other things that the

> findings of fact made by the trial judge were fatally flawed because his treatment of the various kinds of oral histories did not satisfy [certain principles]. The appellants used oral histories in an attempt to establish their occupation and use of the territory, an essential requirement for Aboriginal title. The trial judge, after refusing to admit, or to giving no independent weight to these oral histories, reached the conclusion that the appellants had not demonstrated the requisite degree of occupation for 'ownership'. Had the trial judge assessed the oral histories correctly, his conclusions on these issues of fact might have been different.[10]

Lamer C.J. found that '[b]oth the Aboriginal and common law perspectives must be taken into account in addressing proof of occupancy'.[11] Lamer C.J. dealt with the question of evidence by emphasizing that the courts need to take into account Aboriginal evidence and the integrity of their oral evidence. He stated that the courts must adapt the laws of evidence

> so that the Aboriginal perspective on their practices, customs and traditions and on their relationship with the land, are given due weight by the courts ... this requires the courts to come to terms with the oral histories of Aboriginal societies, which, for many Aboriginal nations, are the only record of their past ... those histories play a crucial role in the litigation of Aboriginal rights.[12] [...] if oral history cannot conclusively establish pre-sovereignty occupation of land, it may still be relevant to demonstrate that current occupation has its origins prior to sovereignty.[13]

Lamer C.J. limited his comments on the matter of the testimony of expert witnesses, stating simply that findings of credibility, including the credibility of expert witnesses, are for the trial judge to make and should warrant considerable deference from appellate courts.[14] In the earlier appeal hearing in the British Columbia Court of Appeal Justice Macfarlane had found that on the question of the treatment of the evidence of experts, the trial judge, McEachern C.J., had no trouble with the admissibility of the evidence but had difficulty with the weight to be given to the evidence. It is of interest to historians that McEachern gave the so-called 'scientific evidence' of archaeology, linguistics and some history more weight than he did the evidence of other experts, including certain historians and anthropologists. McEachern considered that some of the historical and oral evidence could only constitute confirmatory proof of early presence, even though he considered that it did not satisfy him as being direct evidence, thus indicating his opinion of the value of certain forms of historical evidence and oral evidence.

McEachern was apparently impressed by the expert-opinion evidence given by Dr Ray, a historical geographer, based on his interpretation of records kept by early trappers in the area under claim, but he was less impressed with the evidence of cultural anthropologists whose testimony he considered biased because of their close and on-going association with the applicants.[15] These reasons given for his decision on the matter of evidence reflect the value the trial judge placed on so-called 'objective' sources, the historians' analysis of these sources and the apparently higher value placed on the written word. The reasons indicate the judge's failure to understand that both oral and written testimony must be subjected to the same rigorous analysis because they are both likely to be affected by similar biases and influences. Historians must constantly remind themselves of the limitations and dangers of claiming to be 'objective' and the need to problematize both the evidence and the process of historical research in order to avoid the pitfalls of a positivist position in historical research. Most historians are very much aware of the value and the limitations of both oral and documentary sources in historical analysis.

Lambert J., who dissented from the position of McEachern, contributed an interesting observation about the task of the historian and the need to validate the opinions and 'facts' of the expert historian or anthropologist when he stated that

> findings of historical fact based on historical or anthropological evidence given by historians or anthropologists should, in my opinion, be given only the kind of weight that other historians or anthropologists may give to them. There are some historical facts on which all historians agree. But there are many others on which historians disagree about the historical facts or about the interpretation of the events which brought about or followed from generally accepted historical facts. It is a strange situation indeed if a trial judge, in a case such as this, can make a finding on a question of historical fact on the basis of the evidence of one or two historians or anthropologists, particularly if he does not believe one or more of them, with the result that the historical facts become frozen for ever as the basis for any legal decision about entitlement to rights. Historians

[267]

and anthropologists and other social scientists do not always agree with each other. Circumstances change and new raw material is discovered and interpreted. The tide of historical and anthropological scholarship could, in a few years, leave a trial judge's findings of fact stranded as forever wrong.[16]

The process of solidifying the 'historical fact' which Lambert J. outlines resembles the process which occurs when histories are documented in the written word. Changes in interpretation *do* occur and must be taken into account. New material may appear later but the judge can only be guided by the material before her or him. New interpretations or information may well come to light, just as new technologies may throw a different light on the 'facts' in a criminal case. The oral testimony and the historical evidence from documentary sources are both important in native title cases. Commenting on the treatment of the evidence of expert anthropologists in such cases, Richard Bartlett warned of the danger of 'non-aboriginal experts' interpretation and filtering of aboriginal evidence'.[17]

In Australia, the oral evidence of the native title applicants, including Aboriginal-way-of-life evidence, is being used in the court process to determine native title, as is the evidence of expert witnesses, including historians. I now turn to the examination of two native title claims in which a decision has been reached in the Federal Court of Australia and comment on the role of the expert historian and her/his contribution in the proceedings.

On 24 November 1998, Lee J. decided that native title existed in the determination area held by the Miriuwung and Gajerrong people.[18] On 18 December 1998, Olney J. determined that native title did not exist in relation to the areas of land and waters claimed by the members of the Yorta Yorta Aboriginal Community.[19]

These two recent native title decisions give us valuable insights into the nature of the evidence required to prove native title and the role of the historian in the proceedings. The historians briefed in these cases came from very different perspectives and obviously had different briefs and approaches to their work. In court, under cross-examination, not only the written evidence and opinion itself, but even the methodology and the credentials of historian come under further scrutiny.

In *Yorta Yorta* v. *State of Victoria & Others*, in addition to the oral testimony of the witnesses, the applicants relied on documentary historical evidence prepared by an anthropologist. The applicants did not draw on the opinion of an expert historian; instead their historical evidence was included in a report entitled 'Anthropological and Socio-Historical Issues' prepared by an anthropologist.[20] The State of Victoria, however, called two historians and a professional genealogist as witnesses. One of the witnesses called by the State of Victoria identified herself as an ethno-historian whose role, she stated, was to examine historical sources, 'to look at the question of identifying and defining as far as possible on the basis of historical materials available the boundaries of the area occupied at the time of European contact by the group said to be the ancestral group of the present claimants, and to look at the question ... of it in [another report]'.[21] This expert witness considered that what she had written was an ethnography. She was later asked to comment on and guide the court in reading certain historical maps which were among the earliest official maps of Victoria. Under cross-examination particular attention was drawn to the issue of definition of professional boundaries between historians and anthropologists, the work of the ethno-historian and ethnographer. The witness was also called upon to defend her methodology and her reliance on particular sources.

In his reasons for the decision in *Yorta Yorta* v. *State of Victoria &* *Others*, Olney J. was satisfied that the inference that indigenous people occupied the claim area in or around 1788 and when the earliest explorers and settlers first entered the area was compelling.[22] As the applicants had not called an expert historian to provide a history report or an analysis of available historical material which may have been critical in this case, Olney J. had before him the applicants' anthropological report to provide him with a brief sketch of European settlement of the claim area. The failure to differentiate clearly between historical and anthropological evidence, the uncritical use of material from historical sources and the failure of the judge to understand the importance of historical analysis, all had a part to play in the (mis)representation and (mis)interpretation of critical historical evidence of ongoing use and occupation in the Yorta Yorta claim.

A significant piece of evidence to which Olney J. referred was a petition signed by forty-two Aboriginal leaders in 1881 which was tendered as evidence by the applicants in support of their claim. The petition was quoted in full by Olney J., who found that, rather than support the claim, the petition confirmed that 'all land within [the petitioners] tribal boundaries [had] been taken possession of by the government and white settlers', and therefore the claimant group failed Toohey J.'s test of occupation by a traditional society now and at the time of annexation.[23] Olney J. relied uncritically on a limited range of what he considered to be 'historical facts', failing to question the source and the context in which the materials were produced, the influences or biases of the author of the comments, the prevailing attitudes and values of the period, the purpose for the production of the document which was quoted and other important factors which must be considered in the interpretation of historical sources. In this case both the applicants and the judge failed to recognize the value of a nuanced historical analysis of relevant materials, and the importance of expert historical evidence in native title litigation. Olney concluded:

> The tide of history has indeed washed away any real acknowledgment of their traditional laws and any real observance of their traditional customs. The foundation of the claim to native title in relation to the land previously occupied by those ancestors having disappeared, the native title rights and interests previously enjoyed are not capable of revival. This conclusion effectively resolves the application of a determination of native title.[24]

The Miriuwung and Gajerrong people's native title claim is the first claim on mainland Australia in which a determination of native title was made after full trial.[25] Although a number of historians were engaged, both by the applicants and the respondents, to undertake research in relation to the claim, only two historians were called to give evidence as 'expert witnesses', one each by the applicants and the State of Western Australia. Reports by two other historians were uncontested, and they were not called to give evidence in court.

On the question of Aboriginal connection with the claim area at the time of sovereignty, Lee J., drawing on archaeological and historical evidence, concluded that

> the claim area, and surrounding lands, were inhabited by organized communities of Aboriginal inhabitants at the time of sovereignty and that ... Aboriginal people who occupied the claim area at sovereignty functioned under elaborate traditions, procedures, laws and customs which connected them to the land. It follows that the Aboriginal communities which occupied the claim area at sovereignty possessed native title in respect of that land.[26]

Lee J. took account of the historical, linguistic, 'primary' evidence of applicants, and of anthropological and genealogical evidence in his consideration of the question of whether native title continued after the occupation of the claim area by Europeans.

With reference to the historical evidence, Lee J. relied on the evidence of an archaeological report tendered as evidence by the Northern Territory as well as on the published material and evidence of anthropologist and oral historian Dr Bruce Shaw who, in the 1970s, had documented the oral histories of a number of Miriuwung and Gajerrong people, including elders who were ancestors of the current applicants. This material was valuable in showing the continued connection of the applicants to the claim area. Lee J. also relied on reports and evidence obtained under the cross-examination of Dr Neville Green, a witness of the State of Western Australia. From the evidence of Dr Cathie Clement, who prepared a historical report for the Northern Territory's Government, Lee J. concluded that 'Aboriginal people, some of whom were Miriuwung and Gajerrong, occupied the Keep River National Park area prior to 1894 and coexisted on the pastoral leases from which the national park was excised, with a number of them living a "bush" life until at least 1944'.[27] My own evidence assisted Lee J. to conclude 'that although the introduction of the *"Pastoral Award"* in 1968 saw Aboriginal people leave pastoral properties, thereafter the connection with land for Miriuwung and Gajerrong people remained'.[28]

There was an interesting development in this case as it relates to the evidence of the applicants' historian. Counsel acting for the State of Western Australia objected to the acceptance of the report as evidence. One objection was that some of the opinions expressed in the report were based on anthropological and not historical expertise. A second objection was that 'at various places in her report [the witness] expresses opinions on facts which are not disclosed'.[29] Here, again attempts were made to discredit the work of the historian. Eventually the witness was asked to withdraw while the lawyers engaged in legal argument as to the admissibility of the evidence, and, after a long discussion, the reports, with a number of small excisions, were accepted as evidence.

The comments of Lee J. in relation to the admissibility of the evidence are of particular interest, as they place the evidence of the expert witness in the context of best evidence, in this case, the evidence of the applicants themselves:

> in matters like this there is some latitude in relation to secondary material particularly that of an historical nature where it can become the foundation for conclusions being drawn, and I think the concern is that, not through a sidewind should there be an elevation of what could be dealt with by direct evidence into material that's relied upon, having been drawn in through a report of an historian as foundational material, and put in the same class as [*sic*] ... that foundational material, as other historical material from which conclusions could be drawn by the Court in respect to its content.[30]

Here the discussion is about the primacy of the direct evidence. In the original *Delgamuukw* decision the trial judge had given less weight to the direct evidence of the applicants than to some of the evidence given by expert witnesses. In *Ben Ward & Others* the trial judge made clear that he recognized that the direct evidence of the applicants was of prime importance. It appears to be the trial judge's opinion that direct evidence should stand on its own and not be drawn in as evidence through discussions with an historian (or other expert witness, including the anthropologist]. This places a big question-mark on the use of oral history as a method for obtaining otherwise undocumented source material for historical analysis. Documentary historical sources provide only part of the picture in Aboriginal history, primarily because they have been written by and for the non-Aboriginal, and for mainly administrative or personal purposes. It is difficult and extremely time-consuming, though not impossible, to discover traces of Aboriginal presence in and through the use of archival documents and other written material. However, the oral histories of a minority group with a rich oral, aural and visual culture and tradition, must certainly be an important part of the historian's sources. The integrity of the various sources must be examined and respected.

The different discourses of the professions of history and law are highlighted in this situation. It appears that the trial judge wished to reserve for himself the role of interpreter of historical material, including the oral history of the applicants. He was interested in obtaining the 'facts' on which he would base his decision. Discussion of the historian's evidence highlighted the trial judge's view of the weight to be placed on the opinion of the historian in his deliberation of the facts of the case:

> I do not take the expression of an opinion wherever it appears in the report as a matter that would entitle me to extract or rely upon that to the exclusion *of my proper function which is to find the relevant and pertinent and material facts on which the purported opinion could be based.* Indeed, whether in a material such as this, one could be said to express an opinion is, to my mind, a matter of opinion in itself and really can be no more than the highlighting of an available inference that may [be] drawn from material that has been gathered, historical material that has been gathered. Whether such an inference is indeed able to [be] drawn is a matter for me after I determine the facts. So, in short, I will not be relying upon an expression of an opinion as a basis on which I may form other conclusions.[31] [my emphasis]

It is apparent from an analysis of the judgments of Lee J. in *Ben Ward & Others* v. *State of W.A. and Others* and Olney J. in *Yorta Yorta* v. *State of Victoria & Others*, that the role of the instructing solicitors handling the applicants' cases and of the respective counsels who led the evidence-in-chief becomes significant. It is their responsibility to ensure that the evidence on which they will rely is brought before the court and that the evidence is credible. It appears that the legal profession has much to learn about history as a professional discipline, and the value of the processes, method and analysis techniques of professional historians, who are not simply 'gatherers of facts'. In the context of litigation for native title, the legal profession and the courts appear to be leaning towards such a limited view of professional historians as 'gatherers of facts', with the lawyer taking on the role of historian and interpreter of historical 'facts'. Here is an example of the blurring of professional boundaries – a practice of which, in court, lawyers are so critical.

Historical evidence in proving native title

Historical research in the native title context raises complicated questions about the nature of historical evidence. The paucity of existing research on contact history (and Aboriginal–European relations) in Australia leaves serious gaps in the story of regional settlement and its impacts. Consequently, the historical research process often involves intensive search and analysis of primary archival material which had never before been interrogated for that purpose. The evidence assembled by historians and the opinions they formulate are part of an intensely political process in which a number of different perspectives are pitted against each other in court. Often the same historical material may be subjected to a number of divergent and incompatible interpretations by historians working to very different briefs. Another significant aspect is the problem of reconciling the research and the debates with the imperatives of the judicial discourse and its notion that objective truths can be discovered. The rhetoric of objectivity which is at the heart of the judicial treatment of historical evidence obscures the senses in which both the analytical process and the facts it interrogates reflect power relations associated with race, gender, ethnicity, class, etc.

One of the most significant aspects in this discussion is the question of cultural difference and different knowledges. Representations of the past are culturally specific. European historiography and the rules of evidence around which it revolves are grounded in a tradition of positivism and Enlightenment rationalism. Western historiography is embedded in the tradition of written discourse and the idea of linearity, while the conceptions of time, place and story which emerge from Aboriginal epistemology are vastly different, sometimes incomprehensible to Westerners.

The tendency of Western historians to value written traces of the past more than other traces (for example, individual memory, story, dance, visual art, etc.) often obscures minority voices and renders them invisible. However, if the historian is interested in accounting for the absence of Aboriginal voices in archival material particularly important for native title cases, and in illuminating issues of social and cultural oppression, then problematizing orthodox notions of evidence and methodology is likely to be of some importance. Ann Curthoys captures some of the challenge of the historian's work when she

[273]

reminds us that new questions lead to finding new records or the reading of old records in a new way.[32] Inga Clendinnen, another respected historian, suggests that what the historian has to offer is a 'middle voice' in action 'whereby the reader is brought into a constructed, controlled, directed engagement with the texts, and is invited to join the writer's search for their meanings'.[33] Therefore the historian's narrative and credibility are critical.

Conclusions

By way of conclusion I want to refocus on the litigation process, particularly in relation to native title claims, and question the role of historians in this process. Historians can and do discover new material that throws fresh light which can only enhance our perception of the history of Australia. The huge gaps in our understanding of the history of non-Aboriginal occupation of this country are gradually being filled as historical research and analysis are undertaken in relation to native title claims. In the process Aboriginal people have the opportunity to tell their side of the story of the occupation of their lands by non-indigenous people.

Another outcome is that Aboriginal Australians are gaining access to documentary material and archival sources, including photographs, oral history recordings, administrative files, diaries and other records relating to their communities, families and their lands. Until recently most of these sources have been inaccessible to Aboriginal people and their communities because of geographical and cultural barriers.

My review of the use of professional historians in litigation for native title confirms my opinion that we have a long way to go in improving the dialogue between lawyers and historians, between legal processes and historiography. We must continue our dialogue to clarify understanding of our particular professional expertise and professional boundaries. Some lawyers, like many other people, think that 'anyone can do history'. Lawyers therefore must be educated about the uses of history, the value of historical evidence and the professional expertise which historians can offer in court. Historians have a responsibility to prepare themselves for increasing scrutiny of their profession and their methodologies, and to develop the confidence to deal with these issues publicly.

What the native title claims have highlighted for non-Aboriginal Australians are the complexity and richness of the many indigenous traditions across the country; that there is not one but many Aboriginal cultures; and the depth of the Aboriginal connection with the land. Historians of Australian history cannot continue to ignore the presence of Aborigines. The excuse that Aboriginal people are invisible in the archival records is longer tenable. Careful research undertaken for native title claims shows clearly that Aboriginal people were present, despite consistent attempts in the past to render them invisible. Professional historians have contributed to 'breaking open' the archival sources to enable the emergence of new understandings and new meanings in the texts. And this, I believe, is one of our strengths.

Finally, these points raise questions about the place of the discipline of history in the education of future generations of Australians. What stories of Australia do we tell? Not only is Australian history rich in texture but it is many-hued with stories of indigenous and non-indigenous citizens of a range of cultural backgrounds waiting to be told and to be heard. And these are the stories for which each one of us must make room.

Notes

I am grateful to Shawn Hollbach, Anne Sheehan, Michael Barker Q.C., Alex Shaw, Scotty Hammond, David Ritter and Simon Choo for their comments on earlier drafts of this paper.

1 Christine Choo and Margaret O'Connell, 'Historical Narrative and Proof of Native Title', *Land, Rights, Law: Issues of Native Title*, Issues Paper 3:2 (Native Title Research Unit, Australian Institute of Aboriginal and Torres Strait Islander Studies (hereafter AIATSIS), March 2000).
2 *Ben Ward & Others* v. *State of Western Australia & Others* [1998] 1478 F.C.A. (24 November 1998); available online at: http://www.astlii.edu.au/cases/cth/federal_ct/1998/1478.html and *The Members of the Yorta Yorta Aboriginal Community* v. *The State of Victoria & Others* [1998] 1606 F.C.A. (18 December 1998); available online at: http://www.astlii.edu.au/cases/cth/federal_ct/1998/1606.html. Both these decisions have gone to Appeal.
3 *Mabo* v. *Queensland (No. 2)* [1992] 107 ALR.
4 Native Title Act, 1993, No. 110 of 1993 (Commonwealth). Assented to 24 December 1993, implemented from 1 January 1994.
5 *Mason* v. *Tritton* [1994] 34 NSWLR 583.
6 *Ben Ward & Others* v. *W.A. & Others* [1998] 31.
7 *J. Ejai & Others* v. *Commonwealth of Australia*, Supreme Court of Western Australia, No. 1744 of 1993 (unreported: No. 940150, 18 March 1994).
8 *Guidelines for Expert Witnesses in Proceedings in the Federal Court of Australia*, 15 September 1998; available online at: http://www.fedcourt.gov.au/practice.htm#praticed1.htm
9 See Geoff Sherrott, 'The Court's Treatment of the Evidence in *Delgamuukw* v. *B.C.*', *Sasketchewan Law Review*, 56 (1992), 441–50, for a critique of McEachern C.J.'s decision and its implications regarding the use of oral history and other oral evidence.
10 *Delgamuukw* v. *British Columbia* [11 December 1997], *Canadian Native Law Reporter* (1998), 14–97.
11 *Delgamuukw* v. *B.C.* [1997] 17.
12 *Ibid.*, 48.
13 *Ibid.*, 54.
14 *Ibid.*, 51.
15 Sherrott, 'Court's Treatment', 442–4.
16 *Delgamuukw* v. *B.C.* [25 June 1993] 696–7.

17 Richard Bartlett, 'The Content and Proof of Native Title: *Delgamuukw* v. *The Queen in right of British Columbia*', Casenote, *Indigenous Law Bulletin*, 4:9 (1998), 17–18.
18 *Ben Ward & Others* v. *W.A. & Others* [1998].
19 *Yorta Yorta* v. *Vic. & Others* [1998].
20 'Indigenous historians' were not permitted to give evidence as historians in *Yorta Yorta*.
21 *Yorta Yorta* v. *Vic. & Others.*, Transcript of Evidence [7 August 1997] 7564.
22 *Yorta Yorta* v. *Vic. & Others.* [1998] para. 25.
23 *Ibid.*, paras 120–21.
24 *Ibid.*, para. 129.
25 *Ben Ward & Others* v. *W.A. & Others*, Transcript of Evidence [4 December 1997 5 December 1997].
26 *Ben Ward & Others* v. *W.A. & Others*, [1998].
27 *Ibid.*, 44.
28 *Ibid.*, 45.
29 *Ben Ward & Others* v. *W.A. & Others*, Transcript of Evidence [5 December 1997] 5718.
30 *Ibid.*, 5743–4.
31 *Ibid.*, 5758.
32 Ann Curthoys, 'The Proof of Continuity of Native Title: An Historian's Perspective', *Land, Rights, Laws: Issues of Native Title*, Issues Paper 18:1 (AIATSIS, June 1997).
33 Inga Clendinnen, *Reading the Holocaust* (Melbourne, Text Publishing Company, 1998), p. 202.

CHAPTER SEVENTEEN

'Race', gender and nation in history and law

Constance Backhouse, Ann Curthoys,
Ian Duncanson and Ann Parsonson

Comparisons between the histories of settler societies are increasingly advocated but still are all too rare.[1] In their collection *Unsettling Settler Societies: Articulations of Gender, Race, Ethnicity and Class*, Daiva Stasiulis and Nira Yuval-Davis brought a welcome comparative, sociological and historical focus to the study of indigenous and settler/immigrant populations, suggesting directions for future work in comparative histories. Of particular concern to them was the way 'imperialism created new sites for gender struggles and relations between and within' indigenous communities and European men and women.[2] This issue is here taken up by scholars reflecting upon their own work and the histories written of nation–states. The relationship between colonial–postcolonial historical work, on the one hand, and feminist scholarship on the other, proves to be a fraught and complex one.[3]

Constance Backhouse: Canada

I speak as someone whose research and writing have moved over time between gender and race. My research has loosely followed the evolving politics in the Canadian women's movement. I came into the academy in the late 1970s as a feminist activist who saw the world through the lens of gender. I taught women's history and feminist law courses as though gender were a universal attribute, and I saw divisions as neatly drawn between male and female. Where race and class emerged, I looked for commonalities between women, and believed that sexual oppression united women more than other divisions – such as race, class, disability and sexual identity – separated them.

By the mid-1980s, deep-rooted changes had become apparent. Canadian feminist organizations were splitting at the seams over allegations of racism, ableism and homophobia. Feminist writing, academic and otherwise, was beginning to critique gender as a universal theory.

[277]

Some writers were insisting that race, class, disability and sexuality intersected gender to create many 'genders'. The experience of black women, they argued, while sexually mediated, was distinct in multiple ways from that of white, Asian-Canadian and Aboriginal women. They took explicit issue with the 'whiteness' of the Canadian feminist movement in its history, its policies and its activist strategies.

The criticisms needed some years to take effect. By 1991, when I published *Petticoats and Prejudice: Women and Law in Nineteenth Century Canada*, a book which had taken over a decade to complete, I recognized, somewhat belatedly, that there were serious problems with my research methodology and interpretation. Studying the legal history of gender alone had resulted in the invisibility, effectively, of 'race' in my book. 'Racelessness' is really another face of white racial domination. I realized with some chagrin that my book was essentially about white women's legal history.[4]

I decided not to make the same mistake in my next book, originally intended to be a sequel to *Petticoats* which would continue the investigation into the first half of the twentieth century. I now wanted to interrogate gender through the lenses of race, disability and sexuality. I began by doing an extensive search through cases and legislation for issues of race: if I began there, I thought, I would be sure not to miss the racial significance of gender. The result was that the sequel to *Petticoats* turned into an entirely different book: *Colour-Coded: A Legal History of Racism in Canada, 1900–1950* looks at cases of legal discrimination against Chinese-Canadians, blacks, the First Nations and the Inuit.[5]

This new book has as many chapters devoted to men as to women. Gender arises, especially, where women divide on racial questions. It describes, for example, the campaigns of white women's organizations in the 1920s to prohibit Asian-Canadian men from employing white females, and the efforts of the Ku Klux Klan to eliminate racial intermarriage in the 1920s and 1930s in Canada. It also recounts the struggles of black women to eliminate racial segregation in Canadian theatres in the 1940s, examining how they used images of 'respectable femininity' to further their claims. *Colour-Coded* also demonstrates the ways in which sexism is fundamentally altered by issues of race. White women ally themselves with white men to solidify white racial superiority. Women of colour sometimes resist racial oppression in ways different from those used by men of colour.

I have learned a great deal through shifting my focus of research from gender to race and gender. I am, however, left with several queries, as follows.

The separation of race and gender

One of the most obvious difficulties with this research is the constant tendency to think of race and gender as two separate variables. I used to read 'feminist' books; now I find myself reading 'race' books. My sense is that few authors in either category do justice to the other. It is not unusual to find a great divide between people who are extraordinarily sensitive to sexism and people expert in anti-racist analysis.

We live in a world that is overrun with sexual and racial discrimination. It requires a fine-tuned sense of 'upside-down thinking' to get past what exists and imagine what might and should be. I used to read books while honing my critical faculties, looking for the best feminist interpretations. I have to admit that I now believe that I missed the racial analysis completely. I currently read books honing my critical faculties looking for the best anti-racist interpretation. I frequently find I'm missing the gender analysis. It's as if my head can't get around the two issues equally at the same time.

The significance of the separation of gender from race is felt daily by women of colour. Patricia Monture-Angus, a First Nations' legal academic and activist, writes that she cannot separate out the Mohawk part of her heritage from her gender. She often says: 'I am a Mohawk woman – you can't take the woman out of the Mohawk or the Mohawk out of the woman.' Such realities are brilliantly articulated in the title of an African-American women's history book: *The Women Were White, the Blacks Were Men, But Some of Us Were Brave.*

I am left with the following important query, to which I confess I have no answers. How does it distort our thinking to conceive of gender and race as two distinct entities? What would it mean if we spoke constantly of 'genders', meaning 'racialized genders', and of 'gendered races'?

Affixing the labels of 'racism' and 'sexism' in the historical past

The word 'racism' appears to have been coined first in the 1930s, as the scientific construction of racial categories came under intellectual critique. The political urgency of the times was accentuated by Hitler's rise to power in Nazi Germany. Historians frequently argue that it is 'presentist' to attach the late twentieth-century label of 'racism' to events and individuals from the past. They argue that it is unfair to burden historical actors prior to the 1930s with our post-Second World War sense of the horrors of racial hierarchy. This approach is illustrated in the following statements from the writings of Canadian, American and British historians. I do not specify the writers or the texts, since this would not serve any useful purpose, but the authors I quote here represent a cross-section of the most respected and established scholars as well as some of the brightest doctoral students in the field.

[X] seems to have simply accepted the [racial perspective] of his time and culture in a totally uncritical manner. One can't blame him for being a totally nineteenth-century person.

The subject of race inferiority was beyond critical reach in the late nineteenth century.

Until about the third decade of the present century, most people in the so-called western world, including most social scientists and historians, took for granted the hereditary inferiority of non-white peoples.

The various victims of racism had internalised much of the oppressive ideology ... They shared much of the racist world view, including conceptual thinking and language. In hindsight, it is difficult to locate non-racist views ...

Generally speaking the times in which (these accounts) were written made prejudice and ignorance inevitable.

These conclusions strike me as odd. Discrimination based on race goes back hundreds of years at least. Historical societies were not monolithic in respect of the attitude to race; they were not unrelievedly smothered by ideas of racial hierarchy. Some racially subordinated groups and individuals have always resisted racism, and some racially dominant groups and individuals have, to varying degrees, recognized the injustice of inequality. We know too little yet about the historical record of race to make sweeping generalizations about what was known or understood, and what could have been known or understood, about the evils of white supremacy. So why the hesitation to use words such as 'racist' or 'anti-racist' in recounting historical times?

There somehow seems to be less resistance to using the label 'sexist' to describe historical actors, even though this also is a modern addition to our vocabulary. While there is still *some* reluctance, there is a growing acceptance of calling anti-female bias what it is. Why the disparity? What does this say about the balance of power between gender and race in historical research today?

Backlash

In North America we are facing an undeniable political shift to the Right. Under the guise of reducing government deficits and preserving our spot in global competition, we are witnessing growing income disparities between rich and poor, cutbacks to redistribution programmes and social services and the restriction of affirmative action programmes designed to reduce the stranglehold of white, able-bodied, heterosexual males in the workforce. We are also witnessing the unprecedented monopolization of the media, and the restriction of space for progressive and alternative views within the public realm.

Using epithets such as 'femi-nazis' and 'thought police', right-wing zealots are attacking the slim inroads we have made within educational structures for programmes such as women's studies, ethnic studies and native studies. Old-guard historians are complaining that women's history, race history and labour history have 'swamped' the far more important political, military and diplomatic study of historical records.

What threats do we face to our faculty-hiring programmes, research grants and progressive teaching methods from this backlash? What strategies of resistance are open to us? How do we organize to respond to these challenges in the coming years? These are questions to which I can provide few answers, but for the sake of future historians of gender and race I fear we must pursue them with the tenacity and urgency they deserve.

Ann Parsonson: Aotearoa/New Zealand

I speak as a Pakeha woman. This is how I would normally identify myself, and how others identify me at home. 'Pakeha' is a Maori word for non-Maori (of European origin) which has been part of everyday Maori usage for generations, and is increasingly part of everyday usage in the wider New Zealand community.[6] To many Pakeha New Zealanders today, it is a term that also embodies a statement of identity in our evolving society; it indicates an awareness that our cultural identity is constructed alongside and in relation to that of Maori. For some, it means a commitment to biculturalism and to the treaty relationship between two peoples which their representatives entered into in 1840, and the recognition that getting that relationship right today is the necessary basis for the success of the wider multicultural society now developing in our country. The prevalence of the term 'Pakeha' today thus in itself says something perhaps about the context in which our history is written, and not written.

Who should write Aotearoa/New Zealand history?

In Aotearoa/New Zealand there has not been a great deal of history written in the past fifteen years that is focused simultaneously through the lenses of 'race' and gender; we haven't produced a New Zealand version of the Australian text *Creating a Nation*. One important reason for that is the nature of the debate we had in the late 1970s–mid-1980s about who had the right to write about the Maori past. That debate grew out of the particular historical experience of both Maori and Pakeha, and the long dominance by Pakeha of the institutions of state power. In the early 1970s there emerged strong Maori challenges to monoculturalism in a wide range of areas – government, bureau-

[281]

cracy, resource management, education, the media. Maori were especially disappointed in government's failure to address long-standing
Maori grievances in any meaningful way, and by the mid-1970s some
younger leaders were saying this in no uncertain terms – publicly and
angrily, as well as behind the scenes in Wellington. The Waitangi Tribunal was set up in 1975, but at that time it had no power to address
historical grievances, nor had it gained any credibility with Maori.

Tensions were thus growing, and the New Zealand Pakeha public
were becoming conscious for the first time that there *were* Maori grievances – with major protests like the Maori Land March on Parliament
in 1975, and the Bastion Point land occupation in Auckland in
1977–78, from which protesters were finally removed in a massive
police exercise which shocked many New Zealanders. Waitangi Day
became a focus for Maori protest every year; and the Springbok Tour in
1981, which deeply divided New Zealanders, moved the spotlight on to
racism, in New Zealand itself as much as in South Africa.

In this context, the writing of history also became contested. Challenges were issued to Pakeha historians by Maori as to their monopoly
of the historical airwaves and their production of what must be
counted monocultural history in the context of an 'integrationist' yet
still largely monocultural education system. Maori feminists withdrew from the Pakeha feminist movement, where they did not feel
comfortable because 'race' did not seem an issue to Pakeha feminists.
They, too, focused on the writing of history by Pakeha as a tool in
making the Maori experience invisible, or in appropriating, integrating
and misinterpreting it. And so there were criticisms by both Maori
women and men of some of the books, such as biographies of Maori
women leaders, published in this period by Pakeha historians.

One of the most important indigenous critiques of New Zealand
society published in these years was *Maori Sovereignty* by Donna
Awatere, a Maori psychologist. Today she is an MP with the right wing
Association of Consumers and Taxpayers Party, still fighting for Maori
issues; but in the early 1980s she was seen as one of the great radical
leaders.[7] *Maori Sovereignty* examined the historical roots and the
nature of racism and cultural imperialism in Aotearoa, and was successful in waking up both Pakeha and Maori to an understanding of the
impact of colonization on Maori. Awatere's hard-hitting analysis of
Pakeha society and culture, originally published in the feminist period-
ical *Broadsheet* (where it generated some hostile reaction from readers),
included a discussion of the possible allies of Maori in their struggle, all
of whom she dismissed. White women were written off as allies for
being (she argued) more concerned with a struggle against patriarchy
than with racism: 'The first loyalty of white women is always to the

White Culture and the White Way.'⁸ Foreshadowing subsequent Maori discussions of autonomy, she also wrote of the importance of Maori surviving as a nation.

It was in the wake of all these kinds of challenges that many Pakeha historians – women and men – pulled back from writing about the Maori past, as intrusive and unwelcome. It seemed inappropriate even to write about the Maori–Pakeha interface, if there was a danger of demonstrating only partial understanding of the dynamics of cultural interchange. Pakeha – few of whom claimed to be bicultural or bilingual – took on board the criticism that Pakeha ignorance or shallow understanding of Maori culture might lead to their misrepresenting that culture, and thus the nature of cultural change and cross-cultural relations.

On gender issues, in particular, Pakeha historians were hesitant. Maori women – strong, articulate, challenging, fiercely protective of their culture – demanded respect for their views, and were often impatient of attempts by outsiders to categorize their status and roles in society. The impact of this assertiveness was evident in the 1986 collection of essays, *Women in History: Essays on European Women in New Zealand*, edited by three respected women historians.⁹ All of the authors, and their topics, were Pakeha, a fact which did not escape the notice of reviewers. Why was the focus solely on European women? Even in the successor volume *Women in History 2* (which carried the cover-page heading *Essays on Women in New Zealand*), published six years later, the imbalance was merely tentatively addressed: only one of the eleven essays had a specifically Maori focus, while another was a reflective essay entitled 'Maori and Pakeha Women', and both were by Pakeha women.¹⁰

The Waitangi Tribunal and the writing of history
A change in attitude to writing history became evident in the later 1980s, in the general context of the beginnings of government recognition of Maori grievances. In order to redress the pervasive monoculturalism, there was a new emphasis on Maori involvement in decision-making, intended to bring about new initiatives in a whole range of areas. In 1985 the Waitangi Tribunal gained retrospective jurisdiction back to 1840, leading to intensive research for Maori land claims. This research began to produce substantial historical reports which highlighted ways in which Maori had in effect been denied partnership with the Crown throughout their history.

In a less tense social and political climate, there began to be much more co-operation between Maori and Pakeha in historical research, not only for Maori claims against the Crown, but also for new projects such as *The Dictionary of New Zealand Biography*, whose first volume appeared in 1990. The *Dictionary* involved a Maori advisory group, Maori working parties and staff from the beginning, and a substantial number of Maori entries and Maori-authored entries have been written. The *Dictionary* has also been at the forefront of bilingual historical publishing: its Maori entries, as well as appearing in English in the main volumes, have been translated and published in *te reo Maori* (the Maori language) in separate volumes. Co-operation has continued in recent years, particularly, though not exclusively, in the field of biography. In 1991, for instance, in the wake of the successful 1990 commemoration of 150 years since the Treaty of Waitangi (1840), *The Book of New Zealand Women/Ko Kui Ma Te Kaupapa*, edited by one Maori and two Pakeha, was a remarkably inclusive collection of well-researched biographies of, and by, Maori, Pakeha and Chinese women, which aimed to 'tell the story of women in New Zealand through a series of biographical portraits'.[11] A recently published book called *Southern People*, though it commemorates the first organized Pakeha settlement of the conservative southern provinces of Otago and Southland, is a splendid group of biographies of (and by) notable Maori, Pakeha (especially Scottish and English), Chinese, Jewish and Lebanese women and men.[12]

In recent years, much of the most important historical treatment of Maori–government relations has come not in general histories, or in monographs, but in the many detailed research reports written for land, waterways and fisheries claims heard before the Waitangi Tribunal, and in the final Tribunal reports themselves. These are not reports that mention ethnicity up front very much. They are couched in terms of the history of the tribe/subtribe which brought the claim, and the government legislation and policies that impacted on them. But the Tribunal reports are all discussing indigenous grievances which derive from the distinctions which the New Zealand government has made in its treatment of Maori as Maori, particularly of their property rights, and as such they shed a great deal of light on the role of the State in creating conditions for effecting indigenous land and resource loss.[13]

So far, Waitangi Tribunal reports have not shed much light on gender issues. There is, however, a Maori women's claim filed with the Tribunal, spearheaded by the president and past-presidents of the Maori Women's Welfare League, and supported also by prominent individuals such as Lady Rose Henare and Donna Awatere Huata.[14] Though the claim stemmed initially from dissatisfaction with lack of women's representation on contemporary statutory bodies, its scope is potentially much wider.[15] The statement of claim begins with strong assertions of the *rangatiratanga* (authority) of Maori women in 1840 'as leaders and members of tribes, respective families and individuals', and of the integral position of Maori women 'to the political, economic and social structures of tribes and families, particularly in relation to the decision-making processes of hapu self-government'. It goes on to assert that Crown actions and policies systematically deprived Maori women of their well-being in many ways. That claim will doubtless lead to some historic hearings in which the role of women in Maori society over time is discussed by women in many tribal areas – and thus to a Tribunal report which, because it will be rooted in the wisdom and experience of women from rural and urban marae, in a great variety of oral histories, should shed remarkable light on issues of gender and culture, and on racism, in our past. This is the sort of work which in Aotearoa today would be regarded as making an informed and important contribution in this area.[16]

Path-breaking writing outside the scope of the Tribunal's work has also been done, for instance by Ngahuia Te Awekotuku, a sociologist and art historian who is now professor of Maori Studies at Victoria University in Wellington. Te Awekotuku wrote a doctoral thesis some years ago which looked at the historical development of tourism in her tribal area of Rotorua, and focused on the role of Te Arawa women as guides, showing how they reclaimed control of the process of guiding at the outset in a situation in which they might seem at first sight to have been exploited.[17] These insights drew heavily on her own research with Te Arawa women, and their oral histories, and on her understanding of gender roles in her own community. Younger Maori postgraduate students are now continuing to reshape understandings of the Maori past, focusing on issues of identity, leadership and iwi institutions, and iwi histories.

Questions of who should write about our past, and how it should it be written, remain. In Aotearoa the debate has been conducted particularly in the fields of archaeology, tribal histories, and biographical historical writing. Sir Tipene O'Regan of Ngai Tahu worded the challenge in this way:

> Despite the greater hospitality to Pakeha perceptions of the Maori past ... there are some areas into which outsiders, the tauiwi, step at their peril. Those things that are particularly Maori in a cultural sense – our myths, our karakia, our custom – are essential ingredients of our view of the past and are peculiarly 'ours'. Most important of all, there is whakapapa [genealogy] – the key to who we are ... New Zealand's past belongs to all New Zealanders – but first it is ours![18]

Accountability

Recently there has been a shift from an emphasis on ownership of the tribal past to one on accountability. Te Ahukaramu Charles Royal has argued that tribes should take control of the publication of tribal histories and traditions and that, if such publications are to receive the recommendation of the tribe, they should be completed 'under the guidance of the intellectual leadership of the iwi'.[19]

The ripples from such debates have inevitably spread further to impact on historians working in the field of Maori–Pakeha relations. One reviewer, Kerry Howe (interestingly enough, a historian primarily of the Pacific rather than of New Zealand), recently lamented the fact that detailed scholarship in the field of 'race relations' had effectively stopped around the mid-1970s because of Maori opposition, and that Pakeha had only recently been able to return to such research, though only to produce what he called 'politically correct history'. In the meantime, he argued, there had been a 'lost generation of scholarship'.[20] This perhaps is to miss the point of the remarkable changes that in recent years have taken place in the study of and approaches to New Zealand's past. In a recent paper Chief Judge (now Justice) Durie, chairperson of the Waitangi Tribunal, acknowledged a considerable Pakeha contribution to research, and also suggested that traditional and academic evidence depended on each other. At the same time, he stressed how important it is that all those who write history should have a proper understanding of Maori beliefs, core Maori values and Maori custom, lest they fall into the trap of assessing Maori from a solely Western standpoint.[21] The insistence on accountability may be seen less as unwarranted censorship and more as reflecting a deep-held belief among iwi that it is the responsibility of the researcher to take the trouble to understand the dynamics of their society before she or he writes about it.

Accountability was an important issue discussed at a major joint hui held in 1994 between the New Zealand Historical Association and Te Pouhere Korero, a new organization which brought together Maori academic and tribal historians to provide a supportive forum for those studying the Maori past. The New Zealand Historical Association had been a largely Pakeha body; not till 1991 was there substantial Maori involvement in its biennial conference. By 1994 it was decided that it might be helpful to bring together in a workshop members of both organizations who were active and leading researchers in the field. The weekend hui, held at Te Herenga Waka marae at the Victoria University of Wellington, reflected many aspects of the experience of Maori and Pakeha historians. The hui was not without its disagreements, which reflected all the developments in our understanding of our past, outlined above. Some members of Te Pouhere Korero did not attend because they did not think the time was right for such a discussion; others did attend, but expressed the same view. And to Maori participants, the Pakeha historians, despite their shared interests, seemed divided in their views, too. In the words of one Maori historian: 'what separates you is the extent to which you are aware of, and seek to work to, the various conventions which Maori historians themselves [though not all of them] feel constrained to follow'. The nature of some of these conventions was evident at the hui in discussions on the rights of communities as *kaitiaki* (guardians) of their past, the obligations of researchers to those who shared knowledge with them–including the obligation to accept conditions which might be laid down as to the use or publication of material – and the rejection of the idea of a code of ethics to guide those researching the past of Maori communities, on the grounds that agreements which might be made at whanau, hapu or iwi level to guide particular projects should not be overridden. The warmth of the atmosphere throughout the hui – which survived disagreements on a number of matters – itself reflected the nature of relationships among the various participants developed over the past few years.

'National' history in Aotearoa/New Zealand

The deeper understandings of the past that have emerged from the conflict and debate of recent years mean that constructing the history of Aotearoa/New Zealand has never seemed more challenging. On the whole, New Zealand historians have shied away in our writing from explicitly contemplating the building of a nation, paradoxically perhaps, given that many consider the process of hearing and settling Maori claims as denoting the coming of age of a postcolonial nation.

Our recent general histories have been of various kinds. In 1990 Dr Ranginui Walker of Whakatohea, then associate professor in Maori Studies at Auckland University, wrote *Struggle Without End: Ka Whawhai Tonu Matou*, a readable account reflecting the widespread concern among Maori that the historical roots of their position in our society were not understood.[22] It is not a gendered history, though it records the leadership of particular Maori women at various times. But it does draw attention to the fact that by the end of the nineteenth century 'the coloniser deluded himself into thinking he had created a unified nation state of one people', and it explicitly looks forward to the promise of a new nation–state in the postcolonial era.[23] A rather different kind of history is *Standing in the Sunshine*, subtitled *A History of New Zealand Women Since They Won the Vote*, by feminist writer Sandra Coney.[24] This illustrated social history of various aspects of women's lives over the course of a century, handled topically, was researched by a team of women, Pakeha and Maori; Maori women, it stated, had written most of the pieces on Maori women, and a decision was taken to disperse these throughout the book, rather than risk a perception of marginalizing Maori experience by having a separate Maori section. More recently, James Belich published *Making Peoples: A History of New Zealanders*, the first volume of a two-volume history.[25] He, too, avoids the term 'national', calling his a 'general' history. In a work which seems almost defiantly to downplay the role of the State, he focuses in separate parts on the respective cultures and socio-economies of Maori and Pakeha and their colonizations of Aotearoa, and also examines the interaction of their two societies. He is undoubtedly more comfortable in handling the past of Pakeha than of Maori women (though he has not escaped criticism on either count), perhaps because of the greater body of available work which has gendered the Pakeha past.

Issues of 'race' and gender have thus been approached in a variety of ways by historians in Aotearoa/New Zealand. The work of all of them has been shaped by Maori insistence that their past will neither be written out of the script nor appropriated. Perhaps an all-Maori-authored work will before long provide an alternative history of Aotearoa.

Ann Curthoys: Australia

In my career as a non-indigenous historian in Australia, I have moved back and forth between a concern with gender and a concern with race. My doctoral research in the 1960s was on racial politics, ideas and relations in New South Wales in the nineteenth century, but with the increasing influence of women's liberation from 1970 I became fascinated by the implications of feminist theory for the practice of history. In the 1990s, I have returned to my earlier interest in the history of race relations, this time trying to bring my interest in race and gender together.[26] In this I am not alone; indeed the attempt to understand both gender and race has been a focal point of concern in feminist historical scholarship for the last decade.

The impact of feminist scholarship on the writing of Australian history has been enormous. Of all the disciplines in the humanities and social sciences in Australia, it was history which was most transformed by the impact of feminist scholarship.[27] Prior to 1970 there had been remarkably little interest in women, or the relationships between women and men, in the writing of Australian history. All at once, in 1975, four major and foundational texts appeared and, two years later, *Women in Australia: A Guide to Records* indicated the vast quantity of hitherto little-used or unused archival, manuscript and printed material available for the study of gender relations in Australia.[28] Over

[288]

the next twenty years many theses, monographs and journal articles appeared; by the 1990s, women's history and gendered history had become among the most popular of historical topics for investigation.

The nature of this scholarship changed over time. In the 1970s and 1980s, there was a focus on the history of women's work and the role of the labour movement. Women convicts exerted a strong fascination from the beginning and continue to do so.[29] Other areas of investigation included the family, human reproduction, prostitution, education, political activism and 'first-wave' feminism.[30] In the 1980s, there emerged alongside the study of women's history an interest in masculinity. Hitherto, men's gender had largely been treated as natural, and women's gender, their femininity, as that which had to be explained. Marilyn Lake drew attention to the anti-feminist politics of the 1890s, while other historians developed studies of masculinity and violence, the development of male identities, the varieties of masculinity, and masculinity and sexuality.[31]

For two decades, the question of Aboriginal history, and the history of Aboriginal–European relations, hovered uneasily. Many feminist histories had little or nothing at all to say about Aboriginal history. Such histories, I suggested in 1991, continued to explore gender conflict within non-Aboriginal Australian society, and so failed to result in a gendered history of colonial contact and conflict.[32] White Australian feminists, like their counterparts elsewhere, found it very difficult to place themselves on the side of the oppressors, rather than the oppressed. Anne Summers' pathbreaking feminist history text *Damned Whores and God's Police* had the subtitle *The Colonisation of Women in Australia*. The analogy of colonial invasion, exploitation, and dispossession in that text was used, metaphorically, theoretically and rhetorically, to describe the experience of white women. In so doing, it blurred and undermined the possibility of recognizing that white women were themselves colonizers, part of the invading society which dispossessed and exploited Aboriginal women and men.

Yet all this while, through the 1970s and 1980s, the attention to Aboriginal history was growing, from both indigenous and non-indigenous writers. Indigenous writing was most often in the form of personal narrative, either autobiographical or biographical, and very often based on oral histories. Outstanding contributions came from Sally Morgan, whose *My Place* mixed autobiography and oral history, and Jackie Huggins, whose *Auntie Rita* counterposed her mother's oral history with her own memories and historical reflections.[33] There are also the collaborative histories, such as Margaret Somerville with Patsy Cohen in *Ingelba and the Five Black Matriarchs*, and Deborah Bird Rose with many Aboriginal people in *Hidden Histories: Black Stories from*

Victoria River Downs, Humbert River and Wave Hill Station. Aboriginal history came into national public consciousness in an unprecedented way in the context of the Bicentennial Commemoration of 1988, in many ways successfully converting the event from a celebration to a renaming and a re-conceptualization of white settlement itself. Aboriginal testimonial reached its maximum public impact and apotheosis in 1997 in *Bringing Them Home*, the report of the Government inquiry into the 'stolen generations', those indigenous people taken away as children from their parents through most of the twentieth century. The report collected and reproduced hundreds of individual stories, whose effect on public debate was profound.[34]

From non-indigenous historians came a growing body of work telling a discomforting story of invasion, colonization, dispossession, exploitation, institutionalization and attempted genocide. Aboriginal peoples, who had to this point usually made only fleeting appearances in the standard national histories, appeared in these new histories clearly and unambiguously as victims of white aggression and racism, and also as resisters, adapters and survivors.[35] Such histories had their popular counterparts in television series, film, painting, poetry, novel, song and drama.

Despite their widespread influence, these histories also encountered rejection. Especially after the election of the conservative Coalition Government in 1996, and the emergence of the populist One Nation Party, 'race' resurged as a topic for open public debate. Histories narrating a past of dispossession, colonization, brutality and institutionalization were called 'black-armband histories', and were attacked as 'politically correct' one-sided accounts of the past. The historical understanding embedded in the *Mabo* and *Wik* decisions was attacked as deficient. Many non-indigenous Australians did not wish to be told that their society was built on a process of invasion and child-theft; they wanted, instead, to reassert pride in their history, institutions and culture. Prime Minister John Howard articulated this response in October 1996 when he said he sympathized fundamentally with Australians who are insulted when they are told that we have a racist and bigoted past.

The resilience of racism in public debate has prompted some historians to examine its history more closely, while others, motivated in part by a desire to find a white history that is not totally shameful, focused on those people – indigenous and non-indigenous – who had fought racism.[36] Most notably, gendered and indigenous histories have come closer together. The separation Constance Backhouse speaks of is still evident, but is reducing all the time. Two works of synthesis, one, *Gender Relations in Australia*, a substantial collection, and the other, *Creating a Nation*, an ambitious feminist general history of

Australia, registered the growing importance of 'race' in Australian feminist history.[37] In recent years, work has focused on the lives of indigenous women; the sexual dimensions of early contact between Aboriginal and non-Aboriginal peoples in the Australian colonies; white women's nationalism, racism and anti-racism; and the relationships between, and the political activities of, black and white women.[38]

As in New Zealand, land claims have provided a stimulus to historical research. Two legal decisions concerning native title, the *Mabo* decision of 1992 (with the subsequent native title legislation in 1993) and the *Wik* decision of 1996 (which led the conservative Coalition Government to amend the legislation to limit the rights of Aboriginal claimants), have led to extensive historical research for native title claims. Though native title claims in Australia have been more circumscribed than have those in New Zealand, and have proven influential much later and less centrally to historical endeavour generally, they have a similar potential to change the way many Australian historians think and write about the past.

Another consequence of the 'race debate' has been the growth of reflections, sometimes anguished, on the nature of history itself.[39] With the past so hotly contested in a political sense, with even the prime minister getting involved, it is little wonder that historians have been forced to reflect on their own practice. What kind of national history should historians write? Should they write national history at all? Certainly, from the 1950s onwards, Australian historiography has often had a nationalist cast. In breaking away from older forms of historiography that saw Australian history as purely an epiphenomenon of British history, and establishing an Australia-centred history in its place, Australian historians tended to lose their international and comparative perspective. Attention to questions of race and gender has forced a more comparative and international perspective. The political and historical interest in both native title and child-removal has led to an increased awareness of the histories of nations with similar experiences, especially Canada and New Zealand. Canadian history has for example, influenced Australia's best-known historian, Henry Reynolds, in this field.

Nevertheless, despite the growth in thematic, cross-national and comparative history, the desire for a national history has continued to flourish, in both popular demand and professional historical practice. Where Aotearoa/New Zealand historians have been extremely wary of writing national histories at all, Australian historians have tried to write national histories which embody full attention to both race and gender. Whereas the general national histories of the 1950s had little Aboriginal or women's history – and as late as 1974 one edited collection used widely in undergraduate history courses could contain no Aboriginal history at all – attempts (not wholly successful) were made to include indigenous and feminist narratives in the national histories produced for the bicentennial commemoration of 1988.[40] The most recent general history accords both race and gender a significant role in its national narrative.[41]

Ian Duncanson

Gender, class, 'Englishness' and empire[42]

In her book on eighteenth-century England, Kathleen Wilson sees, in the decades 1740–80 on both sides of the Atlantic, a rowdy struggle to define Englishness, culturally and politically. Political conflict was not waged only in Parliament, or only by the enfranchised. The manly patriot was set against effete aristocratic tyranny by even the lowest social class in petitions to Parliament, in written instructions to candidates at elections, in the licensed and unlicensed presses, in theatre and elaborate street theatre, in cartoons and in ceramic mugs and plates. When the British surrendered in America, they surrendered to the thirteen United States. When the war first began, it had aspects of civil war, of the populist free-born Englishman against the new tyranny of the aristocrats and King George. With the failure of the Pitt administration's reforms in 1784 and the refocusing of British imperialism on India, Canada and Australia, the maintenance and projection of Englishness became authoritarian and paternalist.[43]

The struggle over the place of 'the people' in the political nation was resolved apparently differently in the metropolis than in its erstwhile American colonies.[44] If the resolution was to succeed across the new Empire, then three forms of difference presented themselves for assimilation during the course of the new century to the same of the 'Englishman': natives, the labourer and women. Macaulay's aim of 'form[ing] a class who may be interpreters between us and the millions we govern; a class of persons, Indian in colour but English in taste, in opinions, in morals and intellect',[45] was a quite late summary of a policy of cultural assimilationism already begun in British India under Bentinck. Later in the century, Matthew Arnold's antidote to the British working class's apparent threat to order was, again, the cultural integration, thus neutralization, of the other, 'for Culture looks beyond machinery and hates hatred. Culture has but one passion, for sweetness and light. Yes, it has one greater – the passion to make them prevail. It is not satisfied till we all come to be the perfect *man.*'[46]

The social signifiers of native, labourer and woman were, of course, both irrecoverably other and frequently fungible as one moves into the nineteenth century. In the eighteenth century and before, 'native' has the primary meaning of local to a place. The 'genius' of English law might relate to the inborn superiority of the native-born Englishman.[47] In the new Empire, however, the 'Englishman' becomes a more refined social technology of differentiation and exclusion as a nationally focused working class comes into existence, and women, too, argue for inclusion in the political order. Susan Thorne observes that the already vague category of 'race' and that of class were not seen as antithetical categories by the nineteenth century.[48] As late as the early Edwardian era, Susan Kingsley Kent finds Sir Almroth Wright equating the defects of women and natives, both of whom were, in consequence of their inferiority, incapable of governing themselves or of participating in their governance.[49] The route from savagery to civilization which the native must take, according to Walter Bagehot, again linking natives and women, is inevitably a masculinization of social order: the move from the obviousness of matrilineal descent forms to the culturally more sophisticated patterns of patrilineal descent.[50]

The project of empire took a pedagogical turn in the Empire, expanding but now without most of America, which it had not taken earlier. Finding India sunk in depravity even before he had been appointed to the India Council and travelled there, Macaulay told the House of Commons that England's duty was to 'educate our subjects into a capacity for better government'. At a less elevated level than Macaulay's quest for an empire exempt from decay, however, Gauri Viswanathan finds an India Council Minute from one J. Farish, of March 1838: 'The natives must either be kept down by a sense of our power, or they must willingly submit from a conviction that we are more wise, more just, more humane and more anxious to improve their condition than any other ruler they could possibly have.'[51] Viswanathan puts it slightly differently: 'Making the Englishman known to the natives through the products of his mental labor removed him from the plane of on-going colonialist activity. His material reality as subjugator and alien ruler was dissolved.'[52]

Yet another perception, on the motif of the native as a threat of disorder in the metropolis, comes from Jyotsna Singh. The nabobs, she suggests, those East India Company servants whose new wealth was so resented when they returned to England, were considered to have learned their venality and their capacity for the ruthless exploitation of Indians from the Indians themselves. If the natives acquired the moral rectitude and earnestness of purpose associated with the heritage of Englishness, this improvement would serve to protect not only them from the Company's servants, but the Company's servants (and old wealth at home) from them. On the same theme, of order and the habits of thrift and attachment to existing society presumed to flow from education, but displaced this time on to the problem of native disorder at home, we find Macaulay, long returned from India, recommending government finance for education in England. The magistrate with the power to punish incivility has a duty to teach civility, Macaulay argued, contrasting the dissolute English working class with its better-educated, ambitious and presumably more earnest Scottish counterpart.[53]

Contemporary – and later – understandings of empire assumed the centre–periphery diffusion of civilization. The blessings of England's already-accomplishments are to be bestowed upon India. Macaulay, as we saw, speaks of the necessity for introducing 'our' literature and 'our' law to the natives. James Fitzjames Stephen writes of the civilizing mission in terms not of religion itself, but in the theological language of transmitting the peculiarly English 'gospel' of the law. Yet in the construction of the Englishness of Shakespeare, Milton and the rule of law, Pennycook writes, India was a key site for the development of policies that then flowed back to England. Empire was a system that allowed the flow of culture and knowledge produced in the colonial encounter back to the imperial center.[54]

In general Europe's colonies were never empty spaces to be made over in Europe's image; nor were European states self-contained entities that at one point projected themselves overseas. 'Europe was made by its imperial projects.'[55]

It is not clear that there was an 'our' culture or an 'our' law ready-made to which to assimilate the native. If we consider law, the gradual supersession of the governing role of the East India Company involved a conception of gubernatorial sovereignty in India that was not familiar in Britain until much later. The reason why this is not now obvious is that Benthamite positivism, developed in his critique of Blackstone's Vinerian lectures and published as the Fragment on Government[56] in 1776, forms the basis of modern imaginings of law and government.

The aims of Gladstone's Civil Service reforms, designed by Northcote and Macaulay's brother-in-law and former Indian civil servant Trevelyan, were both to reconcile the middle classes to the oligarchic State[57] – offering careers on the basis of merit, and removing the dangerous possibility of middle-class alliances with working-class radicalism – and 'to strengthen and multiply the ties between the higher classes and the possession of administrative power.'[58] The route into the Civil Service was from the public-school sector, reinvigorated by Thomas Arnold, through Oxford or Cambridge and the Civil Service examinations, which might include English studies as well as the classics.

From mid-century ... the public schools ... provided a common education ... an intensive intersocialization for the sons of the gentry and the
upper bourgeoisie ... Reforms at Oxford and Cambridge reinforced these,
generating an academic ethos in which the disinterest of the scholar
mingled ... with those of the aristocrat, and ideals of service subliminally
associated the profession of rule with the rule of the professions.[59]

A bureaucracy firmly attached to the values of the rulers was insurance against the 'irresponsible' legislators a working-class electorate
might choose to represent it. Meanwhile, the regulatory aspects of
education for the 'populace' were clear to Matthew Arnold. In the case
of prisons, he argued, the object is not merely to reform the prisoner,
but to protect the public; and so, too, in schools, the State has another
interest besides the encouraging of reading, writing and arithmetic –
the protection of society. 'It has an interest in schools so far as they
keep children out of the streets, so far as they teach them an orderly,
decent and human behaviour, so far as they civilize the neighborhood
where they are placed.'[60]

English literature as a discipline (as opposed to literary texts),
invented to enable a pivotal class of Indians to recognize themselves as
subjects of the colonists' culture, appeared now in Britain as a convenient ritual narrative of the nation, eliding differences of class and
gender in the constitution of an imaginary racial community of the
same. Silently outside the shared heritage is the colonial other in relation to whom the community of the English heritage is united in its
obligations and patriotism – women seeking political and legal equality
in Britain needed the credentials of equal concern with the men of the
Empire for the condition of Indian women, as one example, and were
thus coopted into the moral justification for imperialism;[61] the working
class could share equally both cultural superiority and pride of ownership in the Empire.[62] Literature led to the location of the literary heritage in the genius of the nation and the 'inherent nobility of the English
spirit', contemplation of which, it was hoped, would strengthen established authority and pre-empt social unrest.[63]

The heritage is, in effect, English extended 'beyond any disciplinary
boundaries to encompass all mental, imaginative and spiritual faculties ... the cultivation of the mind, the training of the imagination
and the quickening of the whole spiritual nature', and practised outside
the school and university, in museums, on statues honouring imperial
exploits and in exhibitions celebrating the diversity and tribute of
the Empire.[64]

The language of empire was used quite naturally to describe the
pedagogic 'missions' and 'colonization' of working-class areas
where, Lloyd and Thomas argue, an older working-class ethics of

self-improvement converged with the paternalist and, of course, politically soporific objectives of the utilitarians and others. 'Culture' in the
sense of knowing one's proper place as a subject 'is not a mere supplement to the state, but the formative principle of its efficacy'.[65] Before
the legal Sovereign State is directly thinkable, there must be the possibility that the subject can identify with the existing relations of privilege and hierarchy which it encompasses. These relations and subject
positions must seem to represent the fundamental identity of the
community and 'the state be conceived ideally as the disinterested and
ethical representative of this identity'.[66]

Coming from a lower-middle class Scottish family living in the
working-class suburbs of an English provincial city, I encountered
'Englishness' personally in the Fabian mission of a boys' state gram-
mar school. As I continued my 'education' I met it again among the
public schoolboys of a prestigious law faculty. From this alienating
experience I then spent several academic years trying to 'place' the
phantasmogoric world of English common law, history and theory in
performance – but whose, and how? As an immigrant to a settler
society, I now find useful leads in cultural studies and postcolonial
theory, where class, gender and ethnicity, 'culture' and geography can
be articulated, relations of domination and subordination theorized,
and resistance plotted.

Conclusion

Stasiulis and Yuval-Davis pointed out how 'few analyses of settler
societies have examined how settler capitalism exacerbated and transformed relations based *simultaneously* on colonialism, capitalism,
gender, class and race/ethnicity'.[67] The inherent complexity of settler
colony populations has meant that most scholars focus on one or other.
While 'the gendered character of nation–state building in settler
colonies' has been addressed by feminist scholars, in this paper we see
a growth in the attempts by historians to grapple with the problem-
atics of racialization including 'Englishness'. Such attempts have led to
a questioning of some of the basic questions in history: the relation
between present values and the way we write about the past; the
responsibility of historians when writing about cultural groups other
than their own; the importance and influence of the political context
within which gendered and racialized histories are written.

Problematizing racial categorization has led many scholars to ponder
the culturally specific nature of history itself. Historical work is
inevitably political, and always contested, but it can also be an important part of indigenous cultural identity. There are significant possibili-

ties for working together to overcome the destructiveness of the colonizing process.[68]

Notes

1 Donald Denoon's *Settler Capitalism*, a notable and honourable exception, is now 16 years' old. A recent discussion on the H-ANZAU email discussion list, to take just one example, revealed just how little comparative work there has been on Australia and New Zealand. [Since the conference at which the papers comprising this book were originally presented, however, such a major comparative work has been published: Donald Denoon and Philippa Mein-Smith, with Marivic Wyndham, *A History of Australia, New Zealand and the Pacific* (Oxford and Malden, MA, Blackwell, 2000).]

2 Daiva Stasiulis and Nira Yuval-Davis, *Unsettling Settler Societies: Articulations of Gender, Race, Ethnicity and Class* (London, Routledge, 1995), p. 13.

3 We provide here edited and updated versions of the papers from the conference discussion. Each of the authors supplied an edited version of her or his conference paper, and Ann Curthoys drew them together.

4 Constance Backhouse, *Petticoats and Prejudice: Women and Law in Nineteenth Century Canada* (Toronto, Osgoode Society and the Women's Press, 1991).

5 Constance Backhouse, *Colour-Coded: A Legal History of Racism in Canada, 1900–1950* (Toronto, Osgoode Society and University of Toronto Press, 1999).

6 Though there is debate on the origin of the term 'Pakeha', its use by Maori to name the first Western arrivals in Aotearoa is generally considered to reflect a definition in terms of fairness of skin. Today it remains a contested term: some exclude themselves from it because they do not wish to be defined by a Maori term; others feel excluded by it because they do not consider it encompasses their ethnicity. The term *tauiwi* (strangers or outsiders) is also used, which some consider more appropriate in that it includes migrants to New Zealand of various ethnicities (European and Asian, though not Pacific Islanders, with whom Maori ultimately claim a relationship through descent). It also encapsulates something of the nature of the relationship between *tangata whenua* and other New Zealanders. But the term is not nearly as common in everyday New Zealand usage.

7 Donna Awatere, *Maori Sovereignty* (Auckland, Broadsheet Magazine, 1984). Awatere, now Donna Awatere Huata, recently noted that she now regrets parts of *Maori Sovereignty*; but as she has very rightly said, it 'did capture the spirit of the times'.

8 Awatere, *Sovereignty*, p. 42

9 Barbara Brookes, Charlotte Macdonald and Margaret Tennant (eds), *Women in History: Essays on European Women in New Zealand* (Wellington, Allen & Unwin/Port Nicholson Press, 1986)

10 Barbara Brookes, Charlotte Macdonald and Margaret Tennant (eds), *Women in History 2* (Wellington, Bridget Williams Books, 1992). The essay on Maori women was by Judith Binney, highly respected for her understanding of Maori society.

11 Charlotte Macdonald, Merimeri Penfold and Bridget Williams (eds), *The Book of New Zealand Women/Ko Kui Ma Te Kaupapa* (Wellington, Bridget Williams Books, 1991).

12 Jane Thomson (ed.), *Southern People: A Dictionary of Otago Southland Biography* (Dunedin, Longacre Press/Dunedin City Council, 1998).

13 In the course of lengthy Tribunal hearings conducted on marae, the involvement of respected Maori Tribunal members, and the evolution of a Treaty jurisprudence which reflects a Maori as well as Pakeha worldview, cross-cultural understanding of our joint history has improved. And as tribes have probed the nature and powers of the nation–state in recent years as they argue their claims before the Tribunal – and the courts – Tribunal reports have increasingly reflected these concerns by considering indigenous autonomy and the impact on our history of government failure to acknowledge indigenous rights.

14 Wai 381, filed in 1993.
15 The bodies concerned included the Treaty of Waitangi Fisheries Commission, charged with distributing quota which Maori received in the Fisheries Settlement of 1992, Te Waka Toi (Council for Maori and South Pacific Arts), and the regional health authorities and Crown health enterprises.
16 A recent report by the Law Commission, *Justice: The Experiences of Maori Women/Te Tikanga o te Ture: Te Matauranga o nga Wahine Maori e pa ana ki tenei* (Wellington, Law Commission, 1999), whose purpose is to assist those involved in New Zealand justice institutions to understand and better respond to the needs and values of Maori women, reflects the same determination to explore the unique understandings of Maori women (here specifically of justice) from the Treaty of Waitangi and Maori cultural values. One of the Commissioners, Denese Henare, notes that 'the concerns of Maori women [as expressed to the Commission in an extensive consultation process] were cultural rather than gender based' (personal communication, 13 June 2000).
17 Ngahuia Te Awekotuku, 'The Sociocultural Impact of Tourism on the Te Arawa People of Rotorua, New Zealand', Ph.D. thesis, University of Waikato, 1981.
18 Tipene O'Regan, 'Who Owns the Past?', in John Wilson (ed.), *From the Beginning: The Archaeology of the Maori* (Auckland, Penguin, 1987), p. 145.
19 Te Ahukaramu Charles Royal, *Te Haurapa: An Introduction to Researching Tribal Histories and Traditions* (Wellington, Bridget Williams Books/Historical Branch, Department of Internal Affairs, 1992), pp. 92–3.
20 Kerry Howe, Review of reissue of Alan Ward's, *A Show of Justice, Listener* (27 May 1995).
21 E.T. Durie, 'Ethics and Values', Te Oru Rangahau Maori Research and Development Conference, Dept. of Maori Studies, Massey University, July 1998, pp. 62–9.
22 Ranginui Walker, *Ka Whawhai Tonu Matou/Struggle Without End* (Auckland, Penguin, 1990).
23 Walker, *Ka Whawhai*, p. 10.
24 Sandra Coney, *Standing in the Sunshine: A History of New Zealand Women Since They Won the Vote* (Auckland, Viking, 1993).
25 James Belich, *Making Peoples: A History of the New Zealanders From Polynesian Settlement to the End of the Nineteenth Century* (Auckland, Penguin, 1996).
26 See Ann Curthoys and Andrew Markus (eds), *Who Are Our Enemies? Racism and the Working Class in Australia* (Sydney, Hale & Iremonger, 1978); Ann Curthoys, *For and Against Feminism: A Personal Journey into Feminist Theory and History* (Sydney, Allen & Unwin, 1988); 'Identity Crisis: Colonialism, Nation, and Gender in Australian History', *Gender and History*, 5:2 (1993), 165–76.
27 See Ann Curthoys, 'Gender Studies in Australia: A History', *Australian Feminist Studies*, 15:31 (2000), 19–38.
28 Anne Summers, *Damned Whores and God's Police: The Colonization of Women in Australia* (Ringwood, Penguin, 1975); Miriam Dixson, *The Real Matilda: Woman and Identity in Australia 1788 to 1975* (Ringwood, Penguin, 1976); Beverley Kingston, *My Wife, My Daughter, and Poor Mary Ann* (Melbourne, Nelson, 1975); Edna Ryan and Anne Conlon, *Gentle Invaders: Australian Women at Work, 1788–1975* (Melbourne, Nelson, 1975); Kay Daniels, Mary Murnane and Anne Picot (eds), *Women in Australia: A Guide to Records* (Canberra, Australian Government Publishing Service, 1977), 2 vols.
29 Deborah Oxley, *Convict Maids: The Forced Migration of Women to Australia* (Melbourne, Cambridge University Press, 1996); Joy Damousi, *Depraved and Disorderly: Female Convicts, Sexuality, and Gender in Colonial Australia* (Melbourne, Cambridge University Press, 1997); Kay Daniels, *Convict Women* (Sydney, Allen & Unwin, 1998).
30 Some examples of this extensive scholarship include: Katrina Alford, *Production and Reproduction* (Melbourne, Oxford University Press, 1984); Kay Daniels (ed.), *So Much Hard Work: Women and Prostitution in Australian History* (Melbourne, Fontana–Collins, 1984); Desley Deacon, *Managing Gender: The State, the New*

Middle Class, and Women Workers 1830–1930 (Melbourne, Oxford University Press, 1989); Rae Frances, *The Politics of Work: Gender and Labour in Victoria 1880–1939* (Melbourne, Cambridge University Press, 1993).

31 Marilyn Lake, 'The Politics of Respectability: Identifying the Masculinist Context', in Susan Magarey, Sue Rowley and Susan Sheridan (eds), *Debutante Nation: Feminism Contests the 1890s* (Sydney, Allen & Unwin, 1993); Ray Evans, 'A Gun in the Oven: Masculinism and Gendered Violence', in Kay Saunders and Raymond Evans (eds), *Gender Relations in Australia* (Sydney, Harcourt Brace Jovanovich, 1992), pp. 197–218

32 See Ann Curthoys, 'The Three Body Problem: Feminism and Chaos Theory', *Hecate*, 17:1 (1991), 14–21.

33 Sally Morgan, *My Place* (Fremantle, Fremantle Arts Centre Press, 1989); Jackie Huggins and Rita Huggins, *Auntie Rita* (Canberra, AIAS, 1994).

34 (Commissioner Ronald Wilson) *Bringing Them Home: Report of the National Inquiry into the Separation of Aboriginal and Torres Strait Islander Children from Their Families* (Sydney, Human Rights and Equal Opportunity Commission, 1997).

35 Henry Reynolds is the best known of these, his many books ranging from *The Other Side of the Frontier* (Ringwood, Penguin, 1981) to *This Whispering in Our Hearts* (Sydney, Allen & Unwin, 1998).

36 Peter Read, *Charles Perkins: A Biography* (Ringwood, Penguin, 1990); Heather Goodall, *Invasion to Embassy: Land in Aboriginal Politics in New South Wales, 1770–1972* (Sydney, Allen & Unwin, 1996).

37 Kay Saunders, Kay Evans and Ray Evans (eds), *Gender Relations in Australia: Domination and Negotiation* (Sydney, Harcourt Brace Jovanovich, 1992); Patricia Grimshaw, Marilyn Lake, Ann McGrath and Marian Quartly, *Creating a Nation* (Melbourne, McPhee Gribble, 1994).

38 Marilyn Lake, 'Feminism and the Gendered Politics of Anti-Racism, Australia 1927–1957: From Maternal Protectionism to Leftist Assimilationism', *Australian Historical Studies*, 29:110 (1998), 91–108; Sitarani Kerin, *'An Attitude of Respect': Anna Vroland and Aboriginal Rights, 1947–1957* (Melbourne, Monash Publications in History, 1999); Alison Holland, 'Post-War Women Reformers and Aboriginal Citizenship: Rehearsing an Old Campaign?', in Joy Damousi and Katherine Ellinghaus (eds), *Citizenship, Women and Social Justice: International Historical Perspectives* (Melbourne, University of Melbourne, 1999), pp. 20–9; Fiona Paisley, *Loving Protection? Australian Feminism and Aboriginal Women's Rights 1919–1939* (Melbourne, Melbourne University Press, 2000).

39 Bain Attwood, *History in the Age of Mabo* (Sydney, Allen & Unwin, 1997).

40 Verity Burgmann and Jenny Lee (eds), *A People's History of Australia*, 4 vols (Fitzroy, Victoria, McPhee Gribble–Penguin, 1998); *The Oxford History of Australia*, general editor Geoffrey Bolton, 4 vols (Melbourne, Oxford University Press, 1986–90); Ken Inglis and Alan Gilbert (gen. eds), *Australians: An Historical Library* (Broadway, NSW, Fairfax, Syme & Weldon, 1987–88); and John Molony, *A History of Australia* (Ringwood, Penguin, 1988).

41 Stuart Macintyre, *A Concise History of Australia* (Cambridge, Cambridge University Press, 1999).

42 As always, a huge intellectual debt is owed to Judith Grbich.

43 Kathleen Wilson, *The Sense of the People: Politics, Culture and Imperialism in England 1715–1785* (New York, Cambridge University Press, 1998).

44 Although both de Tocqueville (*Democracy in America*) and Henry Maine (*Popular Government*) see law as an important check to 'excessive' democracy in the United States.

45 George Otto Trevelyan, *The Life and Letters of Lord Macaulay*, 2nd edn (London, Longmans Green, 1878), pp. 409ff; John Clive, *Macaulay: The Shaping of the Historian* (Cambridge, MA, Harvard University Press, 1973), p. 368.

46 Matthew Arnold, *Culture and Anarchy* (1869), ed. Samuel Lipman (New Haven, CT, Yale University Press, 1994), p. 46, (my emphasis).

47 Peter Goodrich, 'Poor Illiterate Reason: History, Nationalism and the Common

Law', *Social and Legal Studies*, 7 (1992), 1.

48 Susan Thorne, '"The Conversion of Englishmen and the Conversion of the World Inseparable': Missionary Imperialism and the Language of Class in Early Industrial Britain', in Frederick Cooper and Anne Laura Stoler (eds), *Tensions of Empire: Colonial Cultures in a Bourgeois World* (Berkeley, University of California Press, 1997).

49 Susan Kingsley Kent, *Sex and Suffrage in England 1860–1914* (Princeton, NJ, Princeton University Press, 1987), p. 203.

50 Walter Bagehot, *Physics and Politics* (Boston, MA, Beacon Press, [1867] 1956), p. 89.

51 Gauri Viswanathan, 'Currying Favor: The Politics of British Educational Policy in India 1813–54', in Anne McClintock, Aamir Mufti and Ella Shohat (eds), *Dangerous Liaisons: Gender, Nation, and Postcolonial Perspectives*, Mineapolis (Minneapolis, University of Minnesota Press, 1997), p. 113.

52 *Ibid.*, p. 128.

53 T.B Macauley, Speech on education to the House of Commons, 18 April 1847, in *Macauley's Miscellaneous Writings and Speeches*, ed. T.F. Ellis (London, Longmans Green, 1889).

54 Alastair Pennycook, *Englishness and the Discourses of Colonialism* (London, Routledge, 1998), p. 69.

55 Anne Laura Stoler and Frederick Cooper, 'Introduction', in Stoler and Cooper (eds), *Tensions of Empire*, p. 1.

56 Jeremy Bentham, *A Fragment on Government* (Cambridge, Cambridge University Press, [1776] 1988).

57 Peter Cowan, 'The Origins of an Administrative Elite', *New Left Review*, 4 (1987), 162.

58 William Gladstone to Lord Russell, November 1854, quoted in E Feuchtwanger, *Gladstone* (London, Allen Lane, 1975), p. 91.

59 Perry Anderson, *English Questions* (London, Verso, 1992), p. 147.

60 Arnold quoted in Chris Baldick, *The Social Mission of English Criticism* (Oxford, Oxford University Press, 1983), p. 34.

61 Antoinette Burton, *Burdens of History: British Feminists, Indian Women, and Imperial Culture 1865–1915* (Chapel Hill, University of North Carolina Press, 1994).

62 John MacKenzie, *Propaganda and Empire: The Manipulation of British Public Opinion 1880–1960* (Manchester, Manchester University Press, 1984).

63 Franklin Court, *Institutionalizing English Literature: The Culture and Politics of Literary Study 1750–1900* (Stanford, CA, Stanford University Press, 1992).

64 Brian Doyle, *English and Englishness* (London, Routledge, 1989).

65 David Lloyd and Paul Thomas, *Culture and the State* (New York, Routledge, 1998), p. 118.

66 *Op cit*, 47.

67 Stasiulis and Yuval-Davis, *Unsettling Settler Societies*, p. 5.

68 Ann Curthoys,' The Proof of Continuity of Native Title: An Historian's Perspective', *Land, Rights, Laws: Issues of Native Title*, Issues Paper 18:1 (Native Titles Research Unit, Australian Institute of Aboriginal and Torres Strait Islander Studies, June 1997), pp. 7–12.

INDEX

LaVergne, TN USA
24 March 2010
177069LV00002B/4/P